THE EUROPEAN CAMPAIGN:
ITS ORIGINS AND CONDUCT

Samuel J. Newland
Clayton K. S. Chun

June 2011

The views expressed in this report are those of the authors and do not necessarily reflect the official policy or position of the Department of the Army, the Department of Defense, or the U.S. Government. Authors of Strategic Studies Institute (SSI) publications enjoy full academic freedom, provided they do not disclose classified information, jeopardize operations security, or misrepresent official U.S. policy.

About the Cover:

The backdrop of the cover is a photograph of the 28th Infantry Division on August 29, 1944, as they marched down the Avenue des Champs-Élysées, Paris, France, with the Arc de Triomphe de l'Étoile in the background. Their celebration was short, because upon the conclusion of the parade, they proceeded through Paris and moved eastward to maintain contact with the retreating *Wehrmacht*.

The inset photograph is of the key leadership of the European Campaign. It was originally released by the Office of War Information in 1945 and it was captioned: "This is the Brass that Did It." The photo was taken at the 12th Army Group Headquarters, Bad Wildlungen, Germany, May 11, 1945, three days after the German surrender.

Front row left to right, William H. Simpson, George S. Patton Jr., Carl A Spaatz, Dwight D. Eisenhower, Omar N. Bradley, Courtney H. Hodges, Leonard T. Gerow.

CONTENTS

Foreword..vii

About the Authors..ix

Introduction..1

Chapter 1. The European Campaign: Origins.....13

Chapter 2. Was Europe First?..............................53

Chapter 3. 1943: Frustrations and Successes.....101

Chapter 4. D-Day: Planning and Execution......137

Chapter 5. Toward the German Border:
Operations COBRA, The Falaise
Pocket, and Operation ANVIL....................189

Chapter 6. Operation MARKET GARDEN........229

Chapter 7. The Hürtgen Campaign....................271

Chapter 8. The Ardennes Offensive...................305

Chapter 9. The Ruhr or Berlin............................359

Chapter 10. Conclusions and Observations......377

Bibliography..389

Appendix I. Developing Strategy:
A Look at the Other Side...............407

Appendix II. To Supreme Commander
Allied Expeditionary Force..........453

FIGURES

Figure 4-1. The SHAEF Chain of Command.................149
Figure 5-1. "Busting the Bocage".......................197

MAPS

Map 5-1. Normandy Map..................................190
Map 5-2. Breakout after Operation COBRA................208
Map 6-1. Operation MARKET GARDEN.......................245
Map 7-1. The Western Front, Fall 1944..................275
Map 7-2. The 9th Infantry's Attack.....................284
Map 7-3. The Hürtgen Area..............................289
Map 7-4. Showing the Area where 28th Division
    Attacked...293
Map 8-1. The Western Front: December 15, 1944..........317
Map 8-2. Ardennes Offensive............................321
Map 8-3. Allied Counteroffensive Against the Bulge..336
Map 9-1. The double envelopment concept for the
    Ruhr as planned and executed.......................368

PHOTOS AND ILLUSTRATIONS

Lieutenant General Albert Wedemeyer....................33
Admiral Karl Dönitz....................................61
U.S. Army General Dwight Eisenhower....................80
General George C. Marshall.............................103
Admiral Ernest King....................................107
German U-Boat..111
American B-17..119
Morgan & Burrough......................................140
Eisenhower & Tedder....................................150
P-51 Mustang...156
Rommel's obstacles.....................................166
American assault troops................................170
"Rhino"..200

iv

Field Marshall Bernard Montgomery..............................234
V-2 rocket..243
Hans von Seeckt..414
German shortage of mechanized equipment.................418
Hitler...419
Großadmiral Erich Raeder..427
Reichsmarschall Hermann Göring...................................434
Waffen-SS..441

TABLES

Table 8-1. 9th Infantry Division Casualties...................306
Table Appendix 1-1. The "Z-Plan" 430

FOREWORD

Since the end of World War II, there has been a stream of publications about the War in Europe, but despite the volume of literature, interest in the topic remains high. Given the significance of this conflict and the interest in this campaign, the Strategic Studies Institute offers a fresh look at the campaign in Europe. This publication begins with an examination of prewar planning for various contingencies, then moves to the origins of "Germany first" in American war planning. The authors then focus on the concept, favored by both George C. Marshall and Dwight D. Eisenhower, that the United States and its Allies had to conduct a cross-channel attack and undertake an offensive aimed at the heartland of Germany. Following the background provided in these initial chapters, the remainder of the book provides a comprehensive discussion outlining how the European Campaign was was carried out.

The authors, Dr. Samuel J. Newland and Dr. Clayton K. S. Chun, conclude that American political leaders and war planners established logical and achievable objectives for the nation's military forces. Conversely, in the campaign's execution, American military leaders were slow to put into practice what would later be called operational level warfare. For comparisons sake, an appendix is included that covers German efforts at war planning in the tumultuous 1920s and 1930s.

DOUGLAS C. LOVELACE, JR.
Director
Strategic Studies Institute

ABOUT THE AUTHORS

SAMUEL J. NEWLAND is a faculty member in the Department of Military Studies at Washburn University and a lecturer at the University of Kansas. Prior to accepting these positions, he was a faculty member at the U.S. Army War College for 20 years and he also served as a strategic research analyst at the Strategic Studies Institute. In 2005, Dr. Newland served as a visiting Professor at the George C. Marshall Institute in Garmisch, Germany. Dr. Newland is a modern military historian, to include the 20th century American experience, and a modern German historian. He is the author of numerous publications on military history to include two books on the history of the Pennsylvania Militia and National Guard, a book entitled *Cossacks in the German Army, 1941-1945*, and the author of the lead chapter in the commemorative volume, *The D-Day Companion*. Dr. Newland holds a B.A. from Evangel College, an M.A. from Pittsburg State University, an M.Phil. and a Ph.D. from the University of Kansas. He is also a graduate of the U.S. Army Command and General Staff College and the U.S. Army War College.

CLAYTON K. S. CHUN is the Chair of the Department of Distance Education at the U.S. Army War College located at Carlisle Barracks, PA. Before assuming his current duties, he was Professor of Economics at the College. Dr. Chun completed a full career in the U.S. Air Force with assignments to missile, space, acquisition, education, strategy development, and command positions. He has written articles and books dealing with issues related to national security, military history, and economics. He held the Army War College's General Hoyt Vandenberg Chair of Aerospace Studies. Dr. Chun has a B.S. in business from the University of California, Berkeley, an M.A. in economics from the University of California, Santa Barbara, an M.S. in systems management from the University of Southern California, and a Ph.D. in public policy analysis from the RAND Graduate School.

INTRODUCTION

As the world is moving rapidly into the 21st century, some might ask, why another history and analysis of World War II's European Campaign? After all, historians have continuously studied the war and the European Campaign since it ended in 1945. Why should one look back to a time and conflict from the industrial age when terrorism and insurgency are so prevalent today? These questions become increasingly relevant if contemporary military challenges are considered. In particular, during the last 2 decades, America's wars have been limited to short wars against second-rate powers, failed states and, most recently, insurgencies. Since 1945, there has not been another World War II-type conflict. U.S. military forces developed war plans, trained, and designed equipment for such a situation for decades during the Cold War and continuing up to today, but we have never used them. The only wars this nation has waged since 1945 have been conflicts against regional powers that had global implications, but are nowhere near the magnitude of the events of 1941 to 1945. These recent conflicts are hardly comparable to World War II in terms of the scope, stakes, and demands placed on the U.S. military, the economy, and the population. Thus, does yet another study on World War II have any relevance, or is it merely an interesting "fun" read for history buffs or students of past military operations?

The authors contend that despite the passage of time and the absence of major worldwide conflicts comparable to World War II, additional studies of this momentous war still have relevance, particularly to a student of military affairs and strategy. For example, World War II is a classic example of nations developing well-formulated goals, objectives, and strategies to achieve those objectives. More importantly, World War II illustrated how great powers adapted to a changing strategic environment. Formulating America's objectives and developing strategies to achieve them was a formidable task for a nation that had spent the interwar period wrapped in a shroud of isolation and economic desolation. Faced by multiple major-power adversaries, the nation's leadership had a difficult task in preparing for war. The primary concern for American politicians was domestic politics. In this regard, World War II offers many significant insights not only for today's leaders, but for those in the future.

Even evaluating World War II military strategy is a formidable task, at least without some type of analytical framework. One framework to analyze the strategy of that period is to use a simple model formulated by Colonel (Ret) Arthur F. Lykke, Jr. Lykke is a former U.S. Army War College faculty member who believed that military strategy should include three main elements: ends, ways, and means.[1] Each element of this model affected the other two. Lykke illustrated his approach by using a three-legged stool with each leg representing an element, either the ends, ways, or means. The challenge for a strategist is to keep these three legs in equilibrium so that the stool will sit upright. The three-legged stool, like a strategy, should be balanced. Two factors influence the end or strategic objectives for a nation: ways, or courses of action; and the means or the resources like people, funds, and materials. For example, a dearth of means could alter the ways a nation could use its military and may cause the ends of the strategy to be at risk. Without the necessary balance between the elements (or legs), military strategy, like the stool in Lykke's illustration, could become unbalanced and possibly fail.

World War II provides an excellent example of a time when this nation had clear-cut *ends* (goals or objectives) and the *means*, financial and industrial, to achieve those objectives. The strategy, the *way* to accomplish those goals, through the exercise of military power in the Western European Campaign was excellent. The path to achieving the goals was not without problems, but fortunately for Allied military leaders, the ends remained essentially unchanged from the start to the finish of the conflict. The ultimate objective — the unconditional surrender of Germany — was inherent in Allied planning. Events did force the national and military leadership to adjust the ways and means throughout the war. At the onset of American participation in the war, one of Washington's means, the industrial capacity to produce war materials, was hardly adequate. However, once mobilized, American industry proved capable of supplying the needs of its military and assisting the Commonwealth Nations, the Soviet Union, the Free French, and other Allies. German actions and Allied interests affected the ends and ways of American military policy. Thus, British interests in the Mediterranean and other areas affected strategy, as did the goals and priorities of the Soviet Union.

Examining how the United States created a strategic plan that focused first on defeating Germany and then Japan provides a lucid example for the many issues that face national leaders today and will so in the foreseeable future. Assessments and reevaluations of a nation's interests, the changing strategies of an opponent, the impact of senior leaders — both friendly and enemy — and other factors forced the Allied nations to alter their military strategies throughout the European Campaign.

World War II also provides classic lessons in the art of leadership at the tactical, operational, and the strategic levels. Consider, for example, the monumental tasks of Supreme Headquarters Allied Expeditionary Force Commander General Dwight D. "Ike" Eisenhower as he attempted to lead the multinational alliance during the European Campaign. Today's military leaders emphasize the necessity, in present and future wars, of building coalitions and going to war with allies instead of as a unilateral power. If one can find lessons on how to wage war by studying military history, then it would be difficult to find a better example of when multinational allies, bound by a common cause, successfully waged war against a very capable aggressor than during World War II in Europe. Each alliance member had its own national interests and possessed its own agenda, though all were united in their dedication to the defeat Nazi Germany.

Complicating Ike's task was the added problem of personalities that were frequently in conflict. Commanding a large military organization and addressing the opinions and interests of many significant personalities is still a critical skill for today's leaders as they wage alliance and coalition warfare. Eisenhower had to address the differing priorities and often meddling of Prime Minister Winston Churchill, he had to consider the demands of General Charles De Gaulle, and he had to satisfy the requirements given to him by General George C. Marshall and President Franklin D. Roosevelt. Adding to the challenges of working with the senior leadership, Ike had to address the challenges presented by difficult subordinates within his own command like British Field Marshal Sir Bernard Law Montgomery and U.S. General George S. Patton, Jr. He also had to contend with inept leaders such as

General J. C. H. Lee; Eisenhower wanted to relieve him but could not, due to political considerations.

While Eisenhower had to overcome some obstacles, he also had a major advantage. The Allied Combined Chiefs of Staff provided Eisenhower a clear, unequivocal understanding of President Roosevelt's priorities. Eisenhower held a key advantage that many post-World War II leaders have not had; he possessed a crystal-clear, unwavering mission statement, a focused end state, which remained unaltered throughout the war. The Combined Chiefs of Staff issued the following directive to Eisenhower:

> You will enter the continent of Europe and, in conjunction with the other United Nations, undertake operations aimed at the heart of Germany and the destruction of her armed forces. The date for entering the Continent is the month of May 1944. After adequate Channel ports have been secured, exploitation will be directed towards securing an area that will facilitate both ground and air operations against the enemy.[2]

The consistency of this mission statement is in stark contrast to the situation that future military commanders faced in the soon to follow Korean and Vietnam Wars. In Korea, the end state changed several times due to General Douglas MacArthur's own plans that developed in the euphoria of victory, with the acquiescence of the Combined Chiefs of Staff and the President. Then, the ground realities changed, MacArthur was relieved, and the President and the Combined Chiefs changed and re-changed the desired end state. Military leaders faced more confusion in Vietnam with convoluted and contradictory missions and objectives. A more recent example of this problem was the vacillating definition of the end state to the first

Persian Gulf War in 1991. The United States and its coalition partners set an initial goal of forcibly removing Iraqi forces from Kuwait, and then flirted with the defeat of Iraq and the removal of Saddam Hussein. They later returned to the initially agreed coalition goals. The unequivocal mission statement and the consistent end state provided Eisenhower with a luxury that many commanders, since that time, have envied.

Since the task was clear, the question was what type of campaign did the nation intend to fight in pursuit of its goals? With the end state clearly enunciated, was a logical strategy developed to achieve it? Were the means sufficient to meet the strategy? Prior to America's entry into the war, some students of military strategy and operations throughout the U.S. Army proposed to engage in mobile offensive operations or open warfare. American industry helped make this type of warfare possible by producing large quantities of dependable trucks, small arms, general-purpose vehicles, aircraft, tanks, food, and other equipment that was ultimately used by many Allied countries to successfully win the European Campaign.[3] Because Americans were innovative, aggressive, and self-reliant, such an approach seemed to be the type of warfare in which the U.S. Army would excel.[4] After the U.S. entry into the war, the quality and quantity of equipment and supplies that were produced gave the Western Allies the potential to function as a highly mobile force. Did the Army incorporate this significant advantage appropriately? Did the United States fight as a *Blitzkrieg* army across France, or did Washington fail to digest the concepts promoted by J. F. C. Fuller and B. H. Liddell Hart?

The Western Allies, especially the United States, fought this campaign with the best-supplied military force in World War II. American industry also facilitated control of the air by fielding the P-47 and P-51. These two superb aircraft surpassed the *Luftwaffe's* aging air fleet in quality and quantity.[5] Dominance in the air permitted the Army to wage combined operations with sound cooperation between air and ground assets. This command of the air and dominance over the necessary sea-lanes also allowed American military forces to have sufficient logistical capability to conduct a modern war.[6]

What did this mean for the actual conduct of the war? The highly respected historian, Martin Blumenson, in an article published in *Parameters*, questioned the conduct of the European Campaign. Blumenson notes that:

> Surprisingly, the top Allied echelons only occasionally attempted to knock out the enemy. The basic Allied motive was, instead, geographical and territorial. The intention was to overrun land and liberate towns. In which direction were the Allies going? Toward the enemy homelands, specifically, the capitals. Seizing these cities, the Allies believed, was sure to win the war.[7]

Blumenson is not alone in his criticisms. Williamson Murray and Allan Millet also note in their recent study of World War II that there was:

> ... a general lack of preparation for War [in the Allied armies] at the operational level. Throughout much of 1944, Allied generals focused on the immediate tactical problems of landing and buildup, without paying attention to longer-range operational possibilities. When Allied armies broke out in early August, senior

commanders had failed to think through the possibilities offered by a breakout.[8]

In fact, a recent generation of military historians has called to question many decisions involving many operations conducted in the European Campaign. For example, these historians have focused on the operations that were conducted after the successful June 6, 1944, Normandy landings. A student of history might wonder what the true purposes of some of these operations were. The tasking provided by the Combined Chiefs of Staff directed a campaign that was aimed at "the heart of Germany" and secondly, "the destruction of her (German) Armed forces," but British and American commanders all too often focused their attention on the Rhine River, Berlin, or some other geographical objective other than the destruction of fielded German forces.[9] Unfortunately, examples of this type of problem are all to numerous throughout the campaign. General Omar Bradley exhibited far too little drive to destroy the elite German forces following the Mortain offensive, until it was almost too late. British General Brian Horrocks, commander of Montgomery's XXXth Corps, failed to destroy the trapped German XVth Army or secure the important terrain leading to Antwerp, Belgium. He simply explained in his memoirs, "my excuse is that my eyes were fixed entirely on the Rhine, and everything else seemed to be of subsidiary importance."[10] Horrock's British forces had the opportunity to capture or kill over 80,000 Germans, but his focus on geography blinded him to this opportunity. By far the best, or worst, example for an American infantryman was the Hürtgen Forest. American field commanders concentrated on taking an insignificant and unnecessary piece of terrain that overshadowed the destruction of the deployed German forces in the area.

These instances have caused historians like Blumenson and Murray to bemoan the failure of Allied leaders to understand operational thinking and to pursue operational type objectives. Some would say that the criticism of the Allied leadership for failing to understand operational warfare decades before it began to emerge in American military doctrine is unfair. On the other hand, the authors of this volume contend that a key strategic objective reflects an age-old principle of war: to conduct operations aimed at destroying the enemy's military forces. Operational thinking is merely a more efficient method of accomplishing this goal. In the European Campaign, all too often British and American commanders aimed operations at achieving tactical or geographical benchmarks rather than focusing on enemy formations and the enemy's ability to conduct military operations. This focus caused the European Campaign, in the eyes of several modern analysts, to appear like a series of tactical events that were merely milestones on the road to Germany's heartland and victory. Certainly, geographical objectives have relevance in military operations, but one needs to question the wisdom of making geographic or other superficial goals more of a priority than the destruction of the ability of enemy field forces to conduct war.

Questions about operations and the implementation of military strategy have caused critics of World War II to focus on the issue of senior leadership. How well did our senior leaders in the field do in pursuit of their assigned mission, the end state? For this volume, we focus on the Supreme Commander, Allied Forces in Europe, and his immediate subordinate commanders. Obviously, these leaders won the war, but did they undertake operations that quickly and efficiently accomplished the mission assigned by the Combined Chiefs of Staff? Did the United States win the war by swamping the Third Reich with a flood of materials, superior strategy, or better leadership? Did the American military establishment still have much to learn about waging modern war?

Thus, another look at the European Campaign is relevant. Today, students of military history, as well as military leaders, must reflect on how strategy was developed, how a joint and combined campaign was designed, how it was fought, the strengths and failings of the leaders, and the lessons that can be learned from such a study by contemporary students of military history, and practitioners of the art of war.

ENDNOTES - INTRODUCTION

1. Arthur F Lykke Jr., "Toward an Understanding of Military Strategy," in *U.S. Army War College Guide to Strategy*, Joseph R. Cerami and James F. Holcomb, Jr., eds., Carlisle, PA: Strategic Studies Institute, U.S. Army War College, 2001, p. 179. While Lykke is credited with this approach, he noted in his writings that the idea for ends, ways, and means originated from comments by General Maxwell D. Taylor, during the latter's visit to the Army War College in 1981.

2. "Directive to Supreme Commander Allied Expeditionary Force, issued 12 February 1944," *Report by The Supreme Commander to the Combined Chiefs of Staff on Operations in Europe of the Allied Expeditionary Force: 6 June 1944 to 8 May 1945*, Washington, DC: Center of Military History, 1994, p. v. See Appendix II for the complete directive.

3. This requires a caveat. The American M4 Sherman Tank was not the best-fielded tank. It was undergunned, had insufficient armor, and used a gasoline power plant rather than diesel. Nonetheless, it was dependable, much like the jeep and the two-and-a-half-ton truck. Additionally, this fighting vehicle was made in vast quantities that far surpassed German tank production.

4. Dennis Showalter, *Patton and Rommel: Men of War in the Twentieth Century*, New York: The Berkley Publishing Group, 2005, pp. 111-112.

5. The P-47 Thunderbolt was an unbelievably rugged plane, suitable for air-to-air combat as well as close air support and interdiction. The P-51 Mustang possessed much of the same outstanding performance of the P-47, but it excelled in both roles and accelerated the gain of nearly complete air superiority.

6. By the fall of 1944, Allied forces had, in fact, outrun their logistical tail. This was a due to lengthy supply lines rather than lack of supplies. The Combined Chiefs of Staff had tasked Eisenhower to secure adequate channel ports to supply Allied armies, but secure ports that could support the Allied advance eluded Eisenhower and was one of the shortcomings in campaign planning.

7. Martin Blumenson, "A Deaf Ear to Clausewitz: Allied Operational Objectives in World War II," *Parameters*, Summer, 1993, pp. 16-17.

8. Williamson Murray and Allen Millet, *A War to Be Won: Fighting the Second World War*, Cambridge MA: The Belknap Press of Harvard University Press, 2000, p. 445.

9. *Report by The Supreme Commander to the Combined Chiefs of Staff*, p. v.

10. Brian Horrocks' memoirs, as quoted in Cornelius Ryan, *A Bridge Too Far*, New York: Simon & Schuster, 1974, p. 61.

CHAPTER 1

THE EUROPEAN CAMPAIGN: ORIGINS

> Before long I rediscovered the obvious: a journey can be charted only with a destination in mind, and strategy can be plotted only with goals or aims in mind.[1]
>
> Albert Wedemeyer

Casual readers of military history often assume that the U.S. Government approached World War II with a set of clear and unambiguous objectives and that U.S. national and military leaders had set a clear course for victory. This is essentially true, but the paths that led from neutrality to Western Alliance leadership and the decision to wage a military campaign in Europe were not simple ones. One must understand the planning processes and the national priorities of the United States from the early part of the 20th century to understand the European Campaign's origin and how the United States and Great Britain selected Europe as the priority for the Allied exercise of military power.

The planning for joint military activities for possible wars had been part of America's military tradition since 1903. Secretary of War Elihu Root had established several reforms; one was a joint Army and Navy Planning Board.[2] This board relied for help on several organizations, to include students at the Army and Navy War Colleges. The students and faculty received practical problems that the General Staff of the Army and the General Board of the Navy would review, and if these two entities agreed, the Secretary of War and the Secretary of the Navy were given the plans for the two armed services to approve.[3] This planning process continued through the early part of the 20th century and was still in place on the eve of World War II. The process was not without its problems. For example, on occasion military planners sought advice and consultation with the State Department. Military planners sought needed information on national policy in various regions of the world to improve their planning. When planners requested guidance and cooperation from the State Department, these officers received little, if any, help. The State Department did not welcome military interest in national policy, and they regarded such inquiries as unwanted military interference into a civilian domain.[4]

Some U.S. planning was an exercise assigned as part of the studies by students at the two war colleges. The students did not draft the plans in isolation. For example, there was a close relationship between the Army War College War Plans Department and the Army's War Plans Division. In the words of Dr. Henry Gole, formerly a faculty member at the Army War College, "Relations between the Army War College and the General Staff from 1919 to 1940 were very close, with the War College enjoying the best of two worlds."[5] The advantage of using War College students in this fashion, as compared to plans developed by the Army War Plans Division, was that the students could develop plans and concepts that were original or totally "out of the box" rather than following specific concepts or scenarios outlined by senior commanders. In short, plans developed by Army War College students were unrestrained and original. The War Plans Division received original "think pieces." Due to the high level of coordination, it should come as no surprise that the planning process of the two groups and their concepts had many similarities.[6] In the early part of the 20th century, the United States developed a series of color-coded plans, the most famous of which was War Plan Orange, which postulated war with Japan in the Pacific.[7] The Navy repeatedly used Orange as a key element in its planning and in its war gaming. The Army also factored Orange into its plans, although without the same conviction since it was a naval centric plan.

Even though the concept of joint planning and joint operations seems to be a recent development to today's military culture, emerging as it did with the 1986 passage of the Goldwater-Nichols Act, the Joint Army and Navy Planning Board was very active, particularly in the post-World War I period. In 1919, the Army and Navy formed a planning committee to assist the Joint Army and Navy Planning Board with its work. This committee consisted of eight officers, four from the Army War Plans Division and four from the Navy. This committee served as the working group for the Joint Army and Navy Planning Board. The committee and the board, to whom it was responsible, worked on post-World War I plans with particular attention to the possibility of war with Japan—a scenario that seemed the most likely in the 1920s—and other potential conflicts.

In these planning sessions, Navy leaders tended to be the most consistent, certain that the threat facing the nation was a maritime power like Japan. Their angst over Japanese capabilities had begun to grow in the wake of the Russo-Japanese War of 1904-05. The U.S. Navy warily watched the growing military power of the Japanese nation. Many naval officers regarded Japan's growing potential and intentions with misgivings.[8] The U.S. Navy's anxiety over Japan did not diminish during the interwar years, but only heightened after the 1922 Washington Naval Conference that recognized Japan as a major naval power. When the conference attendees agreed on the capital ship building ratios, Japan ranked third, trailing only the United States and Great Britain, the top global maritime powers. This caused the U.S. Navy considerable concern, but diplomats brushed their objections aside. Additionally, the post-war League of Nations mandates that placed the former Imperial German Pacific colonies of the Carolines, Marianas, and the Marshall Islands under Japanese control, created even more concern for U.S. war planners. This action made Tokyo more powerful by giving it additional naval bases in the Pacific.[9]

Some of the other plans developed from 1903 through the early 1920s were European centered, while additional plans concerned the Western Hemisphere. By today's standards, some seem curious since they did not appear to focus on the most likely aggressors.[10] For example, although the United States had regarded Britain as a potential aggressor against the United States through most of the 19th century, by the time of World War I, Britain no longer seemed to be a serious threat. Nonetheless, military planners working during the interwar period created War Plan Red for a possible war with Britain and War Plan Crimson for a war against Canada. Because of the porous southern border, War Plan Green was developed for a potential war with Mexico as well as hyphenated plans like Black-Green, should Germany ally with Mexico (like the Zimmerman telegram of World War I advocated) and Black-Red, should the British and Germans conclude an alliance that threatened America. U.S. war planners assumed that the United States would wage war independently rather than as a member of an alliance. As the planners continued their tasks, three likely scenarios emerged. First, situations could develop in Latin America that would cause the United States to go to war with its southern neighbors. Second, a contingency could erupt somewhere on the shores of the Atlantic that would result in American military intervention. Third, the Japanese might make an aggressive move against American interests in the Pacific, resulting in a conflict there.

Through the first half of the 20th century, the German threat to the United States was a mercurial affair, but the potential for Germany to threaten American interests either through military, political, or economic means was often evident to both services. From the 1890s until 1918, the newly unified Germany had posed a major threat to the United States due to its powerful fleet and its large and well-trained army. Berlin's aspirations in the Pacific, and particularly its meddling in the politics of Latin America, underscored the threat to American interests. At the conclusion of World War I, the German threat receded since that nation lost most of its armed forces through the Versailles Treaty. The Imperial German Navy had become virtually nonexistent due to Versailles and the act of defiance by the German naval personnel at Scapa Flow. In 1918, with Germany no longer a threat, the focus of navy planning returned to a growing rival, Japan.

In short, while the United States had engaged in joint war planning since the early part of the 20th century, there remained many issues on the eve of World War II left to be resolved, despite the years of work on the "color" plans. One of the most significant issues was the different service perceptions concerning which nation posed the greatest threat to the United

States.[11] As late as 1937, service interests and priorities continued to cause fissures in the process. From 1937 to 1938, the Navy maintained a concentrated focus on the Pacific and the danger posed there to American economic interests by the Japanese Empire. This was a logical concern for the U.S. Navy due to the size of the Japanese Navy and that the United States did not have sufficient military or naval forces to protect its Pacific interests and its lines of communication.

Conversely, the emergence in 1933 of a bellicose Third Reich under Adolf Hitler's leadership, which constituted the emergence of an accomplished land power, caused the U.S. Army considerable concern. Germany was primarily a land power. Army planners tended to focus more on Europe and the defense of the Western Hemisphere from any European-based threat. The different opinions on the threat held by the two services—whether the armed services should be prepared to defend the nation and the Western Hemisphere from a European-based threat or undertake a major campaign to defeat an enemy in the Western Pacific—were not easily resolvable. The inability of the services to agree caused the Army and Navy members of the Joint Planning Board to submit separate reports in 1937.

The Navy consistently favored War Plan Orange. This plan postulated war in the Pacific resulting from the Japanese threat to American interests in China and the Philippines. Naval strategists revised this plan in 1938 as the Japanese overran coastal China causing a further deterioration of the world situation.[12] The Joint Planning Board, taking a cue from statements issued by both Secretary of State Cordell Hull and President Franklin D. Roosevelt, directed its planning committee to develop a plan that would be based on the

United States working in concert with allies to fight a two-ocean war against an enemy alliance.[13]

While joint planning was significant in shaping attitudes toward a future war, and where and how to fight it, Roosevelt's concern about the world situation began to have more impact after 1937. This concern was increasingly obvious in the latter part of 1938. In a meeting held in the White House on November 14, 1938, Roosevelt stressed the necessity of expanding defense production. Of particular significance, he stressed the need for more aircraft not only to supply the necessary airplanes to defend the United States, but to aid friendly powers against fascist aggression.[14] This November 1938 guidance was forward-looking because at that time, Germany, Italy, and Japan had not consummated their Tripartite Alliance nor had the German/Soviet Non-aggression pact been created.[15] It seems likely that even though the President was becoming increasingly concerned about the deteriorating world situation, the concept of expanding aircraft production may have resulted from a meeting between the President and then Ambassador to France William C. Bullit on October 13, 1938.[16]

As crises continued to occur with increasing regularity, the Joint Planning Committee worked to complete its most current report, which was ready in April 1939. The committee assessed the likelihood of war and analyzed potential threats to American interests in both Europe and Asia. In many respects, the most significant part of their product was that the United States would wage war as a member of a coalition, fighting a totalitarian alliance or coalition.[17] This meant that by 1939, a distinct change in American policy was emerging since, in the years following the end of World War I, Washington had distanced itself from any involvement in world affairs that might cause it to exercise military power in support of any alliance or coalition. Involvement in European squabbles, for example 1917, was regarded as a mistake by many American citizens. Equally significant, a substantial number of the nation's congressional representatives were determined that American boys would never again shed their blood for foreign interests or for the war profits of American corporations. Granted, the plans emerging in 1938-39 did not reflect a shift in popular sentiment, but they did indicate the recognition that in a future war, the United States simply could not go in alone.

As planners proceeded toward the now famous Rainbow Plans in mid-1939, they agreed on the following assumptions:

> 1. Germany and Italy would take overt action in the Western Hemisphere only if Great Britain and France remained neutral or were defeated.
> 2. Japan would continue to expand into China and Southeast Asia at the expense of Great Britain and the United States, by peaceful means if possible, but by force if necessary.
> 3. The three Axis powers would act together whenever the international situation seemed favorable. If other countries, including the United States, reacted promptly and vigorously to such action, then a general war might well follow.[18]

Planners used these assumptions to create five plans, the Rainbow Plans, that would dominate prewar planning. They were far more focused, compared to the previous color plans, because all were based on the assumption that the United States would be faced by aggression from Germany, Italy, or Japan in concert or as allies. These plans included:

1. *Rainbow 1* assumed that the United States would be at war without major allies. United States forces would act jointly to prevent the violation of the Monroe Doctrine by protecting the territory of the Western Hemisphere north of 10 degrees south latitude, from which the vital interests of the United States might be threatened.
2. *Rainbow 2* assumed that the United States, Great Britain, and France would be acting in concert, with limited participation of American forces in continental Europe and in the Atlantic. The United States could undertake immediate offensive operations across the Pacific to sustain the interests of democratic powers by the defeat of enemy forces.
3. *Rainbow 3* assumed the United States to be at war without major allies. Hemispheric defense was to be assured, as in Rainbow 1, but with early projection of American forces from Hawaii to the western Pacific.
4. *Rainbow 4* assumed the United States was to be at war without major allies, employing its forces in defense of the whole of the Western Hemisphere, but also with provision for the United States to send forces to the southern portion of South America and to be used in joint operations in eastern Atlantic areas. A strategic defensive, as in Rainbow 1, was to be maintained in the Pacific, until the situation in the Atlantic permitted transfer of major naval forces for an offensive against Japan.
5. *Rainbow 5* assumed the United States, Great Britain, and France to be acting in concert; hemisphere defense was to be assured as in Rainbow 1 with early projection of American forces to the eastern Atlantic, and to either or both the African and European Continents; offensive operations were to be conducted, in concert with British and allied forces, to affect the defeat of Germany and Italy. A strategic defensive was to be maintained in the Pacific until success against the European Axis powers permitted transfer of major forces to the Pacific for an offensive against Japan.[19]

As the world situation continued to degenerate from 1938 to 1939, it seemed that the United States might have to execute either Rainbow 2 or 3. In the end, even the casual reader can see that the United States would ultimately base its response on the concepts included in Rainbow 5.

The prewar planning accomplished by the various military entities seemed necessary, given the deteriorating world situation. In the last half of the 1930s, the Japanese showed no tendency to cease their aggression in Asia. In Europe, Hitler had cast aside the military restrictions of the Treaty of Versailles. Germany had remilitarized the Rhineland and by 1938 had taken both Czechoslovakia and Austria. Italy, a junior though active participant in aggression, further disturbed world peace by engaging in its own ventures beginning with the 1935 invasion of Ethiopia. War had raged in Asia throughout the 1930s, and it seemed likely that war would soon erupt in Europe.

Despite the world situation and the various plans that called for a U.S. response to threats against its interests, the mood in the Washington remained clearly isolationistic. America's eyes were focused elsewhere—directly centered on domestic issues. Wall Street fell on hard times during the October 1929 stock crash that ushered in the Great Depression. The economic crisis spread to Main Street and, by the 1936 general election, employment and economic productivity had still not returned to its pre-1929 figures, which meant that domestic issues remained primary in the public's mind. The President, while not oblivious to the international situation, faced a nation in the midst of a major economic crisis and that had an aversion to involvement in foreign wars. Its elected representatives in both houses of Congress shared this aversion. The fact that neutrality was important to the nation and to its elected representatives was evident by the passage of the Neutrality Acts of 1935 and 1937.[20] American public attitudes were also evident through the lack of military preparedness. Consider, for example, the U.S. Army: In mid-1939, General George Marshall estimated the Army's strength at 170,000 adequately armed and equipped Soldiers plus two mechanized regiments. The U.S. Army Air Corps consisted of 56 squadrons.[21] The military establishments of Germany, Japan, and the Soviet Union overshadowed American military forces on land and in the air. Still, with the mood of the nation in the 1930s opposed to entanglements in overseas affairs, it did not seem likely that an expansion of the military services would occur anytime soon.

In 1939 however, the international landscape began to change rapidly. On September 1, 1939, the Germans launched their surprise attack on Poland. After a brief interlude that was termed *Sitzkrieg*, or the "phony war," the Germans launched offensives against Denmark, Norway, the Low Countries, and France in the spring of 1940.[22] In particular, the attack on France, its subsequent fall, and the imminent threat to the British Isles changed the strategic landscape. While U.S. planners worked on the Rainbow plans, they explored the concept that the nation would fight future conflicts with American military forces being a part of an alliance. In Rainbow plans 2 and 5, the United States joined France and Britain, a familiar scenario comparable to America's entry into world affairs in 1917-18, but the events of May to June 1940 meant that France, existing only as a rump state, was no longer a viable ally against the totalitarian powers. In the spring of 1940, it had become a victim of German aggression, and what was left of that once proud nation was the puppet state of Vichy France. Thus, by the end of June, totalitarian leaders of Germany, Italy, and Spain controlled Western Europe. Great Britain, Hitler's next obvious target, was also in danger of falling to the Nazi juggernaut.

Considering the spread of totalitarian rule throughout Western Europe in the last half of 1940 and subsequent events in 1941, planners feverishly worked to address the new situation resulting from German successes in Europe. Two possible threatening scenarios confronted military planners. First, there was a potential threat from Latin America. Throughout the joint planning that was conducted in the early part of the 20th century, planners had considered threats posed to the United States from unfriendly governments and powers in Latin America. A potential foe intruding into America's "backyard" had not been a serious problem since the Civil War period when France, under Louis Napoleon, had installed a potentially threatening government in Mexico. A threat emanating from Mexico was again an issue in 1914 and in 1916 when the United States felt obligated to intervene, militarily, in Mexican affairs.[23] In 1940, the possibility of a threat from the south emerged, because it was feared that German agents, who were in fact active in Latin America, might make substantial inroads in that area. Thus, a situation could result where unfriendly governments, supported by totalitarian countries, would emerge on America's southern border.

The second and equally threatening scenario concerned a possible increase in German naval power. With France's defeat, the question remained, what would happen to that nation's navy? The Vichy government controlled the French Navy, and that government hardly demonstrated that it was a neutral nation. Thus, even though the German Navy in terms of surface ships was in its infancy, if augmented with French ships it could pose a serious threat to freedom of navigation in the Atlantic and in the Mediterranean. Worse yet, the Italian fleet could support the German and French ships, making a serious threat to freedom on the seas.

American planners in general, and Navy planners in particular, had long looked at Japan and the Pacific as the area where the greatest potential threat to American interests existed. The expansion of the Japanese Navy and the consistent pattern of Tokyo's aggression in China throughout the 1930s fed this perception. The fall of Western Europe to German domination caused an abrupt shift in American threat perception by the national leadership since, in a period of weeks, Denmark, Norway, Belgium, Holland, Luxembourg, and France were conquered in lightning-like succession. Given the situation of a beleaguered Britain, American military planners considered the possibility that Britain too might fall, and that the United States could face a Europe totally controlled by totalitarian powers. Due to the lack of American military power when Germany attacked France, American policymakers recognized that the United States could not prevent the German occupation of France. Worse yet, it was theorized that if the Germans attacked the British Isles with their combined forces and, if U.S. forces entered the war, any U.S. effort at that time would be insufficient to prevent the defeat and occupation of the British Isles.

In many respects, the German failure to establish aerial superiority over the British Isles and to launch Operation SEALION in August-September 1940 provided the United States a respite, an opportunity, to prepare both in terms of policy and militarily for any future aggressions. This was extremely important because even though Army and Navy planners had been working on war plans and strategies for several decades, such plans were strictly from the military perspective and were not the priority of the American populace or, for that matter, its elective representatives. Events beginning with Poland in 1939, and later in Western Europe, had gotten the American public's attention, but this did not translate to an acceptance for the entry into another conflict in Europe. As Europe and Asia went to war, many Americans and their elected representatives continued to believe that America was merely a regional power whose attention had to be focused on events at home and in its sphere of influence, the Western Hemisphere.

In 1940, however, several things occurred that reflected America's growing concern over world events, particularly Hitler's aggression in Europe. On September 16, 1940, the Burke-Wadsworth Bill was passed in Congress, the first peacetime conscription in American history. This followed another joint resolution passed by Congress on August 27 that activated the National Guard and the Reserves for 1 year of training. This did not mean that the United States was actively preparing for war against the Third Reich or the Japanese Empire; it meant that the mood of the nation had shifted from neutrality to armed neutrality.[24] The American populace accepted expansion of its military, given the worsening world situation. Planning for hypothetical wars had been, up until this point, largely formed by military minds. In the late 1930s, as the world situation continued to deteriorate, the changing plans and priorities of President Roosevelt began to emerge.

From 1932 until 1938, Roosevelt's attention centered on domestic issues, specifically how to lead the nation out of the Great Depression and restore America's economic vitality. Roosevelt watched with great concern as the prospects for global peace evaporated under a steady stream of totalitarian aggression. However, the President was not anxious to lead the country into another foreign war in either Europe or Asia. Even if he had been so inclined, he faced a Congress led by a large neutrality faction that was determined to keep the country out of war. Nonetheless, by 1938 Roosevelt had begun laying plans to assist nations that were victims of fascist aggression. At the same time, he avoided unduly alarming elements in Congress and in the population as a whole that were wary of any type of U.S. involvement in foreign wars. Thus in 1938, Roosevelt began turning his attention increasingly to international affairs and defense because he believed that the United States was a global power with worldwide responsibilities.[25]

Given the President's interest or intent as described above, and the aggression that occurred between 1939 and 1940, the United States was obliged to reconsider its prewar planning. The color-coded and the Rainbow plans had allowed members of several Army War College classes and officers assigned to the War Plans Division to consider what the basic priorities would be in the event of war. The plans however, were skeletal ones and provided only basic information for waging a war. Several military boards and committees had identified potential enemies and estimated general priorities. Planners did not compute or analyze the force composition, the necessary industrial output, and the sacrifices that the nation might have to endure for a future conflict. Future military staff planning would have to create detailed plans before the United States would go to war. By 1940, the War Plans Division could no longer depend on the assistance of Army War College staff groups to assist them; the school had been closed that same year and its personnel reassigned, actions that indicated the gravity of the situation.

By 1940, the expanding pattern of fascist aggression continued to force the President's attention on matters of national security and the commitment of materials to those countries fighting fascism. Perhaps the most significant factor was the recognition by the President and his key advisors that the nation might once again be pulled into a war as a part of an alliance, a decided change in the government's position, given the post-World War I attitudes toward alliance warfare.[26] Roosevelt indicated his administration's support for America's former allies by a plan for expanding military aircraft production. As early as November 14, 1938, the President announced his desire to build 20,000 aircraft, some of which would be available to Britain and France.[27] In the fall of 1940, the United States Government traded 50 surplus and obsolete destroyers to the British for naval bases in Newfoundland, the Bahamas, Bermuda, British Guiana, Antigua, Trinidad, St. Lucia, and Jamaica. This was hardly a neutral act, a fact recognized by both the American public and the Axis governments.[28] Later, in March 1941, Roosevelt signed the Lend-Lease Act, which pledged American materials to "any country whose defense the President deems vital to the security of the U.S."[29] Increasingly tying the defense of the United States to the continuance of Great Britain as a free and independent nation added another element to the planning processes.

Working with the British in defense matters was an increasingly important policy from 1938 to 1940, but the American public did not share Roosevelt's concerns. While Rainbow Plans 2 and 5 had proposed fighting a war as part of an alliance with Britain and France, the public's attitude toward participating in a foreign war as a member of an alliance made such a concept a future possibility rather than a realistic plan. Simply, Rainbow Plans 2 and 5 did not reflect the public sentiment, neither did the President's drift from neutrality. Still, American intentions, at least within the government, became very clear when Roosevelt's Secretary of War, Henry L. Stimson, met with the two service chiefs, General George C. Marshall and Admiral Harold R. Stark, along with Secretary of the Navy Frank Knox on December 16, 1940. The consensus at that meeting was that eventually the United States would enter into the war.

With a future war increasingly viewed as a coalition or alliance operation, planning and coordination with the British entered a serious phase in late spring 1940. The fall of France and the Low Countries made Britain the next likely target for German aggression. Despite its Pacific focus, the U.S. Navy was an early participant in alliance oriented planning. As early as December 1937, the Navy staff began discussions with their British counterparts regarding the new construction of naval vessels. They also discussed what type of cooperation with other nations might be possible in the Pacific in the event of a war with the Japanese.[30] U.S. Navy senior officers continued their contacts with their British peers into early 1938, with the January meetings referred to as the Anglo-American Naval conversations.

From this point forward, even predating the crises of 1939-40, American and British officers met and shared thoughts on future military demands.[31] The U.S. Navy's leadership also began moving toward an increased emphasis on European affairs, given the seriousness of the German threat to Britain. A clear proposal for what American plans should be regarding British-American cooperation was drafted in a memorandum by Chief of Naval Operations Admiral Harold R. Stark on November 4, 1940 (and revised November 12). Stark proposed several courses of action. He preferred a plan that the United States, in concert with Britain, undertake a strong offensive in the Atlantic, while at the same time be on the defensive in the Pacific.[32] The realization, at least within the American government, that the country was rapidly drifting toward war became very clear during the previously mentioned December 16, 1940, meeting. Stimson, Marshal, Stark, and Knox increasingly believed that eventually the United States would be drawn into the war. It was much easier to recognize the drift toward war as soon as the election of 1940 was over and the issue of American participation in a foreign war was less sensitive for the political leadership.

American and British delegates also discussed military cooperation in London during August and September 1940 at the Anglo-American Standardization Committee meetings. Even more significant were the American British Staff Conversations (ABC) held between January and March 1941. Officials from the two countries agreed that: (1) Germany was the main adversary; (2) in the event of American participation in the war, a coalition between the two nations would focus efforts on that principal enemy with the ultimate goal, the unconditional surrender of Germany; and (3) it was agreed that if a two-front war was to develop, the United States would contain the Japanese until the principle enemy, Nazi Germany, was defeated.[33]

As noted by one writer, however, the British strategy emphasized the use of sea and air power rather than directly engaging the enemy with large ground forces. Such an approach—an indirect or peripheral approach—was an attritional effort to wear down the enemy's strength, which would mean a longer war. The American strategy, while it included both air and sea power, promoted massing the material strength of the nation and more rapidly employing substantial ground forces to win the war as quickly as possible.[34]

These priorities were established not so much because the Germans or their regime were regarded as the most odious; rather, it was because a key element of Roosevelt's policies was the survival of a free and independent Great Britain. The greatest threat to Britain was clearly Nazi Germany. Even if viewed solely from the standpoint of American interests, Britain's survival was vital. If the United States was to wage war against Germany, then the best platform from which American military forces could project power was the British Isles. Britain was a power projection platform that Washington could not do without for either an amphibious invasion of the continent or an aerial offensive against the German heartland. Additionally, one of the key elements in maintaining the freedom of navigation in the Atlantic was the continued existence of the British fleet. If Great Britain were to fall under the heel of German aggression, the Atlantic would become a dangerous area where Berlin could interdict American shipping or strike targets in the Western Hemisphere. Britain, already at war with Germany, was clearly the next target for German aggression. Finally, the Caribbean and Latin America were key long-term American interests. The threat to this region came from Germany, not Japan.

The growing crises prompted an even closer look at America's military forces. Perhaps no one in uniform was more cognizant of the problems facing the military services than George Marshall. The first issue facing Marshall was serious, not hypothetical, war plans. Army officers had created student-authored papers, staff generated think pieces, and other works throughout the 1920s and 1930s, but they were not fully developed war plans for the nation's immediate use. As noted by Charles Kirkpatrick, even the current Rainbow Plans "were actually contingencies that allowed the U.S. to respond to foreign aggression and then to react purely in a military way."[35] Although the nation's military leadership had created a series of notional plans for a number of different possibilities for a future war, they still needed to develop the details for waging an actual war.

The President had to confront conflicting demands on the nation's industrial base due to his desire to assist the British and at the same time rebuild America's armed forces. The nation needed a cohesive plan to develop a strategy that would help prioritize resources. Sensing this need, Marshall ordered Brigadier General Leonard T. Gerow, Chief of the War Plans Division, to formulate a long-range strategic plan for the Army since it seemed to be on the eve of war. A national military strategy did not exist. Gerow had a vital task to accomplish that would shape the future of the war. By today's standards, it was unique. He tasked Army Major Albert C. Wedemeyer to develop the plan. Gerow gave Wedemeyer 90 days in which to complete the plan.

Source: U.S. Army Military History Institute.

Lieutenant General Albert Wedemeyer, who as a major, drafted what has been called the Victory Plan.

Wedemeyer, by today's standards, initially had an undistinguished career. He was a West Pointer who graduated early due to the demands of World War I. Despite his early graduation, he missed combat in World War I. His career seemed at an end in 1922 when his superiors court martialed him due to a drinking incident. Fortunately, this serious disciplinary action did not affect his career. He managed to avoid an abrupt end to his military service and served in a rather nondescript series of assignments in the infantry branch. Aside from company level, command eluded him. Instead, he served an aide-de-camp and in various staff capacities. Prior to his assignment in the War Plans office, the first time he actually did anything particularly notable was the academic record he established during his 1934 attendance at the U.S. Army Command and General Staff College at Fort Leavenworth, Kansas. There, surprisingly, this previously nondescript officer was the honor graduate of the 2-year course. Given his outstanding academic credentials, the Commandant selected him to be the College's exchange student at the prestigious German military school in Berlin, Germany, the *Kriegsakademie*.

In this rigorous 2-year course, Wedemeyer had excelled. He studied a wide variety of topics including contemporary military thought in the rapidly expanding German Army. He moved easily through the German military society of the late 1930s, becoming proficient in his host nation's language and German military thought. He even commanded a German antitank company in one of the obligatory *Kriegsakademie* maneuvers. When he returned to the United States in 1938, he provided a detailed report of his observations on the German Army.[36] This report caught the eye of then Brigadier General Marshall who was serving as the Chief of the War Plans Division. Thus, even before Wedemeyer's assignment to the War Plans Division, Marshall already had a positive impression of him.

Marshall and Gerow's confidence in Wedemeyer's abilities was not misplaced. Wedemeyer produced an insightful 14-page plan that still merits consideration by planners today. The particular merit of his so-called "Victory Plan of 1941" centers on its methodology. In a direct and analytical manner, he approached the problem of preparing a plan by asking a series of questions. By his own admission, he worked like a journalist trying to construct a good newspaper "lead." Thus, his framework focused on answering the questions "who, what, where, how, when, and why."[37] With this methodology, he sought answers to four important specific questions:

1. What is the national objective of the United States?

2. What military strategy will be devised to accomplish the national objective?

3. What military forces must be raised in order to execute that military strategy?

4. How will those military forces be constituted, equipped, and trained? [38]

The establishment of a national objective seemed to be a logical step, but the fact remains that it did not exist. Although Roosevelt had been moving increasingly toward involvement in Europe since 1938, no national objective had been formulated as it related to the relentless advance of totalitarian aggression. Wedemeyer took the initiative and drafted a proposal stating that the U.S. objective should be: "To eliminate totalitarianism from Europe and, in the process, to be an ally of Great Britain; further to deny the Japanese undisputed control of the Western Pacific."[39] By this statement, Wedemeyer established the goal of the U.S. Government for the coming war.[40] He had created the "end" state similar to Lykke's model.

The next step in his system was developing the appropriate military strategy—Lykke's "way"—to achieve this end. While Wedemeyer recognized that exactly planned military operations could not feasibly be arranged at that particular time, a strategy could be developed that would provide the basis for such operations. Rather than becoming bogged down in details for a war that was still on the horizon, Wedemeyer essentially followed the basic concepts—the strategy—outlined in Rainbow 5. This plan proposed that the nation focus its attention on the defeat of Germany and Italy, and do this in an alliance with Great Britain.[41] At the same time, Washington would pursue a strategic defense in the Pacific until the defeat of these two totalitarian nations had been completed. There was nothing new or novel about this concept since "Europe first" in one form or another had been alive and well, at least in Army circles, since the 1930s. Given the rapidity of German expansion and the lethality of their army, it seemed only logical. The next step for Wedemeyer was to determine the "means" to support the "ways" that would ultimately achieve the U.S. goals of the war.

Wedemeyer researched the question concerning how large and what force composition the Army would need to achieve its objective. In so doing, he used the resources of the Library of Congress to examine appropriate historical cases, the experiences of other nations at war, and recent demographical data from studies undertaken by Princeton University. In his "Ultimate Requirements Study," Wedemeyer determined that 12-14 million men in uniform would be necessary for the United States to accomplish its goals. The U.S. Army would need 215 divisions, including 61 armored and 61 mechanized divisions. During the plan's development in the summer of 1941, Wedemeyer used data supplied by the Army G-2's (Intelligence) German section that significantly influenced his conclusions. Germany was at the apex of its military successes, and the United States was just beginning to mobilize. In retrospect, Wedemeyer grossly exaggerated the number and types of divisions that would be required to win the war. This has led some to criticize his work and question his importance to prewar planning. In fairness however, at the time the study was completed, the fate of the Soviet Army was in doubt, considering their losses in the summer of 1941. Had the Soviet Union lost the war or the Axis powers been more successful, his original planning figure might have been too low. In his own defense, Wedemeyer later noted, "the victory plan was never static."[42]

The planning task given to Wedemeyer had to go beyond the Army's traditional ground forces; it also had to include the newest branch, the Army Air Forces (AAF). Through his studies at the *Kriegsakadamie* Wedemeyer clearly understood the importance of airpower, particularly as it related to close air support. He was not however, familiar enough with air power to plan for the AAF. Fortunately, the AAF had the capabilities to accomplish this study due to a March 1941 reorganization approved by General Marshall that authorized a Deputy Chief of Staff for Air. In the summer of 1941, General Henry "Hap" Arnold became Chief of the AAF, and his new office included a plans section that he had authorized to develop AAF branch specific plans and itemize requirements for an annex to the war plan.[43] The annex to the proposed plan was christened "Munitions Requirements of the AAF for the Defeat of our Potential Enemies" or Air War Plans Division/1 (AWPD/1). This plan provided not only a set of long-range production requirements, but proposed a strategy that AAF officers could use to conduct air operations in Europe and the Pacific.

The AWPD/1 drafters had to maintain a delicate balance between supporting the overall Victory Plan while at the same time pursuing one of their more controversial provisions, strategic bombardment as a means to defeat Germany. The air planners sought to promote their favored strategy but, at the same time, they wanted to avoid any political clash within the

War Department's General Staff.⁴⁴ The air planners wanted — actually needed — to avoid any such clash.⁴⁵

Air Force doctrine and strategy during the interwar period reflected theories rooted in the value of strategic bombardment to reduce an enemy's ability and will to fight. The concept of strategic bombardment, the basis of the AAF's future European Combined Bomber Offensive, rested on concepts advanced by the Italian theorist Guilio Douhet and the American, Billy Mitchell. The key concepts advanced by such theorists called for the emerging air arm to be an independent branch of service. According to such theorists, a significant element in future wars would be strategic bombardment delivered by a large fleet of four-engine bombers. Some of America's air power advocates, like their colleagues in other nations, believed that a strategic air campaign could defeat the enemy without the need for major land campaigns, but any claims minimizing other services would decidedly cause conflict with the War Department's General Staff. Thus, air power advocates had to advance their concepts with a degree of prudence. The proposed plan also provided sufficient resources to support an invasion of the Continent and subsequent ground operations to conquer Germany. Developing the type and number of aircraft and personnel needed to fight the air war provided the perfect avenue to shape a force structure that would reflect this AAF view on strategy.

AWPD/1 allowed AAF leadership to argue its ability to conduct strategic bombardment and conceptually test their prewar theories about defeating an industrial nation by attacking vital economic centers. American airmen espoused the industrial web theory that postulated that the demands of a modern war would force an industrial nation to operate its economy at maximum capacity. The destruction of certain targets could force the collapse of an economy and cause the entire country to falter.[46] If strategic bombing could create these conditions, then the will of workers and civilians would degrade to such an extent that surrender would become imminent. The key to the theory was to identify and successfully attack the appropriate targets. If the AWPD/1 planners were correct, then a strategic bombardment campaign could reduce German opposition to a minimum and create conditions where an invasion would not be as costly. At best, strategic bombardment alone might cause Berlin to capitulate.

Although AWPD/1 planners believed that strategic bombardment would work, the AAF would still need adequate aircraft to provide close air support and interdiction for an invasion and subsequent ground operations. Additionally, the AAF would need an interim force while it created an appropriate strategic bombardment capability and to conduct other operations. The interim force would allow the United States to carry out military operations while American industry produced the requisite number of heavy bombers to strike Germany's economy. The AAF's plan focused on conducting a strategic bombardment campaign against Germany in preparation for an invasion; providing close air support for land forces after the invasion; defending the Western Hemisphere; sustaining a strategic defense against Japan; and staging a strategic air offensive against Japan after Germany's capitulation.

The AWPD/1 planners called for a massive increase in AAF resources. Then Major Haywood S. Hansell, one of AWPD/1's authors, recalled that the air component would expand to 2,165,000 personnel and 61,800 aircraft in 3 years.⁴⁷ Hansell forecasted a need for almost 11,000 four-engine heavy bombers alone, with combat replacements of 770 planes per month. This effort would expend a large portion of funds, material, industrial capacity, and people from the country's economic and population base. The AAF strength in 1940 numbered 51,000 officers and enlisted members, and AAF squadrons only contained 6,000 aircraft. If approved, AWPD/1 positioned the AAF to fulfill its goal of demonstrating the value of victory through air power in general, and strategic bombardment in particular.

A critical element for the air plan's success in disrupting the German economy was the selection of appropriate targets. AAF planners needed information on German industrial plants, but obtaining accurate information proved difficult. The AAF did receive copies of Royal Air Force (RAF) target folders and reports, but intelligence officers needed more details. Fortunately, many of Germany's construction projects from 1925-37 had received funding via American banking loans. Blueprints of the newly constructed plants were located in a New York bank vault. These plans contained specifications and locations of critical equipment within the buildings. AAF officers used the RAF and these bank plans to assemble a list of 154 targets. The target list included 30 aircraft assembly and assorted metal production firms. The other locations involved 50 electrical generating or switching plants, 47 key transportation nodes, and 27 synthetic petroleum plants.⁴⁸

The success of AAF bombing plans depended on several crucial assumptions. First, bombers would have to provide precision bombing. This would be a difficult task since the bombing technology of that era allowed only a 5 percent chance of hitting a target 100 square feet in size from an aircraft at an altitude of 3 miles.[49] The AAF would need a massive numbers of bombers to assure destruction of the target. For example, up to 220 bombers would be needed to destroy a small plant in good flying weather. AAF officers could not assure Washington that flying conditions over Germany would have perfect weather conditions.

Second, AAF officers also assumed that the bombers would escape unscathed through enemy air defenses. Unfortunately, as early as 1940, the RAF had proven that unescorted or poorly defended bombers were easy targets. RAF fighter pilots had blunted the *Luftwaffe* bombing campaign in the Battle of Britain by using a well-led fighter force against inadequately escorted German bombers.[50] Despite the recent RAF experience, AAF officers thought the proposed bomber fleet had sufficient defensive firepower, greater speed, flew higher, and their sheer number of bombers might allow the AAF to bomb Berlin or the Ruhr essentially unmolested.[51] Large numbers of German fighter units, however, could still pose a problem, thus AWPD/1 proposed the destruction of the *Luftwaffe* by destroying aircraft plants and by the general degradation of the economy through the bombing campaign. This prerequisite to the strategic bombardment campaign would ensure that the AAF could concentrate its effort to destroy the German economy. Shortages of replacement aircraft, spare parts, and fuel would ground existing *Luftwaffe* units. AAF bombers would ensure air superiority rather than using fighters.

Third, AWPD/1 did not make room for major deviations from the focused strategic bombardment campaign.[52] If Washington diverted bombers to conduct tactical air support or to the Pacific theater, then efforts would likely be diluted and delay victory. AAF pilots might not have the luxury of bombing German industrial plants independently, but instead might be required to conduct operations in conjunction with other forces.

Fourth, the plan also assumed that AAF officers understood the inner workings of the German economy at war. While the *Wehrmacht* was trying to conquer the Soviet Union in 1941, AAF observers and other experts believed the German government had fully mobilized the economy. In fact, the German government and industry had only partially mobilized the economy through 1942.[53] AAF planners believed that bombers would attack the most vulnerable and difficult to replace economic targets as the easiest means to wreck the economy.[54] The AWPD/1 authors concentrated on electrical power plants since the planners assumed they were the key to economic production. Transportation, especially railroads, and petroleum followed in priority. A force of bombers could attack selected targets and paralyze the entire nation. This strategy was supposed to distress the populace and curtail its will to fight. However, the AWPD/1 planners did not have sufficient time to conduct a thorough appraisal of the German economy.[55] The impact of a target's destruction and its effect on the total economy is difficult to assess, even today.

Despite AWPD/1's limitations and concerns, Marshall and Stimson approved the annex in September 1941. The Joint Board also agreed to AWPD/1, despite AAF fears of Navy protests over its resource requirements. Assistant Secretary of War John J. McCloy supported approval of AWPD/1 in part based on the offensive nature of the plan, instead of relying on hemispheric defenses.[56] The AAF offered one of the first opportunities to strike back at Germany. Along with a naval blockade, the AAF's strategic bombardment campaign could soften up Germany and divert resources away from its Eastern Front to try to stop the bombing campaign. AWPD/1 provided an opening that AAF officers could use to press the case of an independent strategic effort. Fears of relegating aircraft to "flying artillery" for ground forces, transportation of men and material, or reconnaissance, motivated AWPD/1 to develop a strategic concept and build an air plan to avoid this fate.[57] Although AAF planners would modify AWPD/1 during the war, its basic intent never changed.

Although much of the planning of the late 1930s and early 1940s was service specific, a thread of continuity is evident in terms of key priorities for waging the war. First, if a war started, it would be Europe—or Germany—first. One might argue that this priority occurred because many American citizens were of European origin or that the President was an Anglophile, but this is not the case. Since Washington enacted the Monroe Doctrine, Latin America and the Caribbean were key American interests. In the 1930s, the threat to these areas did not come from the Pacific; it came from the Atlantic. Secondly, if war spread or was initiated in the Pacific due to aggression by the Japanese, the Pacific would be a secondary or defensive effort until the adversary in Europe was defeated. Some revisionists and postwar analysts have questioned the "Europe first" decision. After all, for most American citizens Japan had initiated the war with the United States by attacking Pearl Harbor, Hawaii, on the morning of December 7, 1941. This line of thought however, ignores Roosevelt's concern for the survival of Great Britain as a free and independent entity that was an extremely important interest for Washington, particularly after France collapsed. Additionally, the United States had consistently drifted away from neutrality and toward close military cooperation with Great Britain.

The drift from neutrality, to armed neutrality, and finally to active participation became evident beginning in the last half of 1940 as weapons from American stores were supplied to the British in the wake of Dunkirk. This was followed in September by the agreement that provided 50 overage destroyers to the British Navy, in exchange for bases in the British Empire throughout the Western Hemisphere. The Lend-Lease Act, enacted in March 1941, exacerbated the slide toward American participation although it focused on supplying war materials rather than troops. By the fall of 1941 the United States was actually engaged in warlike activities against Germany with American naval vessels taking an increasingly war-like path to include escorting vessels in the Atlantic that were menaced by German submarines. Thus, Washington consistently promoted Germany as the first priority through pre-war planning, particularly in the 4 years leading up to the war. As a result of the aggressive actions of the Axis countries and the increasing involvement of the Roosevelt administration in world affairs, during 1940 and 1941, the United States began to slowly but consistently edge toward an active role in the war.

ENDNOTES - CHAPTER 1

1. Albert Wedemeyer, as quoted in Charles Kirkpatrick, *An Unknown Future and a Doubtful Present: Writing the Victory Plan of 1941*, Washington, DC: Center of Military History, 1990, p. 61.

2. In a series of reforms either announced or passed by legislative action in 1903, a General Staff Corps was established, as well as the Army War College, which had an association with the General Staff Corps. As the War College developed over the next several decades, it preformed a planning function for the General Staff Corps. See Russell Weigley, *History of the United States Army*, New York: The Macmillan Company, 1967, pp. 313-325.

3. This board consisted of the Chief of Staff, Chief of G-3, and the Chief of the War Plans Division in the Army. The Navy's board had a similar composition that included the Chief of Naval Operations, the Assistant Chief of Operations, and the Chief of the Navy's War Plans Division.

4. Mark A. Stoler, *Allies and Adversaries: The Joint Chiefs of Staff, The Grand Alliance, and U.S. Strategy in World War II*, Chapel Hill, NC: University of North Carolina Press, 2000, pp. 1-2. As Stoler notes, it was not until the eve of World War II (1938), that the State Department agreed to the establishment of a State-War-Navy Liaison Committee to coordinate the efforts of these three departments of government, p. 3.

5. Henry G. Gole, *The Road to Rainbow: Army Planning for the Global War, 1919-1940*, Annapolis, MD: Naval Institute Press, 2003, p. 19.

6. Not all writers are complementary about the close relationship between the Army War College and the Army War Plans Division. Edward S. Miller stated that the Army's planning, especially for the Pacific, was "sterile of imagination." Perhaps this view was held due to the Navy's belief, in contrast to the Army's, that the Pacific was the primary area of interest for the United States and one where aggression could most seriously threaten U.S. interests. See Edward S. Miller, *War Plan Orange*, Annapolis, MD: Naval Institute Press, 1991, p. 13.

7. War Plan Orange, perhaps the most famous of the color plans, is well covered by Miller's *War Plan Orange* and by Louis Morton's Article, "War Plan Orange: Evolution of a Strategy," *World Politics*, January 1959, pp. 221-250. Note as well that among the plans developed were color plans for war with the other major powers, notably Germany (color coded black).

8. World War I actually added to Japanese power and prestige since the Japanese sided with Britain and France, and their troops attacked and overran some of Germany's Asian and Pacific possessions. Thus, when the war was over, the League of Nations gave Japan control over German Pacific possessions and, as a part of the winning alliance, they took their seat among the victorious powers.

9. Louis Morton, "Germany First: The Basic Concept of Allied Strategy in World War II," in Kent Roberts Greenfield, ed., *Command Decisions,* Washington, DC: U.S. Army Center of Military History, 1984, pp. 13-14.

10. As early as 1904, Army War College students considered the possibility of war with Germany and Japan resulting from unfriendly power influences in the Western Hemisphere and challenges to the Monroe Doctrine. See Gole, p. xvii.

11. There are two ways to assess the threat(s) facing the United States in the 1930s. The most likely adversary that the country would face was the Japanese, but the most dangerous adversary, that is, after Hitler's assumption of power, was National Socialist Germany. The resurgent Germany (and for that matter Great Britain) posed a greater threat to U.S. interests in the Caribbean and Latin America than did Japan. Thus, as one author notes, this was a "clear assessment to the 'Europe-first' approach . . ." Stoler, p. 4.

12. In December 1937, Captain Royal E. Ingersoll, Director of the Navy's War Plans Division, was sent to London to have informal discussions with the British Admiralty. Discussions revolved around the construction program of the two navies and the possibility that they might cooperate in the event of a war against Japan if both nations were involved. Logically, a possible war with Germany was also discusssed with the hope by the British that the U.S. Navy could handle threats in the Pacific, relieving the British who would be fully occupied in the Atlantic. Morton, "Germany First,"pp. 20-21.

13. Military leadership between 1939-41 was able to benefit from Army War College studies that had considered the possibility of a German-Japanese-Italian coalition and the United States participating in defense of the Western Hemisphere as a part of a coalition. See Gole, p. 19.

14. Roosevelt set an objective of a 20,000 airplane Army Air Corps but recognized that he could likely only achieve 10,000 given the mood of Congress. The President ignored the shortages of weapon systems and equipment for ground forces, instead clearly indicating his desire to expand aircraft production for both the Army Air Corps and as a resource for other friendly countries, i.e., Great Britain and France. See Mark Skinner Watson, *The War*

Department, Chief of Staff: Pre War Plans and Preparations in the Series, U.S. Army in World War II, Washington, DC: U.S. Army Center of Military History, 1991, pp. 136-138.

15. It was in a sense forward looking, but as Henry Gole notes, the Army War College Class of 1935 had developed plans for such a scenario. They looked at the prospect that the United States would fight a war in cooperation with allied nations against a German-led coalition that included the Japanese. This scenario assumed that in such a situation, Germany would be the primary enemy and that merely providing funds and supplies to nations threatened by the German coalition would not be enough; Washington would need to send an expeditionary force to Europe. They further assumed that the United States would have to establish a strong naval presence in the Pacific. See Gole, p. xvii.

16. Watson, *The War Department: Chief of Staff: Prewar Plans and Operations*, pp. 131-132. Watson notes that in a meeting with the Ambassador, Bullit noted the French concern about what they perceived was Hitler's unusual confidence exhibited during the Munich meetings and the rapid growth of the German air arm, particularly its fleet of bombers.

17. Of additional significance, on July 5, 1939, the President transferred the Joint Army and Navy Board (as well as the Joint Army and Navy Munitions Board), from the military departments to the newly created Executive Office. Thus, in the future, the Executive Department would have an impact on this function. Eric Larrabee, *Commander in Chief: Franklin Delano Roosevelt, His Lieutenants and Their War*, New York: Simon and Schuster, 1987, p. 16.

18. Morton, "Germany First," p. 22.

19. *Ibid.*, p. 24.

20. These Neutrality Acts were designed to restrict public and private financial assistance to any belligerent nations. If these restrictions were followed, meaning that U.S. businesses would not have a vested interest in the war, it was thought that the United States could perhaps avoid becoming an active participant in another European War. For a good discussion of American attitudes, see Walter Millis, *Arms and Men: A Study in American Military History*, New York: G. P. Putnam, 1956.

21. Edward M. Coffman, *The Regulars: The American Army 1898-1941*, Cambridge, MA: The Belknap Press of Harvard University Press, 2004, pp. 373-374. Coffman also notes that 15 months later, the Army had expanded to 500,000 Soldiers and its air arm to 209 squadrons.

22. The writers acknowledge that in the spring and summer of 1940, the Japanese were also on the offensive. In the later part of the 1930s, the campaign in China had entered yet another and more aggressive phase. When France fell in June 1940, July found the Japanese occupying French Indo China. Japanese aggression, however did not seem to directly threaten the British Empire as did German aggression.

23. The authors acknowledge another potential threat in this region that emerged through the Zimmermann telegram episode, which occurred in January 1917. The telegram, sent by German Foreign Secretary Arthur Zimmermann to the German Ambassador to Mexico, suggested that in the event of a war between Germany and the United States, Germany and Mexico could conclude an alliance. If Mexico would go to war against the United States, Germany would provide it with substantial financial assistance; and with the alliance's victory, Mexico could regain the lost territories of Arizona, New Mexico, and Texas. Though the telegram was threatening, there was little probability or possibility that Mexico would or could take it seriously. See Barbara W. Tuchman, *The Zimmermann Telegram*, New York: The Viking Press, 1958.

24. The Burke-Wadsworth Bill was interesting in that, as noted by one author, congressional sentiment actually ran ahead of the President on this issue. Congress was not committed to any type of action in Europe or Asia, since congressional leaders limited troop deployment to the Western Hemisphere and U.S. possessions. Weigley, pp. 426-427.

25. FDR's plans concerning possible U.S. intervention into a wider scope of world affairs and his seeming duplicity about taking the nation into another war is a complex topic beyond the scope of this volume. As a leader of the nation observing the degenerating world scene, he had experiences that caused him to be

cautious and to not appear to be an interventionist. As a member of the Wilson administration, he had watched that President fail miserably in leading the United States into a more active role in world affairs in the post World War I era. Roosevelt had been elected and reelected on a domestic agenda to which he was committed, but at the same time he recognized that the United States would again become more involved in world affairs. By the end of 1938, it was becoming inescapable.

26. While policymakers were edging toward this reality, Henry Gole notes that beginning in 1934, Army War College classes looked at a two-ocean war with Germany and Japan and included the concept of fighting as part of an alliance. Gole, pp. 39-81.

27. Roosevelt apparently failed to consider how this would initially affect an expansion of America's military forces. With a small army, a miniscule armored force, and no suitable airframes to contest the *Luftwaffe*, this intent undercut the expansion of American military forces. Furthermore, the President's proposal to make arms available to the British after Dunkirk and the establishment of the Lend-Lease program, while both concepts supported a crucial ally, they also worked against the expansion and equipping of America's military forces.

28. Roosevelt's decision to designate some of American production for Britain and France was admirable, but it undercut America's ability to rebuild its military forces that were woefully inadequate in terms of equipment and training. Additionally, as France was on the verge of defeat, Roosevelt released a substantial amount of war stocks to France and Britain, something that helped the British considerably after the Dunkirk evacuation. See Richard W. Stewart, ed., *American Military History: The United States Army in a Global Era, 1917-2003*, Washington, DC: U.S. Army Center of Military History, 2005, p. 72.

29. The text of this act, brief by today's standards, can be found in *United States Statutes at Large Containing the Laws and Concurrent Resolutions Enacted During the First Session of the Seventy Seventh Congress of the United States of America 1941-1942 and Treaties, International Agreements and Other Treaties and Proclamations*, Vol. 55, Washington, DC: U.S. Government Printing Office, 1942, pp. 31-33.

30. The Navy was not changing the direction of its threat assessment since it focused on the Pacific and the danger of a war with the Japanese. Still, in discussions with Royal Navy Captain Ingersoll of their War Plans Division, the increasing threat of Germany to the Atlantic sea lanes did come up. The possibility was raised that if the Germans menaced the sea lanes in the Atlantic, the British would be obliged to withdraw most of their Pacific presence, leaving the United States to take care of that area essentially alone.

31. The two countries pressed for continued coordination between the themselves, which ultimately produced the American-British Staff Conversations (ABC). It was U.S. Navy interest that ultimately produced the talks, rather than U.S. Army pressure. See Watson, p. 120.

32. Louis Morton, "The Basic Concept of Allied Strategy in World War II," in Kent Greenfield Roberts, ed., *Command Decisions*, Washington DC: U.S. Army Center of Military History, 1984, pp. 35-37.

33. There was however, one issue that arose between the British position and that of the United States—Singapore. The British were intent on protecting Australia and New Zealand from any possible Japanese threat and regarded Singapore as being a key bastion that the Allies had to protect, ideally with American Naval assets. In Churchill's view, the Japanese would never venture too far from their home posts as long as the British or Americans maintained superior battle-fleets at Singapore or Pearl Harbor. See Winston S. Churchill, *Their Finest Hour*, Boston, MA: The Houghton Mifflin Co., 1949, p. 691.

34. Morton, "Germany First," p. 43.

35. Charles E. Kirkpatrick, *An Unknown Future and a Doubtful Present: Writing the Victory Plan of 1941*, Washington, DC: U.S. Army Center of Military History, 1990, p. 55.

36. Perhaps one of the most insightful statements in his July 11, 1938, report, was his lead sentence which stated: "For political and economic reasons, Germany must plan for a war of move-

ment which contemplates early decision." Albert Wedemeyer in Keith Eiler, ed., *Wiedemeyer on War And Peace*, Stanford, CA: Stanford University Press, 1987, p. 3. German military leaders whom he worked with understood this; Hitler apparently did not.

37. Alberet C. Wedemeyer, *Wedemeyer Reports*, New York: Henry Holt, 1958, p. 64.

38. Kirkpatrick, *An Unknown Future and a Doubtful Present: Writing the Victory Plan of 1941*, p. 61.

39. *Ibid*, p. 63.

40. Arthur F Lykke, "Toward an Understanding of Military Strategy," *Military Strategy: Theory and Application*, Carlisle PA: U.S. Army War College, 1993, pp. 3-8.

41. Note that at the time the Rainbow Plans were developed, Rainbow 5 called for an alliance war waged in cooperation with both Britain and France. By early September 1941, when Wedemeyer submitted his draft, France had long since been defeated, and the Germans were driving deep into Russia.

42. Wedemeyer, *Wedemeyer Reports*, p. 65.

43. Bernard C McNalty, *Winged Shield, Winged Sword: A History of the U.S. Air Force, Vol. I, 1907-1950*, Washington DC: Air Force History and Museum Program, 1997, pp. 181-182.

44. Bernard C McNalty, et al., *With Courage: The U.S. Army Air Forces in World War II*, Washington, DC: Air Force History and Museums Program, 1994, p. 75.

45. *Ibid.*, p. 75.

46. Robert A. Pape, *Bombing to Win: Air Power and Coercion in War*, Ithaca, NY: Cornell University Press, 1996, p. 62.

47. Haywood S. Hansell, Jr., *The Strategic Air War Against Germany and Japan*, Washington, DC: Office of Air Force History, 1986, p. 37.

48. Geoffrey Perret, *Winged Victory: The Army Air Forces in World War II*, New York: Random House, 1993, p. 51.

49. *Ibid.*

50. The RAF's victory was greatly facilitated by the use of radar to spot incoming German aircraft and the British integrated air defense system which permitted them to efficiently use their limited resources to meet German attacks.

51. Consider that this was well within the concepts of air power theorists from the 1920s and 1930s. Giulio Douhet postulated that two types of aircraft were needed for future wars— battle planes and reconnaissance aircraft. The battle planes, designed for bombing missions, were to be so heavily armed that they would have sufficient firepower to defend themselves. See Clayton K. S. Chun, *Aerospace Power in the Twenty First Century: A Basic Primer*, Colorado Springs, CO: United States Air Force Academy, 2001, pp. 42-43.

52. R. J. Overy, *The Air War 1939-1945,* Chelsea, MI: Scarborough House, 1980, p. 117.

53. R. J. Overy, *War and Economy in the Third Reich*, Oxford, UK: Clarendon Press, 1994, p. 233.

54. Barry D. Watts, *The Foundation of US Air Doctrine: The Problem of Friction in War*, Maxwell Air Force Base, AL: Air University Press, 1984, p. 19.

55. AWPD/1 authors started the plan on August 4, 1941, and completed the project on August 12, 1941.

56. Robert Frank Futrell, *Ideas, Concepts, Doctrine Volume I: Basic Thinking in the U.S. Air Force 1907-1960*, Maxwell Air Force Base, AL: Air University Press, 1989, p. 111.

57. Perret, *Winged Victory*, p. 49.

CHAPTER 2

WAS EUROPE FIRST?

Our first major offensive should be Germany.[1]

Dwight D. Eisenhower

As the fall of 1941 turned into winter, Washington teetered on the brink of war. Throughout the year, the United States had been bolstering its armed neutrality status, preparing for war if those efforts failed. The Roosevelt administration in 1940 had orchestrated the first peacetime draft in American history despite some congressional reservations. Roosevelt also placed the National Guard and Army Reserve on a year of active duty for training. The draft expansion of the armed forces increased the size of the U.S. Army from its prewar strength of 280,000 to 1,638,086. These increases were however, only for one year.[2] In August 1941 the administration asked to extend the term of the 1-year draftees. Congress was uncertain of America's need for such a large military force. The vote extending the reservists' service only passed by a vote of 203-202 in the House of Representatives.[3] Furthermore, the President seemed uncomfortable with the possibility that the United States might again require American soldiers to give their lives for another European war. Instead, he preferred to strengthen the forces of freedom-loving nations (though the inclusion of the Soviet Union into this fraternity was clearly a stretch) with military equipment and supplies, rather than sending America's sons into foreign wars. Hesitant to employ American troops overseas, Roosevelt intended to gradually demobilize 18 National Guard Divisions beginning in February 1942. Marshall advised against this demobilization, but the President ignored this advice and continued to formulate plans to cut back American forces.

America's goals, as enumerated in Chapter 1, remained constant, but the feasibility of the President's ways and means were rapidly becoming questionable. President Roosevelt clearly preferred the United States to serve as the "Arsenal of Democracy," but events of 1941, like the invasion of the Soviet Union, seemed to indicate that this strategy alone would not stop any European or Asian Axis aggression. According to one study, Roosevelt was a president "who still cherished the hope that the United States could escape with something less than full participation. He still hoped that the American contribution could be restricted to naval and air support and material assistance."[4] Even as the Lend-Lease Act provided supplies to Soviet Russia, China, and Great Britain, Roosevelt sought to avoid direct conflict, while German U-boats were diligently working to cut Britain's Atlantic lifeline. As the late fall turned to winter, German troops ringed Leningrad and moved ever closer to Moscow and the fate of Russia's continued existence was uncertain. To make matters worse, China, a traditional area of U.S. interest, had already lost its industrial coastal areas to Japanese aggression. The battle for the control of China and its vast resources continued unabated.

An equally serious problem was the effect that the Lend-Lease Act—Roosevelt's preferred strategic "way"— had on America's military forces. The amount of aid offered to those fighting fascist aggression by the United States clearly had a detrimental effect on the effort to supply the rapidly expanding U.S. military forces.[5] This situation became obvious in the September 1941 Louisiana Maneuvers when American soldiers, in greater numbers than in 1940, had to use cardboard and plywood cutouts for tanks and trucks, while using stovepipes for mortars and cannons. American military units simply did not possess the necessary equipment to adequately supply American Soldiers, Sailors, Airmen, and Marines. In many American training areas, broomsticks had to suffice for close order drill, but these would be no match for German Mauser rifles or, for that matter, Japanese Arisakas if the war became "hot" for the United States.[6] Lend-Lease Act priorities forced industry to supply Great Britain, Russia, and China with military supplies before the U.S. Army and Navy. American forces faced equipment shortages or had to use obsolete equipment into 1943.[7] For the nation's military leadership, too few products from American industry were destined for its own military, but instead they were supplied to other nations that were fighting fascist aggression.[8]

The problem of equipment shortages encompassed all types of materiel, but the root of the problem was not merely the Lend-Lease Act drain. American industry was still on a peacetime path, rather than a wartime mobilization footing.[9] With the nation slowly moving out of the Depression, many people again had jobs and money to spend. Consumer goods were in high demand, and industries were attempting to fulfill those demands. Ford, General Motors, and numerous other automobile manufacturers were already shipping out their new car models. Business was good and was getting better all the time.

This situation drastically changed on Sunday morning, December 7, 1941. The Japanese attack on Pearl Harbor and the declaration of war on the United States by Germany and Italy on December 11 meant that Washington's adversaries had, in effect, determined the level of American participation in this war. Several questions, however, remained. First and most importantly, how long would it take for the American government and industry to mobilize its considerable resources and work with allied countries to achieve victory over the aggressor nations? Second, had American goals, our objective/ends changed? Third, what sort of revisions needed to be made to prewar planning considering the events of the first 2 weeks of December 1941?

The objectives — or the ends — developed by Albert Wedemeyer, remained in keeping with Roosevelt's overall goals, and they remained the key U.S. objectives throughout the conflict. To reiterate, they were "To eliminate totalitarianism from Europe and, in the process, to be an ally of Great Britain; further to deny the Japanese undisputed control of the Western Pacific."[10] The war for the United States began with Japanese aggression against American forces in the Pacific, and the Japanese onslaught would continue unabated well into 1942. Nevertheless, Europe remained the focus of American attention. Furthermore, as Wedemeyer's planning for the war tended to follow the basic concepts included in Rainbow 5, so did the initial plans to prosecute the war. This view required Washington to maintain American forces on the defensive in the Pacific and to develop projections for early movement of units to the North Atlantic. When Army officials could buildup sufficient military strength for an invasion of the European Continent, Washington could consider launching an invasion, in concert with the British. The primary objective remained the defeat of fascist Germany and Italy.

The gap between objectives, plans, and reality, however, was enormous. American public opinion from 1939 through 1941 concerning American participation in another foreign war, the reticence of elected representatives to commit funds or American soldiers to such a conflict, and Roosevelt's vacillations on the size and use of the U.S. military forces meant that America, though it had a clear objective, lacked the means to achieve a quick victory.[11] For example, in 1941 as Albert Wedemeyer developed his so-called Victory Plan, he postulated that the Army should consist of 8,795,658 men or, in terms of force structure, a whopping 215 divisions.[12] While ultimately the Army only required 89 divisions to achieve victory, when the Japanese attacked Pearl Harbor, the recently expanded Army only had 37 divisions. Equally serious, only a few units were fully trained or equipped and thus ready to face any task.[13] The Army's strength had increased, but its equipment levels were far below what was necessary. The Army could not, at any time in the near future, execute its plans to defeat the European Axis powers. The events of December 1941 and early 1942 further eroded inventories and capabilities.

The materials necessary to win the war that the U.S. had recently entered was a difficult task in itself. As mentioned, in 1940-41, the nation had just begun moving out of the Great Depression and demand for consumer goods of all types was rapidly growing. Now that America was at war, it was imperative that industry convert the civilian oriented production, in particular the transportation sector, to wartime needs. This was necessary since the automobile industry consumed 51 percent of the country's annual production of malleable iron, 34 percent of its lead production, and 80 percent of its rubber production.[14] Washington also needed to reorient the aircraft and ship construction industries. On January 16, 1942, by executive order, the President established the War Production Board led by Donald Nelson. Nelson's first action was to cease civilian automobile production, which went into effect on February 10, 1942. The impact of this one action, as it relates to the means for the war, is apparent through the wartime production figures. About 20 percent of the nation's wartime production came from the automobile industry; that included 50 percent of the aircraft engines, 80 percent of all tanks and tank parts, 100 percent of the trucks, and most of the B-24 bombers, one of the main airframes for strategic bombardment.[15]

The resource issue for a larger Army was only one part of a wider conflict involving military leaders. The Army as an institution focused primarily on land power, but the AAF in its AWPD/1 report called for a massive increase in manpower, aircraft, equipment, and infrastructure. No other country's air force had proposed the scope of aerial warfare to the extent of the AAF. Arnold's requirements for forces and the commitment to a massive strategic bombardment were unprecedented. The use of strategic bombardment to defeat an enemy nation was largely unproven and was inherently a rival to the other branches of service. The theory that strategic bombardment could destroy an enemy's economy and will in a relatively short period of time without the aid of surface forces, was an immediate hit with AAF officers looking to revolutionize warfare.[16] Thus, within the Army, ground and air officers disagreed about the necessary allocation of funds, manpower, and material for the coming war. After Pearl Harbor and the string of seemingly uninterrupted Allied defeats, the AAF's leadership had to reconsider its priorities. AWPD/1 required revisions.

At the same time, the U.S. Navy's quest for preeminence through building a two-ocean force was also a significant resource rival to the Army's plans, as well as to the air leaders' efforts to build an air force capable of strategic bombardment. Like the fledgling AAF, the Navy had its own internal battle concerning what would be the major weapon system in that service's arsenal. Since the early 1920s, the Navy's emerging aviation branch pressed hard for its claim that any future war's outcome would depend on the aircraft carrier and carrier borne aircraft. Traditionalists, however, were certain that, despite the virtual inactivity of battle fleets in World War I, the battleship would be the decisive weapon system, particularly in the Pacific where the Navy traditionally assumed a war would occur. Immediately following World War I, carrier advocates faced an uphill battle against traditionalists who wanted the battleship and cruiser to retain their prominence. The Navy's leadership ultimately came to recognize the importance of the aircraft carrier. By December 7, 1941, the Navy had seven carriers in its inventory, and it had begun building advanced *Essex* class carriers.

The U-boat problem was an important lesson from World War I that the American and British military leadership had forgotten or ignored. In World War I, German submarine operations had blockaded Great Britain and created food and material shortages. Britain needed foodstuffs and raw materials from other regions of the world, because without these raw materials, it would collapse. During World War I, German naval commanders estimated that if the U-boat fleet could sink 600,000 tons of shipping per month, starting in February 1917, the German Imperial Navy could cause the British to surrender by June 1917.[17] A concentrated submarine offensive would cause neutral country merchant marines to terminate commerce with Britain, and this, together with heavy losses of commercial shipping, would starve the British into submission. Fortunately, in 1917 this strategy failed, but the possibility that such a strategy could succeed was still very real. If U-boats ruled the Atlantic, then Britain, the base for a cross-channel invasion, could be lost. Planning in Washington had largely ignored any type of significant naval threat by Germany.

Certain elements in the German Navy, however, had not forgotten the lessons of World War I. The U-boat faction led by Karl Dönitz, himself a World War I submarine officer, knew that these underwater weapons had almost brought Britain to its knees in 1917.[18] Although they had a relatively small U-boat fleet in 1939, the German leadership began to quickly expand this arm and disrupt commercial shipping in the Atlantic and Mediterranean, shipping that was necessary for the survival of Britain and the Soviet Union.[19] Obviously, the U-boat threat did not affect all military forces. The AAF could still move its aircraft over the Atlantic to Britain and conduct its favored strategic bombardment campaign, but merchant marine vessels had to carry the bombs and aviation fuel used by strategic bombers to England. Troops and foodstuffs would not get through unless the Navy silenced the U-boat threat. If German submarine forces could sink sufficient cargo and tanker ships, then they could also paralyze the Soviet Union, which needed weapons, food, and raw materials from the Western Allies.

Source: Author's Collection.

Admiral Karl Dönitz, strong proponent of U-Boat warfare, at work planning operations against the Allies.

In a replay of a World War I strategy, the *Kriegsmarine* again sought to turn the tables on Britain. Despite the British advantage in capital ships, Great Britain was still vulnerable to an effective U-boat campaign. Before any combined Anglo-American strategy resulting in an invasion of the continent of Europe could succeed, Allied navies would have to defeat the U-boats. The Battle of the Atlantic would determine if the Germans could isolate and starve Britain or if the

American and Royal Navies could find a way to ensure safe transport across the Atlantic. In 1942, the fate of America being able to execute its military strategy for a European campaign hinged on its ability to undercut the effectiveness of German submarine operations. Adolf Hitler commented in April 1942, "Victory depends on destroying the greatest amount of Allied tonnage..." by the *Kreigsmarine*'s U-boat campaign in the Atlantic.[20]

Germany had a few advantages in conducting a concentrated U-boat campaign against the Allies. Unlike World War I, the Germans had access to naval bases from Norway to France, rather than just the North Sea, and refueling capabilities in Spain as well. This advantage allowed U-boats to strike Allied shipping from several areas that included not only the North Atlantic, but also the entire Atlantic Ocean and the Mediterranean. Additionally, U-boat commanders could proceed to East Africa and disrupt merchant shipping from British colonies in Asia, which could also affect events in the Pacific. The German leadership hoped that its U-boat campaign would destroy a large enough number of ships that the losses would exceed the replacement capabilities of British shipyards. In this early portion of the war at sea, the British did not have sufficient long-range aircraft nor escort capability to thwart submarine attacks. Thus, despite American vessels escorting convoys even before December 1941, German submarines were able to take a significant toll on merchant shipping. In August 1941, German U-boat commanders sank 56 ships, representing a total of 267,618 tons. October's toll of Allied ships from *Kreigsmarine* torpedoes was 63 ships that displaced 352,407 tons.[21] American entry into the war greatly increased naval resources to combat U-boat operations, but immediately after the U.S. entry the Navy was definitely not prepared to defeat the U-boat threat. Naval officers had to create strategies to defeat experienced U-boat commanders, strategies that would ultimately require resources from both the Navy and the AAF. The Navy would have to train merchant mariners to avoid U-boat attacks, since merchantmen still operated fully illuminated ships at night close to shore and generally without escorts.[22] The Navy also had to divide its limited assets to numerous Atlantic routes that rapidly became a killing zone for the U-boats.

Dönitz, commander of the German U-boat fleet, believed that American defenses were so weak that the Eastern seaboard was an unexpected windfall for training inexperienced crews on how to attack shipping.[23] Dönitz saw the potential for U-boat warfare and implored the Naval High Command to build a fleet of at least 300 U-boats to blockade Britain and starve the English, but limited resources consistently forced Germany to restrict U-boat production and operations. Dönitz continued to fight diehard German surface warfare officers who insisted that more ships were necessary for the High Seas Fleet, despite the Royal Navy's quantitative and qualitative superiority. Throughout the war, the miniscule German High Seas Fleet stayed in port at Norwegian or Baltic locations and was never able to challenge the British or American surface fleets, repeating the experiences of World War I.

American Naval leaders also had to contend with advocates for the submarine. The Navy's first significant challenge in the Atlantic, which began before American entry into the war, was neither contesting enemy battleships nor carriers; its first task was countering German submarines. In the "Battle of the Atlantic," U-boats attacked the economic lifeline between the Western Hemisphere and Britain and the Soviet Union,[24] and despite Dönitz's failure to get all the U-boats he wanted, the German submarine fleet wreaked considerable havoc on Allied shipping. From January 14 to March 14, 1942, German submarines sank 1.2 ships per day off the Eastern seaboard. Later, from March 15 to April 20, the toll increased to 2.2 ships per day.[25] Without control of the seas, the United States and its primary ally Great Britain could not hope to ship the requisite men and supplies to consider waging a campaign designed to wrest Europe from Nazi domination.

Despite increasing effort to introduce methods to increase merchant ship protection, like using a convoy system and providing better naval escorts, losses continued to mount. The growing German submarine menace off the Atlantic coast caused the AAF to advocate a role in countering this threat in reaction to the Navy's increased role in anti-submarine activities. The AAF pushed the use of heavy and medium range bombers (up to 640) to conduct anti-submarine and long-range patrol activities from North and South America, Iceland, and the Azores. This, of course, would divert bomber resources to this secondary activity, rather than their preferred strategic bombing campaign. The new Chief of Naval Operations, Admiral Ernest J. King, bristled at the suggestion that the AAF could conduct anti-submarine warfare. King opposed a larger role by the AAF in anti-submarine operations and ultimately exerted pressure to force the AAF to transfer many of these aircraft to the Navy. King also believed that the increased focus on aircraft production would draw limited resources away from needed ship construction. More aircraft under AAF command also clashed with his plans to promote a larger role in U.S. strategy for the Pacific Theater.

American involvement in prewar convoy duty was limited to escort operations by surface vessels, but experience soon proved that effective anti-submarine operations also required long-range aerial search and patrol. This new technique forced the AAF and Navy to dedicate joint resources to conduct effective operations. Thus, the AAF was required to divert aircraft and personnel from its bombardment mission to conduct anti-submarine operations, a requirement that was not in keeping with Air Force plans. At the same time, the Navy believed counter U-boat operations belonged exclusively to it. Interservice rivalry erupted from the start, and Navy and AAF commanders faced numerous practical problems, such as different service procedures, in their attempts to accomplish this mission. AAF leaders saw their Navy colleagues pressing to employ more defensive convoy escort measures that shied away from using aircraft in a hunter-killer role.[26] King suggested that the best path for the U.S. Navy was to provide escort operations for convoys. The Royal Navy vehemently disagreed based on its experience and beliefs about the offensive nature of military forces. British naval commanders wanted to use long-range air power to defeat the Germans.[27] The British and the AAF were successful in advocating the increased role of air power to combat the U-boat forces and the AAF and the U.S. Navy ultimately established the Joint Control and Information Center in New York to conduct anti-submarine operations, including air patrols.[28] The use of aircraft improved anti-submarine operations, but the toll of German submarines increased. Navy leaders improved their operations by the use a fleet of small escort carriers to conduct anti-submarine warfare activities in their convoy duties. Ultimately, AAF leaders transferred their anti-submarine aircraft to the U.S. Navy, allowing the AAF to concentrate on its strategic bombardment mission.

Prior to Pearl Harbor, the only area where American property and lives seem to be under attack was in the Atlantic. American forces were not under direct attack by the Germans, but an undeclared war opened up between the U.S. Navy and U-boats by August 1941. During this undeclared naval war, U-boats sank two American destroyers, the *Kearny* and the *Reuben James*, in addition to merchant ships, before a formal declaration of war between Germany and the United States existed.

For Washington, the early war period began in a fashion that confounded the nation's military leaders, because Roosevelt directed strategies that seemed to contradict prewar planning. While the commitment to "Europe first" did not waver as the accepted strategy, the initial progress of the war caused American participation to proceed in an entirely different path than initially envisioned. For the United States, the war was initially in the Pacific where American forces tried to halt the ongoing Japanese onslaught. After Pearl Harbor, the Japanese advanced into Southeast Asia, besieging the Philippines, Hong Kong, Wake Island, Guam, and other areas. Later, the Imperial Japanese Navy would attempt (and fail) to take Midway. They, not the Germans, also brought the war to the Western Hemisphere by attacking the Aleutian Islands, occupying both Attu and Kiska. Imperial forces came dangerously close to Australia and began conducting bombing raids against Australian installations. Because of the immediacy of the Japanese threat, plans for the necessary buildup of men and supplies for operations in Europe were delayed in order to deal with the deteriorating situation in the Pacific. The strategy did not change, but the circumstances did, causing national priorities to temporarily shift. U.S. Navy leaders were pleased with the increased emphasis on the Pacific.

The level of military operations and troop strengths in 1942-43 clearly reflected the urgency of the situation in Asia and the Pacific. Even though Roosevelt did not waver from the Europe first strategy, by the end of 1942 over half of the Army's existent divisions and more than one-third of America's air groups were in the Pacific. As late as December 31, 1943, only 6 months away from the Normandy invasion in Europe, American national and military leaders had employed 1,878,152 members of the nation's armed forces against the Japanese, but assigned only 1,810,367 for operations against Germany.[29] The balance would rapidly shift in 1944, but from 1942-43 the direct threat to the nation seemed to center in the Pacific. As a contributing factor, two strong personalities from two different services, General Douglas MacArthur and Admiral King, consistently pressed for a higher priority for the Pacific and were successful in achieving at least some of their goals to this point.

Even as circumstances were becoming increasingly grim in the Pacific during the first half of 1942, there were two favorable signs in Europe. The stubborn resistance of the British people, coupled with a steady flow of American supplies, meant that by the end of 1941 the survivability of Britain had improved considerably. U-boats threatened this supply line, but the inability of the Germans to mount an invasion of the British Isles and deprive the United States of its bridge to Europe made future plans for an Allied invasion — the European Campaign—more feasible. Furthermore, Russian military forces stopped the German advance into the Soviet Union at the gates of Moscow. The Soviet Army had rolled back the *Wehrmacht*, inflicting heavy casualties by grinding down the *blitzkrieg* designed force with a slow campaign of attrition. American presence in the Pacific however, was tenuous. Thus, Washington shipped the preponderance of American forces to the Pacific. The immensity of the Pacific theater required significant ship construction, employment of large numbers of aircraft, and troops trained for both conventional ground operations and amphibious landings. Before any type of operations against the heartland of Europe could occur, the American War Production Board would have to complete the drastic shift of American industry to wartime production; Washington would have to create and train multiple ground divisions, and Japanese aggression in the Pacific would have to be stopped, and perhaps even rolled back.

Despite increased attention to the U-boat problem, the unseen battles under the Atlantic were a significant problem for future Allied plans. U-boats had the potential of starving the British Isles. If the German naval strategy of blockade had worked, then Washington would have to face the potential issue of a negotiated peace between London and Berlin. Had Britain folded, American planners would have had a more complicated task in attempting to liberate Western Europe and fight a war against Japan alone (Australia and New Zealand excepted). Long-range strategic bombardment against Germany would have been difficult, if not impossible, with the existing AAF bomber fleet.[30] Control of the Atlantic and the Mediterranean was critical, because of the vast logistical requirements necessary to buildup the Allied base in Britain in order to stage an invasion of occupied France. Ironically, German inadequacies in waging the U-boat war may have saved the British. In September 1939, the Germans only had 56 U-boats.[31] Had their fleet been more robust, the United States might have had to concentrate its attacks only on North Africa and into Italy or southern France, rather than opening fronts against Germany simultaneously from the Mediterranean and Britain. Without the massive supply of weapons and food transported across the Atlantic from America, the Soviet Union could have collapsed, or Stalin might have sought a separate peace with Hitler. Allied planners had to create the conditions necessary to implement their combined military strategy before they could even start any feasible planning or operations to conquer Germany.

The campaigns to neutralize the U-boat threat and the AAF proposed strategic bombardment of Hitler's Germany were important, but throughout most of 1942 the pressure for employing ground forces against the German Army was a major issue. From the onset of planning, an integral part of America's war effort was alliance building. This alliance was firmly committed to the same goal, the destruction of Nazi Germany. At the same time, the alliance had to focus first on the immediate needs—in fact the survival—of its two main allies: Great Britain and the Soviet Union. Britain was a primary concern because it could and did serve as the American staging area for both ground and air operations in Europe. Fortunately, ties with the United States were of long duration and ran very deep. Both nations were firm in their resolve to defeat Nazi tyranny and liberate Europe from German oppression. Even so, the interests of Britain and the United States were decidedly different, as were their experiences. Britain, a highly industrialized and mercantile nation, had a worldwide empire to consider and they had not forgotten the terrible casualties of the World War I, its last significant military venture.

On the other hand, the Soviet Union had been a pariah among the major nations due to its noxious Marxist ideology and, most recently, through its active role in the 1939 dismemberment of Poland, and its subsequent aggression against Finland. Its acceptance into the alliance against Nazi Germany was a marriage of convenience, because the Soviets, above all, sought to survive. The Western Allies desperately needed the Soviet Union to survive, because the Soviets were exacting significant casualties from German armed forces and were tying down *Wehrmacht* resources that could have caused the Western Allies major problems. Conversely, though the immediate goals of the Eastern and Western members of the alliance were comparable, the values and long-term goals and interests of the Soviet Union were diametrically opposed to those of Britain and the United States. In fact, Soviet goals had much more in common with National Socialist Germany than its Western Allies. Still, the continued existence of the Soviet Union with its immense military forces was important for Allied success.

In 1942, the German Army had exerted great pressure on both Great Britain and the Soviet Union. For the Soviet Union, the situation was critical. Since mid-1941, the Soviets had been engaged in a life and death struggle with the German *Wehrmacht*. By any standard, the German commitment to this campaign was staggering. On June 22, 1941, the Germans had thrown 149 divisions, (about 3,000,000 men), 3,332 armored vehicles, and 1,930 aircraft into what was called Operation BARBAROSSA.[32] With great effort, on December 5, 1941, the Red Army launched a counterattack against the overextended *Wehrmacht* that literally stopped the Germans at Moscow's suburbs and hurled them back. The strain on the Soviets however, was still immense, and the spring of 1942 brought no respite; only a renewed German offensive. Most of European Russia was in German hands, the Soviets lost over three million soldiers killed or captured, and the Soviet Air Force had taken staggering losses. The Soviet Union desperately needed help, and the Allies needed that nation as a part of the war effort.

As the Russian military battled German forces, the situation for Britain had improved. Although it was still struggling with the U-boat menace and aerial bombings by the *Luftwaffe,* it no longer faced the likelihood of a full-scale German invasion. The survival of the island nation was crucial for American plans since it was the launching pad for future American operations. A more secure Britain gave the United States the opportunity to begin building the necessary support structure on the British Isles for air and ground operations against the German heartland. Without the necessary men, equipment, and aerial superiority, the likelihood of American military forces conducting a cross-channel invasion of the European continent would be a campaign for the long term, and not the immediate future. Without any impending threat by American ground forces on the European continent, the focus of German operations would continue toward the destruction of what Nazi ideologues called "the home of Jewish Bolshevism," the Soviet Union.

To stage a European campaign and achieve its goals, the redirection of America's industrial priorities was imperative. In the first few months of 1942, the War Production Board began the process of supplying the equipment-starved U.S. Army. Even as it was moving production to a wartime mode, events of the war eroded the likelihood of conducting any kind of a campaign on the European continent in the near term. The priorities for war envisioned by Roosevelt and Wedemeyer's Victory Plan called for a strategic defense in the Pacific and priority for U.S. effort in Europe. Yet from December 1941 through May 1942, American defense in the Pacific was, by necessity, a priority because in the first 5 months of the war, the Japanese advance had consistently pushed American and Allied defenders back toward Australia and Hawaii. This meant that the Pacific was a significant drain on American resources, both manpower and equipment. The fall of the Philippines alone, which was the major American base in the Pacific other than Pearl Harbor, resulted in the loss of almost all of America's Pacific-based B-17 bombers and the bulk of its P-40 fighters. Japan's conquest also resulted in the capture of 12,000 Americans and 60,000 Filipino military members.

The logistics to fight a Pacific war were radically different from one in Europe concerning time and space. For example, a freighter leaving New York could reach Liverpool in 17 days. However, a freighter leaving San Francisco and proceeding to Guadalcanal took 26 days, or 28 days to Sydney, Australia.[33] Freighters, of course, also required naval escorts. It was not until June 1942, when Allied victories at sea in the Battles of the Coral Sea and Midway stopped Japanese advances, that the Pacific front was finally stabilized. But the resource drain continued and actually increased. Rather than maintain a mere defensive posture, on August 7, 1942, American forces went on the offensive with an invasion of Guadalcanal. Offensive operations on this island and in its vicinity assuredly detracted from the Europe first plans throughout 1942.

Despite the operations conducted by American forces in the Pacific and the pressure of a determined U-boat campaign in the Atlantic, the adopted American and Allied strategy continued to demand the presence of United States ground troops in the war against Hitler's Germany. A major factor requiring American operations in Europe was the continued crisis facing the Soviet Union. In the summer and fall of 1942, the survival of the Soviet Union was still in doubt. German units had resumed their advance across the southern steppes, inflicting defeat after defeat on the Soviet Army, but Stalin did not capitulate. Operations by the Western Allies to relieve the beleaguered Soviet Army were crucial.

American plans envisioned a cross-channel assault against Hitler's "Fortress Europe" using Britain as a springboard, but three significant problems emerged for the *way* to achieve the desired *end*. First was the problem of resources: With the drain on resources due to the war in the Pacific and the fact that American industry was slowly switching from civilian to military oriented production, a cross-channel attack in 1942 was hardly feasible. Second, throughout most of 1942, the American Army was in the process of formation. Training for large unit maneuvers (corps level) had not really gotten started until the spring of 1940. In late summer 1940, the U.S. Army extended training on this level to joint Regular Army and National Guard maneuvers. Army leaders tried to establish realistic training despite shortages of equipment and ammunition, at least in part due to Lend-Lease Act requirements. Third, the U-boat campaign continued to undercut the buildup of men and material on the British Isles.

Washington could carry the war to Europe, even at this early stage, through an air campaign. A major goal of the AAF's leadership was to initiate daylight precision attacks on the German economy rather than night area bombing, as practiced by the RAF. At the same time, to establish bases in Britain and prepare crews and aircraft for a campaign required time. The initial American bombing raids on occupied Europe did not begin until August 17, 1942. The first targets were not in Germany but against targets in Rouen, France. The changing strategic environments, rival missions, and other limitations forced President Roosevelt to reassess AWPD/1's requirements in light of naval and ground force demands. On August 24, Roosevelt asked Arnold to estimate the total number of aircraft to gain "complete air ascendancy over the enemy."[34] Arnold directed many of the original authors of AWPD/1 to reexamine AAF needs for the task. Military, political, and economic factors challenged the AAF officers to create: "Requirements for Air Ascendancy" or AWPD/42. Like its predecessor, the authors worked frantically to develop the plan and they completed it on September 9, 1942.

AWPD/42's first task was to conduct an air offensive to render the *Luftwaffe* impotent, which would free the Allied air forces to conduct an unrestricted bombing campaign. In 1942, the *Luftwaffe* was a capable adversary that took a deadly toll on American aircrews. The authors of the AWPD/42 were also required to add a new, higher priority target—German submarine construction yards—to assist with the raging battle of the Atlantic. The major campaign however, that the AAF sought to conduct was strategic bombardment designed to destroy the German economy. Although the AAF officers understood the theoretical basis for strategic bombardment, there was little basis for the planners to estimate the economic underpinnings of their operational strategy. Additionally, the AWPD/42 authors did not possess any extensive experience conducting a strategic bombardment campaign, nor did they have higher-level practice in coordinating joint or coalition warfare. The authors also lacked firm intelligence data on proposed targeting.[35] Nonetheless, AWPD/42 had to forecast aircraft requirements that represented an official statement of what was necessary to fight the Axis powers from 1943 to early 1944.

Competing demands confronted AAF planners and diverted attention away from continental Europe and the planned strategic bombing campaign. In addition to strategic bombing missions, there was also the need to provide air support for ground operations that the Allies could stage in late 1942. AAF leadership also had to contend with the requirements for Pacific operations and the eventual need to establish bases and develop a longer-range bomber for a final offensive against Japan. These issues added to the need for more resources. The AAF also had another significant mission, defending the Western Hemisphere to include aircraft patrols to counter German submarine activities. These activities encouraged AAF officers to request 130,906 aircraft. The AAF projected a need of 75,416 aircraft for their service, about 33,050 for the Navy, and 22,440 for America's allies.[36] The AWPD/42 authors did not coordinate the plan with the Navy, but only estimated their requirements based on AAF projections. AWPD/42 was hardly a strategy that was jointly developed.

AWPD/42 produced a new strategic vision for the AAF. The AAF authors had to reexamine the value of strategic bombardment. In AWPD/1, the military value of strategic bombardment centered on its ability to force Germany's collapse solely by dismembering its economy. It offered the hope that long-range bombers could possibly end the war independent of any surface forces or alliance. By the time planners had completed AWPD/42, the focus of this new plan changed to supporting an invasion only if the strategic bombardment campaign could weaken enemy forces.[37] The AAF now proposed to attack 177 targets with over 66,000 bombers, which they hoped would destroy the *Luftwaffe*, disrupt U-boat activities, and disable the economy. The authors of AWPD/42 envisioned that a possible European invasion would take place by late 1944. Additionally, the AAF slowed provisions for intercontinental bomber production. Instead of conducting bombing operations against Germany from the United States, which would have been difficult considering the range of aircraft, the AAF now planned to use B-17 and B-24 units stationed in Britain. Pacific air bases could eventually strike Japan with a newer airframe, the B-29.

Target priorities also changed. AWPD/42 emphasized the immediate objective of attacking aircraft assembly plants and engine factories to neutralize the *Luftwaffe*. In addition to submarine construction yards, the AAF viewed aluminum and synthetic rubber production facilities as vital targets. Aluminum sources supported aircraft production. The RAF held a different view. The British Bureau of Economic Warfare believed synthetic rubber was the "bottleneck" to transportation of economic production.[38] If the RAF disrupted rubber supplies, then the German transportation network would screech to a halt. AWPD/42 authors still only guessed at the so-called "centers of gravity" for the German economy, but the strategic vision was finally coming into focus. President Roosevelt, who as early as 1938 had promoted aircraft production, compromised with the AAF's plans as outlined in AWPD/42. The President decided to build 107,000 aircraft and devote more resources for naval shipbuilding.[39] These presidential mandates put additional pressure on the American economy.

The use of air offensives against Hitler's Fortress Europe was important because it demonstrated an American commitment to the European Theater. Conversely, air raids did little to satisfy either of America's major allies, the Soviet Union or Great Britain, because these allies needed American manpower on the ground to erode the strength of the German Army. The need became more pressing once the spring of 1942 arrived, because both of America's allies faced German offensives. In May, the German Army, refreshed and revived after the bitter winter of 1941-42, expertly handled a Soviet offensive centered on Kharkov. Once they blunted the Soviet offensive, they counterattacked, encircling the Soviet 57th Army and inflicting massive losses on the Soviets. The German encirclement cost the Soviets 170,958 killed, missing, or taken prisoner, and 106,232 wounded. Soviet tank losses totaled 1,200. In addition, 2,600 artillery pieces were lost. In the succeeding weeks ,the Germans continued to exact substantial casualties from the Soviet Army, and on June 28, 1942 the German Army launched its summer offensive, which sent German, Hungarian, Rumanian and Italian units streaming eastward toward the Caucasus and the Volga. At roughly the same time, from May 26-27, *Generalfeldmarschall* Erwin Rommel began another offensive in North Africa that sent the British and their Free French allies reeling. The German North African offensive threw the Allies into retreat and resulted in Tobruk's fall.⁴⁰ The combined German-Italian force then crossed the border into Egypt.

Stakes were high for the Soviets, who were defending their homeland, but they were also high for the British who were fighting the Axis powers in an area of their long-term interest, the Mediterranean. Britain and the Soviet Union needed immediate help. Marshall commented succinctly that, "the initiative at this time lay wholly in the hands of the Axis." ⁴¹

Unfortunately, there was little Washington could do to relieve the pressure on the Soviet Union other than to send supplies and make future promises for more assistance. In 1942, this was not an easy task. A major lifeline for Lend-Lease supplies ran north along the "Murmansk Run" which subjected Allied shipping to a German manned gauntlet. This route caused unmerciful poundings of Allied shipping from both the Norwegian based *Luftwaffe* and from the U-boat fleet. Another potential supply route existed through the Persian Gulf region in Iran and into southern Russia. As German forces pushed into the Caucasus in late summer 1942, even this route seemed unlikely.

Good intentions aside, through most of 1942 neither the United States nor Great Britain were ready to embark on major combat operations against the main body of the German Army on Soviet soil or elsewhere. Even if they had been, Western Allied troops were not welcome on Soviet soil. The Soviets allied themselves with Imperial Britain and the capitalist United States, but the Soviet ruling elites were paranoid about the danger posed by Westerners adversely influencing their citizens with destabilizing ideas like democracy and freedom of expression.⁴² Large numbers of Western troops on Soviet soil were not likely and, at the same time, they would be difficult to supply. Other than assistance provided through Lend-Lease, Russia would have to go it alone and depend on Roosevelt's "Arsenal of Democracy" in lieu of a full-scale invasion.

As these crises developed in mid-1942, minor fissures emerged between the Allies over the strategy necessary to defeat Germany. These fissures were evident as early as the end of 1941 in the first real wartime strategy conference between the two Western powers. Code-named Arcadia, conference participants came to Washington from December 22, 1941 to January 14, 1942. The attendees were Churchill and his chiefs of staff. Roosevelt and his comparable military advisors hosted the meeting. On the table was the preferred American strategy, or the *way* to destroy Hitler's regime. This conference and subsequent negotiations between the two Western Allies provides a student of coalition warfare with an excellent case study on alliance politics. The American *way* to defeat Germany consisted of building up forces and materials for a cross-channel attack that would aim Allied forces at the heartland of Europe. The plan endorsed by the American leadership, code named Operation BOLERO-ROUNDUP, proposed to muster all available resources on the British Isles for an amphibious operation in the spring of 1943. BOLERO was the codename for the buildup of forces and supplies on the British Isles. American planners designated ROUNDUP as the actual invasion.

Source: U.S. Army Military History Institute.

U.S. Army General Dwight Eisenhower with Members of the War Department, Operations and War Plans Division, 1941.

At this time during the war, operational planning was the responsibility of a rapidly rising officer, Dwight D. Eisenhower. He was a significant new face at Arcadia having reported for this new assignment only a week earlier. As a new staffer in the War Plans Division, Eisenhower described his role at Arcadia as one of the "unimportant" staff officers on the periphery of the conference.[43] American planners, with Eisenhower carrying the flag, became enthusiastic about taking the war directly to the heartland of Europe. The prospects of such a venture seemed feasible since the British seemed initially comfortable with the plan. In his memoirs, Eisenhower notes that there were three options for American military action in 1942:

> 1. Direct reinforcement of the British Armies in the Middle East.
> 2. Prepare amphibious forces to seize northwest Africa with the idea of undertaking later operations to the eastward to catch Rommel.
> 3. Undertake a limited operation on the northwest coast of France . . . capture of an area that could be held against a German attack and which would later form a bridgehead for use in the large scale invasion agreed upon as the ultimate objective.[44]

Although he noted the options, Eisenhower's preferred plan, and that of Marshall, was a cross-channel attack. In addition to ROUNDUP, another plan favored by the U.S. Army's leadership was SLEDGEHAMMER, a proposed assault across the channel in September 1942. It was Marshall's belief that the United States and Britain had to do something in 1942 to relieve the pressure on the beleaguered Russians. Since the American entry in the war, the Soviets appeared to be on the verge of collapse. If the Allies could launch SLEDGEHAMMER, it would relieve the pressure on the Russians and serve the Allied cause by keeping them in the war.

In the meetings that followed, there was no disagreement between the two allies concerning the "Germany first" concept or that Berlin's defeat was the preeminent goal. Once this goal was accomplished, the defeat of Italy and Japan would follow as secondary goals. The agreements reached at Arcadia were:

> 1. Germany was regarded as the most dangerous Axis adversary and would be the primary target, while holding the Japanese in a defensive war.
> 2. A ring or noose was to be drawn around the Axis powers to wear them down, and tighten this ring as

resources mounted. Where limited offensives could be mounted, this too would contribute to weakening German resistance.

3. The ways to attack the most dangerous adversary were clearly in keeping with British thinking. Thus, strategic bombing, continuing military aid to the Russians, encouraging and supplying resistance groups in occupied countries and gaining mastery of the seas, all would weaken the Germans until the Allies could deliver a death blow to Germany.[45]

While "Germany first" was the overriding principle, the key issue that escaped resolution at this conference concerned the timing and location for bringing ground forces to bear against the German Army in the conduct of a Western European campaign. A positive accomplishment, however, was the establishment of the Combined Chiefs of Staff (CCOS), composed of the service chiefs of both nations who were to meet on a regular basis and develop the strategic priorities for the Western Allies.[46]

For American military planners, there was little enthusiasm for the results of the Arcadia meeting. American planners wanted a definitive approval by Roosevelt and Churchill to buildup forces and supplies on the British Isles. After this buildup, these military planners expected to deliver a direct attack on the heartland of Europe through an amphibious cross-channel assault. The British did not show much interest in the plan. Churchill and the British military did not want an immediate invasion. Marshall, in attendance with the U.S. delegation, was extremely disappointed and, at the same time, irritated. In Marshall's mind, any commitment of forces in and around Europe needed to focus on the cross-channel attack. Through such an attack, Allied forces could push across German occupied Western Europe and deliver a deathblow to Nazi Germany. Marshall, representing the Army's military establishment, was firmly convinced that the war effort needed an amphibious attack. His thoughts, included in what was termed the "Marshall Memorandum" (April 1, 1942), were clear and unambiguous. This memorandum, developed in the War Plans Division of the War Department General Staff and written by Eisenhower and Colonel Thomas T. Hardy, clearly stated that a European campaign, including an invasion of France, was "the only place in which the bulk of the British ground forces can be committed to a general offensive in cooperation with U.S. forces" [47]

The Marshall Memorandum proposed a landing of 30 American divisions, with a total of 1,000,000 American servicemen, supplemented with 18 British divisions, in an area between 'Etretat (just north of Le Havre) and Boulogne. The initial assault wave was to consist of 77,000 soldiers on a six-division front. Approximately 2,250 tanks, 18,000 vehicles, and 5,800 aircraft (3,250 of which would be American) would support the invasion. The target date was April 1, 1943. Roosevelt approved the plan. Marshall and Roosevelt's confident, Harry Hopkins, were directed to hand carry this plan to London to get the approval of the British military leadership.

The reception for this ambitious plan proposed by the American military leadership was polite. On April 14, 1942, the British Chiefs of Staff accepted the Marshall Memorandum, but in principle only. The British could, in fact, have been more forthcoming with their misgivings about scheduling such an ambitious undertaking so early in the war. For example, in his diary Field Marshall Lord Alanbrooke noted, "With the situation prevailing at that time, it was not possible to take Marshall's 'castles in the air' too seriously! It must be remembered that we were at that time hanging on by our eyelids."[48]

In 1942, Eisenhower and Marshall pushed hard for a ground campaign in Europe, but the British were at best reticent about the concept of SLEDGEHAMMER. They were even more convinced that a full-scale cross-channel operation in the spring of 1943 was simply beyond Allied capabilities. The British did not immediately point out the problems with the favored American plan; they withheld their reservations about the proposed time schedule for the invasion of the continent.[49]

It was not until early July 1942 that the British Cabinet clearly stated that it was opposed to any type of cross-channel operation, even a limited one. The true British position on an early cross-channel attack came when King, Marshall, and Hopkins traveled to London to get British agreement about the time and place of the invasion. This admission motivated Marshall and King, in meetings held between July 17-22, to propose that if there was no determination on the part of the British to engage in a cross-channel operation against France, then the United States should shift its emphasis and prepare for decisive operations in the Pacific against the Japanese.[50] Roosevelt emphatically vetoed any such idea. It was still to be Europe first; the question was not if, but when.

In retrospect, the British were right. Without aerial superiority (not achievable until early 1944), with a shortage of amphibious invasion ships, plus a strong *Wehrmacht* force in several theaters of war, an invasion of the continent would have been a very risky venture. Furthermore, the Germans, with a rather limited effort, could contain an invasion in a location like the Cotentin Peninsula. An amphibious assault is a direct frontal assault that even with full surprise is a rather risky operation. If the Allies staged SLEDGEHAMMER, as Marshall proposed in order to reduce the pressure on the Russians, then it would likely fail. Failure would likely have resulted in 1942 for many reasons. The U-Boat menace was still present, the Allies were far from achieving aerial superiority in the area where landings were proposed, and an extremely capable enemy had an excellent chance of pushing an invading force into the sea. Still, in terms of good alliance relations, the British should have been much more direct and early in voicing their misgivings.

Since the British totally opposed a 1942 landing along the French coast, Marshall, knowing the British preference for a North Africa operation, drafted a plan for invading North Africa. He discussed the option with King. With King agreeing to the rough draft, the plan for Operation TORCH (the invasion of North Africa) appeared to be on schedule for the first American land operation against the Germans. Marshall scratched SLEDGEHAMMER and postponed BOLERO-ROUNDUP, scheduled for the spring of 1943. Marshall, returning to Washington, hoped he could convince Roosevelt to help reverse this British position, and that the United States could continue plans and preparations for an early invasion in France. On the evening of July 30, in a meeting at the White House, the President made it clear that the Allies should execute TORCH at the earliest possible moment, and the principal objective of the Combined Chiefs of Staff was to assemble the necessary resources to complete the operation.[51]

The predictable reaction to the President's decision from the U.S. military leadership was that Roosevelt's decision was purely political—that politics had overruled military logic. In a sense, they were right, but it was not merely the President bowing to the logic of the British prime minister. Domestic politics also pushed Roosevelt to commit American forces to a military operation against the Germans before the end of 1942. SLEDGEHAMMER was only logical if it prevented the collapse of Russia, but it was acknowledged that it would likely be a failure for American and British forces. This could have been difficult for Roosevelt, given the scheduled November congressional elections.

The British were not adverse to a cross-channel attack, but in their opinion such an operation at this stage in the war boded more for failure than success. Staging a cross-channel attack was still the ultimate plan, agreed to by both the United States and Great Britain, but a limited 1942 invasion as promoted by American military planners and a full-scale 1943 invasion became casualties due to stiffening British opposition. The cross-channel attack favored by Marshall and Eisenhower had to wait.[52] Critics have castigated Roosevelt for the decision to scrap an early cross-channel operation, but even Eisenhower, looking at the decision in retrospect, admitted that "those who held the SLEDGEHAMMER operation to be unwise at the moment were correct in the evaluation of the problem."[53]

From the British perspective, the Allies had to exercise caution about scheduling any amphibious landing too early in the war. At least some of the caution by Churchill came from his experience in 1915 at the Gallipoli failure, the only major amphibious operation in World War I. This had been, by any measure, an unmitigated disaster.[54] Adding to this embarrassment, when World War II started, the British Army suffered a humbling experience at Dunkirk in 1940 when the Germans shoved them off the continent. Their Dunkirk experience, and that of the Battle of Britain in August 1940, made them well aware of German capabilities. The British respect for German defensive capabilities increased when a largely Canadian force landed at the French seaport of Dieppe on August 19, 1942. This raid occurred when, under pressure due to the degenerating course of events in the war, the British decided to stage some raids along the French coast. They focused their raid on Dieppe, a location that they thought was lightly defended by the Germans. Instead, German defenses were well prepared, and the Canadian forces took heavy casualties. The Germans also pushed them off the continent, giving yet another defeat to British forces.[55]

The British remained in agreement with the Europe first concept, but in planning military operations, they had to consider what was necessary to best serve the interests of Great Britain and guarantee the continued existence of the worldwide British Empire. The United States however, only had to consider the security of North America and its national interests. For both countries, the new factor was the entry of Japan into the war and its impact on affected American and British territories. Even though British and U.S. representatives had met repeatedly since 1938 and discussed cooperation, the prewar committees that focused on the possibility of a two-front war, with Germany first, did not anticipate the rapid Japanese drive into the Southwest Pacific. In addition, there were many questions: How would the Allies define a defensive war in the Pacific, what would be the limitations for such a war, and what would it cost to contain the Japanese? No one could answer these difficult questions. The British, though holding fast to Europe first, were deeply concerned about Australia, New Zealand and, in early 1942, Singapore.[56] The Allies needed to devise a defensive strategy for the Pacific; they formed a unified command to protect the interests of both countries. The major issues however, were whether American assets were to be used to bolster the defense of Singapore, Australia, and New Zealand; and the size of the minimum force necessary for defending Pacific interests while preparing to defeat Germany.

In terms of the European war, the British were much more interested in the Mediterranean where Britain already had a ground campaign in progress and where they had long-term interests, including the Suez Canal and oil. Since 1941, British and Axis forces grappled across North Africa in a seesaw campaign, each with the hopes of delivering a *coup de grace* to the other army. The British felt that the correct strategy to defeat Germany was a peripheral one. Thus, the Allies should aggressively pursue the war around the fringes of Germany's Fortress Europe, rather than an attack directly at the heartland. As part of this strategic concept, Churchill believed that there was a "soft underbelly" to Europe exploitable through military action.

There were elements of the British peripheral concept that American planners could easily accept. A bomber offensive to destroy the German economy and bring the war to its leaders and citizens was acceptable on both sides of the Atlantic. It also fit well with the AAF's plans. Another element of the peripheral strategy in which both Western powers could agree was the supply and encouragement of the resistance movements that had sprung up all over Europe and other areas. Finally, both nations understood that the combined power of the American and British navies were necessary to remove the U-boat menace that would also contribute to the erosion of German strength. In all, rather than direct assaults against Fortress Europe, the Allies should strike where weaknesses appeared in the German armor. Such attacks, pressure on the fringes, would wear down Berlin's strength, albeit at a slower pace than those in Washington wanted. When this strategy weakened the once mighty *Wehrmacht*, the Allies could attack the European heartland and drive a stake into the heart of the German beast.

This British approach, conditioned by a lack of resources and the memories of the horrendous losses of World War I, did little to satisfy the needs of the Soviet Union. The British were not fighting a substantial part of the German Army, but were fighting the Germans and their Italian Allies in a theater that Hitler considered a sideshow. The *Afrika Korps*, and particularly its commander, Rommel, thrilled the German media and many of the citizenry with its audacity on the tactical battlefield. However, North Africa was a campaign borne of Italian failures rather than German designs.[57] In mid-1941, Hitler's eyes and the resources of his military were focused on the Soviet Union and the *Führer's* desire to destroy Jewish Bolshevism and the Slavic state that was its home. Hitler's war was on the Russian steppes, the Eurasian heartland, not the hot, desolate North African sands.

Thus, as 1941 faded into 1942, Russia entered a second year of the war virtually alone; a war where each side seldom gave quarter. Stalin wanted and needed help through the establishment of another major front. A second front would force the German military to dedicate forces to counter another threat and, as a consequence, drain the strength of the German *Wehrmacht*. According to Churchill, the proposal for a second front began as early as July 18, 1941. A message from Stalin to Churchill stated:

> It seems to me therefore that the military situation of the Soviet Union as well as Great Britain, would be considerably improved if there could be established a front against Hitler in the west — northern France, and in the North — the Arctic.[58]

According to Stalin's message, the dictator found 1941 to be the "most propitious moment" for the establishment of such a front. From the onset however, Churchill noted the immense problems that were inherent in an amphibious landing in northern France. Limited British forces would face up to 40 German divisions in well-prepared defenses, and would lack the necessary air superiority. The British had faced a similar quandary in 1939 when they pondered how to help Poland, a problem they and their French allies never resolved. Still, as noted by Churchill, this theme, the call for a second front, would "recur throughout our subsequent relations with monotonous disregard, except in the Far North, for physical facts."[59]

Considering this early, but cordial exchange between Churchill and Stalin, it seems evident that from the earliest discussions there were differing priorities about how and where the Allies could win the European war. From the onset of what Churchill called the Grand Alliance, the Soviet leadership felt that Russia, both a participant and a battleground for the European war, was not receiving sufficient support from first the British and later the United States. The absence of another major front to stretch German capabilities, and the inclination of Stalin to distrust two of the world's largest capitalistic countries, led to considerable resentment on the part of Stalin against the Western Allies. Since the second front did not occur until June 6, 1944, Stalin's resentment had a long time to build.

Granted, Stalin was disappointed, but in many respects, this situation merely reinforced his long preconceived distrust of Western democracies and their capitalistic governments. The landings along the North African coast—Operation TORCH—beginning November 8, 1942, were an unqualified success, but they were hardly what Stalin hoped for, since the attack initially focused on the Vichy French forces and never had the potential of tying down large numbers of German units which was the desire of the Soviet dictator. In many respects, the success of TORCH only exacerbated the problem for both the Soviets and the key American strategists that promoted an attack aimed at northern France. For now, the Western Allies fought Axis forces in operations in the Mediterranean, not in France. From the Soviet perspective, the Mediterranean would become a vortex, using more Allied resources, but not tying down sufficient numbers of German divisions. The Allies and Axis powers would not witness a European campaign with any ground actions focusing on northern France in 1942.

ENDNOTES - CHAPTER 2

1. Dwight D. Eisenhower, as quoted in the so-called Marshall Memorandum, authored by Eisenhower and approved by General George C. Marshall, clearly emphasized that the focus of U.S. operations should be Europe to ensure ". . . the security of England, the retention of Russia in the War as an active ally,

and the defense of the Middle East." See Mark Perry, *Partners in Command, George Marshall and Dwight Eisenhower in War and Peace*, New York: The Penguin Press, 2007, pp. 75-76.

2. This Joint Resolution by Congress ordering reserve elements to active duty and the Burke-Wadsworth Bill that authorized Selective Service for a year, limited the employment of troops raised through these measures to the Western Hemisphere and possessions of the United States. See Russell F. Weigley, *History of the U.S. Army*, New York: The MacMillan Co., 1967, p. 427.

3. The Extension Act was highly contentious, focusing on such issues as to whether a national emergency existed that required such an extension or whether the American interest was actually imperiled. Some in Congress felt "a vote for the bill would be political suicide." Robert Bruce Sligh, *The National Guard and National Defense: The Mobilization of the Guard in World War II*, New York: Praeger, 1992, pp. 135-145.

4. William L. Langer and S. Everett Gleason, *The Undeclared War*, New York: Harper and Brothers, 1953, pp. 735, 740.

5. Some events in the European war also intruded into the plans by the Army to rebuild and expand its military forces. The British disaster at Dunkirk in 1940, resulted in the British Army leaving the vast majority of its field equipment on the beach. Thus, the United States released to the British large quantities of rifles, Browning automatic rifles, machine guns, ammunition and TNT from U.S. war stocks. George C. Marshall, *Biennial Report of the Chief of Staff of the U.S. Army to the Secretary of War, 1 July 1939-30 June 1945*, Washington DC: U.S. Army Center of Military History, 1996, p. 39.

6. Tom Brokaw, *The Greatest Generation*, New York: Random House, 2004, p. 359. According to Casper Weinberger, who enlisted in the Army in August 1941, "We were trained with wooden rifles and little blocks of wood painted to look like grenades. We did little live fire because there wasn't enough ammunition."

7. The impact on equipment due to the Lend-Lease Act can be seen through planned aircraft production, which had been a priority for President Roosevelt. Thus, according to the schedule

drawn up in September 1941, the U.S. Army was to receive 4,189 tactical aircraft; Great Britain, 6, 634; Russia, 1,835; China, 407; and other nations, 109. This production was to have been anticipated by June 1942. Weigley, *History of the U.S. Army*, p. 433.

8. Marshall was cognizant of the impact to the ground and AAF units, as he watched supplies go to foreign nations. As Russia sought more and more supplies to halt the German advance, Marshall drafted a rather sharp response to the Secretary of War, indicating the effect that Lend-Lease was having on the AAF. He stated, "In the first place our Air Force is suffering from a severe shortage in spare parts of all kinds. We have planes on the ground because we cannot repair them . . ." Mark Skinner Watson, *The War Department, Chief of Staff: Pre War Plans and Preparations in the Series, U.S. Army in World War II*, Washington, DC: U.S. Army Center of Military History, 1991, p. 329.

9. Through 1941, the nation's economy focused on civilian, not military equipment. In 1941, only 10 percent of U.S. gross national product was geared toward war production. By 1943, 43 percent of production focused on military products. Thus, in 1940-41, the country was not yet on a wartime footing. An added complication for the rapidly expanding American Army was the previously mentioned direction of significant amounts of war materials to our soon to be Allies through the President's "Arsenal of Democracy" concept.

10. Charles E. Kirkpatrick, *An Unknown Future and a Doubtful Present: Writing the Victory Plan of 1941*, Washington DC: U.S. Army Center of Military History, 1990, p. 63.

11. The term "vacillations" on the part of the President may be too harsh. As noted in a recent study, Roosevelt sincerely hoped that America could stay out of another war with Germany. He believed that victory over Germany and its allies was possible by assisting Britain and France, and later the Soviet Union, with the materials of war to accomplish this task. But, the tempo of the crisis was not set in Washington; rather it was set in Berlin, Tokyo, and Rome. Thus, after 1938 Roosevelt had to respond to a consistently deteriorating world situation. See Gerhard L. Weinberg, *Visions of Victory: The Hopes of Eight World War II Leaders*, New York: Cambridge University Press, 2005, pp. 177-179.

12. Granted, the number of divisions estimated by Wedemeyer was excessive, but as noted in his memoirs, on May 31, 1945, the total Army, including the Air Force, consisted of 8,291,336 officers and enlisted men. Albert C. Wedemeyer, *Wedemeyer Reports*, New York: Henry Holt & Company, 1958, p. 75.

13. As war came to the United States in December 1941, the U.S. Army had 37 divisions, 17 of which were technically ready to go to war. Furthermore, these so-called ready divisions lacked radios, weapons, anti-aircraft assets, and anti-tank weapons. Overall, the Army was also suffering from a lack of ammunition. Considering all of the shortages, only one division and one anti-aircraft unit was truly ready to go into a combat zone. See Maurice Matloff, *American Military History*, Washington, DC: Office of the Chief of Military History, 1969, p. 435.

14. The manpower used by the automobile industry was also significant. American car manufacturers employed one out of every 260 Americans in a direct capacity within the automobile industry, while one out of every 19 Americans had an indirect role in this industry. See Alan L. Gropman, *Mobilizing U.S. Industry in World War II*, McNair Paper #50, Washington, DC: National Defense University Press, 1996, pp. 59-60.

15. *Ibid*.

16. Kent Roberts Greenfield, *American Strategy in World War II*, Malabar, FL: Robert E. Krieger Publishing Company, 1982, p. 88.

17. E. B. Potter, *Sea Power: A Naval History*, Annapolis, MD: Naval Institute Press, 1981, p. 224.

18. On the eve of the War in Europe, August 1939, the *Kriegsmarine*, or German Navy, could field 56 commissioned U-boats. Günther Hessler, *German Naval History: The U-Boat War in the Atlantic 1939-1945*, London, UK: Her Majesty's Stationery Office, 1992, p. 1.

19. The *Kriegsmarine* leadership had many internal conflicts over how the Navy should contribute to the German war effort. The leadership, led by Admiral Erich Raeder, was dominated by

a fleet mentality, believing that capital ships would be the Navy's power projection force, not U-boats or aircraft carriers. The older leadership from the Imperial era never strayed too far from Alfred Mahan's concepts. Raeder foresaw a growing naval capability as a means to expand Germany's global position through a greater High Seas Fleet.

20. Richard Overy, *Why the Allies Won*, New York: W. W. Norton, 1996, p. 45.

21. Heinz Magenheimer, *Hitler's War: Germany's Key Strategic Decisions 1940-1945*, London, UK: Cassel, 1998, p. 30.

22. Potter, p. 264.

23. Jak. P. Mallmann Showell, *U-Boats Under the Swastika*, Annapolis, MD: Naval Institute Press, 1973, p. 42.

24. For battleship proponents, the attack on Pearl Harbor must have reaffirmed their belief in the importance of the battleship since Japanese planes struck and severely damaged the battleship inventory of the U.S. Navy. No carriers were lost. Conversely, the Japanese had hoped to catch the three carriers assigned to the Pacific fleet, but the carriers had already left Pearl.

25. Ministry of Defense (Navy), *The U-Boat War in the Atlantic Volume II January 1942-May 1943*, London, UK: HMSO, 1992, p. 14.

26. Timothy A Warnock, *The Battle Against the U-Boat in the American Theater*, Washington, DC: Center for Air Force History, 1992, p. 13.

27. Montgomery C. Meigs, *Slide Rules and Submarines*, Washington, DC: National Defense University Press, 1990, p. 91.

28. Warnock, p. 9.

29. Russell F. Weigley, *The American Way of War: A History of U.S. Military Strategy and Policy,* Bloomington: Indiana University Press, 1973, pp. 270, 271.

30. The enormity of the problem of pursuing the destruction of Nazi Germany without Britain had been highlighted by Admiral Harold Stark in late 1940, early 1941. Although he believed that the British concept of blocking and wearing down the Germans would not in itself win the war, he also believed that the United States had to ensure the continued existence of an independent Britain since the United States would have to have the necessary forward bases that Britain could provide to pursue its strategy for the destruction of Nazi Germany. See Louis Morton, "Germany First: The Basic Concept of Allied Strategy in World War II," in Kent Roberts Greenfield, ed., *Command Decisions,* Washington, DC: U.S. Army Center of Military History, 1984, pp. 34-39.

31. By the time America entered the war, the Germans had 200 submarines and were commissioning 20 per month. Eric Larabee, *Commander in Chief: Franklin Delano Roosevelt, His Lieutenants and Their War,* New York: Simon and Schuster, 1987, p. 176.

32. Troops from Italy, Spain, Romania, and Bulgaria, plus contingents of volunteers from German occupied Europe, bolstered the German commitment to this campaign. See Matthew Cooper, *The German Army, 1933-1945: Its Political and Military Failure,* New York: Stein and Day Publishers, 1958, pp. 268-271. From the middle of 1940 when Hitler began pondering the switch to the East, it was assumed that the campaign against the Soviets would be short and violent, which was the German tradition. When concluded, Hitler could then turn back to problems in the West and in the Mediterranean. See Walter Warlimont, *Inside Hitler's Headquarters, 1939-1945,* Novato, CA: Presidio Books, 1964, pp. 132-137.

33. Marshall, *Biennial Report,* pp. 43-46.

34. Robert C. Erhart, Thomas A. Fabyanic, and Robert Futrell, "Building an Intelligence Organization and the European Theater," in John F. Kreis, ed., *Piercing the Fog,* Washington, DC: Air Force History and Museums Program, 1996, p. 150.

35. *Ibid.,* p. 151.

36. *Ibid.,* p. 130.

37. *Ibid.*, p. 150.

38. *Ibid.*, p. 151.

39. *Ibid.*, p. 131.

40. When Tobruk fell, President Roosevelt asked Churchill what he could do to assist Britain. Churchill requested tanks to replace the British losses suffered from the German offensive. The United States sent 300 new M-4 Sherman tanks to the British. Again, the United States was destined to serve as the "Arsenal of Democracy," even though the U.S. Army was still short on equipment. See Dennis Showalter, *Rommel and Patton: Men of War in the Twentieth Century*, New York: Berkley Publishing Group, 2005, p. 273.

41. Marshall, *Biennial Reports*, p. 52.

42. The Soviets relented briefly in June 1944 when they allowed U.S. aircrews to land at Poltava during Operation FRANTIC. This, however, was one of the few exceptions to the Soviet policy of discouraging the presence of foreign, though allied, troops on Soviet soil.

43. Carlo D'Este, *Eisenhower: A Soldiers Life*, New York: Henry Holt and Company, 2002, p. 288.

44. Dwight D. Eisenhower, *Crusade in Europe*, Garden City, New York: Doubleday and Company, 1948, p. 70.

45. Greenfield, p. 27.

46. The structure of CCOS indicates how Allied planning and communication was facilitated from Arcadia until the end of the war. The membership from the American side consisted of Marshall, Arnold, and King. Their British peers were Field Marshal Alanbrooke, General Sir John Dill, Marshal of the RAF Sir Charles Portal, and Admiral of the Fleet Sir Andrew B. Cunningham. These key officers from all three branches of the service met on a regular basis from Arcadia until May 1945.

47. Larabee, p. 134.

48. Field Marshall Lord Alanbrooke, *War Diaries, 1939-1945*, Alex Danchev and Daniel Todman, eds., Berkeley, CA: University of California Press, 2001, p. 248.

49. According to Wedemeyer, Eisenhower was disturbed in April 1942 because he perceived among the British a "faint but definitely perceptible lack of enthusiasm for the cross-channel concept." Albert C. Wedemeyer, *Wedemeyer Reports*, New York: Henry Holt and Company, 1958, p. 131.

50. Alanbrooke described the meeting, saying "King remained with a face like a Sphinx, and only one idea, i.e., to transfer operations to the Pacific." Alanbrooke, p. 283.

51. According to two notable military historians, "The rationale for the President's decision stemmed from domestic politics. The U.S. had to involve its forces in combat with the Germans in 1942 or else the political pressures for a 'Japan First' strategy might become intolerable." Williamson Murray and Allen Millett, *A War to be Won: Fighting the World War II*, Cambridge MA: Harvard University Press, 2000, p. 273.

52. The decision disappointed Eisenhower. The British proposal, in Eisenhower's view would "eliminate the possibility of a major cross-channel invasion in 1943," the target date for U.S. military planners. Eisenhower regarded the plan to stage Operation TORCH, thereby postponing the cross-channel attack, to be "the blackest day in history." George Patton was equally dismayed, and when Roosevelt heard of the latter's pessimism, he purportedly said, "It must go on; I have promised Churchill that we would fight in Africa." Stanley Hirschorn, *General Patton: A Soldier's Life*, New York: HarperCollins, 2002, p. 268.

53. Eisenhower, *Crusade in Europe*, p. 71. One of the key reasons Eisenhower listed was the limited range of fighter aircraft used by the Allies.

54. Note, however, that the other amphibious operation in the Western Theater in World War I, the German invasion of the Baltic islands of Dago, Oesel, and Moon was highly successful due to sound planning, excellent cooperation between the services, and solid leadership on the ground. See Michael Barrett, *Operation Albion: The German Conquest of the Baltic Islands*, Bloomington, IN: Indiana University Press, 2007.

55. There are many reasons given for executing this raid, *Jubilee*. Whatever the true reason, of the 4,963 Canadians that composed this force, only 2,210 returned to Great Britain. There were 1,946 prisoners of war, and 907 were killed. Churchill and other Allied leaders claimed that it was not a failure due to the lessons learned, but at the same time the Prime Minister was forced to note ". . . the casualties of this memorable action may seem out of proportion to the results." Winston S. Churchill, *The Hinge of Fate*, Boston, MA: Houghton Mifflin Co., 1950, p. 511.

56. The Japanese laid siege to Singapore from January 31-February 15, 1942. King, a shrewd strategist, was a proponent for more assets designated for the Pacific in order to guard American interests. One author noted that King "objected not to the Atlantic-first strategy as such, as MacArthur did, but only to the inference drawn from it that the Pacific could be safely ignored until Germany had been defeated." Larabee, p. 183.

57. One historian has noted, "German intervention in North Africa was originally intended as no more than a holding operation . . . a blocking force, for dispatch to Tripoli with the mission of containing the British while the Balkan offensive took shape." Dennis Showalter, *Patton and Rommel: Men of War of the Twentieth Century*, New York: Berkley Publishing Group, 2005, p. 255.

58. Winston S. Churchill, *The Grand Alliance*, Boston, MA: Houghton Mifflin Co., 1950, p. 383.

59. *Ibid.*, p. 384. In his postwar memoirs, Eisenhower noted as well, that in late June 1942 the American and the British press was echoing the Russian cry for a "second front." Eisenhower, p. 52.

CHAPTER 3

1943:
FRUSTRATIONS AND SUCCESSES

We've got to go to Europe and fight—and we've got to quit wasting resources all over the world.[1]

Dwight D. Eisenhower

In the euphoria of the North Africa landings and subsequent defeat of German forces, Franklin Roosevelt, Winston Churchill, and the Combined Chiefs of Staff (CCOS) met in the newly liberated Moroccan city of Casablanca in January 1943.[2] At the time of the meeting, the North African campaign was not yet over, but it appeared that the campaign would be a success—the ignominious American defeat at Kasserine Pass would not occur until mid February. Both the British and American leadership agreed without dissention on several issues. First, both agreed about the necessity of pressing forward with an expanded strategic bombing campaign in 1943, although the British and Americans had decidedly different viewpoints concerning how the offensive should be staged.[3] A second and equally important problem was the pressing need to erase the U-boat menace so that American men and supplies could reach Britain and Eastern Europe. Without secure lines of communication, the Allies could not undertake a major buildup of men and materiel for significant operations. The third and closely related issue for obvious agreement was the need to continue a solid stream of supplies to support the Soviet Army in the field. The Soviet ability to tie down a substantial part of Germany's elite divisions was critical for the plans of the Western Allies. Fourth,

Roosevelt announced a policy of unconditional surrender that would tie all of the Allies to the total defeat of Germany. This policy provided a demonstrated commitment to Stalin.

Aside from these readily agreed to concepts, two things were obvious. First, the proposed American operations SLEDGEHAMMER and BOLERO-ROUNDUP were the preferred operations for the Americans who had set their sights on a cross-channel attack. George Marshall, Albert Wedemeyer, and Dwight Eisenhower had agreed that this was the logical path to victory over Nazi Germany. Other than the cross-channel attack, they had no alternate plan, no fall back options on how to attack the Germans once the campaign in North Africa was over.[4] As far as the British were concerned, it was simply too early in the war for an invasion of Northern Europe. The Germans were far too strong for the Allies to stage a direct assault on Fortress Europe. At this stage in the war, such an operation was still too risky. The British leadership believed the logical place for the Allies to continue their offensive was in the Mediterranean. Continued attacks in this region could solidify Allied control of the Mediterranean and fully open the sea lanes to Allied shipping. Allied planners did consider other alternatives for a follow up to North Africa including operations against Crete, Greece, the Balkans, the islands of Sardinia and Corsica, or, better yet, Sicily. Due to the British interest in the mythical soft underbelly of Europe, they centered their arguments on the value of Sicily.[5] If British and American forces could take the island, then it could provide a logical bridge to Italy. A successful Sicilian campaign would allow Allied forces to begin working their way up the Italian peninsula, then a war weary Italy would most likely drop out of the conflict.

Source: U.S. Army Military History Institute

General George C. Marshall, the key figure in the U.S. military buildup before World War II.

As could be expected, Marshall was opposed to any plan that would delay landings in northern France — the cross-channel attack. He considered taking the offense against Germany as being the most desirable option to retain the initiative once the North African campaign was over. When asked by Roosevelt when the Sicilian or other option might occur, Eisenhower off the cuff responded, "May 1943," an assessment due more to luck rather than actual insight.[6] Although Marshall consistently pressed Allied leadership for an attack on northern France, it was again Churchill and his military advisors who carried the day. Consequently, once the North African campaign was over, the Allies (beginning to refer to themselves as the United Nations) would invade Sicily, firming up Allied control over the Mediterranean. Operation HUSKY, the invasion of Sicily, not BOLERO-ROUNDUP, would be the next Allied operation. In the eyes of some American planners, this was pinprick warfare or pecking around the periphery, the preferred British strategy. Nonetheless, the Western Allies acknowledged that a cross-channel invasion of France *would* finally occur; the issue still unresolved was exactly when.

For Marshall and Eisenhower, the failure of the British to agree to some type of military action in Europe in late 1942 to early 1943 remained a bitter pill. In their opinion, the only logical way to bring about a quick and decisive defeat of the *Wehrmacht* was a direct attack through France culminating in the destruction of the ability of the German nation to wage war. It seemed that committing American forces to additional action in the Mediterranean was wrong from two perspectives: first, it seemed to commit American forces to support primarily British interests; and second, the selection seemed to support the favored British peripheral strategy, rather than a concentrated attack against the main body of the German military in Western Europe. Still, for perhaps the wrong reasons, the British were right. The German Army, despite the impending disasters at Stalingrad and Tunisia, remained a potent force in the field, as *Generalfeldmarschall* Erich von Manstein's famous "backhand" directed against the Soviet Army in February and March 1943 would show.[7] The *Luftwaffe* was still an extremely capable force and the AAF and RAF would need another year to reduce it as an effective fighting force. Thus, the fact that, in this instance, the President overrode the favored plans of his military advisors was fortuitous.

Neither Marshall nor Eisenhower ever wavered from the strategy that the appropriate route to victory was using the British Isles as a base to buildup the supplies and an appropriate number of troops and then launch a cross-channel attack into northern France. Eisenhower reflected on his firm beliefs on what actions the Allies had to take by commenting, "We can't win by sitting on our fannies and giving our stuff in driblets all over the world, with no theater getting enough."[8] Yet in his opinion, and that of Marshall, the latter was, in fact, occurring.

Many regard the two key decisions of the Casablanca Conference to have been the postponement of the cross-channel attack and the decision to invade Sicily.[9] In many respects, they were. Conversely, often overlooked is a subtle yet significant expansion of the Pacific option. After considerable wrangling about strategy and priorities by the representatives of the two sides, British Air Marshall Sir John Slessor developed a compromise that stated:

> Operations in the Pacific and Far East shall continue with the forces allocated, with the objective of maintaining pressure on Japan, retaining the initiative and attaining a position of readiness for the full scale offensive against Japan by the United Nations as soon as Germany is defeated. These operations must be kept within such limits as will not, in the opinion of the Combined Chiefs of Staff, prejudice the capacity of the United Nations to take any opportunity that may present itself for the decisive defeat of Germany in 1943. [Later a provision was added authorizing plans and preparations, after the capture of Rabaul, for invading the Marshall and Caroline Islands, provided that this did not interfere with an invasion of Burma.][10]

The bracketed provision, added later, proved to be yet another detractor from landings in northern France, in that it played directly into the hands of Admiral Ernest King. The latter, though acknowledging the necessity of an invasion of northern France, was also a proponent for the expansion of major combat operations in the Pacific. King believed that the strength of American industry could provide the necessary materials to support offensives in both theaters. He felt that a drive across the central Pacific could cut the Japanese off from their sources of raw materials in Southeast Asia, with a minimal commitment of additional resources. Through such a move, the United States could seriously erode the strength of the Japanese economy and military. The statement in and of itself did not directly call for a Pacific offensive, but the latitude was there. Plans to expand operations in the Pacific also added to the certainty that landings in northern France in 1943 would not occur, only the continuance of the intent to do so.

Source: U.S. Army Military History Institute.

Admiral Ernest King, Naval Strategist, a major proponent for shifting more emphasis to the Pacific Theater.

American participation in the Mediterranean war, which had begun with Operation TORCH, continued to grow with the invasion of Sicily followed by landings in Italy. The commitment of men and material to this theater continued into January 1944, when American forces executed an amphibious assault at Anzio, that was designed as a classic turning movement.[11] At the same time, King began pursuing his Pacific strategy, driving through the Pacific Mandates controlled by the Japanese and initiating landings on the Makin Islands and a successful, though costly, amphibious landing at Tarawa.[12] Douglas MacArthur also moved through the Southwest Pacific. The war, for American forces, was spreading, but not yet to northern France.

Despite the bitter pill of postponing the 1943 invasion of France, the Mediterranean operations had a strong supporter, Roosevelt. From almost the beginning of what Churchill called the "Grand Alliance," some military officers expressed concern that the President was under the influence of Churchill. Wedemeyer best summarized the rationale of this criticism when he stated, "the virtuoso Churchill led the Anglo-American orchestra, although we furnished practically all of the instruments and most of the musicians."[13] These criticisms grew during the various summits held between the leaders of the two nations, culminating in the bitter disappointment at Casablanca when Roosevelt supported the British proposal for continuing operations in the Mediterranean, rather than holding out for the preferred American solution, an invasion of northern France.

Even though the decision to invade Sicily was a clear disappointment for American Army planners, Eisenhower came away from his private conversations with Roosevelt with optimism. At Casablanca, Eisenhower believed that the President was firmly committed to "our basic concept of European strategy, namely the cross-channel invasion."[14] Roosevelt's commitment to this concept became increasingly evident as the year proceeded. While the President supported the concept, he consistently coordinated actions with Churchill who publicly supported the preferred American strategy, but who, together with his military leadership, dragged his feet on its early implementation. Their preference was to continue the British peripheral strategy, coupled with the bombing campaign, which would wear down German strength, a prerequisite for the planned invasion. U.S. Secretary of War Henry L. Stimson, spent a week in Britain in July 1943, and came home convinced that:

> ... no attempt to cross the channel and 'come to grips with our German enemy' was ever going to be made under British auspices. The heads of their government oppose it; the shadows of Dunkirk and the Somme fell too darkly across their minds. 'Though they have rendered lip service to the operation,' Stimson wrote to Roosevelt, 'their hearts are not in it and it will require more independence, more faith, and more vigor than it is reasonable to expect we can find in any British commander.'[15]

Stimson's conversations with Churchill during his week in London cemented his belief about the British reticence. Upon his return to Washington, he urged the President to exert personal leadership in ensuring that the cross-channel attack remained key to the Allied strategy, and that a commander should be named who whole-heartedly supported this operation. Stimson's preference was Marshall. The President concurred with Stimson's conclusions, and in a subsequent meeting held on August 10, 1943, Roosevelt strongly supported the cross-channel attack. According to one writer, "The cross-channel attack had at last become wholly his own."[16]

For U.S. Army planners, Roosevelt's commitment as a strong proponent of the cross-channel attack was a major coup. But Army planners still had to consider other actions before a campaign in northern France could occur and have a chance to succeed. A prerequisite to wage a European campaign, and one on which the Western Allies agreed, was winning the Battle of the Atlantic. Even though by this stage in the war the Germans posed no major threat through what was left of their miniscule surface fleet, the U-boat menace remained a serious peril. By early 1943, however, the Allies had reached a turning point in the Battle of the Atlantic. Several factors contributed to the defeat of Germany in the Atlantic: superior Allied intelligence capabilities; changes in Allied tactics, advancements in technology; and better organization in addressing the U-boat menace, all began to have their impact. Building on information developed by Polish cryptographers, British intelligence sources had unlocked the German Enigma encrypting device. Allied intelligence analysts would rely on information from this source, which they called ULTRA. It was a goldmine of military information. Through ULTRA, London had access to message traffic from German military higher headquarters to include U-boat operations. This was originally a boon to Allied planners, but in February 1942, the German naval authorities altered their Enigma machines by adding another rotor, thereby changing the code.[17] For 10 months, most of 1942, the Allies were unable to decipher Enigma coded messages. The loss of ULTRA intercepts reduced London and Washington's abilities to reroute convoys, thus avoiding "wolf packs," and to send hunter-killer teams to destroy the submarines. From February until the end of the year, German U-boat commanders inflicted their highest number of casualties on the Allied merchant fleet.[18] Once the new Enigma code was cracked, however, merchant ship losses began to fall and U-boat casualties began to soar.

Other Allied innovations also helped defeat U-boat operations. The Allied navies used improved microwave surface radar; employed magnetic anomaly detectors to find submerged submarines; deployed radio sonobuoy devices; and employed advanced adjustable depth charges. Destroyer commanders employed high-frequency direction finding equipment that would fix the position of a submarine after it made a radio transmission.[19] The U.S. Navy began employing AAF long-range aircraft to spot U-boats a factor that dramatically improved its search patterns.

Source: Jim Haley Collection.

Somewhere in the Atlantic, a U-Boat seeks its prey.

Although German commanders moved operations from the Eastern seaboard into the Gulf of Mexico and the Caribbean, the U.S. Navy's tactics became more effective and efficient in both escort duty and conducting anti-submarine operations. The effect of the Allied anti-U-boat offensive in the Atlantic was devastating to the German submarine fleet. *Kreigsmarine* crews manned 1,175 submarines, but of that number, a total of 781 failed to return to their bases. Over 28,000 U-boat crewmembers died in combat operations, and Allied navies captured another 5,000. These casualties came from a total force of 42,000 men.[20] Germany attempted to counter Allied successes. Submarines started to use radar detectors, and operations were moved out of coastal waters to an area called the "Black Pit," an area south of Greenland and midway between Newfoundland and Great Britain. U-boat commanders formed picket lines and used their typical group attack tactics in an attempt to regain the initiative.

Still, B-24 anti-submarine patrols, enhanced submarine countermeasures, improved communications intelligence, and attacks by RAF Coastal Command against French-based German submarines transiting the Bay of Biscay caused increased losses of submarines. In August 1943, Allied forces sank 41 submarines in the Bay of Biscay and total losses for the year reached 237 boats.[21] By January 1944, Germany had largely abandoned operations west of Great Britain, and only single U-boats attempted attacks on convoys.[22] Despite the cost, German U-boat operations proved very effective since throughout the war they sank over 2,603 merchant ships and 175 naval vessels. More than 30,000 British merchantmen lost their lives due to these attacks.[23] Allied casualties amounted to more than 50,000.[24] Winning the battle of the Atlantic in 1943 was crucial for the Allies because it meant that merchant shipping could begin the buildup of forces for a ground invasion of France.

A second and equally important preparatory campaign, necessary for the invasion of Europe, was a successful air campaign to reduce a number of German capabilities. AWPD/42 had proposed the accomplishment of one significant task in preparation for a successful invasion — achieving aerial superiority over the continent. This proved to be a difficult task for the Allies, because initially the Germans had made a heavy investment in aviation. The Allies hoped that by attacking the production facilities for airframes and aviation power plants, the AAF and RAF could reduce the *Luftwaffe's* effectiveness. At the end of 1942, however, the German Air Force was still a potent adversary. Under pressure to assess the effectiveness of air power, on March 8, 1943, General "Hap" Arnold formed the Committee of Operations Analysts (COA). COA members included former Secretary of the War Elihu Root, Jr.; Edward Mead Earle, military historian from Princeton University; Edward S. Mason, Office of Strategic Services' Research and Analysis; Fowler Hamilton, Chief of the Board of Economic Warfare; and a prominent New York lawyer, Thomas W. Lamont. The committee made a 2-week effort to study German industry. They used specialists that included experts from the Departments of State and Commerce, economists, industrialists, financiers, individuals who had worked in German plants, and assorted others to create a targeting list of 19 key industries.

The study dropped electrical power as a priority, because the Germans used a network of production facilities. The study members believed that disrupting power originating along the Rhine, Ruhr, and central Germany was too difficult.[25] Transportation was also a vital target, but here too significant disruption was hard to achieve. Like AWPD/42, the COA study recognized aircraft, especially plants producing fighters, as the most vital priority. The second most important target was anti-friction ball bearing factories. If the American air power could destroy ball bearing plants, then German industry as well as the *Wehrmacht* would come to a halt.

This new target list forced a change in emphasis for the AAF's strategic bombardment campaign. In keeping with these new priorities, in the summer of 1943 AAF aircraft staged bombing raids on the Rumanian oil fields in Ploesti, German ball bearing plants at Schweinfurt, and the Messerschmitt aircraft plant at Regensburg, making the *Luftwaffe's* destruction a key priority. Although the AAF attacks did create a disruption of the German economy, it proved to be only temporary. Repair, dispersion, and purchases from foreign sources quickly replaced the damaged capacity. The most serious problem resulting from these raids for the Allies was the cost in trained personnel and aircraft. In the August 17, 1943, attacks on Schweinfurt and Regensburg, unescorted American bombers lost 60 of the 306 B-17s that reached the targets. An additional 27 airplanes suffered serious damage.[26] A second attack on Schweinfurt lost a further 60 B-17s out of 291 aircraft. The AAF unescorted bomber attacks against *Luftwaffe* production facilities proved disastrous.[27]

Without long-range escort fighters, victory through strategic bombardment would not come fast, nor would it be cheap. From necessity, American air power advocates had to change strategy again. The AWPD/42 planners had to change their focus to that of destroying the *Luftwaffe* itself as the key priority, and thus forcing a restructuring of American aircraft production. American industry had to increase the manufacture of long-range fighters to escort the bombers and to defeat and destroy German fighters. Additionally, the AAF had to go after German aircraft bases and industries like airplane engine plants. These U.S. fighters would be critical for both escort duties in support of strategic bombardment and for a less favorite mission, conducting tactical operations in support of ground forces. This change diverted more resources away from the manufacture of bombers and training pilots for such missions. In short, the AAF had to move in two different directions by the demand for aircraft and pilots. The preferred mission, strategic bombing—and the pilots and airframes to support it—had to compete with the need for fighters for both escort aircraft and close air support.

An additional issue facing air planners was the different methodologies used by the AAF and RAF in conducting their Combined Bomber Offensive (CBO). The AAF generally operated during the daylight hours in an attempt to destroy their targets with accurate bombing raids, thereby limiting collateral damage. Airmen desired precision, but despite the great effort by AAF aircrews, measured bomb accuracy was in miles rather than feet.[28] The RAF viewed the strategic air offensive through an entirely different lens. Britain's war planners were in agreement with their American peers about the desired ends, the destruction of the National Socialist state. Much like the AAF, the RAF did not initially possess long-range escort fighters to protect its bombers. Most of the RAF's fighter force was composed of short-range interceptors—Spitfires and Hurricanes—aircraft that had served as the backbone of the island kingdom's defense during the Battle of Britain. Defense of the British Empire also forced the assignment of fighters throughout the world from Great Britain to the Far East. When the RAF conducted the initial bombing raids over German territory, unescorted bombers made the attacks. Lacking fighter support, the *Luftwaffe* made the lightly armed, slow RAF bombers pay dearly for the raids. RAF officers recognized the folly of using daylight bombardment missions when faced by a dedicated fighter force. Their solution was to attack at night. Night attacks resulted in far fewer losses, but accuracy suffered as British bombers continued attacks on industrial centers and cities. RAF bombers would eventually have a host of guidance systems to assist their planes in finding targets, but this process was still less accurate than the American daylight raids. RAF officers advocated that their raids should concentrate on two targets: oil and morale.[29] Fortunately, for the British, despite the strength of German fighter forces, German air defenders did not have a centralized control system like the RAF did, nor at the war's onset did Berlin possess effective night fighters.[30]

The AAF and RAF were both convinced that a strategic bombing offensive would irreparably harm the German economy and its military capabilities, and would result in the collapse of the German population's will. Although the AAF realized that it needed to attain air superiority to accomplish its goal of destroying Germany, the lack of long-range fighters forced changes to its prewar plans. The AAF leadership recognized that it would have to target airfields and aircraft production centers as part of the strategic bombardment campaign; however, the realization of a more dedicated *Luftwaffe* fighter force, massed anti-aircraft artillery, improved radar, and the continental nature of the air defenses forced the AAF to put more emphasis on gaining air superiority than was originally planned. The limited number of aircraft devoted to the AAF's bombardment could not suffer additional losses at the hands of enemy air defenses. Additionally, with bombers and fighters diverted to North Africa in late 1942 to early 1943, many AAF officers found it increasingly difficult to gain air superiority.

RAF leadership pushed attacks on targets that were much different in terms of priority and scope from their AAF allies. Their primary focus was on area attacks, delivered at night, to undermine German morale. The RAF did target the petroleum industry, since British intelligence sources estimated that oil was the primary ingredient that powered the economy and military transportation. Unfortunately, the RAF had a difficult time in targeting petroleum plants because of the distance and the inherent inaccuracy of night bombing. The AAF and RAF also differed in their theoretical outlook for a strategic bombardment campaign. While the AAF used Air Corps Tactical School concepts to guide its strategy, RAF officers stressed concepts favored by a senior British officer, Air Marshal Hugh Trenchard.[31] He stressed that attacking targets that could undermine German morale was 20 times more effective than those that focused on material damage.[32]

Prominent RAF officials, like Sir Charles Portal and Trenchard, mistakenly thought that the German population had much less stamina and resilience to bombing than the British population.[33] If aircrews conducted sufficient bombing, townspeople and their officials would pressure Hitler's government to capitulate. Thus, the RAF would still target industrial centers as a part of its nighttime bombing campaign, however inaccurately, but the preferred target was the destruction of the German morale. Churchill allowed attacks on German cities which observers described as "absolutely devastating, exterminating attacks."[34] This focus on the population and its morale might have worked on more liberal, democratic governments, but advocates of surrender or accommodation would not have fared well under the Nazi regime.

The RAF methodology of night area bombing meant that the RAF did not need to develop a precision aiming system, only sufficient navigational expertise to drop its ordinance on a general targeted area. Once pathfinder aircraft preceded the main body of British bombers and marked the general area of the city, precision was not necessary. Anything in the area was vulnerable. Additionally, the British did not have the necessary aircraft resources to focus precision attacks on economic targets. The British attempted to use night attacks on cities to destroy workers' housing, morale and, of course, the workers as well, all of which would hinder German industrial strength.[35] Indirectly, through these attacks, the RAF could test Trenchard's ideas and at the same time support attacks on industrial power. Some RAF officers also suggested that bombing industrial targets or cities would result in retribution by the *Luftwaffe* with chemical or biological weapons. Fortunately, this did not occur. Later in the war, the RAF would be required to add silencing German V-1 and V-2 facilities to its bombing campaign, targets that would require much more precision than mere area bombing.

Source: U.S. Air Force.

A work horse of the Combined Bomber Offensive in Europe was the American B-17. Capable of carrying a healthy bomb load and extremely tough, the B-17 was a superb aircraft.

The AAF and RAF leadership sought to focus their efforts on the strategic bombardment mission as the primary means to make continual direct attacks on Germany. However, they faced increased demands for fighters, medium bombers, and heavy bombers for tactical roles. Tactical aircraft operations were a part of AWPD/1 and later plans for the AAF to support forces after an invasion, but the clear focus for immediate American plans was to produce and employ strategic bombers. The RAF had a different experience. Although RAF Bomber Command had staged numerous raids on German cities, it had the added pressure of conducting operations on German and Italian ground forces in the Mediterranean. RAF tactical aviation had demonstrated its great value by supporting major operations in the highly mobile warfare of North Africa. British tactical air and ground forces cooperated as equal partners to conduct operations against Rommel's vaunted *Afrika Korps*.[36]

The RAF had organized its air power based on function. RAF tactical aviation activities relied on a fighter command to defend the British Isles, with bomber, coastal, and other commands for their specific missions.[37] In contrast, the AAF organized its forces under a single commander, who was under the direction of the supported theater commander. Early in the war, RAF and British Army cooperation did exist, but the relationship focused on artillery spotting, reconnaissance, and limited battlefield bombing. Beginning with the Battle of Britain and followed by the initiation of the strategic bombardment campaign and the growing aerial anti-submarine activities, competition for limited air resources began. During the Battle of Britain, the RAF tactical role languished, at least temporarily. Once the RAF was successful in thwarting German aerial efforts to defeat Britain, therefore the interceptor role was not as heavy a drain, improved close air support to ground forces became more important. Additionally, with the reduction of *Luftwaffe* raids and the infusion of American industrial production, more aircraft were becoming available.

The RAF initiated a policy to provide "Direct Air Support" by tactical aviation for ground units in September 1941.[38] Although many issues involving coordination and control of aircraft remained unanswered, the RAF and British ground forces would evolve into a model of air-ground cooperation that the AAF tactical aviation forces would later adapt for their use.

The November 1942 invasion of Morocco and Algeria under Operation TORCH, provided United

States military forces with needed tactical experience. In North Africa, AAF units operated under British command to gain their necessary experience. The British RAF had an air commander who exercised centralized control of operations and who could prioritize and direct missions to include close air support, air superiority fighter sweeps, interdiction of supply and troop movements, attacking lines of communication, and making long-range attacks. This was in contrast to the scattering of AAF units under command of a ground theater commander. This experience of working under British command would result in the AAF organization evolving into more of a British model where tactical aircraft operations involved one of cooperation and improved support of ground forces. This would ultimately affect AAF operations in North Africa, Italy, and Western Europe.[39] Fighter and tactical bomber aircraft staged strikes against German and Italian forces in North Africa working with ground commanders. Although disputes about the priority of targets continued, tactical aircraft operations became a key element of military activities. Away from European industrial type targets, AAF fighters and medium bombers directly supported surface operations that provided invaluable services to ground forces.

Tactical aircraft operations in the Mediterranean started to force changes in how best to use air power to defeat Axis military forces. The results of employing tactical air power had an immediate and visible impact in the theater as compared to the strategic bombardment campaign, a strategy whose results were more difficult to assess in the short term. As the AAF and RAF gained air superiority over the *Luftwaffe* and the Italian *Regia Aeronautica*, Allied air operations could concentrate on defeating German and Italian ground units in detail. Rather than merely subordinating air forces to ground commanders, a general command structure to fight the war as a joint and combined team evolved which proved more effective in the conduct of the Mediterranean war.[40]

Still, the diversion of aircraft to battlefield support and interdiction missions was not popular with many AAF and RAF officers who were devoted to strategic bombardment. For example, in preparation for the Normandy invasion, Eisenhower and his subordinate invasion force commanders wanted to divert heavy bombers from their preferred mission to support activities in the invasion and breakout of Allied forces in Normandy. Eisenhower's staff wanted to drop more than 45,000 tons of bombs on 101 rail centers in France.[41] This bombing would limit the rail movement of reserve forces and supplies headed toward Normandy to relieve German defenders and force them to use roads or travel farther to reach the invasion site. Tactical air forces alone, both American and British, did not have the capacity to deliver sufficient bomb loads; they needed heavy bomber support. If the Germans moved their military forces on roads in daylight, they would be subject to ruinous strafing and bombing since the Allies would have uncontested air superiority by this time.

Despite the critical nature of this air offensive that would affect the liberation of France and subsequent campaigns in Western Europe, some AAF and RAF commanders balked at the request. These commanders believed the use of strategic resources for ground support was "tragically wasteful."[42] After all, AAF officers had overseen the design and production of medium and heavy bombers to conduct an aerial campaign in the heartland of German occupied Europe to destroy the civilian, military, and industrial infrastructure of Germany. Given the contention over tactical versus strategic employment of airpower, Eisenhower ultimately compromised by planning for coordinated attacks by both strategic and tactical airpower. The conflicts regarding control of the air offensive and the philosophical debate on the appropriate use of airpower at times seemed ready to derail key missions planned in preparation for the Normandy invasion, but in the end Eisenhower's personal leadership and the capability of American industry to produce large numbers of aircraft allowed both types of missions. The philosophical debate over the appropriate use of airpower, however, remained contentious.

After the Normandy invasion, the extended use of tactical air operations posed several new problems for the Allies. Unexpected weather, the need to gain bases close to the battlefield, the coordination of attacks with heavy-bomber support, mechanical problems, logistics, and other concerns created the potential for the accidental bombing of British and American ground forces.[43] Additionally, like the strategic bombardment efforts, many aircrews in tactical aviation units lacked detailed information about targets. Despite these problems, air and ground officers developed air-ground coordination teams with some success. Aerial photography provided some relief to this problem, but this type of intelligence was more fleeting than with strategic targets. Planning attacks against mobile formations or smaller, camouflaged locations was difficult to accomplish. Heavy vegetation often obscured the landscape. Air and ground commanders had to establish proper timing to coordinate aerial and surface fire to avoid wasting limited fire support and ensure maneuver elements could accomplish their objectives without delay. Proper coordination would also reduce fratricide of Allied ground forces by the AAF and RAF.

Throughout the European Campaign, tactical air operations would support ground operations. The joint efforts by air and ground assets were an unbeatable combination. In Normandy, when tactical air power was available, German maneuver was limited and Allied tactical air power was an invaluable key to victory.[44] Allied leadership had to adjust strategic concepts throughout the war regarding its air forces. Although AAF and RAF commanders made several changes to force structure and operations, the flexible nature of employing air power allowed these modifications. Despite the diversion of strategic bombardment efforts, the AAF and RAF tactical forces gave Allied commanders a host of capabilities including close air support, interdiction, and gaining air superiority. Aerial operations complemented the Allied rapid movement in the European Campaign by creating greater momentum and improved tactical mobility.[45] Ground and air leaders had to amend the means and ways to make these changes work.

A consistent issue that plagued those who promoted the strategic bombing campaign was the material and personnel demands for strategic airpower; it was resource and time intensive for both the Americans and the British. Conducting the CBO was initially impossible for the British because in January 1941, the RAF had no heavy four-engine bombers.[46] By midyear, the RAF could only muster 31 heavy bombers. This limited number of aircraft could only *initiate* the process of bringing the German nation to its knees. As the war proceeded, however, from 1941 to 1945 the British aircraft industry was able to produce 14,306 heavy bombers.[47] The American aircraft industry was even more robust and proved capable of outproducing both the British and German industries. In January 1939, before Washington's entry into the war, American aircraft companies were able to field more B-17s, either on contract or completed (52 airplanes), than the RAF flew even after 1 1/2 years into of war.[48] As the United States approached the war, production continued to build with American industry slated to produce 220 B-17s, in the last 6 months of 1941.[49] Washington transferred some of these planes to supplement RAF forces. Even with a two-front war, American aircraft firms assembled bombers not only for the strategic bombardment effort, but also for antisubmarine and tactical air operations. During World War II, U.S. aircraft plants built a total of 30,865 B-17 and B-24 aircraft.[50] Aircraft plants around the nation manufactured more B-24s than any American aircraft type in the conflict. The AAF procured 18,190 B-24s as well as the second most numerous plane, 15,863 P-47 fighters.[51] At the same time, the AAF was also developing and building its B-29 Superfortress that was used to attack the Japanese home islands.

American industry could and did replace the AAF's damaged or destroyed planes despite bomber losses. The AAF and the nation had the resources and the industrial base to conduct the strategic bombardment campaign. Washington could have changed its priority from four-engine bombers to tactical aircraft. Instead, U.S. decisionmakers chose to focus primarily on bomber production, given the AAF's emphasis on bombardment. Retaining the emphasis on four-engine bombers was expensive since the average cost of a B-24 bomber was $304,391 as compared to a P-47 fighter at $105,594.[52] AAF planners could have built almost three P-47s for the cost of a single B-24. By 1944, at peak production for each aircraft, the ratio was 2.51:1.

Aircrews were another story. Producing qualified crews took time and effort. Both the B-17 and the B-24 required a crew of 10 as compared to a fighter, which required only the pilot. Thus, the AAF suffered even heavier personnel losses than just the aircraft losses of 1943. Since American airspace was under control, aircrew training was never an issue. With skies safe from enemy attacks, the AAF trained more than 193,000 pilots, 45,000 bombardiers, 297,000 gunners, and 50,000 navigators for the war.[53] Pilot training was so successful that by December 1943, the United States was overproducing aircrews. By that time, the AAF had over 74,000 pilots in uniform.[54] Pilot training slowed in 1944, despite the massive CBO activities, but the AAF could and did produce more than enough flight crews.

Despite differences in strategic, operational, and tactical approaches, the CBO remained a major element in the AAF's offensive against Germany and its forces in the European Theater. The AAF and RAF began CBO attacks in January 1943 and continued to the last days of the war in Europe in May 1945. The RAF never strayed from its reliance on night attacks even though immature radio and radar guidance resulted in inaccurate bombing. Despite the inherent inaccuracy, the RAF's area bombings began to immolate cities and the weight of British efforts did affect German capabilities. Even though the RAF regarded night attacks as safer than daylight missions, the Germans countered with improved German air defenses and developed a robust night fighter capability. From January 1943 to March 1944, the RAF Bomber Command lost 5,881 aircraft, either due to anti-aircraft flak artillery or night fighters.[55]

The AAF continued daylight raids, but at a much heavier price. By the spring of 1943, the *Luftwaffe* commanders assigned over 70 percent of their fighters to the West.[56] The myth that heavily armed bombers could survive missions without fighter escorts over German defenses quickly evaporated. Early in the war, AAF leadership believed strongly in a strategic bombing campaign with self-defending aircraft that did not require fighter escorts. Bomber units quickly found this belief to be erroneous. As the pace of Allied bombing increased, *Luftwaffe* fighter and anti-aircraft artillery units took a heavy toll on unescorted daylight bomber raids. Bomber losses over heavily defended industrial targets like Schweinfurt, Regensburg, and others compelled the AAF and RAF to modify their strategy: First, American fighters, initially P-47 Thunderbolts and ultimately P-51 Mustangs, were fitted with long-range fuel tanks and escorted four-engine bombers into the heartland of Germany where they effectively engaged German fighters. Even with the introduction of long-range fighter escorts, bomber losses were significant. Secondly, Allied fighter production increased to higher levels to gain control over European skies allowing a continuation of the bomber offensive as well as providing support over the future battlefields in Western Europe. Third, the AAF started to attack and defeat the *Luftwaffe* in the air and on the ground with its improved tactical aviation forces.

From February 20 to 25, 1944, AAF leaders concentrated their efforts on the enemy's aviation industry under an offensive titled Operation ARGUMENT. The AAF designed this campaign to reduce the *Luftwaffe's* ability to defend the Reich and challenge Allied air power. The 8th Air Force from England and the 15th Air Force in Italy struck German, Austrian, and other aircraft manufacturing and component plants. The RAF supported this "Big Week" by hitting cities at night where aircraft factories were located. At least 3,800 AAF bomber sorties supported by 3,500 fighter escort sorties dropped 10,000 tons of bombs on targets. This effort destroyed some factories and forced dispersal of the German aviation industry, inhibiting its ability to supply aircraft and maintain existing fighter forces. Further, German aircraft manufacturers could not maintain production schedules and plans to introduce modified or new weapons, like the Me-262 jet fighter. Coupled with the increasing strength and quality of Allied long-range fighters, dwindling oil supplies and the lack of a stable training base to replace heavy casualties among aircrews forced the *Luftwaffe* into a tail spin from which it would never recover.[57] The Big Week destroyed almost 75 percent of the industrial facilities that sustained 90 percent of German aircraft production.[58]

All of this was possible because the United States had the population and training base to replace losses and to supply more crews into the European and Pacific Theaters. For example, in September 1943, the AAF had 373 combat ready heavy bomber crews operating in Western Europe; by June 1944, the effective strength grew to 1,855 crews, despite significant losses.[59] Increased emphasis on employing fighters to escort bombers allowed the Allies to continue the CBO. Additionally, more pilots and airframes later provided invaluable assets to tactical forces conducting close air support and interdiction missions when Allied forces invaded France.

Despite high losses, the CBO provided other dimensions to the Allied offensive against the *Luftwaffe*: The continual bombing diverted great numbers of *Luftwaffe* aircraft away from the Eastern Front and other theaters in order to protect German cities. German aircraft losses and expanded defensive requirements forced German officials to reallocate their dwindling economic resources to produce additional weapons for the air war instead of tanks, vehicles, artillery, or other armaments. From June to December 1941, Germany lost 3,157 aircraft of all types, which represented 55.8 percent of its force. During January to June 1944, the *Luftwaffe* lost another 10,137 aircraft, an astounding 137.1 percent of authorized aircraft strength.[60] Experienced crews became a rarity that forced increased training demands and even higher losses as the AAF and RAF grew in strength and skill. Anti-aircraft artillery requirements also ballooned, increasing from 791 batteries deployed in the Reich in 1940 to 2,132 in 1943. Without the CBO, Germany could have released these assets for use by ground forces.[61]

The losses to the German economy and the impact on its morale caused by the CBO are difficult to measure, but there was an impact. Airpower theory developed in the wake of World War I's trench warfare carnage, postulated that wars could be won by using strategic bombardment to destroy infrastructure and morale. The AAF and RAF devoted vast resources and effort into turning their prewar concepts of strategic bombardment into an air campaign, but results in both the Battle of Britain and the CBO leave the accuracy of the strategic airpower theory open to question. One can only estimate the potential loss of economic production. Reductions in German economic efficiency by disrupting working schedules and dispersion of industries certainly had an impact. The American and British air campaign, which commenced in 1943, did affect German production, but determining the total effect on the economy is difficult. Berlin had not fully mobilized the economy until well after the start of the war. German industrial production accelerated in 1943 and actually reached its peak in August 1944. Diversion of resources to higher priorities also skewed production. Conversely, attacks on petroleum and transportation networks did slow German military activities. The impact of the CBO on German morale is more difficult to measure, but as any G.I. fighting in the spring of 1945 would attest, it was not decisive.

Despite the emphasis on building four-engine, long-range bombers, the AAF and RAF had to support a number of ongoing operations worldwide, build and train an adequate force, and wait until conditions were suitable to begin striking at the heart of Germany. Although the CBO did not achieve its prewar predictions of swiftly defeating Germany, it did add an essential dimension to the Allied campaign. The campaign contributed to the softening up of the Germans, aided the European ground campaign, and added pressure on the German production capability.

ENDNOTES - CHAPTER 3

1. Dwight D. Eisenhower, as quoted in Eric Larabee, *Commander in Chief: Franklin Delano Roosevelt, His Lieutenants, and Their War*, New York: Simon & Schuster, Touchstone Ed., 1988, p. 135.

2. American and British officials did not snub Stalin through the lack of an invitation. He was, in fact, invited but declined. In January 1943, Russia was going through a significant period in its war. Stalingrad had been ringed, and the primary business for the Russian dictator was ensuring the death of Hitler's 6th Army and its attached units.

3. The British firmly believed that nighttime aerial bombing was the only logical strategy given the staggering casualties that the *Luftwaffe* could inflict on bomber forces, while the American bombing campaign concentrated on daytime precision bombing. As succinctly noted in the official Air Force history, "For them [Generals Arnold and Eaker] daylight precision bombing was an

article of faith." The British leadership was not adverse to letting the Americans go their own way, but the RAF had little interest in the daylight bombing tactic. Bernard C. Nalty, ed., *Winged Shield, Winged Sword: A History of the United States Air Force*, Washington DC: United States Air Force, 1997, pp. 224-226.

4. Note that Wedemeyer's role in planning was still significant. At the time of this conference, then Brigadier General Albert C. Wedemeyer was still involved in war plans as were Eisenhower and Marshall. Much like Ike and Marshall, Wedemeyer viewed the British "victory" in focusing 1943 operations on the Mediterranean as a grievous error, later stating, "We lost our shirts . . . we came, we listened, and we were conquered." Richard M. Leighton and Robert W. Coakley, *The War Department: Global Logistics and Strategy, 1940-1943*, Washington, DC: Center of Military History, 1995, p. 686.

5. If Alanbrooke is accurate, the debate ultimately settled on the advantages of Sicily vs. Sardinia. According to Alanbrooke, joint planners believed Sardinia had important advantages because opposition on the beaches would not be as heavy and when taken, Sardinian Airfields would be a better springboard for air operations against Italy. Field Marshall Lord Alanbrooke, *War Diaries, 1939-1945*, Alex Danchev and Daniel Todman, eds., Berkeley, CA: University of California Press, 2001, p. 358.

6. Dwight D. Eisenhower, *Crusade in Europe*, New York: Doubleday, 1948, p. 137. Eisenhower later noted that this was his "most miraculous guess of the war" and that a short time later he related this to the General Sir Harold R.L.G. Alexander, who smiled and said he had given the date, May 30.

7. Friedhelm Klein, und Karl Heinz Freiser, "Manstein's Gegenschlag am Donec: Operative Analyse des Gegenangriffs der Heeresgruppe Süd in Februar/Määrz 1943" ("Manstein's Counterstroke on the Donets: Operational Analysis of the Counterattack of Army Group South in February/March 1943"), Militärgeschichte: Zeitschrift für Historische Bildung, Heft 1, 1 Quartal, 1999, 9th Ed., pp. 9, 12-18. See also the excellent study by Bruno Kasdorf, *Oberst der Bundeswehr, The Battle of Kursk: An Analysis of Strategic and Operational Principles*, Carlisle, PA: U.S. Army War College, 2000. Note: This is an unpublished paper available through the Defense Technical Information Center.

8. Carlo D'Este, *Eisenhower: A Soldier's Life*, New York: Henry Holt & Co., LLC, 2002, p. 293.

9. Though for the purpose of this book this postponement was highly significant, of equal importance was the announcement that the Allies would pursue the policy of unconditional surrender.

10. Eric Larabee, *Commander in Chief: Franklin Delano Roosevelt, his Lieutenants and their War*, New York: Simon and Schuster, 1987, p. 186.

11. A turning movement is an action designed to cause the enemy force to turn away from its intended area of effort and address the threat designed by your force. In the case of Anzio, Allied planners designed the invasion to cause German defenders to turn away from their formidable defenses known as the Gustav Line and address the Allied threat to their own lines of communications to the rear of the Gustav line.

12. Larabee, *Commander in Chief*, pp. 187-188.

13. General Albert C. Wedemeyer, *Wedemeyer Reports,* New York: Henry Holt and Company, 1958, p. 170.

14. Eisenhower, *Crusade in Europe*, p. 138.

15. Larabee, *Commander in Chief,* p. 147.

16. Henry L. Stimson and McGeorge Bundy, *On Active Service in Peace and War*, New York: Harper and Brothers, 1949, pp. 430-439.

17. Timothy A. Warnock, *Air Power Versus U-boats: Confronting Hitler's Submarine Menace in the European Theater*, Washington, DC: Air Force History and Museums Program, 1999, p. 7.

18. E. B. Potter, *Sea Power: A Naval History*, Annapolis, MD: Naval Institute Press, 1981, p. 266.

19. Ronald H. Spector, *At War At Sea: Sailors and Naval Combat in the Twentieth Century*, New York: Viking Press, 2001, p. 244.

20. *Ibid.*, p. 254.

21. *Ibid*, p. 252.

22. Gunter Hessler, *German Naval History: The U-Boat War in the Atlantic, 1939-1945*, London, UK: Stationery Office Books (TSO), 1989, p. 41.

23. David Mason, *U-boat: the Secret Menace*, New York: Ballantine Books, 1968, p. 154.

24. R. Ernest Dupuy and Trevor N. Dupuy *The Harper Encylopedia of Military History: From 3500 B.C. to the Present*, 4th Ed., New York: Harper Collins, 1993, p. 1222.

25. Robert C. Erhart, Thomas A. Fabyanic, and Robert Futrell, "Building an Intelligence Organization and the European Theater," in John F. Kreis, ed., *Piercing the Fog*, Washington, DC: Air Force History and Museums Program, 1996, p. 155.

26. Bernard C. Nalty *et al.*, *With Courage: The U.S. Army Air Forces in World War II*, Washington, DC: Air Force History and Museums Program, 1994, p. 204.

27. Stephen L. McFarland, and Wesley Phillips Newton, "The American Strategic Air Offensive against Germany in World War II," in R. Cargill Hall, ed., *Case Studies in Strategic Bombardment*, Washington, DC: Air Force History and Museums Program, 1998, p. 204.

28. Conrad Crane, *Bombs, Cities, and Civilians: American Airpower Theory in World War II*, Lawrence, KS: University of Kansas Press, 1993, p. 64.

29. John Terraine, *The Right of the Line*, Hertfordshire, UK: Wordsworth Editions, 1997, p. 263.

30. W. A. Jacobs, *The British Strategic Air Offensive Against Germany in World War II* in R. Cargill Hall, ed., *Case Studies in Strategic Bombardment*, Washington, DC: Air Force History and Museums Program, 1998, p. 113.

31. The Air Corps Tactical School (ACTS) concepts emphasized targeting economic and or military targets rather than undermining morale. This inherently pressed them to focus on precision bombing raids rather than area bombing. This was in contrast to the Douhet inspired concepts proposed by Air Marshal Trenchard.

32. Richard J. Overy, *Why the Allies Won*, New York: Norton, 1996, p. 106.

33. *Ibid.*, p. 264.

34. Terraine, *The Right of the Line*, p. 260.

35. John Buckley, *Air Power In the Age of Total War*, Bloomington, IN: Indiana University Press, 1999, p. 157.

36. Daniel R. Mortensen, *A Pattern For Joint Operations: World War II Close Air Support North Africa, 1940-1943*, Washington, DC: Office of Air Force History and U.S. Army Center of Military History, 1987, p. 48.

37. David R. Mets, "A Glider in the Propwash of the Royal Air Force," in Daniel R. Mortensen, ed., *Airpower and Ground Armies: Essays on the Evolution of Anglo-American Air Doctrine, 1940-1943*, Maxwell Air Force Base, AL: Air University Press, 1998, p. 63.

38. Vincent Orange, *Getting Together: Tedder, Cunningham and Americans in the Desert and Tunisia*, in Mortensen, ed., *A Pattern For Joint Operations*, p. 12.

39. R. J. Overy, *The Air War 1939-1945*, Chelsea, MI: Scarborough House, 1980, p. 69.

40. Williamson Murray, *Strategy For Defeat, The Luftwaffe 1933-1945*, Maxwell Air Force Base, AL: Air University Press, 1983, p. 162.

41. Geoffrey Perret, *Winged Victory: The Army Air Forces in World War II*, New York: Random House, 1993, p. 297.

42. Martin Blumenson, *The Battle of the Generals: The Untold Story of the Falaise Pocket—The Campaign That Should Have Won World War II*, New York: Morrow, 1993, p. 133.

43. Will A. Jacobs, "The Battle for France 1944," in Benjamin Franklin Cooling, ed., *Case Studies in the Development of Close Air Support*, Washington, DC: Office of Air Force History, 1990, p. 264.

44. Robin Neilliands, *The Battle of Normandy 1944*, London: Cassell, 2002, p. 194.

45. David N. Spires, *Air Power For Patton's Army: The XIX Tactical Air Command in the Second World War*, Washington, DC: Air Force History and Museums Program, 2002, p. 293.

46. Jacobs, *The Battle for France*, p. 97.

47. *Ibid.*, p. 100.

48. Mauer Mauer, *Aviation in the U.S. Army, 1939-1939*, Washington, DC: Office of Air Force History, 1987, p. 436.

49. Michael S. Sherry, *The Rise of American Air Power: The Creation of Armageddon*, New Haven, CT: Yale University Press, 1987, p. 105.

50. Stephen L McFarland, and Wesley Phillips Newton, *The American Strategic Air Offensive Against Germany in World War II*, in R. Cargill Hall, ed., *Case Studies in Strategic Bombardment*, Washington, DC: Air Force History and Museums Program, 1998, p. 185.

51. Irving Brinton Holley, Jr., *Buying Aircraft: Matériel Procurement for the Army Air Forces*, Washington, DC: U.S. Army Center of Military History, 1989, p. 550.

52. *Ibid.*, p. 560.

53. Nalty *et al.*, *U.S. Army Air Forces in World War II*, pp. 171, 173.

54. *Ibid.*, p. 173.

55. Murray, Table XLI Bomber Command Losses, January 1943-March 1944, p. 220.

56. Overy, *The Air War 1939-1945*, p. 118.

57. Replacement of aircrews was a serious issue. As Allied aircraft became a common sight over Germany in late-1943 to early-1944, there were few safe places to train potential pilots. Then again, there was the issue of resources. The *Luftwaffe*, in terms of numbers of aircrews and aircraft, was not robust. Thus, when crises occurred demanding more airpower, planes and instructors were pulled out of the training bases to fill in the gaps. In the process, futile operations, like the Stalingrad airlift, wrecked the *Luftwaffe's* training base.

58. Nalty *et al.*, *U.S. Army Air Forces in World War II*, p. 226.

59. Murray, Table XLIX Bomber and Fighter Strength, Eighth Air Force, p. 234.

60. *Ibid*, p. 304.

61. Williamson Murray and Allan R. Millet, *A War To Be Won: Fighting the Second World War*, Cambridge, MA: The Belknap Press of Harvard University Press, 2000, p. 332.

CHAPTER 4

D-DAY:
PLANNING AND EXECUTION

> Soldiers, Sailors, and Airmen of the Allied Expeditionary Force. You are about to embark on the great crusade towards which we have striven these many months.[1]
>
> Dwight D. Eisenhower, June 6, 1944

A cross-channel attack to initiate the European Campaign remained the linchpin of American strategy for taking the war to Germany and defeating its armies in the field. This approach remained the centerpiece of Allied strategy despite the feared casualty rate from a dedicated German resistance, and the fact that the neither the British allies nor U.S. President Franklin Roosevelt would support an early implementation of this plan as originally proposed in mid-1942. Thus, American and British military leaders had to delay the invasion from 1943 until the spring of 1944. Participants at the January 1943 Casablanca conference reaffirmed the commitment to this event, even though in some of the meetings Admiral Ernest King continued to press for greater emphasis on Pacific operations.[2] At Casablanca, a significant decision was made: the necessity of establishing a joint Anglo-American planning staff, to be located in London. In actuality, the first significant Allied planning group had been the Allied Force Headquarters (AFHQ) commanded by then Lieutenant General Dwight D. Eisenhower. In a dual-hatted role, Eisenhower had been responsible for conducting the Operation TORCH invasion and, at the same time, he commanded the European Theater of Operations,

United States Army (ETOUSA), a headquarters that was responsible for all American forces stationed in Great Britain. While Eisenhower was absorbed with command of Operation TORCH, it was necessary for him to have a deputy to actually run the British operations. Once Operation TORCH had succeeded, Eisenhower's span of responsibility increased considerably. He split these two functions, retaining command of AFHQ while delegating the actual control of ETOUSA to Lieutenant General Frank M. Andrews.

Another important strategic decision from the Casablanca conference was the role of strategic airpower in the European Campaign. Even prior to Casablanca, Allied leaders determined that a necessary preparatory phase for a successful European ground campaign was "the heaviest possible air offensive against the German war effort."[3] Beyond this general statement, a number of questions remained. For example, what were the priorities of such an offensive? Would it be directly coordinated with ground forces operations or would it be a largely independent operation? Finally, what would be the level of coordination between the AAF and the RAF, and whose tactics would be used to pursue this air offensive? British Prime Minister Winston Churchill's support settled the latter issue: The RAF would have the ability to pursue its nighttime area bombing campaign, while the AAF would pursue its controversial daylight precision bombing campaign.[4] Air operations emanating from Britain would be under the overall control of the RAF, but each air force would have the latitude to pursue the bombing campaign, using its own nationally determined tactics. General targeting concepts were agreed upon. Since no Allied ground troops were on the main body of the continent, the preparatory phase for the campaign would be independent of, and not coordinated with, ground forces. At the same time, per agreements between General George Marshall and RAF Air Chief Marshal Sir Charles Portal, the air emphasis would switch to the support of ground operations when the invasion started.[5]

The necessity to appoint a staff clearly tasked to focus on planning for an invasion, rather than provide this function as an additional duty, was evident, given the size and importance of the task. The establishment of a new allied command was initially a slow process at least in part due to the vague nature of its charter at Casablanca. Nonetheless, the process of putting together a staff started in early 1943. Allied leadership appointed Lieutenant General Sir Frederick Morgan as the commander. A highly respected British officer, Morgan's task was to build a planning staff that would lay the foundation for the cross-channel attack. Morgan's actual title was Chief of Staff to the Supreme Allied Commander (COSSAC). American and British leaders had not appointed a supreme commander for the campaign yet, but in his role as Chief of Staff, Morgan had the responsibility of planning the actual attack.[6] Morgan arrived in March 1943 and received a less than an enthusiastic overview of his duties: Chief of the Imperial General Staff Field Marshal Alanbrooke gave the overview, summarized Morgan's task, and concluded with the statement, "Well, there it is. It won't work, but you must bloody well make it."[7]

Source: U.S. Army Military History Institute.

Frederick Morgan was one of the original planners for a cross channel attack. He is shown here (on the left) with Admiral Sir Harold Burrough in May 1945 in Reims, France.

As Morgan formed his staff, his goal was to achieve a good balance by using both British and American officers. He believed that the supreme commander would be British and thus had the basic command structure set up on a British model with a British Chief of Staff. Under this command umbrella, he envisioned having British, Canadian, and American headquarters that would handle the administrative work for their respective armies. Morgan had an American, Brigadier General Ray W. Barker, as his Deputy Chief of Staff. For air operations, he secured the services of American Carl Spaatz and from the Royal Air Force,

Air Marshal Arthur Travers Harris, as well as Air Chief Marshal Sir Trafford L. Leigh-Mallory. While both Britain and the United States had ample representation in airpower, on the Navy side the primary planner was initially Commodore John Hughes-Hallet. Hughes-Hallet's experience included being a planner for the Dieppe raid, not exactly a comforting fact. Despite limited naval assets, Morgan and his staff had the task of planning for a major cross-channel attack. At the same time, they were to have a contingency plan available to rush troops to Europe if it seemed likely that the German army was weakening or disintegrating, and thus the Allies might conduct a landing with limited resistance.[8]

Morgan and his staff, though they were operating with limited personnel, worked diligently on the enormous task that faced them. Morgan regarded the COSSAC role as that of a coordinating body which was in fact "... the embryo of the future Supreme Headquarters Staff."[9] One of the key tasks for COSSAC was to determine where the invasion would take place. To accomplish this task, he gave his American contingent the task of researching the possibility of landing the assault force on Normandy, while the British staffers were to look at the advantages and disadvantages of Pas de Calais. The choice was in many respects difficult. Both staffs assumed the Germans would have heavy defenses at both landing sites. They thought Calais would have more defenses than the Normandy region. Calais, however, had a certain number of advantages. It was closer to Great Britain and led to excellent terrain for mobile warfare. Furthermore, Calais was on a direct route to Northern Germany, the path had a good east-west road network that led straight to the strategic prize, Berlin. Calais, with its proximity to Britain, was an obvious choice to the Allies, but to the Germans as well. Normandy also had a good road network leading inland. Both proposed landing areas had beaches that were acceptable for amphibious landings. Normandy, though obviously further from Germany, offered one significant advantage: If the Allies made successful landings near the Cotentin Peninsula, and American and British forces occupied the Peninsula, then the Allies would have a suitable port, Cherbourg.[10]

In the end, there were few significant advantages of one site over the other. Thus, additional staff work was necessary to develop a recommendation that COSSAC could forward to the upper echelons of command. The staff thinking was crystallized in a conference held by Admiral of the Fleet Louis Mountbatten, who invited Morgan to what has become known as the "Rattle Conference." This joint and Allied conference, almost an old world gentlemen's party, was characterized by both serious meetings and by innumerable social occasions and outings. Attendees included 20 general officers, 11 air marshals and air commodores, and 8 admirals. Attendees came from American, Canadian, and, of course, British services. Mountbatten enthusiastically chaired the meetings which included a myriad of social events. The group reached a final consensus: the location for the cross-channel attack would be Normandy.[11]

These ranking officers had worked through this planning process; higher authorities would approve the final decision, the actual landing site. It would be a decision by the highest-level officials at the next Allied conference scheduled for Quebec in August 1943. Even here, after 2 years of meetings between representatives of the American and British governments, there was still some friction on the issue of when a cross-channel attack would occur. The British preference was still to delay until peripheral operations could wear down the German strength through actions such as the CBO or operations in Italy and the Mediterranean. By 1943, the Soviet Army's resistance to the Germans created increased numbers of casualties throughout the *Wehrmacht*, another factor that weakened Berlin's strength. Casablanca participants had agreed to conduct detailed planning for the "second front" which, of course, resulted in the creation of COSSAC.[12]

Some thorny problems remained for the Western Allies, despite their excellent record of ironing out national differences. At the Arcadia conference in December 1941, attendees had agreed that a single Allied commander would be appointed for each theater of operations. In keeping with prior agreements, once COSSAC began to operate in 1943, its plan called for the invasion force to consist of three divisions, two of which were to be British (and supported by a single airborne division).[13] Since the majority of the force proposed for the invasion was British, it followed that the Supreme Commander, Allied Expeditionary Force would come from that nation.[14]

Those familiar with amphibious operations would quickly recognize that this was, at best, a conservative number of divisions for such an undertaking. Conversely, Morgan and his staff faced significant resource constraints such as the availability of landing craft, men, and supplies. British senior political and military leaders were also cognizant of the reality facing the island nation. Planning an amphibious operation, a direct assault against prepared German defensive positions, brought back ghosts from the past. British leaders recalled the specters from World War I; Gallipoli and the Somme. Adding to the problems posed by those unpleasant memories, there was a physical limit to what Britain could contribute on the ground. The British had been fighting German aggression since September 1939, and by the end of 1941, with the addition of the Italian and Japanese foes, Britain and its Commonwealth nations had reached their limit of the supply of additional divisions. Simply, they were running out of men. As the buildup of forces and supplies continued, it became increasingly evident that the preponderance of the invasion force would have to be Soldiers in the service of the United States Army.

Churchill had originally promised the position of Supreme Commander to Field Marshal Alanbrooke. The invasion force's national composition, however, logically caused reconsideration. Given the increasing number of American units in the landings, it seemed obvious that an American would become the Supreme Commander. Churchill and Roosevelt recognized this in August 1943 at Quebec when they agreed that the changing circumstances meant that an American would have to be in command. Before the conference was completed, Churchill informed Alanbrooke that the command of the Expeditionary Force was going to go to an American, General George C. Marshall. This decision was a good one for the Alliance, but likely fueled Alanbrooke's dislike of many American senior leaders.[15]

The choice for the Supreme Commander, agreed to by Churchill and Roosevelt, was Marshall, but other decisions resulted. When Marshall assumed this command, Roosevelt planned for Eisenhower to take Marshall's position as U.S. Army Chief of Staff.

Eisenhower had impressed many American and British leaders with his work on American war plans and at several Allied Conferences. Problems, however, emerged with Marshall as the selected commander, at least in Roosevelt's mind. Marshall's competence was beyond question and he had earned this combat command. The President initially seemed willing to reward Marshall with this coveted command, but at the same time, he seemed uncomfortable with a Washington without him. Thus, in the weeks that followed the pivotal Quebec conference, the President did not make any announcement concerning who would command the growing American force in Great Britain. However, military staffs entertained the widely rumored belief that it would be Marshall. In the late fall and early winter meetings, at Tunis, Tunisia, and Tehran, Iran, Roosevelt seemed to intentionally spend time with Eisenhower, in a sense sizing him up before he made the final decision.

There are many speculative reasons as to why Eisenhower received the command, rather than Marshall. As Chief of Staff, Marshall had learned to navigate through the political minefields in the nation's capital, but he was brusque and cold with people, even trusted subordinates, something that Eisenhower could easily attest. Thus, the President could talk to "Ike," but Marshall did not want anyone to call him "George." When later asked by his son, James, why he appointed Eisenhower instead of Marshall, the President stated, "Eisenhower is the best politician among the military men. He is a natural leader who can convince other men to follow him, and this is what we need in his position more than any other quality."[16] Churchill, when asked for his opinion by Roosevelt about nominating Eisenhower vice Marshall stated,

"... that we had also the warmest regards for General Eisenhower and would trust our fortunes to his direction with hearty good will."[17] On December 7, 1943, Roosevelt met with Eisenhower at Tunis and simply stated, "Well, Ike, you are going to command OVERLORD." Eisenhower's response was simply, "Mr. President, I realize such an appointment involved difficult decisions. I hope you will not be disappointed."[18]

Dwight D. Eisenhower, a man who had limited command experience and who had no combat experience in World War I, was now set to command the largest amphibious operation in World War II or, for that matter, in all of history! This operation was also against an army that the Allies regarded as their most serious adversary. Choosing an officer with such limited combat experience made Eisenhower's appointment curious to some. Ike however, had shown many excellent leadership qualities and had gained the confidence of both Marshall and the President through his performances as Chief of the War Plans Division, commander of ETOUSA, and Commander of Operation TORCH. The press announced he official appointment on Christmas Eve, 1943. In the time that elapsed between his appointment and the official announcement, Eisenhower worked to provide a smooth disengagement from his duties in the Mediterranean. He was aware of the basic concepts of Operation OVERLORD and he had been briefed on the OVERLORD plan (as developed by COSSAC) to include the strength of the force and the intended landing site — Normandy. From the onset, he was dissatisfied with the lack of combat power in the invasion force. Simply, three divisions on a small frontage would be insufficient for a successful invasion. He immediately called for a larger force. Although Roosevelt and Churchill appointed him in December, his official tasking for this new assignment came on February 14, 1944. He was to complete the following:

TO SUPREME COMMANDER
ALLIED EXPEDITIONARY FORCE
12 February 1944

1. You are hereby designated as Supreme Allied Commander of the forces placed under your orders for operations for liberation of Europe from Germans. Your title will be Supreme Commander Allied Expeditionary Force.

2. *Task.* You will enter the continent of Europe and, in conjunction with the other United Nations, undertake operations aimed at the heart of Germany and the destruction of her armed forces. The date for entering the Continent is the month of May 1944. After adequate Channel ports have been secured, exploitation will be directed towards securing an area that will facilitate both ground and air operations against the enemy.

3. Notwithstanding the target date above you will be prepared at any time to take immediate advantage of favorable circumstances, such as withdrawal by the enemy on your front, to effect a reentry into the Continent with such forces as you have available at the time; a general plan for this operation when approved will be furnished for your assistance.[19]

Once appointed as Supreme Commander, Eisenhower exercised his prerogative and began to put together a list of people he wanted for his key staff. His understanding of political sensibilities was evident from the onset because, even though he wanted General Sir Harold Alexander on his staff due to their excellent working relationship in the Mediterranean, he recognized that this was clearly a British decision. In spite of Eisenhower's preference, Churchill gave him the Commander of the British 8th Army, Field Marshall Bernard Law Montgomery, hero of El Alamein. When assigned to Eisenhower's staff, "Monty" became Commander of the British 21st Army Group and Commander of all Allied ground troops until a lodgment was secured. Once Allied forces seized the lodgment, Eisenhower planned to take personal command of all ground troops in France. That he desired to work with Montgomery, who could be, to say the least, difficult, was evident as early as December 27, 1943. At that time, Eisenhower called for a meeting with Montgomery to discuss Operation OVERLORD. They quickly concurred that they had to strengthen the COSSAC plan since three divisions were insufficient. In addition, the planned front was too narrow, a factor that would allow the Germans to concentrate their efforts much more effectively. Ike's first meeting with his British subordinate was an unqualified success.

Eisenhower's staff selection continued to show an excellent grasp of joint and combined arms command. Beginning in 1942, his experience in working with the British allies, through his dual-hated command of AFHQ and ETOUSA, made him familiar with the British political terrain and many of the principals. His deputy Supreme Commander was Air Chief Marshall Arthur W. Tedder, and Eisenhower used a British military aide, Lieutenant Colonel James Gault. His Chief of Staff was an American officer whom he had come to trust in the Mediterranean, Major General Walter Bedell Smith. Eisenhower also absorbed the COSSAC organization into his staff to include Morgan. Morgan's experience in the initial planning of the operation made him a logical choice for one of the Deputy Chiefs of Staff. Eisenhower designated a British Officer, Admiral Sir Bertram H. Ramsey, for the position of the Allied commander for naval forces. The Allied Commander-in-Chief of Air Forces, Air Marshal Sir Trafford Leigh-Mallory was also British. See Figure 1 for the SHAEF Chain of Command.

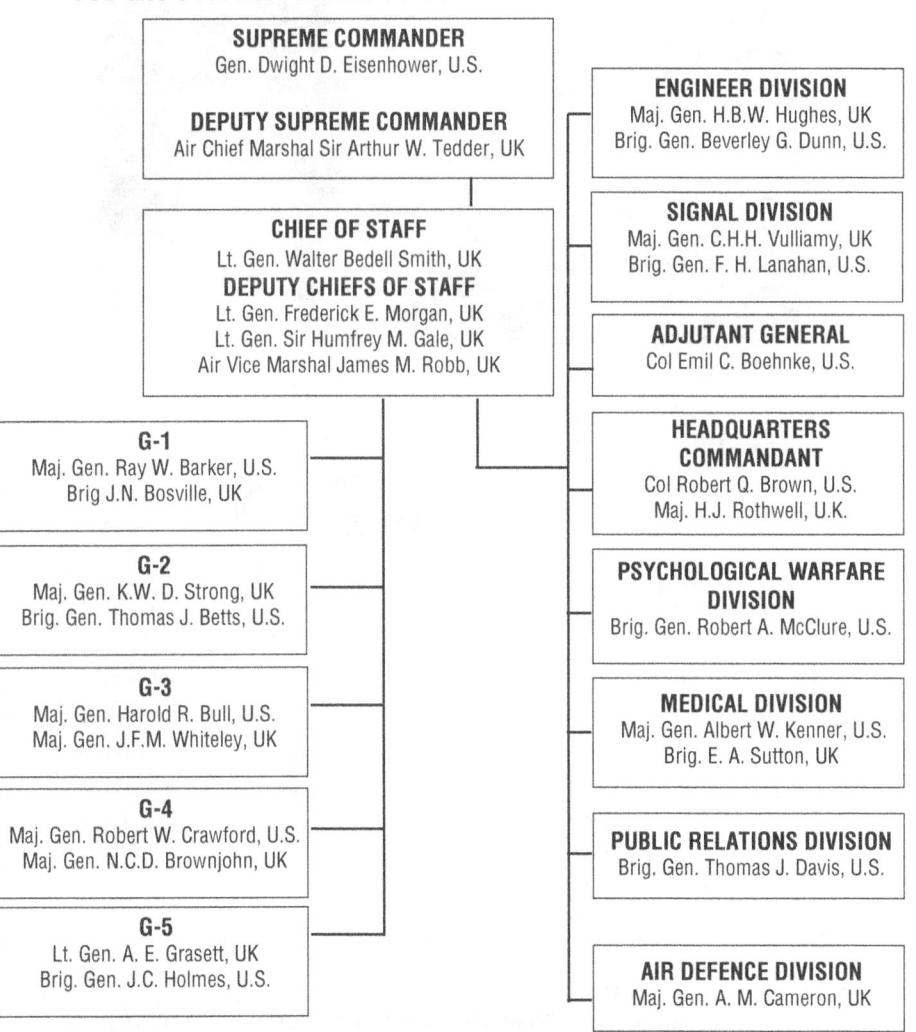

Figure 4-1. The SHAEF Chain of Command.

Source: U.S. Army Military History Institute.

General Dwight Eisenhower, Supreme Allied Commander and his British deputy, Sir Arthur Tedder.

Working with Allies, even English-speaking ones with a common purpose, could be and was often an arduous task. In some respects, one of Eisenhower's consistent problems was British Prime Minister Winston Churchill. The two men shared a good deal of mutual respect, and Churchill seemed proud that he was "half American."[20] The problem was that Churchill, despite his long political career, was also a trained and experienced military leader. He was a graduate of Sandhurst, and a man who would have undoubtedly relished his own command.[21] Throughout the war, Churchill frequently sought to interject his strategic concepts into those proposed by his reluctant subordinate commanders or his American Allies. From the Prime Minister's active mind came a litany of peripheral strategies and ideas including potential invasions of Italy, Greece, Rhodes, and Norway. Eisenhower recognized this potential problem of interference by the Prime Minister as early as 1942, but he also recognized the importance of a strong working relationship with the British. Ike, as the Supreme Commander, had one major advantage; Churchill liked him and the two men genuinely respected each other and shared some common interests. Thus, in innumerable meetings, conferences, and private get-togethers, Eisenhower was cordial despite some irritations. Though Churchill frequently interjected his pet strategies, Eisenhower never lost sight of the goal he and Marshall had agreed to in 1942. Eisenhower worked on scheduling and launching, as soon as feasible, a cross-channel attack. He accepted few distractions to the task which he had planned for and which the Combined Chiefs of Staff had tasked to him on February 12, 1944.

With the task clearly specified, and the location of the attack already agreed to, Eisenhower's immediate objective was to accelerate the buildup of men and materiel to stage the invasion. First, it was imperative to decide what the size of the invasion force would be since COSSAC's plan had been deemed insufficient. American and British invaders were to assault a well-defended coast with no flanks to turn and no way to maneuver for advantage. As an additional problem, for an invasion of the magnitude envisioned by the Allies, the invading force needed a port to provide a logistical base for the lodgment and sustained operations. Typically, defending forces can protect a port better than open beach areas like stretches of the Normandy coast.[22] The Allies would need time to seize a port.

In an excellent example of inter-Allied cooperation, Montgomery took control of the planning for the invasion and the subsequent seizure of the Normandy peninsula. Montgomery's plan called for five divisions for the landings. Adding to the strength of the ground forces was the plan to drop three airborne divisions, making the total assault force eight divisions.[23] In addition, the new Operation OVERLORD plan enlarged the landing area, because the ill-fated Dieppe operation was a perfect example of how the enemy could concentrate against a force that landed on too narrow a front.

Another problem that concerned Eisenhower and Montgomery was the additional resources needed for Operation ANVIL. Allied leaders at the Tehran conference in November 1943 finalized planning for Operation OVERLORD and called for a secondary attack against southern France, Operation ANVIL, later known as Operation DRAGOON. Planners intended the latter operation to be a three, then later a two-division assault. Properly executed, this would place the Germans in a pincer movement from the north and south of France, severely stressing their resources. As an added bonus, when Marseilles fell into Allied hands, the addition of this port would improve the supply situation for the advancing Allied armies. Conversely, when the original COSSAC plan had been strengthened by adding two additional ground divisions and two airborne divisions, this meant that the resources necessary to conduct two separate but supporting invasions had increased considerably. Despite the increased demands, Eisenhower believed that Operations OVERLORD and ANVIL were complementary and supporting operations. He was unwilling to drop Operation ANVIL to strengthen Operation

OVERLORD, although his British peers consistently stressed that ANVIL was a questionable operation.

Military leaders had to support adequately the Operations ANVIL or OVERLORD landings with a strong commitment of air and naval assets. From the onset, however, there was resistance from the AAF to switch its priorities from its strategic based CBO to supporting ground units. Beginning with the Casablanca conference in January 1943, the senior leadership had agreed that an important part of wearing down Hitler's military might was the CBO. At the same time, the method by which the commanders were to conduct the campaign to erode German strength was contentious. For some British officers, including the Prime Minister, this air campaign, the efforts of the Soviet Army, and peripheral operations by the Western Allies would all contribute to wearing down the German national leadership and military. This attrition would allow a successful landing against a weakened German Army. In the opinion of both AAF General Carl "Tooey" Spaatz and RAF Air Chief Marshal Sir Arthur Harris, an opinion shared by many of their colleagues, an air campaign could bring the Germans to their knees.[24] Spaatz and Harris were not in total agreement on how to wage the campaign, since Harris believed in conducting area bombings at night, and the American approach was daylight precision strikes. Ultimately, however, the CBO by the RAF and AAF was complementary. The two air arms conducted a round-the-clock effort with the British hitting major German cities during the night and their American peers conducting "precision" daylight attacks against German industrial targets during the day. AAF planners did undercut the effectiveness of their tactic by too quickly switching targets, hitting the ball bearing industry, the aircraft industry and then shifting to the petroleum facilities with a desire to cripple the German synthetic fuel industry. Daylight precision bombing could have been much more effective if it had consistently maintained focus on a single vital German industry. Although British and American air power advocates had differing opinions on how to wage their air campaigns, both were loath to shift away from the agreed upon strategic bombing campaign to targets in support of the proposed ground campaign. Despite their desire to focus on their designated targets, Eisenhower was determined. In his opinion, a critical element to the success of Operation OVERLORD was dedicated air support from both the strategic and tactical air forces.

Eisenhower's concept was not simply using strategic air assets for tactical close support. It included interdiction, focusing the heavy bombers on targets that would have direct and indirect effects on the tactical battlefield. Key to the success of the Allied invasion was the ability to stop the Germans from moving reinforcements and supplies to the Normandy area once Allied landings began. Thus, he backed the so-called Transportation Plan, which fighter commander, Air Chief Marshal Sir Arthur Leigh-Mallory had developed to destroy rail and surface transportation networks.[25] RAF staff planners designed the actions to bring the German transportation system to a halt. Fighters and bombers were to freeze German transportation assets all over northern Europe and especially near Normandy. Eisenhower gave his preliminary approval of this plan, which called for targeting 101 rail centers in France and Belgium, on February 1, and gave it final approval on March 26, 1944.[26] With strong support from the Combined Chiefs of Staff and despite strong objections from Allied air leaders, from April until September 1944 the strategic bomber force would be temporarily placed under Eisenhower's direct command to support tactical air operations.

Prior to this handover of strategic air to Eisenhower's control, the Allied air forces had already achieved a significant accomplishment in preparation for the Allied landings. In the 5 months prior to D-Day, the Allies were successful in achieving an extremely important prerequisite for a successful landing, aerial superiority over the *Luftwaffe*. This was by no means an easy task, because *Luftwaffe* fighters had managed to exact significant casualties on Allied air forces throughout 1943. The pace of air raids over occupied Europe increased in intensity before D-Day. Allied fighters intentionally drew the *Luftwaffe's* interceptors skyward in the latter's attempt to stop the destruction wrought by massive day and night attacks. Despite the extensive experience of German pilots, the AAF and RAF outclassed the *Luftwaffe* in terms of aircraft. By the fall of 1943, the P-47 Thunderbolt had been fitted with drop tanks, increasing its range, and in December of 1943, the P-51 Mustang entered service. Both aircraft had significant advantages over the aging German airframes, both in terms of armament and performance. From January to June 1944, 2,262 German pilots were killed. In March, 56 percent of the available German fighters were lost. Germany could not sustain these losses, and it was virtually impossible to replace destroyed and damaged airframes and pilots, given the increasing pressure on the German armed forces.[27]

Source: U.S. Air Force.

The P-51 Mustang was the ultimate piston-driven fighter developed in World War II. Its speed, armament, and range allowed the AAF to deliver a death blow to the *Luftwaffe*.

The issue of naval support for Operation OVERLORD was something new. Marshall had two Pacific theater veterans experienced in the problems associated with amphibious landings assigned to Eisenhower's command. Major General J. Lawton "Lightning Joe" Collins had commanded the 25th Infantry Division on Guadalcanal, Solomon Islands, but sought from Marshall a corps command. Marshall had Collins assigned to the European theater and given command of the U.S. VIIth Corps. The War Department also assigned Major General Charles H. "Pete" Corlett to the European theater in April 1944 to Command the U.S. XIXth Corps. Corlett had extensive Pacific experience, having commanded the 7th Infantry Division in the landings on Kwajalein Atoll in the Marshall Islands. Collin's memoirs do not indicate any irritation regarding his acceptance into the "European fraternity." In fact, he stated, "Though a newcomer to the theater, I was greeted warmly and accepted as an equal by those who had served in North Africa and the Mediterranean."[28] Conversely, Corlett, who had led successful landings on opposed beaches at Attu Island off the coast of the Aleutian Islands of Alaska and the Kwajalein Atoll, claimed that Eisenhower and Omar Bradley did not deem the lessons learned from his experiences in the Pacific relevant. According to Corlett, "anything that had happened in the Pacific was strictly bush league stuff."[29] Whether General Corlett's criticism is valid or not, Bradley's irritation with the competing priorities of the Pacific theater is evident in his own postwar memoir where he states:

> . . . I found it difficult to understand why this single most decisive attack of the entire war should have to compete with the Pacific for its minimum means [He refers to the supply of landing craft]. Naval bombardment support had been rationed to OVERLORD on an equally tightfisted basis. And while I knew nothing of the Navy's commitment to the Pacific war, I was irritated by this disposition of the Navy to look on OVERLORD as a European stepchild.[30]

Williamson Murray and Allan Millet also noted a failure of the OVERLORD planners to learn from the Pacific experience:

> The most significant lesson from the Pacific that Bradley and his senior planners passed up was the importance of naval gunfire support for the troops storming the beach. As a result of Bradley's obtuseness, U.S. troops at Omaha and Utah beaches would receive di-

rect support from only 2 battleships, 4 light cruisers, and 18 destroyers. By comparison, at Kwajalein the 7th Infantry Division alone had attacked with the support of 7 battleships, 3 heavy cruisers, and 18 destroyers over a far longer bombardment period.[31]

The necessity for having strong fire support for the landings was recognized by Operation OVERLORD planners, but the plan counted on the effectiveness of using strategic air assets to suppress German defenses rather than an extensive bombardment by naval gunfire.[32] Apparently, Allied leadership had convinced themselves of bomber accuracy claimed by air power advocates, that pinpoint daylight bombing could destroy German defenses. The experience of June 6, 1944, failed to validate these claims.

One problem that the COSSAC staff seemed to agree on was the shortage of landing craft. Marshall in his report on the period 1943-1945 stated:

> Here [planning for the cross channel attack] the Western Allies faced a shortage which was to plague us to the final day of the War in Europe—the shortage of assault craft, LST's, LCI's, and smaller vessels. . . . [A]ll the resources in England and the U.S. were searched for vessels and barges that could be employed in the Channel. Outboard motors and marine engines in pleasure craft in the U.S. were appropriated for this purpose.[33]

The problem of how to procure the necessary number of landing craft for the invasion was no small task. As Eisenhower and his staff were planning for the cross-channel attack, the war in the Pacific and in the Mediterranean had been consuming enormous amounts of naval assets. For example, in 1943 alone, American military forces were involved in the Solomon Islands campaign, the retaking of the Aleutians, and the landings on Sicily and Italy. Shortly after Eisenhower took command, the stress on the landing craft supply was further complicated by the amphibious assault at Anzio, Italy, on January 22, 1944. When the United States entered the war, it had little experience with such things as landing craft. The British had already developed the Landing Ship Tank (LST) and the Landing Craft Tank (LCT). Both of these were effective for vehicles, but what the Allies needed was the development of a suitable craft that could be mass-produced and used for landing troops in amphibious operations.

The answer came from a New Orleans, Louisiana, entrepreneur named Andrew Higgins. Higgins had developed shallow draft boats for the oil industry and was familiar with small boat design and construction. Higgins developed a plywood landing craft with a readily deployable front ramp, which was ideal for landing troops. He also developed a mass production capability that permitted him to manufacture some 20,000 of these craft during the war. Eisenhower once asked historian Stephen Ambrose if he knew Higgins, and when the latter responded no, Ike said, "That's too bad, he is the man who won the war for us."[34] While acknowledging the contribution of Andrew Higgins, the conflicting demands for "Higgins Boats" was an important factor that caused Eisenhower to delay the invasion of the continent from his original date of early May to early June 1944.

The Higgins Boat, or landing craft vehicle, personnel (LCVP) was an excellent technical solution for transport and landing soldiers on the beaches. Despite the clever design of this craft and of the LSTs and LCTs, however, the essential problem for Allied Planners was the shortage of landing craft, particularly LSTs. The Pacific demanded landing craft; Anzio consumed some of the supply; and the expansion of the OVERLORD operation called for more. Obviously, with each amphibious landing there were losses due to accidents and enemy fire. Eisenhower faced a quandary. In his area of responsibility, he needed landing craft for two separate invasions, Operations OVERLORD and ANVIL, and the demand outstripped available supply. In addition, America's British allies were not supportive on the secondary invasion, Operation ANVIL. A front already existed in the Mediterranean, the Italian Campaign, and the addition of yet a third front was problematic. This operation would stress German capabilities; but it would stress Allied forces as well. To conduct Operation ANVIL, Allied commanders would need to pull out experienced troops from Italy and would have to withdraw landing craft used for Anzio.[35] A debate between Washington and London raged during the first 3 months of 1944 as to whether the Allies should retain, reduce, or postpone Operation ANVIL. The British were highly skeptical of ANVIL's necessity and its probability of success. Eisenhower negotiated the issue with the British Chiefs of Staff. On March 22, 1944, with mounting evidence of limited resources to conduct two simultaneous invasions, Operation ANVIL was postponed.[36]

Aside from the landing craft issue, another major problem for the proposed amphibious operation was the issue of supplying the landing forces. Operation BOLERO, the original buildup of men and supplies for the landings in northern France, was in many respects an accomplishment of great magnitude. The British, Canadian, and American military landing on Normandy Beach owes its success to Operation

BOLERO. While acknowledging that the United States had the industrial and agricultural capacity to supply the Allied armies, two significant problems existed: The landing site initially chosen by COSSAC, Normandy, did not have immediate port access to provide logistical capability. Granted, the plan called for the seizure of the Cotentin port of Cherbourg, but how would the initial invasion force and the follow-on forces be supplied until the peninsula could be secured and the port opened.[37] The enormity of the problem was highlighted by Eisenhower who noted that "on D-Day and D-Day+1 [we planned] to land 20,000 vehicles and 176,000 personnel. The vehicles included 1,500 tanks, 5,000 other tracked fighting vehicles, 3,000 guns of all types, and 10,500 other vehicles from jeeps to bulldozers."[38]

For the landings and the development of a secure lodgment, the amphibious assault phase, which was code-named Operation NEPTUNE, planners endorsed an innovative solution. Drawing from concepts developed in World War I, the Allies explored the idea of constructing giant portable harbors. Engineers could build these harbors, and naval forces would then tow them to the Normandy coast. These so-called "mulberries," essentially artificial harbors and docks, would provide a location where smaller vessels could bring in supplies and unload them.[39] As the plan evolved, engineers and logisticians augmented the concept of mulberries with another structure, "phoenixes." These devices were towering hollow concrete caissons that, together with the mulberries and intentionally sunken vessels, essentially created artificial harbors. The task to create these artificial harbors was monumental. For example, the phoenixes, designed for ship crews to sink and create a breakwater, consisted of some 146 caissons. Building the phoenixes required 330,000 cubic yards of concrete and 31,000 tons of steel.[40]

Mulberries could alleviate the immediate supply issue, but the Allied armies were mechanized units and became the largest consumer of fuel in the European Campaign. Thus, as an important part of the process, planners had to address the problem of how to supply the enormous amounts of fuel necessary for the Allied breakout and pursuit phase. Planners were equally innovative in solving this problem. Attributed to Lord Louis Mountbatten as early as 1942, a program called pipe line under the ocean (PLUTO), was initiated. However, since the Germans controlled the French coast, the construction of a pipeline could not really get underway until the Allies secured a lodgment. Engineers did not complete PLUTO until August 12, over 2 months after D-Day. This was fortuitous, though, since the completion of the pipeline was in time to fuel the pursuit of retreating German forces in the area during August.

While one must give Allied planners credit for their innovations that enhanced logistical support for the landing sites, they were unable to provide for the demands of future operations. These innovations alleviated the immediate problems, but the Allied plan for the European Campaign failed to resolve the problem of supplying the armies in motion. The plan to drive westward, take the Cotentin Peninsula, and secure the port of Cherbourg (according to the plan, D-Day +15), was only a partial solution, since Cherbourg lacked the necessary capacity to adequately supply the Allied armies. Taking Cherbourg was also a curious move considering that it required the Allies to attack in the opposite direction of the goal, Germany, and the main body of the German Army. Allied commanders faced further complications about the supply problem since they had to clear the entire Brittany Peninsula in order to gain the port of Brest before turning the full Allied might eastward toward Germany.

While the port situation was a problem that was never actually solved, the massing of supplies for the invasion was an unqualified success. The British Isles, in particular south eastern Britain, became a gigantic warehouse for the Allied armed forces. Allied military leaders made great strides between 1943 and mid-1944 to create this situation. Over 60,000 U.S. engineers and 75,000 British workers built six and a half million square feet of covered storage and shops and requisitioned an additional 13,500,000 square feet of storage for Allied supplies. The Allies also used another 43,500,000 square feet of open storage for the necessary buildup. In these facilities, as well as many others, were 450,000 tons of ammunition, 175,000 tons of fuel oils and lubricants, and parking locations for 50,000 vehicles.[41]

The U.S. Army's Service of Supply task was to funnel enormous amounts of supplies into British facilities. General Brehon Somervell was responsible for ensuring that American forces had sufficient supplies in the various theaters around the world. His commander in Britain was Lieutenant General John C. H. Lee, an old friend from Somervell's World War I days. Eisenhower inherited Lee. Somervell had appointed Lee to command the American supply effort for Europe in 1942, long before Eisenhower's assumption of command. The success of Operation BOLERO, the buildup for the invasion, was likely *in spite of* its commander, rather than due to him. Lee was unpopular in Eisenhower's command because he was pompous and self-righteous, whose religiosity caused him to be nicknamed "Jesus Christ himself Lee" by his many detractors.[42] Eisenhower's Chief of Staff, Bedell Smith, said of Lee, "He didn't know much about supply organization," and found him to be a "stuffed shirt," one of the "crosses that we had to bear."[43] From Eisenhower's assumption of command until the end of the campaign, accountability for materials remained a serious problem in Lee's command, in part due to mismanagement and in part due to the thriving black market. The problem within Lee's command would finally climax after the campaign was underway, with scandals in black marketeering in Paris, France. Despite all of these problems, Eisenhower never attempted to relieve Lee due to the latter's strong political connections in Washington.[44] In the end, the American supply system was robust enough to make up for Lee's ineptitude and the inappropriate funneling of supplies into the black market.

Though logistics would emerge as one of the shortcomings in planning for the European Campaign, the deception campaign was completely the opposite; it was a resounding success. A robust deception plan was necessary because the Germans were preparing for the invasion with increasing seriousness. As early as the end of 1941, the Germans began constructing defenses along the Atlantic coast of France, recognizing the likelihood that the Allies would try to invade the continent. They had also created a high command element in the west to coordinate the defense of Western Europe. Yet for all practical purposes, the German defense in the west did not truly begin to take shape until 1943. Prior to late 1943, the Germans had created a series of bunkers and strong points, but a systematic defense of the most likely landing zones, from Calais to the tip of the Brittany Peninsula, was not well developed.[45] The catalyst for renewed German preparation occurred when on October 25, 1943, Hitler's commander in chief in the West (or OB West), *Generalfeldmarschall* Gerd von Rundstedt, submitted an assessment of German defenses for Hitler's consideration. Rundstedt stated with certainty that the Allies would invade the continent and predicted that the first landing would come at Calais, followed by Normandy. Direct and brutally frank, Rundstedt noted that to defend these most likely landing areas, Germany would need much more than just strong points; rather it would need a defense in depth with adequate mobile reserves for counterattacks.

Critics did not meet Rundstedt's assessment with the scorn and derision as so often happened when officers gave Hitler unfavorable reports. Instead, the *Führer* ordered that increasing assets be provided for the defense in the west.[46] In addition to providing more assets to the west, Hitler provided Rundstedt another asset, a new subordinate commander. Hitler appointed *Generalfeldmarschall* Erwin Rommel as Commander, Army Group B, with responsibility for the garrison in the Netherlands and the 15th and 17th Armies that were positioned in Normandy and in the vicinity of Pas de Calais. Despite their different backgrounds and styles of command, Rundstedt and Rommel surprisingly worked well together. Rommel surveyed the defenses in his command and was disturbed by the overall German unpreparedness. He tackled this problem with the same energy that had given him his reputation as commander of the *Afrika Korps*. Rommel estimated that, in addition to the fortifications or strong points built, engineers would need to create extensive minefields to slow any invasion force to allow time for a counterattack. As a credit to his energy and that of his engineers, between October 1943 and May 1944, German military and civilian labor scattered over four million mines along the French coast.[47] In addition to the mines, Rommel also had improvised obstacles installed both on the beaches that were potential landing sites and in the open fields where gliders could land troops. After observing the existing gun emplacements, he ordered many of them further strengthened and had additional positions built.

Source: Author's Collection.

A USAF reconnaissance photo taken at first light on May 19, 1944 (and at low tide) showing Rommel's obstacles designed to rip the bottoms out of Allied landing craft.

Rommel firmly believed that the only way to defeat the Allied invasion was to stop it on the beaches. To do this, the *Wehrmacht* needed two capabilities: a strong and mutually supportive system of fortifications, and a strong mobile reserve. Positioning armored units close to the coast as a mobile reserve was imperative. Those reserve forces would rush forward to push the Allied troops back into the sea. Rommel, who had personally witnessed the growing Allied airpower in North Africa, was totally convinced that unless reinforcements, especially armored units, were close to the coast Allied air supremacy would make it impossible to get to the invading force in time. His strategy was countered by the commander of armored forces in the west, *General der Panzertruppen* Leo Geyr von Schweppenburg, who believed that the armored reserves had to be kept far to the rear and thus out the reach of tactical air and naval gunfire.[48] Because of these two different philosophies on how armored units should respond to the coming Allied invasion, there was considerable friction between Rommel, Rundstedt, and Schweppenburg. Instead of exercising firm command over the three respected officers with a clearcut decision directing where they would locate mobile reserves, Hitler and Rundstedt allowed the controversy to simmer and in the end essentially split the control of armored units in France, rather than assigning firm command authority over armored reserves. Events would show that Rommel was correct.

Rommel was convinced that the invasion was going to hit in the Calais vicinity and that it would come at high tide.[49] Thus, German defenders spent a considerable amount of energy focused on this region. After all, it was close to Britain, and it led to the best terrain for mobility and the most direct route to Berlin. The commander of *Kriegsmarine* in the West, Admiral Theodor Krancke, placed the likely invasion site further west but could not decide with any degree of certainty where it might occur. Hitler vacillated on exactly where the landings would occur, but he was certain that the invasion would come soon.[50]

All of this demonstrates that from late 1943 to early 1944, the Germans knew the Allied invasion was coming. They were planning for the day an Allied armada would appear somewhere off the coast of France. The only remaining questions were when and where the Allies would land. Since the coming invasion was no surprise, it was crucial for the Allies to devise a plan that would deceive the Germans about the time and place of the invasion. American and British military officers created a deception plan called Operation FORTITUDE. Its overall objective was to convince Hitler and his high command that Operation OVERLORD was going to occur at locations where it was not, and at the same time, convince them that landing activities in the Normandy vicinity were actually a feint. Operation FORTITUDE used a number of methodologies to accomplish a classic deception. False information was fed through the former German agents to the *Abwehr*, the German military intelligence service. Allied commands created ghost divisions, complete with shoulder patches, to convince the Germans that many new divisions were poised for the invasion. Radio operators transmitted false radio traffic regarding equipment supplies and men to convince the Germans that many more units existed than actually did. In Scotland, an Operation FORTITUDE plan focused its attention on convincing the Germans, through a stream of messages, that Allied commanders were prepared to invade Norway. In the southern part of Britain, Operation FORTITUDE used phony message traffic, inflated rubber tanks, landing craft, and dummy aircraft to show the supposed buildup in the area opposite Pas de Calais. The most disturbing threat projected to the Germans was the existence of a First Army Group (FUSAG), commanded by General George S. Patton, which seemed poised to strike the Pas de Calais area. Of course, Allied leaders had scheduled a command under Patton for activation, but Patton was not to be a part of the invasion force. Rather, Eisenhower scheduled it as an element for exploitation, once the landings were successful and breakouts from the beachhead were executed.

As military leaders consider future operations against the nation's adversaries, they should carefully consider the significance of Operation FORTITUDE. The campaign was one of the finest examples in modern warfare of the importance of designing and executing a well-planned deception plan. The use of multiple assets from all services, both the intelligence services and the combat arms, convinced the key German commander on the ground that the invasion would come near Pas de Calais.[51] Thus, the deception plan was a success in convincing the Germans of the wrong location for the invasion. The bomber offensive, whose targeting pattern was deliberately diffuse, made it difficult for the Germans to ascertain the exact focus of the Allied air preparations. These activities enhanced the deception.

When American and British forces launched the invasion, Allied landing forces were under the command of Field Marshal Montgomery, the commander of the 21st Army Group. The 21st was composed of the U.S. First Army commanded by Lieutenant General

Omar N. Bradley, and the British Second Army commanded by Lieutenant General Sir Miles Dempsey. The three airborne divisions for the invasion had key missions. The U.S. 82nd and 101st Airborne Divisions would land behind Utah Beach and shield the rear of the landing zone from the expected German counterattack. The British 6th Airborne Division's scheduled drop was in the vicinity of Caen where it was to stop expected reinforcements from the German Fifteenth Army that would likely hit British landing forces. Bradley and his U.S. VIIth Corps would land on Utah Beach, and the U.S. Vth Corps would hit the beach on a sector known as Omaha Beach.

Source: U.S. Army Military History Institute.

American Assault Troops Landing on Omaha Beach, D-Day, June 6, 1944.

The invasion of the northwest coast of France was a monumental achievement for the Allied forces. From the onset, they sought to conduct an amphibious invasion that was, in terms of its mass, unprecedented. In 1 day's time, June 6, 1944, Allied leaders intended to land 150,000 men and massive amounts of equipment on the continent. To do this, it was necessary to employ over 800 vessels to transport the soldiers and supplies to the area of the assault. Additionally, the number of transport aircraft necessary to drop the airborne divisions was great. According to the Supreme Commander's report, the U.S. IXth Troop Carrier Command alone dedicated 1,662 aircraft and 512 gliders to this effort.[52] Since the Germans had liberally strewn the Channel with mines, the Allied navies needed 287 minesweepers to clear these deadly obstacles. Maritime commanders also required a vast armada of warships, landing craft of various types, and small smaller coastal vessels of over 7,000 ships.

Despite superb planning, D-Day had a number of significant shortfalls. Giving Eisenhower control of the strategic bomber forces in the weeks immediately prior to the invasion was a key decision. Strategic air was literally able to strangle the German transportation system in occupied France and virtually prohibited the rapid transportation of reserves to the Normandy area. By June 1944, the French railway system barely functioned; the interdiction campaign had succeeded. At the same time, the use of strategic air to support ground forces proved to be highly ineffective. Two problems contributed to this ineffectiveness: First, the aircraft used by the American 8th Air Force were designed for strategic campaigns like the CBO and were built to operate effectively at high altitudes.

The famed B-17 had a service ceiling of 35,800 feet, and the B-24 could operate at 28,000 feet. Despite all claims of that time and since the war, at that height even the fabled Norden bomb-sight was incapable in delivering precision bomb loads. Further complicating the problem on D-Day, scattered clouds were present as low as 2,000 feet, and at 20,000 feet solid cloud cover existed, totally obscuring the battlefield. American bombers belonging to the 8th Air Force had to target by instruments, and this was even more inaccurate than observed runs.

American military leaders sent 329 B-24 bombers to drop 13,000 bombs to soften up the defenses near Omaha Beach before the invasion. This ordnance, however, failed to hit German defenses and, in fact, fell as far inland as 3 miles.[53] The bomber preparation of Omaha Beach was a total failure, and German defenses on Omaha Beach were intact as American troops came ashore. At Utah Beach, the bombers were a little more effective because the IXth Bomber Command was using B-26 medium bombers. Wisely, in preparation for supporting the invasion, maintenance crews removed Norden bombsights from the bombers and installed the more effective low-level altitude sights.[54] Even though the preparatory bombing on Utah Beach was more effective, even here about one-third of the bombs fell seaward, and some of the pilots were unable to locate their targets due to the overcast.[55] From the beginning of the European Campaign, senior Allied leadership used a questionable tactic; employing strategic aircraft for tactical purposes, a purpose for which they were never intended. Allied military leaders would repeatedly return to this questionable use of strategic bombers throughout the European Campaign, often producing debatable results.

The air force was not the only service whose preparation of the battlefield was lacking. The American and British navies did not have sufficient "battlewagons" that could lay down a heavy carpet of fire to soften German defenses. Insufficient naval forces also translated to inadequate fire support for the invading troops.

At Omaha Beach, where bomber preparation had accomplished little except to inflict damage on French agriculture, all too many things went wrong. Planners had recognized that infantry directly assaulting well-prepared defenses would need armor to support them. Thus, ground force officers planned to employ amphibious tanks to support the infantry. On D-Day, however, of the 32 tanks modified for amphibious use, 29 sank, partly due to the weather but largely due to the Navy's decision to launch them over 6,000 yards from shore.[56] Six-wheeled amphibious trucks (DUKWs) were a partial answer. Crews loaded the DUKWs with 105mm artillery pieces to allow troops to have artillery support, but heavy seas and German guns meant that the two artillery battalions that were supposed to support the 116th Infantry on Omaha Beach lost 16 of their 24 artillery pieces in a matter of minutes.[57] The Navy also launched many of the Higgins boats some 16 to 20 kilometers off shore, too far from the beach. The infantrymen then had to endure a lengthy and perilous journey through heavy seas and under heavy enemy fire. When sailors dropped the ramps, many American Soldiers went into water up to their necks or at least their armpits, and many drowned. Once unloaded, this led to a dash over about 300 yards of tidal sand because landings occurred at low tide, and then another 100 yards of beach. In short, infantrymen at Omaha Beach had a literal gauntlet of fire to run through before they could begin their arduous task of tackling the German defenses.

Royal Army leadership offered to American planners additional equipment designed to tackle German defenses. Montgomery had ordered Major General Sir Percy Hobart to offer one-third of their special equipment to the Americans. Hobart commanded the British 79th Division, elements of which accompanied the assault units going ashore on D-Day. Hobart's 79th had special Sherman tanks called "Crabs" which engineers equipped with flailing chain arms to explode mines. The British also had "Crocodiles," tanks equipped with flamethrowers, to overcome German pillboxes and fortifications. Additionally, the 79th had Armored Vehicle Royal Engineers, multi-purposed vehicles based on the Churchill Mark IV chassis and mounting a mortar designed to destroy fortifications, as well as a bridging device to cross ravines. Despite the offer to share these novel "gadgets" to help unravel German defenses, Bradley and his staff were not interested.[58]

A major contributing factor to the near failure on Omaha Beach was a significant intelligence oversight. In the final stages of Allied preparations for the landings, American intelligence staffs had identified the German 716th Division as the defenders of the Omaha Beach sector. The 716th was not a highly rated division in terms of its combat power. However, the 716th was not the primary adversary of American troops at Omaha Beach. The 352nd Division that had moved into this sector was a much more competent division. Thus, on D-Day there were elements of two German Divisions near the landing site. Although not all of the 352nd Division was positioned for defense of the beach, it gave American troops an extremely difficult time and, had the full division been manning the defenses, it could have been catastrophic.[59] Small unit and individual soldier courage and initiative on the beaches ultimately compensated for these shortfalls. Despite heavy casualties, Omaha Beach became a success.[60]

In the other landing zones, the experience was quite different for both the British and the Americans. For example, on Juno Beach, the 3rd Canadian Division was the assault force and suffered the misfortune of coming in late and at higher tide, making the German obstacles more effective and exacting a heavy toll of landing craft. Despite initial determined German resistance, however, the Canadians were able to break through the German defenses and move inland to a depth of 10 kilometers on the first day. On Gold Beach, the results were similar. There the Royal Navy gave the Germans a heavy shelling, but the Germans still succeeded in putting up a heavy resistance until the determined British landing force punched through the crust of coastal defense and actually advanced to the outskirts of the city of Bayeux. The remaining beach, code named Sword, also had the luxury of a heavier naval bombardment that successfully suppressed some of the German fortifications. British assault forces did have to contend with several major fortifications, as well as accurate artillery fire originating from the rear of the German mainline of defense. Still, they were able to establish a firm foothold, link up with British airborne elements, and prepare to move on Caen. By day's end, the British and Canadian troops had a firm hold on their beaches.

Of the two American beaches, only Utah was an unqualified success. On Utah Beach, the medium bombers had been more accurate than their heavy cousins at Omaha Beach. Another assist from the air came when elements of the 101st Airborne Division were successful in destroying some of the German artillery positions that could have exacted heavy casualties on the Utah Beach assault forces.[61] A notable mistake, landing 4th Infantry Division troops about two kilometers south of their assigned landing area, turned to an advantage since German defenses were weaker in that area.

Another significant problem that emerged on D-Day was the dispersion of the American paratroopers and glider forces. The Allies had decided to drop three airborne divisions at night, rather than at first light. When the transports began taking off, the weather was cloudy, and it was dark. German ground fire over the landing sites was intense in many areas, and the darkness, poor weather, and inexperienced pilots caused many of the airborne units to miss their assigned drop zones completely. In fact, the paratroopers of the American 82nd and 101st Airborne Divisions were widely scattered, robbing the airborne units of their ability to concentrate and quickly accomplish their assigned missions. While poor drops could have been a major problem, ironically, these errors in dropping the paratroopers were, in the end, an advantage. Poorly executed drops totally confused the Germans because they were simply unable to determine the paratrooper's areas of concentration and thus their mission.

Despite the errors and the usual fog of war, D-Day was an unqualified success. An objective and detailed analysis of what happened on the various beaches on that day would provide numerous examples of heroism, initiative, and leadership, but while praising the ground forces for what they had accomplished, readers should remember that this was a joint accomplishment. In the years preceding D-Day, the Allied navies had effectively neutered the German Navy. By 1944, for all practical purposes Germany no longer had a surface fleet; their remaining ships were kept close in port for fear of venturing to sea and meeting with virtual destruction. The last foray of a German capital ship, the *Scharnhorst*, had ended in disaster, and the Allies bottled up what was left of the miniscule German fleet. Even the U-boat menace, which had caused the Allies many anxious months in 1941-42, had diminished considerably. By 1944, improved air and naval tactics and the cracking of the *Kriegsmarine's* Enigma code through ULTRA meant that U-boats had become the hunted, not the hunters. German E-boats and patrol torpedo craft, which had caused so much consternation and casualties at Slapton Sands, Devon, England, were largely absent at Normandy in part due to heavy seas and in part to the hesitancy of Admiral Theodor Krancke to commit them. Thus, naval supremacy meant that the Allies were able to muster their invasion fleet and transport men and supplies across the Channel with no opposition. The German Navy's only significant effort on D-Day was when four E-boats made a run on the invasion fleet and sank a Norwegian destroyer. Other than this brief foray, the *Kriegsmarine* was conspicuously absent.[62] The Allies had achieved naval supremacy.

Command of the air was another important factor for D-Day and the days following the actual invasion. Granted, the use of heavy bombers had been relatively ineffective for direct support of the landings, but the CBO that followed the "Transportation Plan" was an unqualified success. The French/German transportation network was so badly damaged that the German reserves, so necessary to defeat the invasion on the beaches, could not counterattack immediately against the invasion force. Of the elite units that could have helped German defenders contest the control of the beaches, only the 12th SS *"Hitler Jugend"* Division was able to move up rapidly, but it did not get into action until June 7, at which time the Canadians had a firm foothold on their assigned beach. The 17th Panzer Grenadier Division had to move by road and, due to Allied air dominance, it took them 5 days to cover 200 miles.

Importantly, German fighter aircraft were not major factors in any defensive operations against the invasion fleet and the beaches in part due to the attrition of pilots and aircraft in the first 6 months of 1944. In addition, *Luftwaffe* commanders had recalled many German fighters to protect the Reich from the Allied bombing raids. Only a handful of fighter aircraft were available when the landings occurred, making the task for Germany's *Jagdkorps II* extremely difficult, if not impossible. The classic example of fighter shortages was the case of the famous German ace Lieutenant Colonel Josef Priller. Priller had watched, in dismay, as 124 aircraft from his 26th *Jagdgeschwader* were moved from the vicinity of Lille, France, on June 5. On the next day when the invasion forces appeared, he had two fighter aircraft available. Nonetheless, his higher command ordered him to take his "squadron" and attack the beaches.[63] In comparison, over a 24-hour period, the Allied air forces flew 14,000 sorties to support the landing forces. Allied tactical air forces could rely on 2,434 fighters and fighter-bombers and some 700 light and medium bombers for the Normandy landings.[64] Allied control of the air over the coast of France was complete.

D-Day, the invasion of the continent of Europe, was without question an unqualified success. In 1 day alone, the Allies had landed eight divisions and three armored brigades on German occupied France. Broken down by nationality, over 75,100 British and Canadian troops and 57,500 American Soldiers had landed on the European continent from the sea. In addition, 23,000 airborne troops had also dropped into France. Through the efforts of all three branches of service and the combined efforts of two nations, Eisenhower, and his joint and Allied staff had successfully completed the first part of their assigned task. Allied forces had ". . . entered the continent of Europe." The Allied armies were now poised to undertake the second and equally important part of the task, to "undertake operations aimed at the heart of Germany and the destruction of her armed forces . . ."

ENDNOTES - CHAPTER 4

1. Dwight D. Eisenhower, as quoted in Jane Penrose, ed., *The D-Day Companion: Leading Historians Explore History's Greatest Amphibious Assault*, Oxford, UK: Osprey Publishing, 2004, p. 13.

2. According to Alanbrooke's diaries, on January 14, King proposed more emphasis on the Pacific, and again on January 18 was described as being "wrapped up in the war of the Pacific at the expense of everything else." Field Marshall Lord Alanbrooke, *War Diaries, 1939-1945*, Alex Danchev and Daniel Todman, eds., Berkeley, CA: University of California Press, 2001, pp. 359, 361. King's position, as described by Albert Wedemeyer, who was present at this conference, was that the Japanese were capable of holding their gains in the Pacific. With the United States only committing 15 percent of its resources to the Pacific war, the danger existed that the Japanese could shift their operations toward Australia or India. Albert Wedemeyer, *Wedemeyer Reports*, New York: Henry Holt and Company, 1958, p. 177.

3. Winston S. Churchill, *The Hinge of Fate*, New York: Houghton Mifflin, 1950, p. 692.

4. Churchill, in his multivolume history of the war, was quick to point out that he had a luncheon with General Ira Eaker, the U.S. 8th Air Force Commander who vigorously defended the U.S. concept of daylight precision bombing with "Flying Fortresses." Churchill, however, did not endorse this idea; he merely ceased to oppose it. *Ibid.*, p. 680.

5. Maurice Mattloff, "Strategic Planning For Coalition Warfare," in Kent Roberts Greenfield, ed., *U.S. Army in World War II*, Washington DC: U.S. Army Center of Military History, 1959, p. 29.

6. Morgan, in briefing his staff on the duties of COSSAC, pointed out that he was to develop plans, but he did not want his organization to become just a planning staff. In his opinion, "The term 'planning staff' has come to have the most sinister meaning — it implies the production of nothing but paper. What we must contrive to do somehow is to produce, not only paper, but ACTION." Historical Sub-Section, Supreme Headquarters, Allied Expeditionary Force, "History of COSSAC, Chief of Staff to Supreme Allied Commander," N.P. May, 1944, p. 4. (Henceforth "History of COSSAC.")

7. Alanbrooke, *War Diaries*, p. 395.

8. The number of plans or variations of plans produced by COSSAC are admirable. Operations COCKADE, TINDALL, RANKIN, WADHAM, and STARKEY were other plans or sub plans that were considered. "History of COSSAC," p. A-8.

9. From the first meeting of the COSSAC Staff on April 17, 1943, as quoted in Gordon A. Harrison, "The European Theater of Operations: Cross Channel Attack," in Kent Roberts Greenfield, ed., *U.S. Army in World War II*, Washington, DC: Office of the Chief of Military History, 1951, p. 51

10. Note, however, that one major obstacle to Allied progress in the exploitation phase seems to have escaped the planners. In Normandy, the bocage, the century-old system of hedges and

berms, posed a significant obstacle to Allied breakout and pursuit. The other obvious problem was that since Allied armies were moving east and needed logistical support, it made seizing port cities in the opposite direction rather illogical.

11. Duncan Anderson, "Remember this is an Invasion," in Jane Penrose, ed., *The D-Day Companion: Leading historians explore history's greatest amphibious assault*, London, UK: Osprey Publishing Co, 2004, p. 37.

12. Although Churchill agreed to the need to expeditiously plan for the cross-channel attack, at the same time he had inserted in the minutes of the conference the requirement for a staff study on the feasibility of an invasion of Norway as an alternative. The peripheral strategy, the indirect or pecking away at the periphery, did not die easily. Russell F. Weigley, *Eisenhower's Lieutenants: The Campaign of France and Germany, 1944-1945*, Bloomington, IN: The University of Indiana Press, 1981, p. 33.

13. COSSAC's plan called for three divisions the first day, five divisions on D+2, and a total of nine divisions on D+8. Cherbourg was the only sizable port near the landings, but as Allied strength grew to 25-30 divisions and Cherbourg was in Allied hands, it was insufficient to support a force of this size. Robert W. Oakley and Richard M. Leighton, *Global Logistics and Strategy, 1943-1945*, Washington, DC: U.S. Army Center of Military History, 1968, p. 182.

14. COSSAC did the original planning for Operation OVERLORD under Morgan's direction. His plan assumed that the commander would be British, thus the chain of command structure was more suited to British concepts. When an American Army was on the continent, a British Army Group would exercise field command until either the Brittany peninsula was liberated or an American Army Group could be formed. Harrison, "The European Theater of Operations: Cross Channel Attack," p. 107.

15. Alanbrooke, *War Diaries*, p. 441. Alanbrooke found Marshall to be "... a pleasant and easy man to get on with, rather overfilled with his own importance. But I should not put him down as a great man."(p. 246). Of Eisenhower, he said, " I'm afraid Eisenhower as a general is hopeless. He submerges himself in politics

and neglects his military duties, partly I'm afraid, because he knows little if anything about military matters."(p. 351). Eisenhower, despite Alanbrooke's comments, some of which reached the British press, tended to take the high ground and avoid commenting negatively about a fellow senior officer.

16. This was as reported by James Roosevelt in *My Parents: A Differing View*, Chicago, IL: The Playboy Press, 1976, p. 176.

17. Winston S. Churchill, *Closing the Ring*, Boston, MA: Houghton Mifflin, 1951, p. 418.

18. Dwight D. Eisenhower, *Crusade in Europe*, New York: Doubleday & Company, 1948, p. 207.

19. Dwight D. Eisenhower, *Report by The Supreme Commander to the Combined Chiefs of Staff on the Operations in Europe of the Allied Expeditionary Force, 6 June, 1944 to 8 May, 1945*, Washington, DC: U.S. Army Center of Military History, 1994, reprint of 1946, p. v.

20. Sir Winston's mother, Jennie Jerome, was an American and, interestingly enough, his grandmother, Clara Hall, was one-quarter Iroquois Indian.

21. Churchill entered the Royal Military Academy at Sandhurst in 1893 as a Cavalry Cadet. He completed his studies there in 1894. He saw service in the Boer War, and, at the onset of World War I, he was First Lord of the Admiralty, by that time having transitioned to political life. He returned to military life during World War I, serving as a lieutenant colonel commanding the 6th battalion of the Royal Scots Fusiliers.

22. The port problem was never actually solved. The construction of artificial ports, the now famous mulberries, resolved the problem for the initial landings, but supplies to support the advancing Allied Expeditionary Force were consistently a problem until the Allies opened the port of Antwerp in November 1944.

23. Carlo D'Este, *Decision in Normandy*, New York: Konecky and Konecky, 1994, pp. 62-104. Note, however, that even though Eisenhower and Montgomery agreed to a considerable increase in strength in the invasion force, Monty repeatedly opposed Opera-

tion ANVIL that Eisenhower promoted as a critical part in weakening German defenses.

24. Max Hastings, *Bomber Command*, New York: Dial Press/J Wade, 1979, p. 327. There was a conviction on the part of Spaatz and Harris that Germany was "already tottering on the edge of collapse from bombing." Thus, why should the Allies conduct the Operation OVERLORD landing when strategic air had, in fact, brought the Germans to their knees? Apparently, neither Spaatz nor Harris knew or wanted to acknowledge that German industrial production actually increased beginning in 1943 and peaked in the first half of 1944.

25. Leigh-Mallory was the head of this bombing committee, but the actual plan was developed by Solly Zuckerman, a one time Professor of anatomy! The concept was bitterly opposed by leading American and British Airmen and, interestingly enough, by Winston Churchill. Churchill found the plan to bomb rail centers throughout France to be inhumane, due to the number of French casualties that would result. Conversely, Charles DeGaulle, when briefed on the plan, accepted these casualties as necessary to defeat the Germans.

26. Edward Mark, *Aerial Interdiction: Air Power and the Land Battle in Three American Wars*, Washington, DC: Center for Air Force History, 1994, pp. 223-230.

27. Richard Hallion, *D-Day 1944: Air Power Over the Beaches and Beyond*, Washington, DC: U.S. Government Printing Office, 1994, p. 2.

28. J. Lawton Collins, *Lightning Joe: An Autobiography*, Novato CA: The Presidio Press, 1994, p. 181.

29. Charles H. Corlett, *Cowboy Pete: The Autobiography of Major General Charles H. Corlett*, Santa Fe, NM: Sleeping Fox Publisher, 1974, p. 88.

30. Omar N. Bradley, *A Soldiers Story*, New York: Henry Holt and Company, 1951, pp. 220-221. Not directly stated in Bradley's comments but certainly an issue, was the difficulty in prying capital American ships dedicated for Pacific operations from Admiral King's firm grip.

31. Williamson Murray and Alan Millet, *A War to be Won: Fighting the Second World War*, Cambridge, MA: Harvard University Press, 2000, p. 419.

32. This concept predates Operation OVERLORD; it can be found in COSSAC documents. The COSSAC wartime history mentions the use of two R-class battleships which were to supplement air bombardment in neutralizing the German batteries and mentions the need for diverting a considerable proportion of the heavy bomber effort from strategic targets to objectives related immediately to cross-channel operations. "History of COSSAC," p. 19.

33. George C. Marshall, *Biennial Reports of the Chief of Staff of the U.S. Army To The Secretary of War, July 31, 1943-June 30, 1945*, Washington, DC: U. S. Army Center of Military History, 1996, p. 113.

34. Stephen E. Ambrose, *D-Day June 6, 1944: The Climactic Battle of World War II*, New York: Simon and Schuster, 1994, p. 45.

35. Churchill and General Sir Henry Maitland "Jumbo" Wilson were opposed to Operation ANVIL because of its effect on the Italian campaign. Italy, despite being a part of the so-called "soft underbelly," was a tough battlefield for the Allies. With the failure of Anzio to provide a breakthrough, the British were determined not to let American plans weaken this theater any further. Churchill, *Closing the Ring*, pp. 510-514.

36. Ever critical of American leadership, Alanbrooke could only comment, " I now hope that at last all may be well and that the American Chiefs of Staff will at last see some wisdom." Alanbrooke, *War Diaries, 1939-1945*, p. 533.

37. One author notes that the plan ultimately called for 29 divisions to be landed in the lodgment area and that, even with the capture of Cherbourg, there were insufficient port facilities to support a force of this size. See Harrison, "The European Theater of Operations: Cross Channel Attack," p. 73.

38. Eisenhower, *Report by The Supreme Commander to the Combined Chiefs of Staff on the Operations in Europe of the Allied Expeditionary Force*, p. 11.

39. Allied officers seriously discussed the issue of artificial harbors at the LARGS conference held June 29-July 4, 1943. Participants talked about the mulberries, including the floating concrete caissons called phoenixes, and the possibility of using sunken ships as part of the breakwaters. "History of COSSAC," p. A-40.

40. Andrew Gordon, "The Greatest Military Armada Ever Launched," in Penrose, ed., *The D-Day Companion,* p. 133.

41. Duncan Anderson, "Remember this is an Invasion," in *Ibid.*, p. 45.

42. Even Omar Bradley, who was generous on the professional capabilities of Lee, had to admit, "[Lee] suffered from an unfortunate pomposity that caused others to underrate his skills." He also had to admit that Lee, known for his love of creature comforts, undoubtedly negatively affected supply operations when he moved his entire headquarters forward to Paris on August 30, 1944. At that time, there was a supply crisis for the Allied forces pushing the German forces back to their prewar borders. Lee and his headquarters also took sumptuous quarters in Paris, which Eisenhower thought should be reserved for troops on furlough. Bradley, pp. 405-406.

43. Walter Bedell Smith, as Interviewed by Forest Pogue, Military History Institute, Carlisle, PA.

44. Lee's connections were considerable. He not only was well-respected by Sommervell, he also was thought well of by Marshall himself. Thus, despite his many failures and downright foolish actions, Bedell Smith could not talk Eisenhower into relieving him. Patton was clear in his opinion, calling Lee "a pompous little son-of-a-bitch only interested in his own self advertisement." See Carlo D'Este, Chap. 3, *Eisenhower: A Soldier's Life*, New York: Henry Holt and Company, 2002, pp. 483-484, 590-592.

45. According to *Generaloberst* Alfred Jodl, Hitler took personal interest in the construction of these fortifications, specifying that ports should receive first priority. He also had a map

produced showing completed fortifications, under construction and projected fortifications. *Generaloberst* Alfred Jodl, *Invasion and Normandy Campaign*, Foreign Military Studies, MS# A-913, U.S. Army Europe, Historical Division, 1945, pp. 1,2.

46. Walter Warlimont, *Inside Hitler's Headquarters, 1939-1945*, Novato, CA: The Presidio Press, 1964, p. 400-402. Warlimont notes that on November 3, 1943, a German Army (OKW) directive began the process of shifting some of the thinking from the struggle against Bolshevism to the defense in the west. On December 28, Hitler ordered that there would be no additional transfers of men and equipment from the Western Front to the Eastern without his express permission.

47. This number of mines, while substantial, was actually short of what Rommel wanted. He had proposed a series of minefields several kilometers wide and five to six miles inland. As interpreted by the general in command of engineer troops for Army Group B, Rommel's mining plans would actually call for 200 million mines for the French coast. B.H. Liddell Hart, ed., *The Rommel Papers*, London, UK: Collins Press, 1953, p. 455.

48. Schweppenburg wanted a large armored reserve based in the environs of Paris, believing that the Allies might make a deep airborne drop to seize Paris, a possibility that Rommel logically dismissed. *Ibid.*, pp. 468-469.

49. In discussion with his close associate, General Fritz Bayerlein, Rommel stated, "The focus of the enemy landing operation will probably be directed against the Fifteenth Army's sector [The Pas de Calais], because it is from this sector that much of our long-range attack on England and central London will be launched." General Fritz Bayerlein, as quoted in *Ibid.*, p. 453.

50. Hitler in an address on March 20, 1944, to the Commanders in Chief in the West stated, "It is evident that the Anglo-American landing in the west will and must come. . . . The most suitable and hence the most threatened areas are the two west coast peninsulas, Cherbourg and Brest, which are very tempting and offer the best possibilities for the formation of a bridgehead." *Ibid.*, p. 465.

51. As an interesting side light, Carlo D'Este noted in his excellent work on D-Day that Sir Basil Liddell Hart thought that Rundstedt was more deceived by his own logic because, as a classically trained German General Staff Officer, the logical strategy for the Allies would have been to attack near and take Calais, thereby giving them the best terrain and a port. At the same time, D'Este acknowledges that Operation FORTITUDE undoubtedly strengthened this preconception. D'Este, *Decision in Normandy*, p. 117.

52. The British 38th and 46th Groups dedicated 733 aircraft and 355 gliders for their part of the effort. Eisenhower, *Report by The Supreme Commander to the Combined Chiefs of Staff on the Operations in Europe of the Allied Expeditionary Force*, p. 22.

53. Harrison, "The European Theater of Operations: Cross Channel Attack," pp. 300-301.

54. Goeffrey Paret, *Winged Victory: The Army Air Forces in World War II*, New York: Random House, 1993, pp. 304-305.

55. Harrison, "The European Theater of Operations: Cross Channel Attack," p. 301.

56. In contrast, on Utah Beach, 28 of the 32 Amphibious tanks made it ashore where they were extremely important in providing supporting fire to the infantrymen that were attempting to consolidate their foothold. Williamson Murray, "A Visitor to Hell: On the Beaches," in Penrose, ed., *The D-Day Companion*, p. 156.

57. Flint Whitlock, *The Fighting First: The Untold Story Of the Big Red One on D-DAY*, Boulder, CO: The Westview Press, 2004, p. 141.

58. Weigley, *Eisenhower's Lieutenants*, p. 79.

59. As bad as it was on Omaha Beach, it could have been much worse. Fortunately for the G.I.s, only part of the 352nd was manning the German defenses. The division commander had retained the rest of the division further inland.

60. As Omar Bradley later noted, " Although Omaha had squeezed through a crisis, she was still on the danger list. With neither depth, artillery, or tanks, we might easily be dislodged from our precarious footing and thrown back into the channel by counterattacks." Bradley, *A Soldier's Story*, pp. 273-274.

61. Perhaps the best known action of the 101st Airborne Division in support of Utah Beach assault troops occurred with Lieutenant Richard Winters, Easy Company, 2nd Battalion, 506th Parachute Infantry Regiment. Winters and a handful of his men assaulted a German artillery battery at Brecourt Farm that was sited on the landing area and would have caused considerable casualties, had it been allowed to operate. See Stephen Ambrose, *Band of Brothers: E Company, 506th Regiment, 101st Airborne From Normandy to Hitler's Eagle's Nest*, New York: Simon and Schuster, 1992, pp. 77-83.

62. Fifteen additional E-Boats did weigh anchor and head for the invasion fleet, but they turned back because of the rough seas.

63. Priller and his wingman, both with severe hangovers from the previous night, obeyed orders and made a single pass over the beaches at about 50 feet and then headed for the clouds. Both survived this exercise in futility.

64. Hallion, *D-Day 1944*, p. 7.

CHAPTER 5

TOWARD THE GERMAN BORDER: OPERATION COBRA, THE FALAISE POCKET, AND OPERATION ANVIL

> We shall continue attacking, never give him a chance to rest, never give him a chance to give in.[1]
>
> General Omar Bradley

Allied planners had done an exceptional job in the planning and execution of Operations BOLERO, NEPTUNE (the naval aspects included in Operation OVERLORD), and OVERLORD. In terms of senior leadership, from inception to planning and then execution, Morgan, Eisenhower, and Montgomery had performed their roles in an exemplary manner. Eisenhower, in particular, deserves special credit for his difficult decision on June 5, 1944, when, despite the weather, he uttered the simple, but decisive words, "Let's go." The fact that the weather was questionable even added to the Allied deception and thus to the Allied success. Enhancing the leadership shown by the senior officers was the bravery and small unit leadership on all five beaches by Allied soldiers which, in all cases, made up for the shortfalls already noted in the planning or execution. Planning for the European Campaign, however, had focused on making a series of successful landings, establishing a secure lodgment, and then building up the forces within a secure area. Once this was completed, the Allies could execute a breakout from the beachhead area, closely followed by a pursuit phase. Exploitation and pursuit of the German defenders, lacked the careful planning that was evident in Operations BOLERO, NEPTUNE, and OVERLORD. As historian Russell Weigley noted, however, "Operation NEPTUNE [and OVERLORD] planning" [and for that matter execution] "had been tactical and technological, rather than operational."[2]

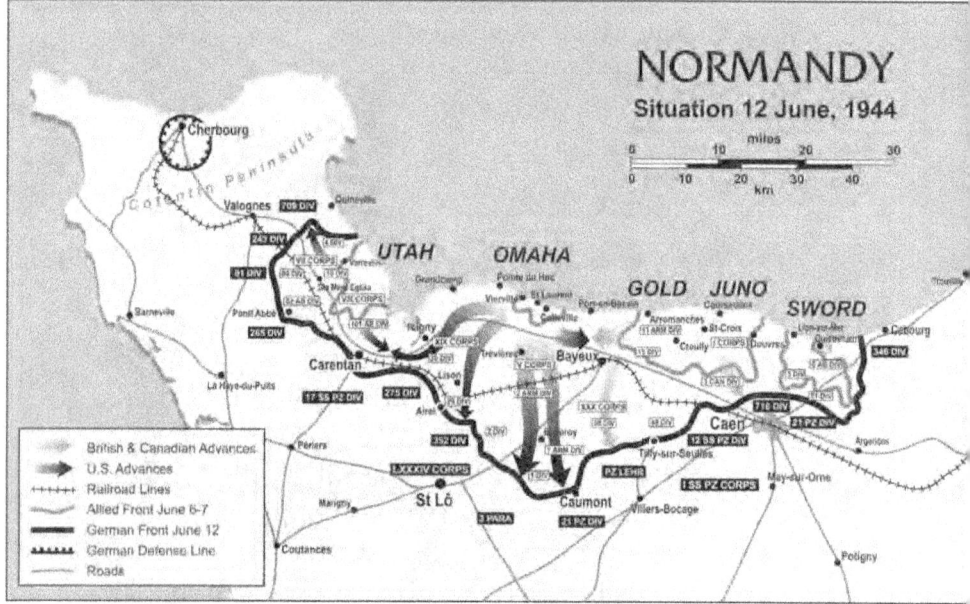

Map 5-1. Depiction of the situation in the Normandy area on June 12, 1944. In all cases, the beach is secure and troops have moved inland. Note, however, that Caen is still held by stubborn German resistance.

The essential problem of the exploitation phase was that it lacked the detail and the forethought that had so characterized the previous operations. Planners had designated phase lines depicting the desired progress of American units, but detailed planning was at best sketchy. There were other troubling factors as well. The British and Canadian landings put the British 2nd Army[3] on the edge of flat open terrain, good terrain for mobile operations, which actually led to the heart of Germany. Even so, some of the immediate terrain tended to favor the defender as events near Caen would show. Landing the British/Canadian Army here seemed logical because these landing areas were closest to the home islands. Since the British were still using a substantial number of Spitfires, a Battle of Britain era aircraft with limited range, being close to the home islands was important for tactical air support. Conversely, the U.S. Army was the most mobile army in the world, but the British 2nd Army, which would become the 21st Army Group, was British and Canadian, not American. Instead, American elements that would become the 12th Army Group landed in an area that was not immediately favorable to maneuver warfare. In the first 2 months of the European Campaign, the U.S. Army would show itself to be increasingly capable in tactical operations, making some mistakes, but learning and adapting rapidly to the realities of combat on the continent. As noted by one historian, however, "The United States Army was the most mobile army in the world in 1944, but American commanders had yet to prove whether they could translate the inherent ability of the American units to move into effective maneuver on the battlefield."[4] In short, the U.S. Army had yet to prove itself in operational warfare.

Institutionally, the U.S. Army had yet to discover operational warfare. Individual officers, such as General George S. Patton intuitively understood it, but the Army, by training or doctrine, had yet to emphasize operational thinking. Consider, for example, Bradley's 12th Army Group formed after the landings. The 12th would consist, for most of the European Campaign, as an entity composed of 29-31 divisions. In the campaign, the 12th was one of three army groups that had the prime responsibility of destroying Adolf Hitler's armies. Commanders did not receive proper guidance about army groups from the doctrine of the period because, according to this guidance, an army group "is a tactical unit." Its commander "may be designated by the theater commander or by the war department."[5] Initially there were two, later three, Army groups that functioned under the theater commander which again, according to doctrine, were tactical entities. The absence of the term operational in the larger unit field service regulation is not as significant as the use of "tactical," in reference to larger combat formations. Most significant is the fact that most Allied commanders, particularly at the start of the European Campaign, tended to conduct their operations in the field tactically, rather than operationally.

Neither the British-Canadian forces nor the American Army, both of which had been so unbelievably successful on June 6, were able to quickly transition to the pursuit phase. The Allied drive toward the heartland of Germany almost immediately bogged down. The reasons for the initial inability to breakout from the lodgment were varied. Montgomery and his 21st Army Group faced an extremely capable enemy force, the 15th German Army, which had a significant amount of elite panzer units. Indeed, because the Germans believed the Allied deception, *Wehrmacht* leadership positioned their strongest defenses and defenders to oppose landings in the Pas de Calais region, closer to the British landing areas than the American ones. Thus, the Canadians had to contend with the crack 12th SS *Hitler Jugend* Panzer Division and the British with the 21st Panzer and the Panzer *Lehr* divisions. Montgomery had optimistically planned to take Caen on D-Day, but despite all of his optimism, the Germans stalled his drive and although Caen was only 15 kilometers from the beaches, the city was not cleared of Germans by British troops until their final drive, July 18 to 21. From the beginning of the campaign, there seemed to be a hesitancy in executing decisive operations by Montgomery and some of his key leadership. Operations that had merit were proposed, but there was a distinct tendency to avoid risks, preferring conservative approaches on the field of battle.[6]

Part of this was likely due to the constant concern about the shortages of manpower, which was a significant British problem. At this time during the war, Britain's manpower situation was bleak and London could not offer many more soldiers for the campaign, nor could it afford to take heavy losses. They could not throw increasingly more divisions into the fight because their army was not nearly as robust as the American Army. Simply, the men were not there. British reticence to undertake operations that were risky or that might result in significant casualties had previously more than once caused friction among the Allied leadership. Adding to the manpower shortage was the inadequacy of some basic weapon systems available to the British and Canadian armies. British Cromwell tanks were no competition for upgraded German Mark IV, Panther, or Tiger tanks. The British were also short on anti-tank capabilities, having no weapon system comparable to the German 88mm gun. The British Piat anti-tank system — a hand-held, spring launched rocket — was hardly a modern weapon system. Even the bolt-action rifle available to the average "Tommy" was reminiscent of the weapon his father carried in World War I. British ordnance never replaced it, despite 6 years of war. In short, for a variety of reasons, to include the capabilities of German units and some poor British leadership on the ground, the British army's advance quickly halted.

As the attempt to break through German defenses continued, there developed an interesting episode to inter-Allied relations. From June 6 through the end of the month, British and Canadian forces attempted to take Caen and unravel the determined defense, but to no avail. At the end of the month, Montgomery would claim that the strategy agreed between he (as ground component commander) and Eisenhower was for the British forces, in position short of Caen, to fight a determined campaign and serve as a magnet, holding around Caen the preponderance of the tough German reserves. This would allow Bradley, once Cherbourg was in Allied hands, to breakout on the right. Bradley as well contributes to this fiction of Montgomery's magnet strategy in his postwar memoirs, but the evidence indicates that neither was forthcoming about what actually transpired. In his memoirs, Eisenhower notes a June 30 directive from Montgomery that states the latter's intention to "attract the greatest portion of enemy strength while the American forces, which had captured Cherbourg 4 days before, would begin attacking southward with a view to final breakout on the right flank."[7] Curiously, on several occasions, records show Eisenhower expressing concern that British forces were stuck near Caen and seemed to be unable to breakout. Did Eisenhower want Montgomery's forces to breakout or serve as a "magnet?" Rather than following a carefully crafted strategy, it appears that Montgomery was stuck in the Caen environs and was not able to advance in a timely fashion and exploit the fine maneuver terrain.[8]

Montgomery's magnet strategy was a fiction as evidenced by Eisenhower's continued encouragement for Montgomery to take Caen, his D-Day objective, then break out and exploit the favorable terrain. Thus, on July 7, Montgomery made a serious attempt to unravel German defenses, attacking German positions with three divisions, which the RAF Bomber Command supported by a massive preparation. Although the effect of the bombers was devastating, the cratering of the ground made the movement by tanks extremely difficult. Even though British forces made some progress, after a month of fighting, Caen was still not in Allied hands. The essential problem again seems to have been caution on the British part, caution to commit too many troops and risk heavy casualties.

The British were not alone in their inability to break the hard crust of German defenses. In the area of American operations, problems for the breakout and pursuit phase also emerged. One of the first goals for American forces, once they had consolidated their hold on the enlarged beachhead, was to take the port of Cherbourg. Securing this major port, though inadequate, would become even more important after June 18 when a major storm hit the coast and wrecked some of the temporary unloading facilities, including the Omaha Beach mulberry and other structures that had served as a lifeline for Allied troops. With an urgency to occupy the port, since logistics officials had to ration ammunition, on June 15, U.S. General Joseph Collins launched his drive to cut off the Cotentin Peninsula, depriving the German defenders of Cherbourg of supplies and reinforcements. By June 17, Collins had cut across the peninsula and isolated the German defenders from any land-based reinforcement. After a brief pause on June 22, he initiated a three-division attack to take Cherbourg. American troops faced heavy fighting from determined German units, but on July 1, Cherbourg surrendered. Regrettably, the port was in ruins and was not immediately usable.[9] This was, however, the first of several offensives that would allow Collins to earn the nickname "Lightning Joe" and establish his reputation as one of the handful of American senior officers that could practice what we now call operational warfare.

Although the logistical problem was far from resolution, Cherbourg was a step in the right direction. At the same time, the Cherbourg operation, as successful as it was, did not resolve the problem facing the U.S. Army; how to breakout of the area that the Germans fully intended to contain and, in Hitler's mind, erase from the face of the earth. Initially, American units had shown more initiative and greater mobility than British forces, but attempts to breakout and attack eastward found the Americans to be in a very difficult position. In addition to dedicated German defenders, American forces had to contend with extremely poor terrain. To attack eastward and drive into the heartland of Germany required American units to contend first with the Norman bocage (hedgerows).

In the Norman countryside, farmers had divided the small fields into blocks of land by earthen berms that were roughly 2 to 3 meters high and between 1-2 meters thick. The bocage contained thickets of hawthorn; the G.I.s called them hedgerows. American infantrymen had difficulties crossing these earthen berms, and German soldiers could create highly effective defensive positions. Eisenhower described the situation as "Our whole attack has to fight its way out of very narrow bottlenecks flanked by marshes and against an enemy who has a double hedgerow and an intervening ditch almost every 50 yards as ready-made strong points."[10] Often these hedgerows were even more difficult to traverse by roads that wound through the area, roads that bordered the berms and were worn deep by centuries of traffic.

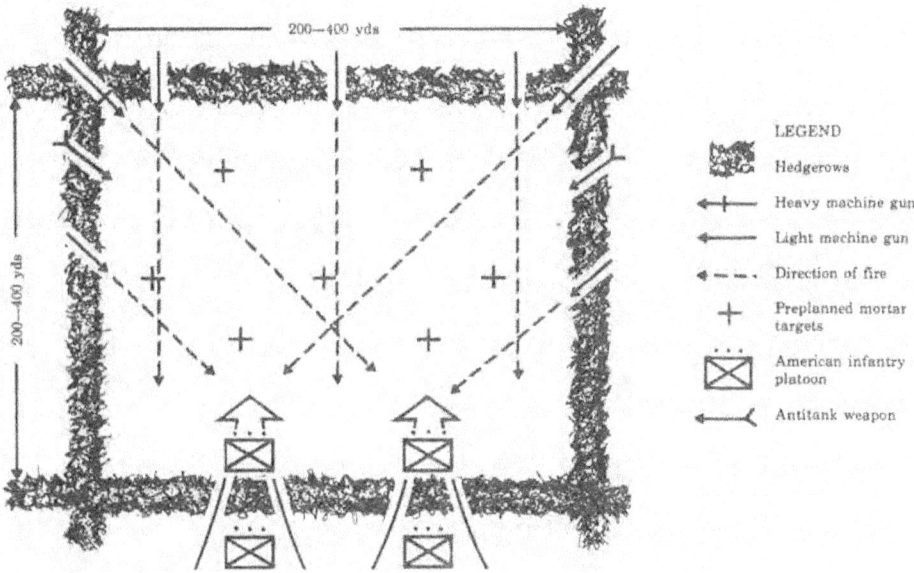

Source: Michael D. Doubler, *Busting the Bocage: American Combined Arms Operations in France 6 June-31 July 1944*, Ft Leavenworth, KS: Combat Studies Institute, 1988.

Figure 5-1. While at Ft. Leavenworth, Captain Michael D. Doubler devised a notional depiction of the formidable defense developed by the Germans in the Bocage area of Normandy.

The German Army was well known for its excellence in maneuver warfare but often forgotten is its excellence in defensive tactics.[11] German units made these so-called hedgerows interlocking belts of defense that stymied American advances. Figure 5.1 shows a typical German defense of one of these enclosed fields. U.S. armor could not initially break through the bocage at the base of the Cotentin peninsula. Here, the bocage terrain transitioned to some low-lying fields that could be and were flooded to make the terrain difficult, if not impossible, for mechanized forces to cross. Even nature, in the form of rainfall, could turn the fields into soggy marshlands. Soldiers encountered fields that had causeways, but the low-lying ground through the efforts of nature or man became all too swampy.[12]

The terrain problems in this area should not have been a mystery as the bocage was an obvious terrain feature shown through aerial reconnaissance and, of course, it was nothing new at all to the locals; it had existed for centuries. Allied planners had focused their attention on the landings and consolidation of the beachhead and not on any stabilizing operations afterward. Patton, who knew the French terrain well, was not involved in the planning process because he was in the proverbial "dog house" over the face slapping incidents in Sicily. Staff officers had not considered the low-lying marshy terrain and the hedgerows. Allied forces also did not have any specially trained assault troops or special equipment to break through this inhospitable terrain. Instead, when American units attacked the bocage, the terrain seemed to come as a surprise to Allied leadership. For the problems associated with the breakout through this region, they were simply unprepared.

For Allied military leaders and their soldiers the bocage became an expensive learning experience. To break through this terrain, American military units required modified equipment, additional firepower, strong combined arms cooperation, new tactics, and sound leadership. At the outset, few of these were available. Allied forces had increasing numbers of tanks, but the standard U.S. Army medium tank, the M-4 Sherman, could not easily break through the bocage. When the M-4s did penetrate one of these natural defensive lines, all too often they were targets for well-placed German anti-tank positions. From the onset of the campaign, the Sherman proved to be inadequately armored and undergunned. Equipped with a gasoline engine, rather than a diesel, it earned its appropriate nickname, "Ronson," after a popular brand of cigarette lighter. U.S. Army units, attempting to smash German defenses, lacked the firepower that their German adversaries possessed. In terms of small arms, the M-1 Garand rifle was far superior to anything the Germans had, but there were no American equivalents to the standard German machine guns, MG-34 or MG-42. Those machine guns provided the withering firepower that had inflicted many casualties on Omaha Beach. To their credit, American noncommissioned officers (NCOs) and company grade officers led from the front and attempted to provide the necessary leadership. The heavy vegetation also muted the Allied advantage in air power.

Finally, field alteration of equipment, like the makeshift bulldozer blade made from German steel obstacles from the invasion beaches and mounted on the front of Sherman and other tanks, did result in vehicles being able to slice through the thickets. Even so, the limited number of these tanks and the number of German defensive positions meant that, without any way to bypass or overcome the bocage, any American advance was going to be a lengthy and expensive process. For the best part of 7 weeks, American units slogged through the bitter attritional warfare in the bocage region, as commanders watched the casualty lists grow.

Source: U.S. Army Military History Institute.

While planners had failed to consider the obstacle posed by the Bocage, American Soldiers devised a plow, nicknamed the "Rhino," crafted from German beach obstacles, to break through the hedgerows.

After weeks of fighting and slogging through the worst terrain, the senior American commander in the field, General Bradley, was discouraged. Bradley and his superior commander on the ground, Montgomery, conferred on July 10. Bradley expressed concern about the lack of progress in his area of responsibility, but at that time, he did have a notional concept for a breakout that would become Operation COBRA. While Bradley was planning for Operation COBRA, British

General Sir Miles Dempsey, commander of the Second British Army, proposed that the British stage their own offensive. The British began organizing their own operation, GOODWOOD, which jumped off with a massive aerial bombardment on July 18. Eisenhower showed great enthusiasm about the prospect of a British breakthrough, telling Montgomery that "This operation will be a brilliant stroke which will knock loose our present shackles. Every plane will be available for such a purpose."[13] Operation GOODWOOD, however, was disappointing and lasted only 3 days. Regrettably for the Allies, it ended without a breakthrough. In the 3 days of fighting, the British lost 469 tanks and 3,600 men to determined German defenders. Though Montgomery failed to achieve a breakthrough, his offensive had occupied the attention of six crack German divisions.[14] Operation GOODWOOD contributed to the ability of American units to breakout a few days later with their own operation.[15]

After six weeks slugging it out against stubborn resistance in the bocage, American forces took the key crossroads town of St. Lo on 18 July. They were finally in a position to breakout from Normandy and begin the sweep to the east. The plan Bradley's staff devised for the breakout was termed Operation COBRA, which initially called for a two and later a three-division assault. Army division commanders would launch initial attacks after a saturation bombing parallel to the Periers-St. Lo Road, where American troops were again up against tough German resistance. Saturation bombing had not worked well for Montgomery's July 7 attack, in part due to the hesitancy of his commanders, but also due to the heavy cratering from 500-pound bombs that made mobility extremely difficult. In planning Operation COBRA, AAF Major

General Elwood R. "Pete" Quesada, Commander of the IXth Tactical Air Command, attempted to have the ordnance size reduced to 250-pound bombs to avoid this problem. However, Collins, commander of the VIIth Corps, overruled Quesada since he wanted the desired blast effect of the 500-pound bombs. Staff officers completed planning for Operation COBRA in draft form on July 13. On July 18, Army commanders intended to initiate the operation, but fortunately, the senior Allied commanders recognized that this was too soon, and rescheduled the start for July 24.

Operation COBRA was the third instance in the European Campaign where planners called for strategic airpower in a tactical role; these aircraft had to conduct a mission that they were not designed or equipped to accomplish.[16] Given the intended operational ceiling for heavy bombers, the results were predictable. The bombers were supposed to fly parallel to the Periers-St. Lo Road and drop their bomb loads, but there ensued several tragic errors. The weather was poor on July 24, and, as a result, Allied leaders had to postpone the operation. Only about two-thirds of the heavy bombers received notification of the mission's cancellation and over 300 bombers dropped their bomb loads, approaching the target area perpendicular to the front lines rather than parallel.[17] AAF P-47s also made their scheduled preparatory runs. Many of the bombs fell short. Casualties resulting from the Allied air attacks on the American 30th Infantry Division included 25 men killed and 131 wounded. To add insult to injury, because American troops had pulled back from their original lines to avoid "shorts," the Germans moved forward and took some of the originally American-held terrain. Before the offensive could commence, American forces had to attack in the afternoon to regain their original ground. Again, commanders had to reschedule the attack for the following day, and this time the heavy bombers and tactical aircraft came in on schedule. In the period of an hour, 1,495 heavy bombers dropped 4,406 tons of high explosives along the front.[18] The bomb runs of July 25 used the same bombing pattern as the previous day. While the German lines were hard hit, friendly fire caused 111 American deaths and 490 casualties. These casualties were in all three of Collin's assault divisions and included a high profile visitor, Lieutenant General Leslie McNair, former commander of U.S. Army Ground forces who had, unbeknownst to Bradley, slipped into the front lines to observe the effect of the aerial pounding on German positions. McNair died as a result of the bombing, and Soldiers witnessed a blast throwing his body over 65 feet. He was only recognizable due to the three stars on his collar.

The effect of the bombing on German defenses was staggering. AAF aircraft upended tanks and self-propelled guns and destroyed the communication network. American assault troops reported German soldiers wandering around babbling incoherently, bleeding from their ears due to the enormous concussion produced by the 500-pound bombs. The psychological damage to the German defenders seemed more serious than the physical.[19] Despite the criticism of the air attacks, air power did deliver a devastating blow. Regrettably, the German forces quickly recovered, and survivors from the 5th Parachute Division and the Panzer *Lehr*, both elite units, put up tenacious resistance despite their heavy losses of both men and equipment. As the day ended, many American Soldiers were discouraged because, despite all of the ordinance delivered, the German defenses had failed to crack. Collins, however, had a keen sense of the battlefield and he understood that the bombing and subsequent attacks had pushed the Germans to the limit. In his memoirs, he stated: ". . . but noting the lack of coordination in the German reaction, particularly their failure to launch prompt counterattacks, I sensed that their communication and command structure had been damaged more than our troops realized."[20]

On the following morning, he committed the three divisions to continue the attack and, although this did not result in a total German rout, American forces broke through the defenses and the German line gave way. Through Collins' keen sense of the battlefield, and the excellent tactical performance of the U. S. Army Soldiers, particularly of the 2nd Armored Division, an opportunity emerged for American forces. American Soldiers had cracked the German defenses, and American units began moving south, east, and west to exploit the attack. They did not race, because the object of Operation COBRA was to break through the German defenses, and the operation's tremendous success seemed to come as a surprise to both Collins and Bradley. However, the end of the battle for Normandy was finally in sight.

Once American forces had punctured the German lines, logic seemed to dictate that American units would proceed eastward into the heartland of France and press the German military. Pre-invasion planning, however, called for a different axis of advance. On August 1, Eisenhower officially activated Patton's 3rd Army which advanced according to Operation OVERLORD's original plan. Elements of two corps moved south, west, and east to begin the exploitation east toward Germany and at the same time cut off and overrun Brittany. The newly activated 3rd Army did not have the singular purpose of concentrating and moving eastward toward the German heartland. Rather, it had multiple missions of securing the Cotentin peninsula, taking Britanny, Brest, and beginning the drive to the Seine River. Units from the heavy VIIIth Corps moved west into Britanny. At the same time, Eisenhower also made Bradley the commander of the newly formed 12th Army Group, consisting of the 1st and 3rd Armies, which became the main maneuver element of the U.S. Army for most of the European Campaign.[21] At this stage in the campaign, the senior Allied ground command remained with Montgomery who was now dual-hatted as commander of the 21st Army Group and head of all Allied ground forces in the region.

Future planners and strategists will find the period immediately following the breakout an interesting study. The tasking given to Eisenhower on February 12, 1944, by the Combined Chiefs of Staff indicated that Allied armies should proceed east toward the heartland of Germany and destroy Germany's armed forces. At the same time, the major logistical problem of feeding the Allied war machine had hardly been resolved, and supplies still came from the Normandy area. Allied logistics officials continued to use temporary port facilities established for the June 6 invasion. American and British leaders hoped that control of both the Cotentin Peninsula and Brittany would improve the supply situation. The possession of these two regions only had the potential to improve the situation, not solve it. It would take weeks for the Allies to take all of the area's ports and months to get them rebuilt and ready for use. Allied officers could not answer the logistical and port problem by using areas in western France alone. Supply problems would drag on. Eisenhower would only see relief when Marseilles, France, and Antwerp, Belgium, were in Allied hands and were fully functional.

Neither Bradley nor Eisenhower seemed to recognize the tremendous opportunity provided by Collin's breakout. Eisenhower, as late as July 21, was firm in insisting on early control of Brittany stating, "We must get the Brittany Peninsula. From an administrative point of view, this is essential."[22] Had operational thinking been in vogue in the American Army, driving east and then swinging north for a junction with Montgomery's forces would have been a more logical option, but controlling the two peninsulas with their ports remained their priority. Interestingly enough, Montgomery thought that changing circumstances meant that the priority of capturing the Brittany area was lower, and the Allied command should use a much stronger force for the drive to the heartland of Germany. He recognized that if Allied forces could concentrate and focus on a drive to the Seine River, then the potential for an operational movement resulting in the encirclement of a significant number of German troops existed. Of course, experience in the European Campaign would demonstrate that Montgomery was much better at recognizing opportunities than executing them.

By August 3, Bradley would slightly alter the emphasis of his operations hoping to use a minimum force to clear the Brittany Peninsula, but ultimately the emphasis of the 12th Army Group remained there. Bradley was firm in his adherence to the original plan that called for Brittany's seizure. The American forces moved rapidly to do so. By August 7, American forces had moved the entire length of the peninsula, but they were unsuccessful in securing Brest. German forces defended Brest much better than they had Cherbourg. Brest did not fall until September 19 and by the time it fell into Allied hands, the port was destroyed by German sabotage, Allied air raids, and the fighting around the port. Nearby, Allied forces bypassed German garrisons at Lorient and St. Nazaire which held out until the end of the war.

As American forces rapidly exploited Collin's breakout, American units moving west, south, and east presented an open flank. Hitler recognized this was an opportunity and intervened. Although his senior commanders counseled caution considering Allied mastery of the air, at the end of July, Hitler was in no mood to take much advice from his senior military commanders. On July 20, several German officers attempted to assassinate the *Führer*, causing him to distrust even more the traditional military establishment. Hitler regarded the offense to be the epitome of military operations and saw no future in remaining on the defensive, fending off Allied initiatives. He therefore ordered *Generalfeldmarschall* Günther von Kluge, Commander of Army Group B, to mount a counterattack aimed at Avranches, which, if successful, would take German units back to the Atlantic, establish a new defensive position, and cut off supplies and reinforcements to American units pushing south, east, and west from the beachhead. To accomplish this task, Kluge had to throw together four Panzer divisions to lead the German counteroffensive. The German Mortain offensive jumped off on August 7 with the intent of driving through the Avranches area to the sea and, in the process, cutting the road over which U.S. 3rd Army's supplies moved.[23]

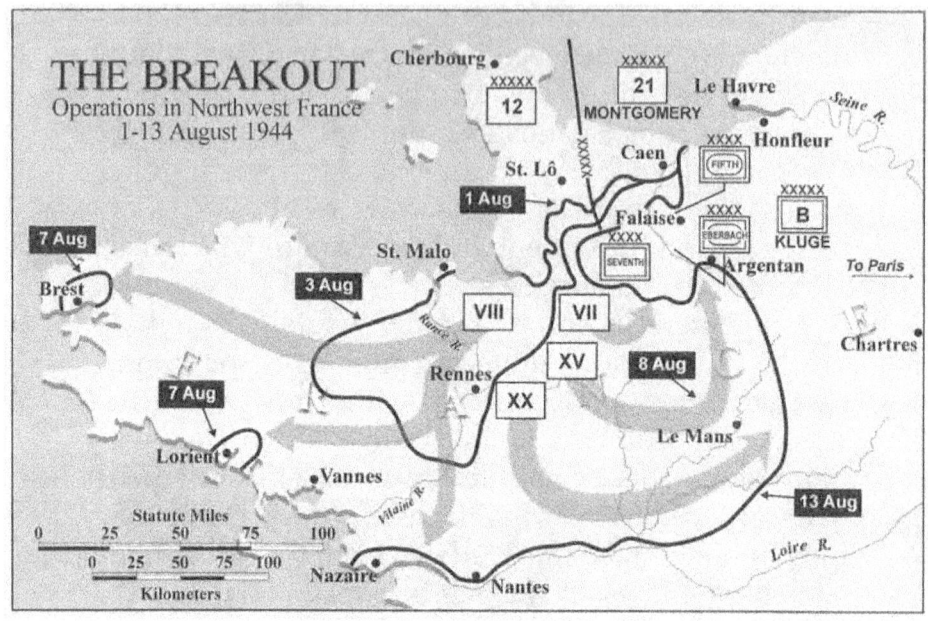

Map 5-2. This map depicts the breakout after Operation COBRA and the potential "bag" at Argentan/Falaise.

When the Germans attacked, the offensive created a minor crisis for the U.S. Army. It caught the U.S. 30th Infantry Division by surprise, even though the 12th Army Group headquarters was aware of German activities in the area. Although the attack inflicted serious casualties on the 30th Division, this American division did a superb job of using good defensive terrain and was successful in blunting the German attack. Elements of the American 120th Infantry Regiment controlled the salient geographical feature in the area, Hill 31. The Germans found movement difficult without a rain of observed artillery fire. To complicate the Germans' task, by late morning of the offensive's opening, the sky over their advancing armored units was full of Allied aircraft. The dreaded AAF *Jabos*, the fighter bombers that dominated the skies throughout the European Campaign, pounded the Germans daily.

After 5 days of hard fighting on both sides, a unique opportunity existed for the Allies. Hitler's offensive, and it was exclusively his, had developed a long salient into American lines, inviting a response by Allied leaders, a response that subordinates should have exploited, given Eisenhower's task of destroying the German army. This is particularly true, because the German counterattack did not come as a surprise to Bradley.[24] From the beginning of the European Campaign, senior American officers had one of the unique capabilities ever offered to a group of general officers—the ability, through ULTRA, to read the enemy high command's message traffic daily. The deciphered information did not reveal all German operational intentions, but it regularly revealed order of battle information. Thus, when Kluge began throwing together his assault formations for the offensive, German intentions were revealed. Mortain, for the Allies, was no surprise; the Germans were going to attack.[25]

Montgomery had also hit the Germans with two offensives in the early part of August. Dempsey and his British 2nd Army were on the offensive, trying to crack the German defenses. The Canadian First Army had jumped off on August 8 with another offensive called Operation TOTALIZE. With this offensive, Montgomery sought to attack through the Caen-Falaise Road that would, if successful, put Canadian, Polish, and British troops in the town of Falaise. At the onset, Montgomery was not thinking of countering the German attack. He wanted to punch though the German lines and swing east; taking advantage of the road network that had Caen as its hub. Once on this road, he intended to move eastward to the Seine River. Hitler, who had created a salient stretching toward the sea, was unwittingly providing the Allies with a unique opportunity: the potential for bagging and destroying an entire German army, see Map 5-2.

With the German 7th Army's salient pointing toward Avranches, it invited the potential for an Allied classic double wing envelopment, with elements of the 12th and 21st Army Groups pinching off the entire German 7th Army. Since the breakout had already occurred, the Allies had hoped that Patton's 3rd Army and elements of Montgomery's 21st Army Group could drive eastward and trap the retreating German forces along the banks of the Seine River. The Germans recognized that this area contained an excellent defensive position, and the German military leadership had hoped to build a defensive position along the Seine to contain the Allies when they advanced from Normandy. Fortunately, for Eisenhower and other Allied officers, the rapid Allied advance prevented the Germans from devising a good defensive position tied to the Seine. At the same time, if the 12th and 21st Army Groups could drive east to the Seine River and then link up on the west bank of the river, they would again have the opportunity for a long double wing envelopment, offering the possibility of destroying Army Group B as well as the 5th Panzer Army. The German army could ill afford to lose these forces. The long envelopment was problematic, given the supply situation, but at the same time, the Allied forces had a chance.

The possibilities for the Allies, however, grew on August 8 because, with the Germans developing a salient that stretched toward the Atlantic, there was also the potential to execute a short envelopment to pinch off the German salient at its base. If Allied military units could execute either event, then this success could propel Eisenhower well on the road to completing his specified task of destroying the German army. On August 8, with the German offensive only a day old, there was an important meeting held at Bradley's headquarters. Present at the meeting were Eisenhower, Secretary of the Treasury Henry Morgenthau, Bradley, and his key staff officers. As participants discussed the plans, a three-way phone conversation with Montgomery began.[26] With Operation TOTALIZE in progress, military officers observed that a great opportunity had emerged. If the XVth Corps of Patton's 3rd Army, commanded by Major General Wade Haislip, turned left at Le Mans and attacked toward Argentan, the German 7th Army could be bagged, see Map 5-2.

At the meeting, Bradley took an aggressive and optimistic stance. He recognized the opportunity stating, "This is an opportunity that comes to a commander not more than once in a century. . . . We're about to destroy an entire hostile army."[27] The German army that he wanted to destroy consisted of approximately 100,000 soldiers. Montgomery conferred with Bradley on July 10 and expressed concern about the lack of progress in his area of responsibility. After the conference, Dempsey had proposed that the British stage their own offensive designed to take British units from Caen to the town of Falaise. In short, advances by both armies provided a unique opportunity that the Allies could take advantage of if they had the necessary resources to do so. Bradley may have undercut his desire to accomplish this by sending the U.S. Vth Corps racing for the Seine River, rather than adding muscle to his branch of the short envelopment he was hoping to accomplish. Patton clearly saw the opportunity, but would have preferred a longer envelopment, with elements of the XVth Army swinging north near Chartes, rather than Lemans for a deeper envelopment.[28]

Before the German attack, the Allies had been advancing east with the goal of reaching the west bank of the Seine River. With American forces holding firm at Mortain, on August 10, the XVth Corps executed a left turn and began to advance north toward Argentan. This was the town where Montgomery had planned for the two armies to meet. Montgomery's Canadians were facing stiff opposition from the Germans in their drive south toward the same town, and they had made little progress since August 8. Heavy resistance from the Germans was logical because it became obvious to Hitler and his high command that the Panzer forces would not be able to clip the 3rd Army's lifeline. Thus, the shoulders were, in fact, getting stronger since the Germans were no longer trying to execute a breakout to the Atlantic but rather to extricate their forces from the salient of their own making.

Kluge knew what was happening with his units in the pocket or, as the Germans called it a *kessel*, that was rapidly forming to put up stiff resistance to the Canadian and American advances. At the same time, he was attempting to hold the shoulders and extricate units, like the 116th Panzer, 2nd Panzer, 1st SS Panzer, and 12th SS Panzer Divisions, which the 7th Army could not afford to lose. He was having difficulty with Hitler, who demanded a renewed German offensive to the Atlantic. By August 12, Haislip's XVth Corps was close to securing the town of Argentan but was encountering heavy resistance. Still, he had essentially achieved his objective, and consequently, Haislip sought new orders. By August 13, Bradley provided the new orders; he halted Haislip's advance.

As early as August 12, it was obvious that the Canadians would not be able to close the 25-mile gap and put a cork in the narrow bottleneck that the Allies had created. Only a couple of days into the operation, Bradley identified the slow advance of the Canadian First Army and expressed his concern to Montgomery. In his traditional style, Patton attempted to override Bradley's orders by telling Haislip to take Argentan and then slowly proceed toward Falaise. When Bradley learned of this situation, he quickly halted the XVth Corps.[29] Even by this time in the campaign, friction existed between the commander of the 21st Army Group and his American colleagues. Eisenhower was also displeased that the combined British and Canadian force remained in the Caen area, particularly because they had the best maneuver terrain. Bradley joined the legion of officers who simply did not like Montgomery; he only tolerated him. As early as the Sicilian campaign, Patton had a definite and often expressed dislike for his British colleague. These personality and national rivalries came into focus at Argentan and Falaise.

Patton tried in vain to get Bradley to relent and let the XVth Corps renew its attack, but the 12th Army Group commander would not move. On the evening of August 12, Patton called Bradley and declared, "We've got elements in Argentan. Let me go on to Falaise, and we'll drive the British back into the sea for another Dunkirk." Bradley responded, "Nothing doing, you're not to go beyond Argentan. Just stop where you are and buildup on that shoulder."[30] Bradley seemed to think that Patton could make the link up, but that the narrow ribbon of U.S. troops would not be able to hold against determined counterattacks by German units trying to break out of the pocket. He also expressed concern about the potential dire consequences of the two armies colliding and the potential for fratricide. Thus, in his memoirs he stated, "I much preferred a solid shoulder at Argentan than a broken neck at Falaise."[31] Eisenhower, who knew of German attack intentions through ULTRA, was present when the Germans initiated their Mortain attack because he had established a forward headquarters in France on August 7, a short distance from the Norman city of Bayeux. From his headquarters, Eisenhower observed, but did not intervene in the American response to the German attack. He totally supported Bradley's decision to halt the XVth Corps at Argentan.

Hitler reluctantly authorized the German withdrawal on August 14, and German units began streaming eastward through the bottleneck. Canadian units completed the capture of Argentan on August 16, but a gap remained in Allied lines through which the Germans could and did retreat. Allied forces finally closed the gap on August 19 with German resistance continuing until August 22. Within the pocket, American and Allied forces took roughly 50,000 Germans prisoner. Allied intelligence sources estimated 10,000 Germans died and approximately 50,000 escaped. Those that escaped took very little with them; their tanks, trucks, and self-propelled guns were a tangle of wreckage. About 50 German divisions had been involved in the fighting, but after August 19, German commanders had only 10 organized divisions remaining in existence, and those forces were scattered elements. Even as this episode of the European Campaign was ending, Allied units were already moving eastward to their next objective, the Seine River. At the same time, they were harrying the remaining elements of the 7th Army and the 5th Panzer Army, trying to block the German retreat over the Seine River. One can gauge the severity of the breach in German defenses in western France through the speed of Patton's progress. By August 26, Patton gleefully reported he was on the Seine. Regrettably, however, the battered remnants of the *Wehrmacht* also achieved one of their finer accomplishments in this European campaign by successfully extricating the remnants of their forces across the Seine. From there, beaten German units began their short retreat into the frontiers of the Reich.

Through the operations beginning June 6, resentment had begun to grow between the British and the American leadership. It may have begun early in the campaign when Montgomery was unable to achieve his first day's objective, the capture of Caen. Then once Caen fell, a review of Map 5-2 shows the reader that after Operation COBRA, American forces advanced rapidly, but the British-Canadian Army seemed to move agonizingly slow against the Germans. This caused even Eisenhower to complain about the slow progress of British forces. The British and Canadian force was up against an extremely capable armor heavy adversary, but at Caen and later in the environs of Antwerp, Eisenhower became very irritated with the slow progress by the British.[32] At the same time, Montgomery responded bitterly on July 26 because of Eisenhower's complaints. The Americans had reached their objective, i.e., Argentan, and they had to wait for the slower moving British and Canadian force, which caused any number of recriminations about who was responsible for letting far too many Germans to escape to fight another day.

The Falaise Gap episode was the first of several significant disagreements between the Western Allies. While this disagreement was occurring at the theater and operational level, yet another was emerging at the Supreme Commander's level. Eisenhower fully believed in launching a second invasion front after the Normandy landing was secure, and on June 24, he rescheduled the invasion of southern France for August 15. The discord over a second front in southern France started at the May 1943 Trident conference in Washington, DC.[33] The British were at best reticent, and at that time they wanted to convince their American counterparts that an invasion in southern France was premature. Later in the spring of 1944, Eisenhower grudgingly postponed Operation ANVIL due to resource constraints, but he was unwilling to cancel the operation entirely. Months later at the Tehran conference, Churchill made impassioned pleas to forego any efforts to invade southern France. His attempts to undermine the proposed operation continued until only 5 days before the actual landings.[34] Ultimately, the British reluctantly agreed to the operation. Later Allied discussions showed that political and military leaders considered the issue far from being resolved. Churchill feared American military leaders would drain their divisions and other Allied assets away from his primary focus of Italy. Therefore, the Prime Minister continued to push the benefits of continued operations in the eastern Mediterranean to include other favored peripheral schemes.

American planners, to include both the Supreme Commander and the Joint Chiefs, took a decidedly different view. Allied difficulties in the Normandy hedgerows and available amphibious forces after the June 6 invasion allowed Eisenhower to reschedule the invasion of southern France, the long awaited Operation ANVIL. Allied planners selected an August 15 landing date with troops and supplies loading for the operation on August 10. In this charged atmosphere, a German attack in progress and an Allied landing impending, Churchill arrived on the continent intending to dissuade Eisenhower from executing Operation ANVIL.[35]

Churchill knew that to execute ANVIL, Allied military commanders would reduce forces from the Mediterranean Theater of Operations, specifically from Italy. It would also mean that the Mediterranean strategy that Churchill had consistently promoted would again be the victim of the American Northern Europe focus. Churchill was totally opposed to Operation ANVIL, but from the onset, Eisenhower viewed Operations OVERLORD and ANVIL as closely connected and complementary. On the afternoon of August 7, Churchill discussed, actually argued, for some 6 hours over the problems that would occur if Washington conducted this operation. He even resorted to an emotional plea stating that the beaches were going to run red with Allied blood, "and if that series of events should come about, my dear general, I would have no choice but to go to his majesty the King and lay down the mantel of my office."[36] This was the most acrimonious debate on strategy between the Supreme Commander and the Prime Minister that occurred during the entire war. Eisenhower firmly believed that it was important to fight on as many fronts as possible to stress and stretch the limited German resources. Whether he was right or wrong regarding a multiple front strategy, the Allies badly needed a high capacity port like Marseilles. As the meeting wore on, Eisenhower expanded his vocabulary, learning many different ways to say no to the agitated and insistent Prime Minister.

Churchill was angry about the whole affair. In a letter to the Chief of Staff of the Army on August 11, 1944, Eisenhower told General Marshall, "He [Churchill] seems to feel that the United States is taking the attitude of a big, strong, and domineering partner rather than attempting to understand the viewpoint that he represents. I have never seen him so obviously stirred upset and even despondent."[37] In an earlier July 6 memorandum to Major-General Sir Hastings Ismay, Chief of Staff to the Minister of Defense, Churchill revealed his feelings about American leadership. He believed that "we have been ill-treated and are furious" due to American behavior.[38] Given his bitterness about Eisenhower ignoring British priorities, the Prime Minister asked that Eisenhower rename ANVIL as Operation DRAGOON since Churchill believed that he had been "dragooned" into the action.[39] Certainly national or personal pride was an element in this extended, but generally polite argument. American dominance in key decisions for the European Campaign had been an established fact since early 1944. This was due to the preponderance of U.S. land, air, and naval forces for the campaign. The British had taken a back seat to the United States in strategic decisions and, of course, Eisenhower, the Supreme Commander, was American. Churchill tried unsuccessfully to retain some focus on his favored peripheral operations, notably the Mediterranean. American leadership was not interested in the British peripheral schemes, which included London's postwar political considerations.[40] Churchill threatened to resign over the matter on August 9.[41] Roosevelt, as well, refused to support Churchill's position.[42]

Casting aside national interests and priorities, an invasion of southern France offered several advantages for the Allies. The invasion would divert German forces from opposing the main American and British thrust in Normandy. This action would further stretch the beleaguered *Wehrmacht*, forcing it to fight on still another front, and would increase the opportunity for a clear breakthrough in the German defenses. Much more important, if American forces could capture the port of Marseilles in southern France, that port had greater capacity than any other port along the Normandy coastline. Securing Marseilles and the area's railways, roads, and waterways (like the Rhône River) would add a needed logistical center to support Allied armies as they advanced into Germany. This debate over a second invasion, if nothing else, underscored one thing: the United States was the dominate power in the war's strategy. The debate over Operation ANVIL strained Allied relations; however, there was never a threat of a permanent rift. As a complement to both men, Eisenhower and Churchill retained their pre-Operation ANVIL respect, and the operation proceeded as the Supreme Commander planned.

The initial planning for Operation ANVIL had begun under the auspices of the U.S. 7th Army in late December 1943. By March 2, 1944, the planning was under the direction of Major General Alexander M. Patch who, like U.S. Generals Collins and Charles Corlett, was a Pacific veteran and familiar with amphibious operations in that theater. The planning was coordinated with the Free French and the actual assault, consisting of three American infantry divisions (the U.S. VIth Corps) was under the command of Major General Lucian Truscott. The assault divisions would be reinforced later with six French colonial divisions. The invasion was supported by an ad hoc Anglo-American 1st Airborne Task Force, the Canadian-American 1st Special Services Force, French special assault groups, and French resistance members.[43]

Perhaps learning from the Normandy experience, the Allied armada launched its airborne attack in daylight hours. Close to 400 transport aircraft lifted off from Italian airfields in the early morning hours. The aircraft dropped their troops without the loss of a single aircraft. On the beaches, casualties were remarkably light. In the first 2 weeks of the operation, there were only 2,700 American and 4,000 French casualties. The problems with expanding the lodgment like had occurred at Normandy, or the threat of the Germans pushing Allied forces into the sea, simply did not exist. One can see the success of this operation not only through the light casualties and the rapid exploitation of the beachhead, but by the Allied capture of two desperately needed key ports, Toulon and Marseilles. Both ports surrendered on August 28, a mere 2 weeks after the landings. Despite German sabotage efforts, Allied military forces opened Marseilles on September 15. Toulon followed 5 days later.

One reason behind the rapid advance in southern France was an uncharacteristic decision by Hitler, a retreat. With the Allied operation only 2 days old, messages decoded through ULTRA on August 17 and 18 revealed that Hitler had ordered Army Group G to evacuate the invasion area and join up with Army Group B on defensive positions on the Sens-Dijon Line.[44] The German XIX Army retreated up the Rhone Valley with its 11th Panzer Division as a rear guard. Constant monitoring through ULTRA also assured the Allies that no counterattack, like the Mortain offensive, was forthcoming. *Generaloberst* Johannes Blaskowitz's Army Group G successfully withdrew from southern France, eluding Truscott's attempts at encircling his Army Group. However, as he retreated out of the area, he lost over half of his force of 250,000 men.[45] As a result, with operations in southern France being less than a month old, on September 11, the American and French forces from southern France met elements of Patton's 3rd Army. Operation DRAGOON, originally known as Operation ANVIL, allowed the Allies to push the Germans out of France faster, buildup their logistics capacity, and establish airfields to attack into southern Germany. Eisenhower characterized the move into southern France as decisive. In his opinion, there was no other single development as influential in the defeat of the Germany forces as Operation DRAGOON.[46]

After the war, some British leaders continued to level criticism about the American decision to proceed with ANVIL. These officers speculated that if the divisions pulled out of Italy for Operation ANVIL had remained, then the Allies would have been more successful in the Italian campaign. American and British forces could have driven through the Po River Valley and into the Alps, maybe even into Austria. Apparently, such critics had never studied the Austro-Italian Campaigns of World War I or the old axiom that one should not attack in an area where the terrain clearly favors the enemy force. Events of 1943-44 should have shown that neither Italy nor the Balkans were suitable for highly mechanized armies to fight and maneuver.

American contentions that Operation ANVIL/DRAGOON was a highly successful operation is obvious, then and now. Russell Weigley best summarized the contributions of Operation ANVIL/DRAGOON as:

As the American Seventh Army approached a junction with the Third Army in Mid September, the pace of the Allied advance since the Cobra breakthrough was about to create a crisis in supply. Without the southern French ports, this crisis would have been insurmountable. Without the southern French ports, a tactical crisis yet to come would have been far more desperate than it proved to be.[47]

The August 7 discussion concerning Operation ANVIL/DRAGOON was significant because it resolved which nation would dominate in developing the strategies for the remainder of the war. The "end," the objective of defeating Germany, had always been clear, but the "ways" to attain this objective had at times been contentious. At SHELLBURST on August 7th, Churchill's attempts to convince the Americans of using a peripheral strategy reached a conclusion.[48] After those discussions, British leadership could propose changes in the war's direction, but American might, both in terms of manpower and industrial production, along with Eisenhower's position, meant that America's leadership could trump any major changes. The United States was clearly not a junior partner in the Alliance.

ENDNOTES - CHAPTER 5

1. Omar N. Bradley, *A Soldier's Story*, New York: Henry Holt and Company, 1951, p. 318.

2. Russell Weigley, "From the Normandy Beaches to the Falaise-Argentan Pocket," *Military Review*, September, 1990, p. 46.

3. For the doctrinal description of an Army Group, see *Field Manual (FM) 100-15, Field Service Regulations: Larger Units*, Washington, DC: U.S. Government Printing Office, 1942, pp. 45-46.

4. Peter R. Mansoor, *The G.I. Offensive in Europe: The Triumph of American Infantry Divisions, 1941-1945*, Lawrence, KS: University of Kansas Press, 1999, p. 160.

5. FM-100-15, pp. 45-46.

6. A classic example of a great opportunity and pitiful execution was Dempsey's attack on June 12 west of Caen on an open German flank. It had all of the earmarks of a great victory, but the sluggish British followup after the initial attack resulted in a disaster for the British. Carlo D'Este, *Decision in Normandy*, New York: Konecky and Konecky, 1994, p. 196.

7. Dwight D. Eisenhower, *Crusade in Europe*, New York: Doubleday, 1948, p. 268.

8. In his excellent study, *After D-Day*, James Carafano objectively lays out the arguments of both Montgomery's admirers and detractors regarding Caen and the controversy over Montgomery's so-called strategy. He ultimately concludes, "No one has found a historical 'smoking gun' to resolve the debate to every one's satisfaction, but the balance of the historical arguments seems to weigh against Montgomery." James J. Carafano, *After D-Day: Operation Cobra and the Normandy Breakout*, Boulder, CO: Lynne Reiner Publishers, 2000, p. 200. In his memoirs, Hans von Luck, commander of a German Combat Group engaged with Montgomery's forces, also questions Montgomery's magnet theory, noting that Canadian soldiers who were captured on July 18-19 stated that Montgomery had told his soldiers, "To Falaise, boys, we're going to march on Paris." Hans von Luck, *Panzer Commander: The Memoirs of Hans von Luck*, New York: Dell Publishing, 1989, pp. 200-201.

9. J. Lawton Collins, *Lightning Joe: An Autobiography*, Novato CA: Presidio Press, 1994, pp. 210-226.

10. Dwight D. Eisenhower, in a July 5, 1944, letter in *Dear General: Eisenhower's Wartime Letters to Marshall,* Joseph P. Hobbs, ed., Baltimore, MD: Johns Hopkins Press, 1999, p. 195.

11. An excellent study on this subject is Timothy A. Wray, *Standing Fast: German Defensive Doctrine on the Russian Front Dur-*

ing World War II, Prewar to 1943, Combat Studies Institute Research Survey No. 5, Ft. Leavenworth, KS: U.S. Army Command and General Staff College, 1986.

12. It is interesting to note that the Germans as well ignored some of the terrain issues. Panzer *Lehr*, commanded by Lieutenant General Fritz Bayerlein, moved from the Caen area to attack American positions in early July. Ignoring terrain issues, the German tanks and self-propelled guns faired no better than the Americans in the wet lands, restricting mobility and resulting in significant casualties in tanks and self-propelled guns.

13. Alfred D. Chandler and Steven Ambrose, eds., *The Papers of Dwight D. Eisenhower: The War Years*, Vol. III, Baltimore: Johns Hopkins Press, 1970, p. 2002.

14. Martin Blumenson, *Breakout and Pursuit*, Washington, DC: U.S. Army Center of Military History, p. 193.

15. Operations COBRA and GOODWOOD were coordinated operations, spaced 3 days apart, because both required significant air assets and commanders could not conduct them simultaneously. Montgomery, it should be noted, learned from his offensive staged on July 7. He ordered only fighter-bombers used in the area where armor was to advance.

16. This use of strategic air to reduce tactical defenses so soon after Montgomery's unsuccessful use of the same tactic on July 7 is indeed curious. It gained little for Montgomery, and thus it is puzzling as to why Bradley thought it would serve the U.S. First Army any better. Nonetheless, on July 19, Bradley flew to England and received assurances from air commanders that 1,800 heavy bombers, 300 medium bombers, and several hundred fighter-bombers would hit the German lines in preparation for the attack. See the Diary of Major Chet Hanson, entry of July 19, Carlisle, PA, U.S. Military History Institute.

17. Thomas Alexander Hughes, *Overlord: General Pete Quesada and the Triumph of Tactical Air Power in World War II*, New York: The Free Press, 1995, p. 209. Note that Bradley was irate over the AAF's failure to bomb in what he thought was the agreed pattern, i.e., parallel to American lines. "Pete" Quesada, however, stated

that "The human truth is that people heard what they wanted to hear" at the planning sessions for Operation COBRA.

18. *Ibid.*, p. 216.

19. Patton, however, was unimpressed by the effects of the bombing. On July 28, he was flown over the lines and caustically observed, "One of the innocent sufferers . . . was the cow. The whole countryside is covered with enormously distended cows, which will eventually be buried. Pending internment, they smell to high heaven, or at least to 300 feet high, as that was my altitude." Martin Blumenson, ed., *The Patton Papers, 1940-1945*, New York: Da Capo Press, 1996, p. 489.

20. Collins, *Lightning Joe*, p. 242.

21. Bradley had initially served as the commander of the U.S. 1st Army. With Bradley commanding the 12th Army Group, Lieutenant General Courtney Hodges received command of the 1st Army.

22. Chandler and Ambrose, eds., *The Papers of Dwight D. Eisenhower*, p. 2018.

23. In his memoirs, Oscar Koch, Patton's G-2, refers to this narrow corridor as the Avranches Gap. Oscar Koch, G-2, *Intelligence For Patton*, Atglen PA: Schiffer Military Publications, 1999, p. 77.

24. Nor did it come as a surprise to Patton. *Ibid.*, p. 77.

25. Bradley knew the Germans had planned some action since Allied signals intelligence personnel picked up their intentions on August 6. Ralph Bennett, *Ultra in the West: The Normandy Campaign, 1944-45*, New York: Charles Scribner's Sons, 1979, pp. 113-115.

26. A reader might logically ask the question, what was the U.S. Secretary of Treasury doing in France so close to the front lines? Morgenthau was extremely interested in the campaign in Europe and in the reconstruction of Europe once the war was over. Morgenthau had penned a plan for the reconstruction of

Germany as a pastoral and agricultural nation. Visiting the front was a popular activity. As Operation COBRA preparations were in the final stages, Secretary of War Henry Stimson, then 77, flew to France to visit Bradley's headquarters. Diary of Major Chester Hanson, entry of July 17, 1944.

27. Omar N. Bradley, *A Soldier's Story*, New York: Henry Holt and Company, 1951, p. 375.

28. Martin Blumenson, ed., *The Patton Papers, 1940-1945*, New York: DaCapo Press, 1974, p. 509. Patton's concept was ". . . getting the XX Corps moving on Dreux and the XIIth Corps on Chartes and the XVth Corps remaining where it now is. In this formation, I can turn north to southeast without crossing columns and can shift divisions and Corps at well. . . . It should be a very great success, God helping and Monty keeping hands off."

29. Bradley admitted that "Patton might have spun a line across that narrow neck, I doubted his ability to hold it." Bradley, p. 377.

30. *Ibid.*, p. 376.

31. *Ibid.*, p. 377.

32. Chandler and Ambrose, eds., *The Papers of Dwight D. Eisenhower: The War Years*, Vol. IV, p. 2215. Despite the importance of Antwerp as a port, a careful review of all of the records seems to indicate that in September, Eisenhower's first priority, the clearing of the estuary, was not always communicated to all subordinates.

33. Jeffery J. Clark and Robert Ross Smith, *Riviera to the Rhine*, Washington, DC: U.S. Army Center of Military History, 1993, p. 5. Other sources reference the first discussions of this operation in April 1943 and at the First Québec Conference in August 1943.

34. Russell F. Weigley, *Eisenhower's Lieutenants: The Campaign of France and Germany, 1944-1945*, Bloomington, IN: Indiana University Press, 1990, p. 218.

35. The British initially attempted to dissuade the Americans through the Combined Chiefs, proposing to take the Operation ANVIL divisions and invade Brittany. The Combined Chiefs quickly dismissed the argument. In their discussions, Eisenhower correctly told Churchill that he was looking at the invasion from a military perspective. If Churchill wanted to argue against Operation ANVIL from political considerations, then he needed to discuss the issue with Roosevelt. Clarke and Smith, p. 21.

36. John S. D. Eisenhower, *General Ike: A Personal Reminiscence*, New York: The Free Press, 2003, p. 199.

37. Eisenhower, *Dear General: Eisenhower's Wartime Letters to Marshall*, p. 198.

38. Winston Churchill, *Triumph and Tragedy*, Cambridge, MA: Houghton Mifflin, 1953, p. 692.

39. Thomas Buell *et al.*, *The Second World War: Europe and the Mediterranean*, Wayne NJ: Avery Publishing Group, 1989, p. 194.

40. For example, the Mediterranean was a key trade route through the Suez Canal to the British Empire on the way to the Far East and oil routes in the Persian Gulf. Clarke and Smith, p. 4.

41. Buell *et al.*, p. 348.

42. Stalin also strongly supported Operation ANVIL as an effort to conduct a large pincer movement to crush the Germans in France. His position and intercession in the American and British disagreement on strategy was a factor in forcing Churchill to back down. Field Marshall Lord Michael Carver, *The Imperial War Museum Book of the War in Italy 1943-1945: A Vital Contribution to Victory in Europe*, London, UK: Pan MacMillan, 2001, p. 107.

43. See *Southern France*, Washington, DC: U. S. Army Center of Military History, n.d., p. 6.

44. Captain Donald Bussey, 7th Army ULTRA officer, received and forwarded Hitler's order before Johannes Blaskowitz had the opportunity to read it. Colonel (Ret.) Donald Bussey disclosed this information in an interview with Dr. Sam Newland at the U.S. Army War College on February 20, 1994.

45. Clarke and Smith, p. 197.

46. Buell *et al.*, p. 350.

47. Weigley, *Eisenhower's Lieutenants*, p. 237.

48. Maurice Matloff, "The Anvil Decision," *Command Decisions*, in Kenneth Roberts Greenfield, ed., Washington, DC: U. S. Army Center of Military History, 1959, p. 387.

CHAPTER 6

OPERATION MARKET GARDEN

But Sir, I think we might be going a bridge too far.[1]

    Lieutenant General Frederick Browning
    to Field Marshal Montgomery

Following the breakout from the Normandy lodgment and the successful landings in southern France, it seemed as if the once vaunted *Wehrmacht* had lost its ability to organize a coherent defense. Initially, the speed and size of the Allied breakout throughout northwestern France denied German military units the ability to regroup and establish a strong defense against Allied advances. Adolf Hitler's Mortain offensive only exacerbated the problem. Neither Eisenhower or the SHAEF staff anticipated the speed of the Allied advance as they prepared their projections for success. Montgomery and Bradley pushed the German forces out of the Normandy area, and with Patton's 3rd Army, American ground forces advanced over a broad front to liberate France and inflict substantial casualties on the retreating German military. Victory seemed in sight.

The Germans had hoped to create a defensive position along the Seine River, but the lack of resources and the quick Allied advance made it impossible to create a new defensive line to hold the Allies in place. With no prepared defensive positions on the Seine, the German retreat continued through the end of August and into the first week of September. The relentless pressure from the Allies pushing eastward, and their dominance in the air, kept the Germans off balance throughout the month of August. The axis of the British 21st Army Group extended across northern France into Belgium. The American 12th Army Group moved eastward toward southern Belgium, Luxembourg, and central and southern Germany. After the Operation ANVIL/DRAGOON landings on August 15, another line of advance proceeded from the south, and a third army group, the 6th, was organized opposite Alsace-Lorraine. Eisenhower's broad front strategy, though in many ways unimaginative, had severely stressed the *Wehrmacht's* capabilities. The crises facing German commanders went beyond events in France, because even though the *Wehrmacht* could achieve some tactical victories on the Eastern Front, the Russian steamroller moved relentlessly forward, crushing everything in its sight.

Eisenhower's decision to press the pursuit was correct and demonstrated a good sense of the battlefield, but the rapid advance put stress on the limited Allied logistical system. Consider the OVERLORD planner's original timetable. Some American staff members thought that Bradley's 12th Army Group would reach the German border by D+96, but other SHAEF analysts estimated that reaching the German border would take until D+300.[2] The Operation COBRA breakout and pursuit phase lasted only 47 days. The Allies had a tremendous material and manpower advantage over the Germans, but as the pursuit phase proceeded, the logistical tail from Cherbourg and Le Harve became dangerously long. There were other ports in France. Unfortunately, the Germans still held a number of these ports, and Allied forces encircled these port cities rather than dedicating the resources to capture them. In early September, the only major French ports in Allied hands were Cherbourg and Marseilles. These were simply inadequate for Allied needs. All other significant French ports were still in German hands, and since they were on the Atlantic coast, they offered little to resolve the supply crisis. At the same time, capturing ports, wherever they were located, did not always result in having an immediately usable facility. American and British forces also faced the consequence of taking a defended French port that had suffered destruction of its facilities through either intentional sabotage or an unintended consequence from the battle. Landing supplies, organizing distribution, and establishing proper transportation required a tremendous effort to get thousands of tons of supplies to combat and support forces every day.

Eisenhower recognized this, and one of his important goals was to take possession of a major useable port, specifically Antwerp, Belgium.[3] If Allied forces could accomplish this task, then the logistical system for the Allied armies might increase and expand combat operations throughout the area. The success of Operation ANVIL/DRAGOON and the subsequent capture of Marseilles and Toulon was a tremendous boon, but still the supply problem seemed to elude resolution.

Ports, however, were only a part of the problem. Even if the Allies could capture ports quickly and make them operational, the linking transportation network was often awry. The success of the AAF and RAF Transportation Plan meant that Allied units could not immediately use large sections of the French railway system.[4] Like the effort against German-held ports, the AAF and RAF attacks had savaged the French rail system. Air interdiction and strategic bombing missions had severely damaged or destroyed rolling stock, rail-lines, bridges, and other critical infrastructure. The U.S. Army in particular, demonstrated its usual innovative tendency by creating the Red Ball Express, a truck-bound transportation system which rushed supplies forward 24 hours a day from the beaches to the troops in contact. Obviously, Allied logistical officials used great amounts of gasoline and vehicles for this temporary expedient, but it helped to ameliorate at least some of the crisis. Motor transportation and the laying of pipelines for gasoline were consistently a prime concern. Although PLUTO functioned well by transporting gasoline from England to the continent, they only brought fuel to the French coast. Distribution into the continent's heartland was a weak link in the Allied logistical system.

Gasoline became a limiting factor for American and British forces that were trying to maximize the advantage of mobility, a force multiplier provided through having highly mechanized forces. One can see the logistical impact on Allied efforts by looking at Patton's 3rd Army. In August 1944, the 3rd Army alone was using about 400,000 gallons of gasoline a day. By the end of the same month, the allocation had dropped to 32,000 gallons.[5] These shortages effectively immobilized Patton's drive toward southern and central Germany. To provide at least some assistance to the creaking logistical system, Allied leaders stripped select new British and American units of their trucks and other transportation assets in order to supply units in combat. The demand for gasoline from truck transportation alone consumed 300,000 gallons daily.[6] Without gasoline, the advance into Germany halted. The supply system provided the U.S. 1st Army with 3,300 tons a day, while Patton's 3rd Army could rely on a mere 2,500 tons.[7] These resources amounted to only about half of their allotted requirements. An inadequate supply system began to dictate strategy.

The failure to develop an appropriate logistics infrastructure slowed the ability of Allied forces to develop depots that could directly support combat operations.

One major factor in the logistical problem was not only the lack of suitable ports; it was also the success of Allied forces in the period from July 25-September 9, 1944. As American and British forces rapidly liberated France, it became obvious that the French economy and the civilian supply network was also a casualty of war. Time was required to reestablish the civilian sector infrastructure. At least for a period, Allied forces would have to dedicate some of their logistical capabilities to supplying the French and later the Belgian populations. The result of the military and civilian demands on the inadequate transportation network were such that by the end of August 1944, the Allied offensive in the west was slowly but surely, coming to a halt.

In the midst of these Allied victories and the growing list of shortfalls, there was a significant change in the Allied command structure. On September 1, Eisenhower assumed the role of ground component commander from Montgomery while retaining his role as Supreme Commander. From June 6 until September 1, the commander of ground forces had been Montgomery. Montgomery wanted and felt he deserved this command. Eisenhower's assumption of command, serving in a dual-hatted capacity, resulted in a dispute, at times bitter, between Eisenhower and Montgomery. This dispute was enduring, even outlasting the war. Eisenhower's broad front strategy, or called by some the strategy of general advance, was also a point of contention between Montgomery and Eisenhower. Both Montgomery and Eisenhower's long time friend, Patton, were highly critical of the broad front strategy.

Both of these officers favored focused and powerful thrusts toward the heartland of Germany because both believed that through focused thrusts the Allies could destroy the German military and end the war quickly. Patton, though he grudgingly followed Eisenhower's direction, repeatedly pushed for a more imaginative approach to the European Campaign, but to no avail.

Source: U.S. Army Military History Institute.

Field Marshall Bernard Montgomery, center, hero of El Alamein, increasingly became a thorn in General Eisenhower's side as the European Campaign progressed.

It was from senior commanders of the British Army, particularly Alanbrooke and Montgomery, that Eisenhower suffered some of the worst barbs.

Alanbrooke considered Eisenhower to be a failure as Supreme Commander. Like Montgomery, he was opposed to Ike's dual-hatted command. In addition, he did not at all believe in the broad front strategy.[8] There were sharp divisions among the Allied military commands.

It was Montgomery however, that continued, sometimes subtly and on other occasions openly, to voice criticism of Eisenhower's strategy and leadership. Montgomery was determined to prove that a different strategy would be more effective in defeating the German military. In early September, he and his staff began developing a new option. British units were on some of the best terrain for mobile warfare. Good terrain, however, had not resulted in a British rush to the Rhine area. In late July, British and Canadian forces had pushed across northern France and were ready to liberate Belgium and the Netherlands. On August 17, Montgomery suggested to Bradley that his combined British and Canadian force could advance through Belgium above the Ardennes. Using 40 divisions, including Bradley's American units, they could drive across the Ruhr River.[9] Montgomery believed this mass of force would be unstoppable, especially against a weakened and disorganized foe. This operation would allow Allied forces to reduce war munitions production and create a path toward Berlin, via the North German Plain. This drive to Berlin could end the war by December 1944. A successful British drive to Berlin might allow the Western Allies to occupy most of Germany and parts of Poland, thereby decreasing the Soviet Union's role in this region.

Montgomery's plan could not have come at a more propitious time. Eisenhower's broad front strategy had stretched German capabilities and had resulted in exacting heavy casualties on innumerable German formations. At the same time, the broad front strategy, and the second landings in southern France, had also stretched American capabilities. As the prewar German border was reached and attritional warfare seemed on the horizon, Eisenhower explored options to avoid a stalemate. In many respects, at least a part of the problem confronting him was the gamble taken earlier by Marshall. The Chief of Staff had taken a significant risk by assuming that a 100-division American Army would be sufficient to win the war to include the Pacific Theater and other obligations. While Marshall had planned for the 100-division Army, in reality the War Department capped the Army's strength in 1943 at 88 divisions (the number actually reached was 89). More serious than the actual number of divisions was the ratio of support troops to combat troops. In March 1945, the U.S. Army's strength reached 8,157,386 officers and enlisted men. Subtracting the 2,308,849 in the AAF and the Women's Army Corps, 5,848,537 Soldiers were in the Army's ground forces. Of this number, only 46 percent, or 2,711,969, were serving in combat, combat support, or combat service support units. Thus, the number of enlisted Soldiers assigned to the 89 combat divisions was not significantly different from the number serving in the 73 combat divisions in service in December 1942, 1 year after the war had begun.[10]

The manpower problem was recognized by McNair before his untimely demise in the Normandy area. He was unable to resolve the problem. Bradley, in one of the more candid and insightful sections of his post war memoirs, recalled:

> Prior to the invasion, we had estimated that the infantry would incur 70% of the losses of our combat forces.

By August (1944) we had boosted that figure to 83% on the basis of our experience in the Normandy hedgerows. The appalling hazard of an infantryman's life in combat was illustrated at St. Lo where in 15 days the 30th Division sustained 3,934 battle casualties. At first glance those casualties would seem to imply 25% losses for the division. That figure is deceptive. Because three out of every four of those casualties occurred in a rifle platoon, the rate of loss in those platoons exceeded 90 percent. [11]

Granted, as the campaign in Europe proceeded, the combat power of American units, in many respects, increased because the American Soldier had become a seasoned and competent element on the battlefield and one the Germans and British started to respect. At the same time, as the fall proceeded, a serious manpower shortage developed. During the beginning of the European Campaign, manpower shortages had been a British problem. However, in autumn 1944, the same problem plagued the American Army as well, particularly in the availability of combat infantrymen. If the Allies were to conclude the war more quickly and effectively, then other approaches other than a strategy of general advance might need to be explored. The question remained, could the American Army's leadership take a different approach to defeat the Germans other than this broad front strategy. As noted by one author, "American generals had demonstrated their tactical competence, although their ability to craft tactical engagements into larger operational strategy to close with and destroy the enemy remained questionable."[12]

Montgomery was uncertain that the Americans could make these adjustments, and he sought to show American generals, particularly Eisenhower, how to fight more efficiently. Montgomery's desire to take center stage in the campaign, in many respects, had a certain degree of irony. His record on Sicily and at Caen made it questionable as to whether he could deliver Rommel or Patton style advances that could end the war more quickly, but nonetheless he was determined to try.

Critics could see the most recent example of his slow and meticulous nature at Antwerp. This port city was an important decisive point on the map for Eisenhower and the Allied war effort. Taking this port, together with Marseilles, could have resolved the Allied supply problem that got worse since the beginning of the campaign. Montgomery's 30th Corps did an excellent job of reaching the port on September 5 and found it in unbelievably good condition. Antwerp, however, lies inland from the coast, up the Scheldt Estuary. Without possession of the river, to include both banks and the Walcheren and South Beveland Islands, Antwerp was useless to the Allies. By taking Antwerp, the 30th Corps action not only secured it for the Allies, it also essentially trapped the German XV Army. Only a narrow escape route existed, and cutting that should have been the 30th Corps immediate task. Instead, the British drive into Antwerp, which originally showed such promise, lost momentum at this critical time.[13] At least part of the reason for this missed opportunity was the fact that Montgomery's thoughts and plans were on another operation. This hesitation gave the Germans a necessary respite. Much like the situation on the Seine River, the Germans proved themselves masters of organization and improvisation. Between September 4 and 22, the XV Army's commander, *General der Infantrie* Gustav von Zangen, succeeded in evacuating over 80,000 men and a substantial amount of their equipment to join up with the main body of German forces on the Dutch mainland. The British

Army did not secure the Schledt or seal off the XVth Army's retreat.

As this opportunity slipped through Allied hands, Eisenhower's quandary was becoming even more serious. His adversary was now fighting on interior lines, its front had constricted considerably, and the German soldier was defending home territory. If Eisenhower wanted to keep the enemy off balance, he had two main options: He could attempt to maintain his broad front advance, even though he was faced with declining resources, and push into Germany, albeit more slowly. His other option was to concentrate his attack on a narrow path to drive across the Rhine and into Germany. If Allied leaders chose the latter option, either the 12th or the 21st Army Groups could be given this mission, but resources were not available for both to take the initiative. Only one army group would have sufficient logistics to conduct the single attack. Further complicating the problem, the only reserve manpower immediately available on the continent were airborne units. Marshall and the AAF's Arnold, had expressed concern about the two elite American airborne divisions, the 101st and 82nd, sitting idle and pressed Eisenhower to use these divisions to conduct an airborne assault.[14] Eisenhower had planned to conduct airborne operations after the Normandy campaign, but the pace of advance from August to early September made it difficult to plan such operations since objectives were taken before airborne assaults could be executed.[15]

Montgomery, miffed about Eisenhower's assumption of ground component command, proposed to take the initiative. On September 4, he sent a message to Eisenhower proposing a full-scale effort on the North German Plain aimed at Berlin. Montgomery's concept was to shift the weight of Allied efforts to his command; troops and supplies included. Eisenhower, in response the following day, was not convinced that the full weight of Allied power should focus on Montgomery's operations.[16] At the same time, from the campaign's onset, staff officers recognized that the northern France-Low Countries' terrain was conducive to armored operations. It also led directly to the North German Plain, excellent maneuver ground, which was the most direct route to Berlin. If American forces maintained their pressure on the German fortified line known as the Siegfried Line, then British forces had the best shot at pushing straight to Berlin and ending the war by Christmas.

Some might ask, why not send the undisputed American master of maneuver warfare, Patton, on a mission to unravel the Reich's defenses? The answer was simply that Patton was occupied in a bitter campaign of reducing the defenses of Metz and was incurring significant casualties in the process. Terrain was not on his side. Bradley, who did not like Montgomery, later countered with a proposal to attack Germany with his 12th Army Group. Using Patton's 3rd Army, Bradley planned to push through Lorraine and then punch a hole through the Siegfried Line.[17] The 1st and 3rd Armies could then attack through the Frankfurt Gap and as the two armies moved into Germany, the 1st Army would press its attack in a more northerly direction.

Given the terrain, Montgomery's plan seemed to offer better prospects than the attack planned by Bradley. Montgomery's staff had actually created several plans to cross the Rhine River, a major obstacle to entering Germany. One plan, Operation COMET, proposed that an airborne force drop into Germany and take the town of Wesel, on the Rhine. If successful,

Operation COMET would allow Allied forces to pour into Germany. Montgomery later strengthened the original forces under Operation COMET and moved the objective west.[18] His revised plan included three and a half airborne divisions. Instead of taking Wesel, British and American airborne forces would land in Holland. The main goal was to take a series of bridges that would cross several rivers to include the Rhine near Arnhem. Once Allied forces took the bridges, a British ground column would race towards the bridges to consolidate these gains and secure access across the Rhine.

On September 10, Montgomery met with Eisenhower in Brussels, Belgium, to discuss future operations. The meeting had all of the earmarks of discord like the meeting between Eisenhower and British Prime Minister Winston Churchill in August. In this case, it was not between the American commander and the Prime Minister; the argument was between a British Field Marshal and his superior. Montgomery was extremely vocal in expressing his displeasure about the broad front strategy and essentially sought full logistical support for the 21st Army Group, to the supply starvation of the others, in order to conduct a rapier-like thrust toward Berlin. He essentially lectured Eisenhower as if he were a subordinate, finally causing Eisenhower to reach over, place his hand on Montgomery's knee, and say, "Steady Monty! You can't talk to me like that. I'm your boss."[19] This was Eisenhower, as Supreme Commander, at his best. Twice in essentially a month's period, he had endured confrontations with the British leadership and despite severe irritation, he kept his temper and successfully worked with two highly opinionated British leaders.[20] Despite Montgomery's arguments, Ike's decision was firm; the broad front strategy remained in place.

All the same, desiring to placate the British and to seize, if possible, the Rhine crossings, Eisenhower authorized Operation MARKET GARDEN. Montgomery was given priority for logistics, but American forces would continue their operations, albeit more slowly.

For the British in particular, this operation was critical, since its success would give the Allies control of Holland and potentially the north German coast. Only 2 days before this meeting a new weapon, a V-2 ballistic missile, hit a London suburb carrying its one-ton warhead. German missile crews launched V-2s from sites in Holland and could strike a number of key political, military, and industrial sites in England. Unlike the earlier V-1 jet propelled cruise missile, the V-2 was not detectable by radar and hit the target at supersonic speed.[21] There was no warning. This new terror bombing campaign put pressure on SHAEF to act quickly and, if at all possible, seize the launching sites, putting an end to this threat. Operation MARKET GARDEN gave Eisenhower and Montgomery what they wanted. For Eisenhower, the operation used airborne troops and offered the possibility of early crossings over the Rhine River. At the same time, it gave Marshall a deep airborne envelopment, something that he wanted. For Montgomery, it offered him the center stage in the campaign. The Allied command assigned logistics priority to the 21st Army Group, much to Bradley's dismay. Speed was essential. MARKET was the airborne portion of the operation, which required the first British and American paratroopers to land on September 17. GARDEN was the ground link-up. Operation MARKET GARDEN concepts required planners to turn their ideas into workable plans and actions. The 21st Army Group commanders had only 7 days to organize, equip, plan, and execute this campaign. While the Normandy campaign had been preceded by months of training and preparation, Montgomery was directed by Eisenhower to move out quickly in this daring attack. Montgomery's plan did have an element of brilliance. Russell Weigley noted, "If MARKET GARDEN was to succeed, however, it would most emphatically demand tactical execution as bold as the strategic concept." Regrettably, it did not.

Source: U.S. Army Military History Institute.

The V-2 rocket, a significant German "miracle weapon," which Hitler hoped would change the course of the war.

Operation MARKET GARDEN had three main objectives: First, by outflanking the Siegfried Line, the Allies would avoid the German entrenched positions;

second, it would allow the Allies to have access to the North German Plain and better maneuver country; and, third, if properly executed, it would allow Allied troops to cutoff those German units still in Holland. The commanding officer of the ground portion of Operation MARKET GARDEN was British Lieutenant General Frederick "Boy" Browning. He was an officer who had never jumped in combat, though he did have some airborne experience. Browning was also the primary planner for this airborne operation. Even though the American airborne forces committed to MARKET GARDEN outnumbered the British, the operation was Montgomery's brain child and thus Browning was chosen. National considerations seemed to outweigh the fact that the American commander of the XVIII U.S. Airborne Corps, Major General Matthew B. Ridgeway, had much more experience. The 1st Allied Airborne Army was under the command of an American, Lieutenant General Lewis H. Brereton, an AAF officer with a dubious record.

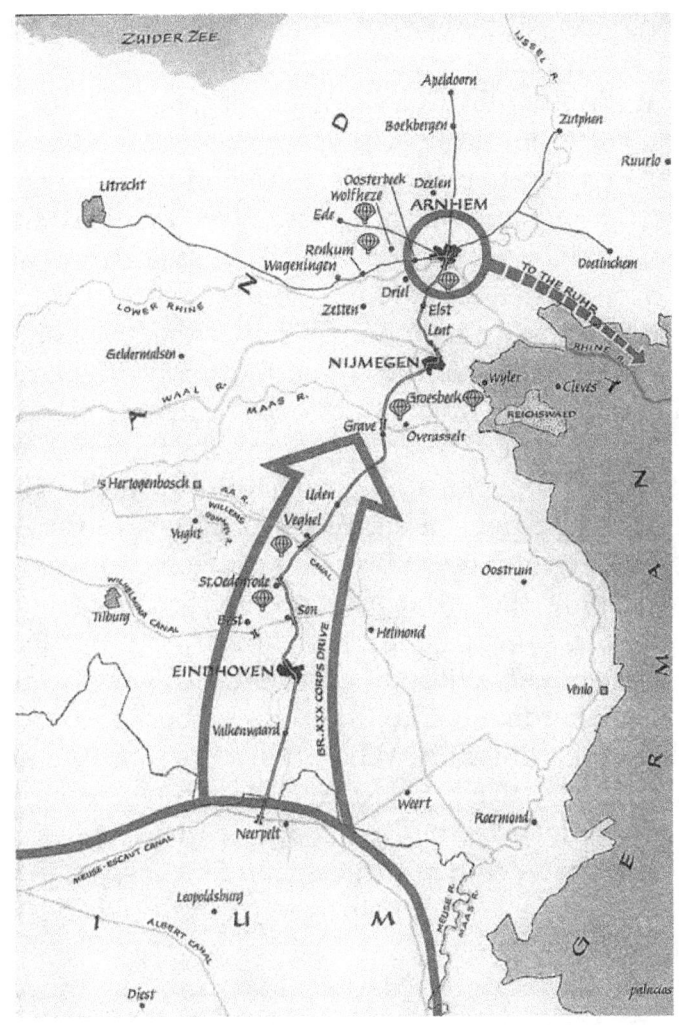

Note: The plan for Montgomery's master stroke, Operation MARKET GARDEN, shows the air drop sites, the advance of Horrock's XXX Corps, and the subsequent planned drive into the Ruhr Valley.

Map 6-1. Operation MARKET GARDEN.

Brereton and his staff completed the plan's air portion. His plans created the first problem for the operation. A critical element of the plan was to ensure a sufficient number of troops would land on the first day. Despite using both AAF and RAF transport units, the planned airborne assault still did not have sufficient lift capability to land all of their forces with one drop. Instead, Brereton would have to land the airborne forces in increments, rather than in a single massive drop. Given the Allied mastery of the air, he had the capability to conduct two sorties per plane on the first day, thereby strengthening the light airborne forces, as well as lessening casualties to the aircrews due to the element of suprise. Nonetheless, Brereton ruled that option out.[22] Brereton did accept some risk by dropping the airborne forces in broad daylight, despite fears of up to 40 percent attrition, but landing paratroopers without sufficient forces or supplies would jeopardize the ability of the airborne troops to achieve their mission. When Allied military leaders executed MARKET GARDEN, Brereton's transport forces would take the first 3 days to land necessary airborne units on their targets. Allied transport pilots would then use the fourth day to resupply the airborne forces.

Complicating the MARKET portion of the operation, Brereton ordered the RAF's 2nd Tactical Air Command to remain away from areas where the transport and resupply missions were conducted.[23] Fears of disrupting the transport aircraft with tactical combat aircraft forced the 1st Allied Airborne Army to lose critical close air support capabilities during the initial and later stages of the campaign. Major General R. E. "Roy" Urquhart, British 1st Airborne Division commander, would have found close air support in the initial days of the Arnhem operation "invaluable."[24] Inadequate artillery, limited anti-tank capabilities, and the use of airborne troops—inherently light infantry—translated to a lack of firepower to contest enemy armor and other activities. Brereton's failure put Allied airborne forces at a severe disadvantage without tactical airpower. Allied successes against German forces in France had depended heavily on AAF and RAF close air support and interdiction missions. Close air support could have given those forces an added capability. Restricting tactical air support for Allied forces was paramount to surrendering the air space to the *Luftwaffe*.

A major error that eroded the chance of success for the operation was selecting the British 1st Airborne Division for the task of taking the Arnhem Bridge and appointing Urquhart as the division's commander. The division's forces had not participated in the Normandy campaign. The division was also relatively inexperienced, compared to the combat tested American 82nd and 101st Airborne Divisions. Seizing and holding the bridge was a critical and very difficult task. The RAF made it even more difficult. Initially, the operation's plan called for the bulk of the 1st Airborne's troops to land in the vicinity of the bridge. The RAF's Air Vice Marshall L. N. Hollinghurst objected due to the location of German anti-aircraft and forced a change of the drop zone to an area outside Arnhem. The drop zone selected was over six miles from its objective. This modification required British troops to move quickly across six miles of enemy territory without the necessary ground transportation and seize a major roadway bridge. They also had to leave some of their limited force to secure the landing site for further drops, supply missions, and glider landings. Deployment of this smaller force made the success of taking or holding the Arnhem bridges problematic. Browning selected troops from the 1st Polish Independent Parachute Brigade to support the British forces in Arnhem, but not on the first day's drop.

To coordinate the movement and progress of the various moving parts in this operation required reliable communications between the divisions and their component elements. Radio sets provided to the British 1st Airborne Division, however, had only a three to five mile range.[25] These radios would likely be out of range to units approaching Arnhem. Any requests for artillery or, if possible, close air support, would probably go unanswered. Coordinating all of the necessary actions would be difficult, if not impossible.

A more critical problem was the distance between the British 1st Airborne Division and their commander, Browning of the I British Airborne Corps. Browning was to land at Nijmegen, the Netherlands, a distance that would put him out of radio range with Urquhart. Without communications, Browning did not know the division's status and was unable to coordinate support or relief action for the Arnhem forces. His decision to land his entire staff was also a major error since it required 34 gliders for the staff and their equipment. Urquhart's 1st Airborne Division could have put some of these craft to better use to land additional support for its exposed troops. Browning had also dismissed much of the strategic intelligence concerning German military units in the region and did not pass this information forward to his subordinate division commanders.[26] If the divisional commanders, especially those earmarked for Arnhem, had known about the presence of the II SS Panzer Corps, they could have taken or arranged for effective anti-tank capabilities.

Urquhart's division had three major initial objectives. Its primary goal was to seize the bridges at Arnhem. South of the city, there was a major bridge for motor vehicles and foot traffic. West of Arnhem is a railroad bridge over the Rhine River. Capturing one or both of the bridges would provide the necessary passage into Germany.[27] The next objective was to take the territory south of Arnhem with the 1st Polish Independent Parachute Brigade. This would allow the British XXX Corps to pass forward in a northerly direction through Arnhem. If transportation delays occurred in landing, then the British 1st Airborne Division and the Polish brigade could ensure the control of this area. The last objective included clearing the immediate area of any anti-aircraft defenses. These measures would allow AAF and RAF aircraft to reduce the threat to aircrews, while they resupplied the ground forces and provided air support to the deployed forces on the ground.

An experienced airborne officer would have vehemently objected to the drop zone that was located over six miles from Arnhem. On September 14, Urquhart briefed his plan to Browning and the other division commanders. Major General James Gavin, commander of the 82nd Airborne, turned to his G-3, Colonel John Norton, and said, "My God, he can't mean it," and Norton replied, "He does, and he is going to try to do it."[28] After the operation was over, the experienced German 1st Parachute Army commander, *Generaloberst* Kurt Student, concluded that the decision to drop the British 1st Airborne west of Arnhem, so far from their objective, was "the most important" reason for the failure of Operation MARKET GARDEN.[29]

According to the British plans, when the Arnhem bridges had been taken by the Allies the RAF and AAF were scheduled to take the British 52nd (Lowland) Division (air transportable) north of Arnhem, projected for the 5th and 6th days, to consolidate Allied control over areas north of Arnhem and allow Montgomery to control a major *Luftwaffe* airfield near Deelen, Holland.[30] Capturing Deelen could give the British a forward operating base for air transportable supplies and forces. It would also provide a valuable airstrip to conduct tactical air operations across the Rhine River.

The drops scheduled for the two American divisions were much more logical in that the drop zones were close to the objectives and were in good open country. Allied planners assigned the American 101st Airborne Division to deploy near Eindhoven and the division was to secure several bridges. Its companion 82nd Airborne Division would drop further north near Nijmegen and capture bridges over the Maas (Meuse) River, Maas-Waal Canal, and the Waal River. Seasoned airborne commanders led both of these combat experienced divisions.

Once the British airborne forces seized control of the Arnhem bridges, the 2nd British Army under General Sir Miles Dempsey was supposed to advance to the area where airborne troops had secured the bridges and relieve them. The 2nd Army would then advance past Arnhem and exploit this breakthrough, driving into Germany. This portion of the operation was code-named GARDEN. The British XXX Corps, under Lieutenant General Brian Horrocks, would have to dash through Belgium and Holland to take control over the critical bridges for the airborne forces. Successful capture of the bridges depended on a series of coordinated actions that commanders would have to complete within a few days. If the airborne forces failed to capture the bridges or if the structures sustained any damage, then a serious delay might create conditions where a German force could counterattack.

If GARDEN was successful, then XXX Corps and the 21st Army Group were free to exploit several options. British forces could drive southeast and try to surround the Ruhr and cutoff the western industrial center of Germany, capturing an essential piece of the German war economy. Armored forces could also drive northeast and make a dash for Berlin, an action that could end the war. Either of these courses of action could draw German forces from the West Wall and other defensive positions, potentially creating an ideal situation for Allied forces. If the German defenders tried to use their limited forces to stop a British advance, then the American 12th Army Group would have a better opportunity to pierce a crumbling defensive line and advance along a broad front.

Allied intelligence sources, using ULTRA, had identified some of the German forces in the area where Operation MARKET GARDEN was to take place. For example, the old adversary of British forces in the earlier stages of the campaign, the German XV Army was in the vicinity. This German army had been pushed out of the Brussels area, escaped from the Schledt area, and had settled into northern Holland. Many of its subordinate units had survived an escape from the Falaise Pocket. Commanders of some of these units, remnants of decimated German divisions, had organized these shattered pieces into improvised battle groups or *Kampfgruppe*. The *Kampfgruppe* did not have a standardized size, but instead they were an ad-hoc collection of men and equipment, loosely organized, some no larger than battalion strength. Their main purpose for being in Holland was to refit, although as the Allies would find out, they had the ability to put up a stiff resistance. Allied intelligence was concerned about the presence of the II SS Panzer Corps. In addition, the 9th and 10th SS Panzer Divisions had moved into the Arnhem area to reorganize and replace losses. Relentless Allied attacks had weakened the 9th SS Panzer Division. Its strength had dropped from an authorized 18,000 soldiers to less than 3,500 effective combatants. SS tank crews only had 20 Mark V Panther vehicles available, as opposed to their normal complement of 170.[31] The 10th SS Panzer Division had even fewer assets and less than 3,000 soldiers. Although the two *Waffen*-SS units had sustained horrendous casualties, they represented a dedicated and experienced defensive force that could descend on Arnhem and contest British 1st Airborne Division plans to capture and hold the bridge over the Rhine River.

Generalfeldmarschall Walther Model's Army Group B had units positioned in the general area where Operation MARKET GARDEN was scheduled to take place. Within this Army Group were the 15th Army and 1st Parachute Army. Other German support organizations located throughout Holland also offered additional units to defend the area. Granted, the leaders of these depleted German divisions could not withstand a sustained attack by similar Allied armored divisions, but they were in place and they too were composed of many seasoned veterans. Unfortunately for the Allies, the SS forces near the vital Arnhem area would offer the most serious challenge to the success of Operation MARKET GARDEN, especially against light airborne units.

Montgomery did know about the presence of the II SS Corps via several sources. He dismissed all of these reports. Eisenhower had also learned about this potential threat through his chief of staff, Bedell

Smith. Smith suggested landing a second airborne division near Arnhem, but concerns about changing the operation and angering Montgomery caused Eisenhower to defer the decision to the 21st Army Group commander. Smith also conveyed the information to Montgomery, but the British commander ignored the warning.[32] The prevailing attitude among senior commanders, based on German performance over the previous month, was that the German units were greatly weakened by their combat operations and would not pose a serious problem. Determined Allied attacks through their lines by XXX Corps would easily shatter their thin defenses.

A key element to GARDEN was a rapid advance of the XXX Corps to reach the paratroopers holding the bridges. Since the airborne units were lacking heavy weapons, their reinforcement by conventional forces was crucial. To accomplish this rapid advance, armor and infantry units had to move across terrain that essentially canalized the attackers. The proposed advance was over a solitary main road that led through Eindhoven to Nijmegen and finally to Arnhem. The road was the only way to pass through land that could not support major cross-country armor movements. The land surrounding Nijmegen contained canals, waterways, and other water obstacles that could delay any major efforts to bypass the road system through overland operations. The limited road system and the unsuitable surrounding terrain restricted the range of maneuver for British ground forces. A determined German defense, if given time, could focus on this narrow corridor of advance and slow if not stop any British progress north.

Initial elements of Operation MARKET GARDEN started on the evening of September 16. Brereton was still concerned with the *Luftwaffe's* ability to use its remaining fighters and anti-aircraft defenses to bring down his transport aircraft. Given this concern, the RAF Bomber Command launched several raids using Lancaster heavy bombers and smaller nimble Mosquito light bombers to strike airfields that operated German interceptors. The RAF hit one *Luftwaffe* facility where Germany officials based their newest fighter, the Me-262 jet. RAF aircraft severely damaged the runway, making it difficult for the Me-262 pilots, with its tricycle gear, to operate.[33] The RAF also attacked potential anti-aircraft artillery positions throughout the region.

Allied air forces also conducted operations to destroy enemy air defenses on the day of the invasion. On the morning of September 17, AAF and RAF fighters and bombers struck *Luftwaffe* and coastal defense batteries throughout Holland. The RAF sent bombers and escort Spitfire fighters to disrupt the operations of flak ships. The AAF sent a 1,000 B-17 and fighter escort force to bomb and strafe 112 anti-aircraft artillery locations.[34] Through these air attacks, commanders believed that they had significantly reduced the enemy air resistance. RAF 2nd Tactical Air Force pilots also hit troop barracks at Arnhem, Nijmegen, and other locations to reduce any threat by enemy ground forces to the airborne landings. These critical assaults were necessary to reduce a number of threats, but they also alerted the German military command of a potential airdrop in the near future. The AAF and RAF used 1,418 bombers and escorts to prepare the area for paratroop and glider landings. Only seven Allied aircraft were lost throughout the night and early morning raids. In less than a day, American and British bombardiers dropped over 4,000 tons of bombs in support of the landings.

Brereton arranged for the bulk of the transport fleet to begin their take-offs at 10:25 am. Pathfinder groups preceded the main body of transport aircraft and gliders. Two transport aircraft groups arrived over Holland. The initial plan for the airborne force included 1,545 transport planes and 478 gliders originating from 24 airfields across England. Aircrews actually flew 1,174 aircraft on Operation MARKET GARDEN's D-Day, and of those aircraft launched, 338 either aborted their drops, were lost, or were damaged.[35] The initial drop was a superb achievement on the part of Allied air forces, with approximately 20,000 troops accurately inserted into Holland within a window of 80 minutes.[36] Despite this huge air armada, the airborne divisions could only land part of their forces due to the space limitations of the aircraft. The fact that only part of the troops could be transported with available aircraft coupled with the refusal of air transport leaders to conduct a second drop the same day would have a profound effect on the operation. The limited transport caused the British 1st Airborne Division to limit its landing of light artillery to a mere 24 of their 75mm pack howitzers. This restricted fire support would have to last until XXXth Corps could arrive with heavier artillery. Brereton, again, compounded the fire support problem by effectively grounding close air support, an essential tool to counter enemy armor and troop concentrations.

Transport aircraft flew either a northern or a southern route. Aircraft with the northern route dropped the British airborne forces on the Arnhem area and the American 82nd Airborne Division on Nijmegen. The route avoided the concentrated flak units based throughout the Walcheren Islands along the channel coast, the Rotterdam area, Nijmegen, and Arnhem. Pilots flying on the southern route were above terrain controlled by the 21st Army Group for most of their flight. Units from the U.S. 101st Airborne Division still had to cross over heavy flak areas when their planes flew across Eindhoven. Despite the Allied bombing preparations and strafing missions, the *Luftwaffe* was able to send interceptors against the transports. Allied air losses included 68 transport aircraft, 71 gliders, and 20 fighters on the first day. These casualties, for a daylight drop, were far less than the 40 percent anticipated losses. Paratroops and glider units began landing around 12:30 pm and continued into the early afternoon.

The RAF dropped British airborne forces in their designated areas northeast of Arnhem. By 1:50 pm, approximately 5,000 British airborne troops had landed in Holland.[37] Urquhart's forces then faced over a six-mile march as they moved toward their objective; Arnhem. They encountered some delays as they tried to organize themselves and move out toward their assigned objectives. Jeeps sent in by gliders were their only motorized transport equipment. These light vehicles did provide a limited reconnaissance capability and could tow the few anti-tank weapons onto the battlefield.

Although the German military had indications that a major airborne operation was about to occur, they knew few specifics about when and what objectives the Allies would take. As a result, the airborne landings took the defending Germans by complete surprise. Model's Army Group B, with headquarters near Oosterbeek, the Netherlands, was very close, a mere three miles away, to Urquhart's landing zone. As the paratroopers began landing, Model retreated to the II SS Panzer Corps headquarters since he believed that his capture was the airborne operation's objective.

Despite the German presence throughout the region, coordinating a dedicated defense against this surprise attack was at first difficult. *Obergruppenführer und General der Waffen*-SS Wilhelm Bittrich, commanding the II SS Panzer Corps, did manage to identify the airborne force's mission of seizing the bridges over Arnhem and Nijmegen. Bittrich ordered the 9th SS Panzer Division to protect the two Arnhem bridges, survey Arnhem and Nijmegen for enemy activity, and attack any enemy forces in the Oosterbeek area. He also ordered the 10th SS Panzer Division to occupy the bridge near Nijmegen. Bittrich requested Model's permission to destroy any bridges once they were under German control to deny their use to the Allies. Model did not concur. He thought the Allies would move against German defenses east of Arnhem. If the Germans destroyed the bridges, then German military forces from Holland could not support any counterattacks or defensive activities. Thus, destroying the bridges would only support the Allies' mission.[38] This decision on the part of the German senior commander was fortuitous for the Allies.

After some opposition and delay from the landing sites, the British units managed to move toward their objectives. Elements from the British 1st Airborne Division reached Arnhem's outskirts and approached the railroad and roadway bridges. Before they could take the railroad bridge, German forces used explosives to demolish it. The only other bridge was the main roadway bridge south of Arnhem. British paratroops did find a ferry that could cross the Rhine River, but they failed to use it. The paratroopers took the northern end of the roadway bridge that same evening after clashing with German forces rushing south to Nijmegen. Unfortunately for Urquhart, an armored car unit from the 10th SS Panzer Division controlled the southern end of the roadway bridge. The British had managed to move a battalion into Arnhem, but German units moved quickly and efficiently to cutoff any reinforcements. British defenders had no choice but to take up a defensive posture and wait until the XXXth Corps or other elements of the airborne division scheduled for the second drop on the following day relieved them. If the 1st Airborne had been dropped closer to their objectives, Urquhart's forces might have taken all of the bridges. Due to the distance from the objective and the time it took Urquhart's men to get organized, British paratroopers were faced with a major task of dislodging elements of the 10th SS Panzer Division that controlled the southern end of the Arnhem roadway bridge.

American paratroopers of Major General Maxwell D. Taylor's 101st Airborne Division had to capture the city of Eindhoven and then take a highway bridge over the Wilhemina Canal. Taylor also had to occupy a 15-mile stretch of road to allow the XXXth Corps to advance northwards. This roadway north from Eindhoven linked the 101st and elements of the 82nd Airborne Division. Paratroopers needed to capture several other crossings and bridges independently and push north ahead of the XXXth Corps. The lightly armed paratroop and glider forces had to disperse to control this road and hold out against any enemy opposition. The stretch of road was nicknamed "Hell's Highway" by the U.S. Soldiers. Taylor dispensed with his assigned artillery and ordered his infantry units to land first on September 17. Since the division contained only light artillery, Taylor thought his artillery could not support the dispersed airborne forces along the road.[39] This scheme might have worked if the XXXth Corps elements had made rapid progress through the initial German defenses, and German engineers had not blown-up any of the bridges, but this was not the case.

The 101st landed without opposition and quickly took most of their objectives. The exception was the crossing over the Wilhemina Canal. American forces attempted to take a crossing over the canal at Son, the Netherlands, but Taylor also assigned a force to take a rail and road crossing west of Son. Unfortunately, German forces had destroyed both bridges. No advance over the canal could occur until the XXXth Corps could provide appropriate bridging and engineering support to span the waterway. The Allied advance northwards towards Arnhem faced a delay.

The 82nd Airborne had several objectives upon landing. Paratroopers were to advance south of Nijmegen and take a bridge over the Maas River. Other objectives included taking bridges across the Maas-Waal Canal and another key bridge north of Nijmegen over the Waal River. Altogether Gavin's 82nd had to take six bridges, control the roadway north, and advance through hilly, wooded terrain southeast of Nijmegen. Gavin believed control over the region and bridges depended on his Soldiers' ability to control the Groesbeek Heights, a wooden ridgeline that ran north to south of this hilly area.[40] The 82nd needed to dominate this ridge, because from it German defenders could stage a counterattack against any of the six bridges or cut the access to the roadway.

Without the division's full resources, limited by the initial landing transportation allocations, Gavin had to make a choice. His forces could take all of the six bridges, but without control of the wooded ridgeline, a German counterattack could sweep the Americans away from their initial gains. Gavin decided to take the bridges over the Maas River and the Maas-Waal Canal and accept the risk of attack from the wooded ridgeline. American airborne forces had to wait for the British XXXth Corps to make a combined attack on the bridge near Nijmegen. Through no fault of its own, the lack of mass for the 82nd Airborne Division affected the operation's success. The XXXth Corps was running into difficulty.

Operation GARDEN's fate rested on XXXth Corps moving the 64 miles from Neerpelt to Arnhem. Horrocks's Corps first had to breech German defensive positions and then rapidly drive towards Eindhoven. Launching the GARDEN portion of the operation from Belgium, Horrock's force crossed the Meuse-Escault Canal near Neerpelt, Belgium. The initial attack by British ground forces, with RAF and artillery support, broke through the German *Kampfgruppe*, and XXXth Corps was able to push ahead. The exploitation, however, was not as easy as had been believed. When the lead Irish Guards Division pushed into enemy territory, within 1,000 yards of its start, German defenders used their anti-tank weapons to destroy nine tanks. Thus, despite a massive artillery barrage and RAF close air support, the German defenders managed to delay the push north. After the first day, the XXXth Corps had advanced only six miles. Initial plans had called for the XXXth Corps to make the drive to Arnhem within 2 days. After the first day's delays, this goal was out of reach. The 1st Allied Airborne Army units would have to defend their positions and wait. Resupply of these units might allow them to hold on to their captured bridges and areas, but heavy first-day casualties and the potential for a reinforced German counterattack could create a catastrophe for the British and American forces.

The slow start on September 17 disappointed American and British commanders. Since the Germans had initially stalled the XXXth Corps advance, on the second day of the operation, an alerted foe had the potential of attacking at any point from the Belgium border to south of Arnhem to stop the invading Allied force. German soldiers had already delayed the Allied advance by demolishing some of the bridges. The Allied ground advance also had to contend with moving through crowded urban areas filled with ecstatic Dutch civilians recently liberated after years of occupation.

Insufficient forces on the ground, poorly chosen landing zones, too many objectives, insufficient firepower, limited routes to advance, and incorrect assumptions about the capabilities of the German defenders all played a part in preventing airborne and ground forces from taking all of their objectives. Montgomery had ordered the British XIIth and VIIIth Corps to make advances to the left and right of the XXXth Corps, but these forces also moved slowly partly due to a lack of fuel and logistics. The only possibility of salvaging something from Operation MARKET GARDEN was a determined advance up the main but vulnerable highway by the XXX Corps.

The drive north to relieve the 1st Allied Airborne Army units became mired in delays due to enemy attacks all along the path to Arnhem. Despite their depleted and weakened status, several German *Kampfgruppe* began converging on the British and American units. Many experienced senior leaders led German units, and they were on familiar terrain, a distinct advantage. The only option available to the Allied airborne units was to dig in and wait for the relief force. This option was a difficult task, especially for British airborne troops that held the most contested area, the city of Arnhem. The roadway bridge south of the city became the most critical battle in the operation. British 1st Airborne Division soldiers were able to maintain a tenuous presence at the northern end of the bridge, but German forces were able to surround them which meant that units from the XXX Corps would have to cross the Rhine River against opposition. SS units used the Arnhem ferry, disregarded by the British, to move units south of the Rhine River. Bittrich organized several German units and counterattacked the British. Through these attacks, the Germans were able to isolate many of the British units. The Germans relentlessly attacked the British defenders from September 17 to 21. British defenders successfully resisted an attack on the bridge on September 18 by elements of the 9th SS Panzer Division's reconnaissance battalion. The 9th's commander attempted to rush the bridge, but concentrated fire from British anti-tank weapons, grenades, and small arms fire stopped the advance. Still, the situation for the British 2nd Parachute Battalion holding on to one end of the bridge became increasingly desperate. At the same time, the Germans were able to infiltrate the drop zone for the 1st Airborne and, because the British did not have effective radio communications, efforts to adjust resupply drop zones were hampered. Dropping supplies to reach British airborne forces became problematic, if not impossible. Casualties, reduced ammunition, and few anti-tank weapons meant that by September 21st British airborne units were in dire straits.

Allied forces hoped for far more success from D+1. On September 18 aerial resupply missions and additional paratroop landings started after a delay due to weather conditions in England. Poor weather in England delayed the Polish paratroop brigade's deployment into the Arnhem area. Eventually, the Polish units landed, but the entire brigade did not get airlifted until September 21. Although the weather worked against supply and reinforcement drops, XXX Corps and the 101st Airborne Division were able to capture Eindhoven with its important bridge, and pushed toward Son. By evening on the 18th, British engineers had built a temporary bridge over the Wilhemina Canal and could move forward toward Nijmegen. On September 19, the XXX Corps reached elements of the 82nd Airborne Division near the Waal River. The operation to link-up with British paratroopers at Arnhem, however, faced repeated delays. The paratroopers continued to hold Arnhem and denied the II SS Panzer Corps from reinforcing German forces in Nijmegen. Still, if the Germans could forestall XXX Corps from breaking through to Arnhem, then the 9th SS Panzer Division and other units could destroy the British paratroopers whose perimeter was increasingly shrinking. A possibility still existed that Operation MARKET GARDEN might succeed, but the chance was slowly slipping away.

The German military's quick reaction and interpretation of the operation's goals created conditions that would deny an Allied victory. The *Luftwaffe* was a shadow of its former self, but in opposing Operation MARKET GARDEN it exhibited considerable resilience. German aircrews had 425 Bf-109 and FW-190 interceptors available to attack the AAF and RAF cargo and troop carriers.[41] *Luftwaffe* fighters strafed British positions and both air and flak crews disrupted glider and paratroop drops with accurate fire. Further, enemy opposition and poor communication with troops on the ground resulted in much of the ammunition and supplies dropped for Arnhem being lost, because aircrews mistakenly dropped them over enemy controlled territory.

Airborne division commanders had to make difficult choices. Urquhart's positions near Oosterbeek and surrounding areas allowed German forces to attack them piecemeal. British forces had to withdraw. Urquhart reformed his units, but the British forces in Arnhem controlling the bridge were separated by German defenders. Meanwhile, south of Arnhem, lack of resources to reinforce the American 82nd Airborne forces had delayed them from taking the Nijmegen roadway bridge. They would need the British forces to support an attempt to seize the bridge. Although the combined American-British effort was successful, taking the bridge on September 23, this was far too late to save the operation. After a heroic defense, the British 1st Airborne Division forces in Arnhem had surrendered on September 21. Urquhart still had a sizeable force near Arnhem, but casualties and limited supplies made the chance of capturing the bridge virtually impossible. The only realistic option was to withdraw these remaining British troops. The Allied forces withdrew during the night of September 25. In the meantime, XXX Corps had broken through the Belgian border and had reached the Rhine River, but despite this belated success, German resistance had stiffened, and there was no clear corridor for an attack toward the North German plain.

The concept of using airborne forces to seize vital objectives and using ground forces to relieve them was valid and bold. Early German examples in Holland during 1940 and the successful Allied Normandy drop validated these concepts. Dashing ahead and seizing bridges over the Rhine River to place Allied soldiers across the Rhine, if it had been successful, had the potential of significantly shortening the war. Conversely, it would be difficult to find an operation that could serve as a better example of what *not* to do when planning an operation, than Operation MARKET GARDEN.

From the very beginning, planning and tactical execution of the operation was badly flawed. First, there was the issue of leadership. Since it was Montgomery's operation, he chose to use British officers with little or no airborne experience to plan and lead the operation. As a British conceived operation, he would not use the more experienced American airborne leaders like Ridgeway or Gavin. Second, ignoring the available intelligence from various sources that indicated the presence of elite German units in the drop areas was extremely foolish. In his memoirs, Montgomery later admitted his error in underestimating the capabilities of the 2nd SS Panzer Corps. In his defense, he would only be the first of several Allied generals in the fall of 1944 to underestimate the fighting power of the *Wehrmacht*.[42] Third, the operation was hurriedly planned, with authorization being given on September 10 and execution performed on September 17. This was a rather short planning period, to say the least, considering that this was the largest airborne drop in World War II. Fourth, the planners based the operation on the success of interconnected events. Any one failure would doom the operation.

Failure came in many forms. The failure to schedule a second drop on the first day of the operation resulted in the paratroopers having insufficient combat power to achieve their objectives. Operational security was compromised when Kurt Student's forces captured a copy of Operation MARKET GARDEN's plans. This error was entirely American because, against orders, an American officer had a full copy of the MARKET GARDEN orders with him on the glider ride that claimed his life. This compromised the entire operation. Perhaps the most serious error was dropping the British 1st Airborne too far from its objectives, compounded by the narrow corridor of advance for the British XXX Corps.

Any one of these issues could have affected the success of this operation. Taken together, they proved to be a recipe for disaster. In his memoirs, Montgomery acknowledges several of these errors, but it is interesting that the first problem he noted was that full priority for logistics was not given to Operation MARKET GARDEN as Eisenhower wished. Using Chester Wilmot as an authority, he indicates that Patton had really not been stopped on the Meuse, and that full priority for operations had not been given to Dempsey and Courtney Hodges, commander of the U.S. 1st Army, both important commanders on the Allied left.[43] This provides some credence to Montgomery's claims, but it is small credence indeed. Montgomery concludes that if he had the logistical support from the operation's inception, he would have succeeded, despite his admitted errors.[44] His most intriguing comment is included in his immediate post war book where he stated that the operation "was 90 percent successful."[45] Given that the stated objectives for this operation, which were not achieved, and the fact that the British 1st Airborne Division had been wrecked, it is difficult to understand how anyone could make such a statement.

Though failing in its operational objective, Operation MARKET GARDEN did focus Allied attention to opening Antwerp; Montgomery's "90 percent success" had, in reality, created a salient that had to be defended and may have diverted forces to the effort. But it was indeed fortunate for the Allies that the Germans did not have the available strength to make this salient a target for counterattack.

ENDNOTES – CHAPTER 6

1. Frederick Browning, as quoted in Cornelius Ryan, *A Bridge Too Far*," New York: Simon and Schuster, 1974, p. 9.

2. Charles B. MacDonald, "The Decision To Launch Operation Market Garden," in Kent Roberts Greenfield, ed., *Command Decisions*, Washington, DC: Office of the Chief of Military History, 1960, p. 432.

3. As he stated, " . . . (it) was our imperative need for the large port of Antwerp, absolutely essential to us logistically before any deep penetration in strength could be made into Germany." Dwight D. Eisenhower, *Report by The Supreme Commander To the Combined Chiefs Of Staff On The Operations In Europe of the Allied Expeditionary Force 6 June 1944 to 8 May 1945*, Washington DC: U.S. Army Center of Military History, 1994, p. 62.

4. Williamson Murray and Allan R. Millett, *A War To Be Won: Fighting the Second World War*, Cambridge, MA: The Belknap Press of Harvard University, 2000, p. 427.

5. Stanley P. Hirshson, *General Patton: A Soldier's Life*, New York: Harper-Collins, 2002, p. 529.

6. *Ibid.*, p. 528.

7. Roland G. Ruppenthal, "Logistics and the Broad Front Strategy" in Greenfield, *Command Decisions*, p. 423.

8. Field Marshal Lord Alanbrooke, *War Diaries, 1939-1945*, Alex Danchev and Daniel Todman, eds., Berkeley, CA: University of California Press 2001, pp. 343, 363, 677, among numerous others. In his diaries on p. 352, he is very clear, stating, ". . . it is equally clear that Ike knows nothing about strategy and is quite unsuited for the post of Supreme commander as far as running the strategy of the war is concerned."

9. Anthony Farrar-Hockley, *Airborne Carpet Operation Market Garden*, New York: Ballantine Books, 1969, p. 17.

10. Peter Mansoor, *The G.I. Offensive in Europe: The Triumph of American Infantry Divisions, 1941-1945*, Lawrence, KS: The University of Kansas Press, 1999, p. 36.

11. Omar Bradley, *A Soldier's Story*, New York: Henry Holt and Company, 1951, pp. 445-46.

12. Mansoor, *The GI Offensive in Europe*, p. 180.

13. It is only fair to note that at a meeting between Eisenhower and Montgomery on September 10, the former admits he ". . . authorized [Montgomery] to defer the clearing out of the Antwerp approaches in an effort to sieze the bridgehead [over the Rhine in the Arnhem region] I wanted." Dwight D. Eisenhower, *Crusade in Europe*, New York: Doubleday, 1948, p. 307. Still, Montgomery's eyes were focused on the operation he wished to stage, rather than the final clearing of the port area.

14. Charles B. MacDonald, *The Siegfried Line Campaign*, Washington, DC: U.S. Army Center of Military History, 1963, p. 119.

15. *Ibid*. It is important to note that, after Normandy, a total of 18 separate airborne operations had been planned, five of which were in the final stages, before Allied troops reached the German border. The rapid advance caused each one to be scrubbed before execution.

16. Alfred D. Chandler and Steven Ambrose, eds., *The Papers of Dwight D. Eisenhower: The War Years*, Vol. V, Baltimore, MD: Johns Hopkins Press, 1970, p. 2128.

17. Farrar-Hockley, *Airborne Carpet Operation Market Garden*, p. 22.

18. Operation COMET was conceived in the latter days of August and was cancelled on September 10. On the same day, Montgomery approached Eisenhower with the strengthened plan which became known as Operation MARKET GARDEN. MacDonald, *The Siegfried Line Campaign*, p. 120.

19. Carlo D'Este, *Eisenhower: A Soldier's Life*, New York: Henry Holt and Company, 2002, p. 607.

20. American military leadership at the time, however, would likely not have concurred with the authors' assessment. Giving logistical priority to the British by allowing Montgomery to stage his own pet offensive was regarded by some as a prime example of Eisenhower's weakness. He too easily deferred to the British.

21. Clayton K. S. Chun, *Thunder Over the Horizon: From V-2 Rockets to Ballistic Missiles*, Westport, CT: Praeger Press, 2006, p. 52.

22. A. D. Harvey, *Arnhem*, London, UK: Cassel, 2001, p. 39.

23. John Terraine *The Right of the Line*, Hertfordshire, UK: Wordsworth, 1997, p. 670.

24. Harvey, *Arnhem*, p. 51.

25. Ryan, p. 179.

26. Murray and Millett, *A War to be Won*, p. 440.

27. W. F. K. Thompson, "Operation Market Garden," in Philip de Ste. Croix, ed., *Airborne Operations*, New York: Crescent Books, 1978, p. 112.

28. James Gavin, *On To Berlin: Battles of an Airborne Commander, 1943-1946*, New York: The Viking Press, 1978, p. 150.

29. Harvey, *Arnhem*, p. 43.

30. Stephen Badsey, *Arnhem 1944: Operation 'MARKET GARDEN,'* London, UK: Osprey, 1993, p. 27.

31. Peter Harclerode, *Arnhem: A Tragedy of Errors*, London, UK: Caxton, 1994, p. 37.

32. *Ibid.*, p. 39.

33. MacDonald, *The Siegfried Line Campaign*, p. 137.

34. Farrar-Hockley, *Airborne Carpet Operation Market Garden*, p. 72.

35. U.S. Army Air Forces, IXth Troop Carrier Command, "Air Invasion of Holland: IX Troop Carrier Command Report on Operation Market," January 1945, p. 80.

36. The U.S. Air Force, *USAF Airborne Operations: World War II and the Korean War*, Washington DC: USAF Historical Division, 1962, p. 60.

37. Harvey, *Arnhem*, p. 56.

38. *Ibid.*, p. 65.

39. MacDonald, *The Siegfried Line Campaign*, p. 144.

40. *Ibid.*, p. 156.

41. Thompson, *Operation Market Garden*, p. 121.

42. Bernard Montgomery, *The Memoirs of the Viscount Montgomery of Alamein, K.G.*, New York: The World Publishers, 1958, p. 266.

43. Chester Wilmot, *The Struggle For Europe*, Old Saybrook, CT: Konecky and Konecky, 1952, pp. 528-530. Wilmot discusses in some detail the supply situation and the fact that full priority had not actually been given to Montgomery's effort, and attributes this to the failure of the American leadership to concentrate the efforts of its forces.

44. Montgomery, *Memoirs*, pp. 266-267.

45. Field Marshal the Viscount Montgomery of Alamein, *Normandy to the Baltic*, Boston, MA: Houghton Mifflin Publishing, 1948, p 153. Wilmot, previously cited, states that "This claim is difficult to support unless the success of the operation is judged merely in terms of the number of bridges captured." (p. 153)

CHAPTER 7

THE HÜRTGEN CAMPAIGN

> Unlike other battles in Europe so far, we sacrificed our ground mobility, our tactical air support, and we chose to fight the Germans under conditions entirely to their advantage.[1]
>
> Major General James M. Gavin

BACKGROUND

As the third week of September 1944 ended, Allied armies had not advanced past the prewar German borders, and parts of Holland had yet to be liberated.[2] The Allied problem with supply had slightly improved because of Operation ANVIL/DRAGOON and the seizure of Marseilles and Toulon, France, but the final resolution of the supply problem still eluded Allied commanders. At least a part of this problem was because of the priority that Eisenhower had originally attached to Antwerp, Belgium, which had fallen by the wayside due to Operation MARKET GARDEN. Throughout September, Eisenhower regularly prodded Montgomery to finish the Antwerp operation, but his authorization of Operation MARKET GARDEN clearly undermined large-scale operations against the Germans holding the Scheldt Estuary. Thus, Allied leaders consigned Antwerp to the status of an unusable port, even though its docks and facilities were in good condition. When Operation MARKET GARDEN failed, the priority for British forces returned to the task of clearing the Scheldt Estuary and opening the port. Still, Antwerp was not functional until late November because the German control of the Scheldt Estuary totally negated Allied possession of Antwerp.

After Operation MARKET GARDEN, American and British forces had to clear German forces out of the Scheldt area. This effort did not commence until October 2, 1944.[3] Montgomery was only willing to dedicate the 1st Canadian Army to the task, an army that consisted of only two corps. Compounding the problem, the Canadians did not receive the necessary priority for supply to allow them to accomplish this task.[4] In early October, Eisenhower became more insistent with Montgomery to take Antwerp. In a letter to Marshall on October 15, Eisenhower was able to report:

> We are having a sticky time in the North, but Montgomery at last has seen the light and is concentrating toward his west, left flank in order to clear up the Antwerp situation.[5]

The Allies were also confronting an additional problem. German resistance was increasing. A number of factors contributed to the ability of German units to resist. The *Wehrmacht* had suffered tremendous losses in both manpower and equipment throughout 1944, but by September, the area that German units had to defend had been substantially constricted. From late 1943 into the first half of 1944, Albert Speer's reorganization of Germany's war industry had produced significant results. German production of airframes, tanks, and even small arms reached its peak. Manpower was also increased, since September, by a decree from Adolf Hitler, the *Volksturm* organization, the People's Army, was established mobilizing males from 16-60 to defend the Reich's borders.[6] *Volkssturm* soldiers were not given the level of training that regular army soldiers received, and they lacked heavy weapons systems to support their units. Still, these new soldiers were additional resources, which provided the German Army with additional combat power. Finally, the German soldier was defending his home terrain, a factor that tended to stiffen resistance. Despite the Allied CBO and the German losses on all fronts, the German soldier remained a formidable opponent. Operation MARKET GARDEN provided a hint of this capability; it would become even more evident in a place called the Hürtgen Forest.

Even as Montgomery was attempting to regain the priority that he had for Operation MARKET GARDEN, Bradley, commander of the 12th Army Group on his southern shoulder, pondered the potential strategies that he thought were available to Eisenhower:

> (1) He could dig in with his 54 divisions across the 500 mile Allied front that now extended from the North Sea to the Swiss border. By postponing a November offensive he could wait until the following spring when a host of fresh U.S. divisions and a vast reserve of tonnage at Antwerp would insure him sufficient resources to strike a knockout blow by winter 1945;

> (2) Or, he could start a November offensive with the troops he already possessed and bank on adequate logistical support through existing supply lines.[7]

According to Bradley's analysis, a cessation of Allied operations would afford the Germans with the opportunity to strengthen their defenses, to better train their new recruits, and to buildup the necessary war supplies, which would result in even tougher resistance to Allied advances. The key western German defense position, the Siegfried Line, was largely intact, and German jet fighter production was underway. Without Allied pressure, time would only allow the Germans to reconstitute their forces. Throughout the remainder of the year, Eisenhower continued to promote the broad front approach, a strategy of general advance, which would keep consistent pressure all along the line and prevent the Germans from reorganizing their defense. Eisenhower, however, had to face continued criticism from some of his subordinates about his strategy. Beginning with Operation COBRA, two of Eisenhower's senior officers, Patton and Montgomery, pushed for a change in strategy. They advocated for sharp focused thrusts against the Germans rather than a linear approach. The grumbling over Eisenhower's strategy continued into the fall of 1944 and winter 1944-45.

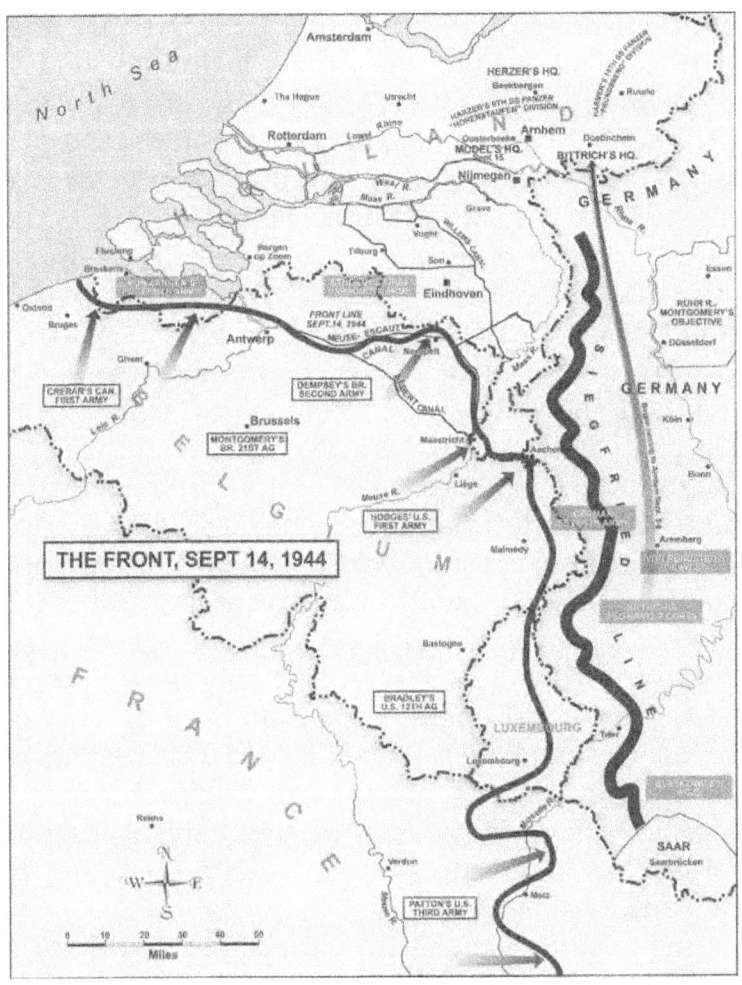

Map 7-1. The Western Front, Fall 1944, about the Time of Operation MARKET GARDEN.

Both subordinate commanders could not dissuade Eisenhower from his broad front strategy because it exerted heavy pressure on the limited German resources. Additionally, an appraisal of the battle maps from that period demonstrates that Eisenhower was unable to attack the Germans across their entire front. A review of ongoing operations in the fall of 1944 shows that Montgomery was holding the Operation MARKET GARDEN salient. He also had the specified task of attempting to clear several pockets of German resistance in Holland. Bradley's 12th Army Group had two major operations in progress in 1st Army's area: attacks against Aachen, Germany, and the division level assaults in the Hürtgen Forest. In short, the 1st Army was oriented toward the northern end of the Ruhr and the North German Plain. Further south, Patton's 3rd Army was engaged in an arduous campaign to take the fortress of Metz. The campaign to take Metz would cost Patton considerable casualties and did not afford him with the ability to engage in maneuver warfare, which was his specialty. There existed in the terrain between the 1st and 3rd Armies, a lightly held area where the 12th Army Group did not have sufficient strength to stage any type of offensive action. Despite both the 1st and 3rd Armies being under Bradley's command, the two armies attacked in a fashion that was in no way mutually supporting; rather they pursued operations that were more like two uncoordinated attacks.

In the south, a new Army Group, the 6th commanded by U.S. Army Lieutenant General Jacob L. Devers, was adding significantly to German woes and Allied fortunes. Allied units with aggressive American commanders and more than adequate supplies pushed the Germans through southern France and into the age-old disputed area known as Alsace. One notable element in Devers' command was the American 7th Army commanded by Lieutenant General Alexander Patch. During this time, French troops belonging to the 2nd French Armored Division and assigned to

Patch's Army, elated the population of France in late November by taking back the revered Alsatian City of Strasbourg from the Germans. Despite its strength, the 7th Army, was unable to clear the entire area of Germans, since the latter were able to hold on to the "Colmar Pocket" throughout the remainder of the year. Nonetheless, the 6th Army Group's operations added pressure on the beleaguered German defenders, but not without a cost to the Allies. The 6th Army Group's operations further added to the broad front and stretched the limited logistical resources even further.

Despite Devers' success, he, and for that matter his 6th Army Group, would never receive the accolades or command emphasis like that of the 12th or 21st Army Groups. At least some of this was likely due to personal animosity. In the summer of 1943, Devers, who was a West Point classmate of Patton, was serving as commander of American Forces in Britain. In this role, he blocked Eisenhower's request to transfer four medium bomber groups from Britain to North Africa. Devers was never in Eisenhower's close circle of friends, and crossing Eisenhower on this request did not in any way improve relations. For the remainder of the war, Eisenhower tended to be overly critical and certainly cool to Devers. He did not seem to value Devers' advice, as compared to that given by Bradley. In the European Campaign, Devers and the 6th Army Group tended to be a backwater of the overall effort.

As German resistance increased and a solid German defense line formed, Eisenhower faced a quandary. Where and how could he stage the necessary attacks to maintain Allied momentum and drive the Germans back into their heartland? There were no flanks to turn; a vertical envelopment would have been desirable, but where could Allied forces accomplish this task, and who could punch a hole through German lines to link up with those light forces? Besides, both British and American airborne forces were not available since Allied commanders had not recalled them from the Operation MARKET GARDEN area, and the two American divisions would be in combat there until early November. Patton was heavily involved in the Metz area and Montgomery's 21st had as their priority the finishing the Antwerp task. Seemingly, the most logical location for a new offensive was directly north of the Ruhr in the U.S. 1st Army's area of responsibility. The area that dominated Bradley's thoughts and those of Lieutenant General Courtney Hodges appeared to be the Stolberg corridor in Germany, which could lead U.S. forces to the Rhine. This corridor led to a great portion of the country suitable for maneuver warfare and could lead to a single wing envelopment of the Ruhr industrial sector; or if the American commanders so desired, a shot at Berlin. For the American Army, the hope for a rush to the Rhine River in the fall of 1944 seemed to center on Hodges and his 1st Army.

The Battle for Aachen.

The initial task that Allied troops had to confront was the penetration of the Siegfried line, a belt of defensive fortifications that started at the Swiss border and stretched up to the vicinity of the Dutch border. The defensive line consisted of anti-tank Dragon's teeth, barbed wire, mines, and pillboxes, a formidable fixed defense. An equally arduous task facing the 1st Army was the taking of the city of Aachen. This was the first major German city American troops would attack. Aachen held an allure for American commanders. Regrettably, it also had great value for the Germans as well; Aachen was *Aix-la-Chapelle*, the city of Charlemagne, an historic capital that its defenders had to hold at all costs. Due to its significance, Hitler ordered that the German military defend the town of 160,000 to the last man.[8]

The 1st Army plan was logical given the task at hand, encircling the city through a double wing envelopment. Aachen was not heavily fortified. Still, Aachen was a medieval city that made it ideal for defense; few sensible commanders would want to stage a direct attack that would result in bitter house-to-house fighting. Thus, the plan called for Corlett's XIX Corps to break through the Siegfried line and when it reached the vicinity of the German town of Würselen, it was to turn south in preparation for meeting the U.S. VII Corps. The VII Corps was also to have punched its own hole through the Siegfried line south of Aachen. When it was east of Aachen's environs, its units were to swing north and link up with the XIX Corps near Würselen. On October 2, 1944, the Americans launched their offensive. In the first 5 days, American units were successful in making substantial progress. The following week, the Germans were able to prevent the Americans from linking up as planned near Würselen. Still, on October 16, the encirclement was complete and for the next 5 days, American units hammered the defenders from both the ground and the air. The city surrendered on October 21 and the Allies were rewarded with the capture of the first major German city of the war. Aachen was a shattered hulk. At the same time, the two U.S. lead divisions, the 1st and the 30th, had also taken substantial losses in their rifle companies. The Allies breeched the Siegfried line, but the rising losses meant that Allied strength was declining.

While the battle for Aachen was being fought, the 1st Army was further dissipating its strength in another offensive. A series of attacks in a wooded area south of Aachen and north of the Ardennes, the Hürtgen Forest, would return the U.S. Army to warfare reminiscent of World War I. The attacks on the Hürtgen Forest remain one of the most puzzling episodes in the European Campaign. In the official history of the 1st Army, "the original source of the idea of clearing the forest cannot be determined."[9] The 1st Army Commander, Lieutentant General Hodges, Major General William B. Kean (Hodges' Chief of Staff), and VIIth Corps commander Major General Joseph Collins were all concerned about the threat that a German force could pose to the flank of the VIIth Corps as it advanced up the Stolberg corridor. To protect the flank, Hodges and his VIIth Corps commander proposed to clear the forested area of German units in an operation strangely reminiscent of the Argonne Forest in 1918.[10] In spite of all of the information available today, it is still difficult to understand why the Americans waged a battle there. Part of the problem was that the objectives changed during the course of the battle; and after the war senior officers who were involved created a fiction about the campaign and its objectives.

As the campaign continued from September into October, a realization seemed to emerge that the Roer Dams might be important military objectives. The Americans had to take the Hürtgen Forest, because it was the gateway to the Roer Dam complex. It was not until the first week of November that the dams had been clearly identified as a threat, and thus that they had to be captured.[11] If these dams were not taken, then the Germans could blow them and flood the area where 1st Army elements intended to advance.[12] Now in the second month of the campaign, the Roer Dams had become the primary objective, rather than that of preventing a German incursion into the VIIth Corps' flank.[13]

Conventional military wisdom, then and now, emphasizes that it is unwise to attack at a time and place where the enemy force holds a clear advantage. The American campaign in the Hürtgen Forest ignored this traditional military wisdom because in this dank forest, the defender held every advantage. A study published by the U.S. Army's Combat Studies Institute noted, "The configuration of the terrain which had sharply defined roller coaster like ridges and valleys, and gorges compounded the stupefying effects of fighting in the woods."[14] This naturally defensible terrain contained numerous well-prepared bunkers and pillboxes. Forests dominated the terrain and the road network was often poor in some areas and nonexistent in others. The German defenders were defending a foreboding forest, a manmade forest, dark and dense, planted before the war. One veteran of the campaign, Ralph Johnson from the 28th Division Service Company, described it this way:

> The Huertgen Forest was a dank dark and impossible place; a pine forest with trees so thick that the sun did not penetrate until about 10:00 a.m. and disappeared again at 3:00 p.m. The ground underfoot was 10 inches deep in wet pine needles and moss.[15]

Such terrain was hardly the place one would expect the most mobile, the most mechanized army in the European Theater to attack since it negated the key advantages of mobility and tactical airpower, which the U.S. Army had available.

The failure to understand the problems attributable to the terrain may have been just one part of a larger failure by the 1st, 5th, and 7th Army headquarters.

The Allies believed that the German Army was on the verge of collapse, and that the end of the war was very near. Granted, the German Army had taken massive losses, however, its soldiers were no longer fighting in France; they were now defending their home. What had happened to Allied armies in Operation MARKET GARDEN and in the stiff defense of Aachen failed to teach the Allies very little about German capabilities. As American Army planners prepared for attacking into the Hürtgen, intelligence officers thought that the forest was held by weak units composed of fatigued soldiers and young boys. Granted, in September when the 9th Infantry Division's attack was launched, the German 353rd Infantry Division had a hodgepodge of units in the Hürtgen which were second tier troops. By October, when operations in the Hürtgen began in earnest, the 275th Infantry Division was responsible for its defense. Staff officers did not regard this division as a crack German unit. One author noted, "What the German division lacked in combat power, it recouped in the advantages the forest gave to the defender."[16] 1st Army planners failed to recognize that even second tier units can perform extremely well in terrain that is highly defendable. Regrettably, for far too many American Soldiers, it would take two bitter lessons, the Hürtgen and the Ardennes, to reinforce the fact that the Germans were not yet defeated.

The Experience of the 9th Infantry Division.

The first division to attack into the Hürtgen was the 9th Infantry Division, commanded by Major General Louis A. Craig. Collins had hoped to punch a hole in the Siegfried line before the onset of winter. He ordered Craig to clear the northern section of the Hürtgen and take the villages of Hürtgen and Kleinhau. By so doing, the 9th would prevent a German attack into the flank of the 3rd Armored Division which was attacking south of Aachen into the Stolberg area.

Craig's attack jumped off on September 14. Even though the American division made progress by taking the villages of Zweifall and Schevenhütte, the 9th was tasked by their higher headquarters with competing priorities. Two of Craig's regiments were reassigned to assist the attack on the Aachen suburb of Stolberg. Thus, the 9th's attack became the responsibility of only one regiment, the 60th Infantry. As Craig's attack into the Hürtgen was in progress, on the Allied left flank two other operations were ongoing, the attack into Aachen and Operation MARKET GARDEN, all focusing on the terrain north of the Ruhr River. Fighting by 9th Division elements continued into the third week of September, seemingly with the original objective of the 9th's action being obscured by a series of tactical milestones that became the norm in the dank forest.

In early October, the attention of the 9th was again focused on the Hürtgen as Collins ordered the resumption of the attack, this time with two regiments. Collins retained the 47th Regiment for support to the 3rd Armored Division. At this stage of the operation, the 9th Infantry Division's G-2 analyzed the region and suggested that the Roer Dams were important. However, the 1st Army staff dismissed his report.[17] Instead, the VIIth Corps ordered two regiments from the 9th Infantry Division to attack through the forest and seize Vossenack and Kommerscheidt, with the ultimate objective of the town of Schmidt. The attack began shortly before noon on October 6. Mud, the dark forest, bunkers, and both mortar and artillery fire caused the attack to falter. The American forces did slog through the miserable terrain, with infantry units finally reaching the outskirts of the town of Germeter

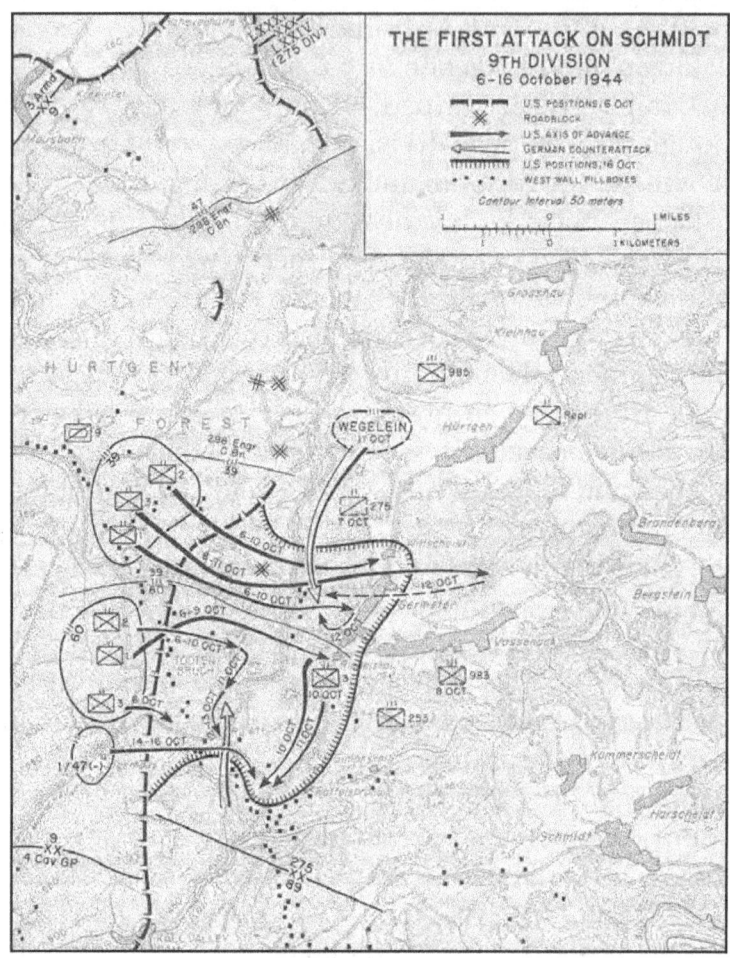

Source: U.S. Army Center of Military History.

Map 7-2. The 9th Infantry's Attack.

on October 9. The two regiments had little chance of reaching either Vossenack or Schmidt. Bitter fighting ensued for the next 4 days with attacks, counterattacks, and reinforcements arriving on both sides.

By October 13, a classic stalemate had emerged on the battlefield. The goal of the division remained the major road junction in the town of Schmidt, but this objective was far beyond their reach. Altogether, elements of the 9th Division were in the Hürtgen Forest for almost 30 days. When the division left the front, it had suffered some 4,500 battle and nonbattle casualties. Despite the sacrifices of its Soldiers, it had only gained a little over 3,500 yards of forest.[18] Even more disturbing, it had not cleared the Hürtgen of German troops, neither had it taken the key town of Schmidt. Given the unusual and puzzling American interest in this area, the Germans continued to add reinforcements for the defense of the Hürtgen.

The failure of the American drive into the Hürtgen Forest was only one of the problems that faced the 12th Army Group, and the U.S. 1st Army in particular. In October, the 1st Army was dangerously low in supplies. Ammunition was in short supply and, in particular, the limited number of artillery rounds caused considerable concern as it resulted in a restriction of support to troops in contact with the enemy.[19] Shortages, however, went beyond ammunition. 1st Army had limited supplies of rations, trucks, and tanks. Part of the problem was the transportation of supplies, since Antwerp was not yet open, and it was a long distance from Normandy to the Hürtgen. Eisenhower's desire to keep up the pressure along the front, and Bradley's direction to have both the 1st and 3rd Armies in an attack mode contributed to significant shortages for 1st Army.[20]

The 28th Infantry Division Attack: Background.

Following the failure of the VIIth Corps to seize the stated objectives in the Hürtgen, the second, and in many respects the most puzzling, phase of the Hürtgen fighting was initiated. This phase was a part of a plan devised by the Headquarters, 12th Army

Group, which called for an attack through the Stolberg corridor designed to put American troops on the west bank of the Rhine River and, if American troops were fortunate enough to seize a bridgehead over the Rhine River. Hodges' 1st Army was responsible for conducting this attack, and two Army corps were designated to provide the necessary firepower, the Vth and VIIth Corps. Collin's corps would take the main effort. The VIIth Corps was to attack the northern part of the Hürtgen through the Stolberg corridor. Corps boundaries shifted in late October and Gerow had the responsibility for the next attack. The Vth Corps leadership directed the 28th Infantry Division to initiate a supporting attack for the VIIth Corps main effort. The 28th began moving into an area east of Rott, Germany, on October 25, replacing the exhausted 9th Infantry Division. The Vth Corps headquarters gave the 28th the following direction:

1. Relieve the 9th Infantry division on October 26-27.
2. Prepare to attack the Germans, with the significant objectives being Kommerscheidt and Schmidt.[21]

Unlike the 9th Infantry Division, the 28th was able to employ all three of its regiments, actually regimental combat teams (RCT), to achieve its objectives. Each RCT from the 28th would have specific objectives.[22] The 109th RCT would attack toward and capture the town of Hürtgen. The division staff sent the 110th RCT to advance toward the town of Simonskall. The third RCT, the 112th, was to secure the ridge that led to Vossenack. The overall objective for the 28th, however, was to secure the town of Schmidt and draw German attention and reserves away from the VIIth

Corps main effort. Again, as designed, the 28th's action was supposed to be a supporting attack rather than the main effort.[23]

The Vth Corps commander and his staff developed the overall plan for the 28th Division's attack. All available evidence seems to indicate that the 28th Infantry Division commander, Major General Norman "Dutch" Cota and his staff, had little input on the plan, and Cota objected to the plan. The Corps staff ignored his objections.[24] Despite the issues, problems surfaced. The VIIth Corps was unable to get prepared to conduct the main effort on November 5, as initially planned. The Corps staff rescheduled the attack for November 10 and then postponed it for an additional 6 days. Despite the VII Corps delays, the Corps did not cancel or reschedule the 28th Infantry Division's drive. Instead, it began as ordered on November 2, even though it was supposed to support a main effort that, by that time, was nonexistent. This meant that on November 2, the 28th's attack was the only push along a 27-mile section of the front and for only a few days. For a few days, the division's attack was the only one on the 170-mile Western Front.[25] This allowed the Germans to focus their attention on a solitary division action, rather than on the collective elements of two corps.

As was typical of many major U.S. offensives in the European Campaign, the 28th Infantry Division staff believed that they would receive significant air and artillery support, but such plans merely demonstrated army and corps planner's ignorance of the Hürtgen's terrain. The heavy forest prohibited accurate close air support and, for that matter, the forest and the terrain complicated observed artillery fire. In addition, at the time the division commander wanted to attack, the weather was poor. Planners did recognize the tough task assigned to the 28th, and the Vth Corps did provide additional assets to the 28th. The 707th Tank Battalion, equipped with Sherman M4A1 tanks, and the 893rd Tank Destroyer Battalion, equipped with M10 tank destroyers, provided additional firepower on the ground. Given the strength of the German position and the terrain, the 117th Engineer Group, three artillery battalions, and a 4.2-inch mortar battalion were attached to the division as well.

The 28th's Full Division Attack.

Even though the combat power of the 28th Infantry Division was significantly enhanced as a result of these attachments, the attack plan developed by the VIIth Corps diminished the strength of this ill-fated division because it dissipated, rather than concentrated the division's combat strength. The plan called for the main effort to be conducted by the 112th RCT, but the corps' scheme of maneuver required the other two RCTs to attack in different directions than the 112th. The 109th RCT attacked north toward Hürtgen, an entirely different axis. The 110th was to attack in the opposite direction from the 109th, with its geographical objective the town of Simonskall. The corps plan was at least in part affected by the experiences of the 9th Infantry Division whose units had suffered from a withering counterattack on their northern flank by *Kampfgruppe* Wegelein on October 11. To prevent the potential of a similar flank attack, division staff put the RCTs in motion on both flanks of the 112th. This plan meant that the 28th's three regimental attacks were not mutually supporting. The principle of concentrating combat power and mass, on a clearly defined, decisive, and obtainable objective seemed to be a foreign concept to the corps planners.

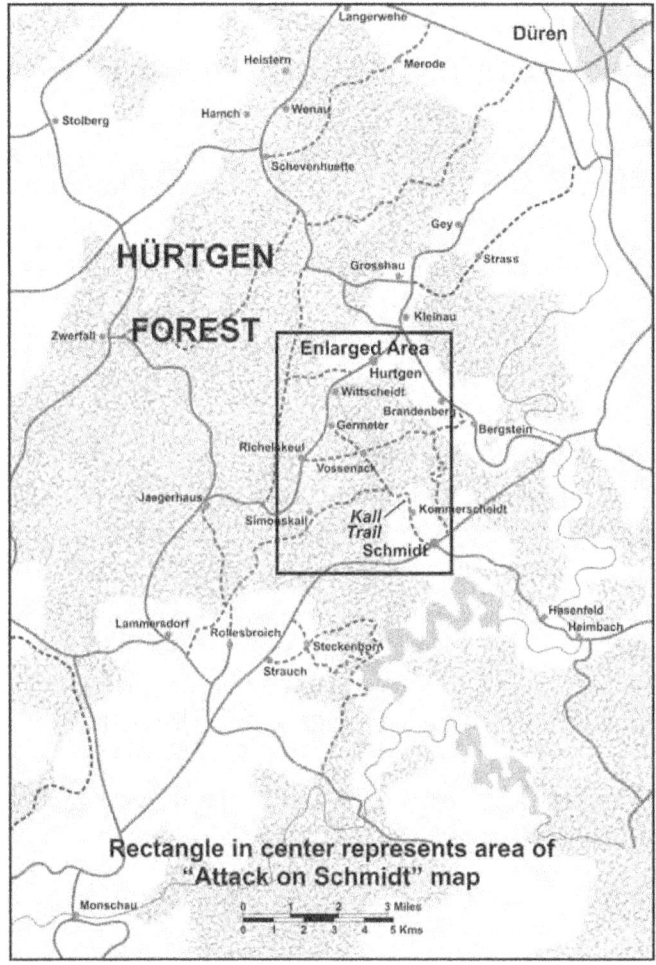

Source: U.S. Army War College.

Map 7-3. This map shows the Hürtgen area in general and the key locations for the Hürtgen campaign.

Unknown to Cota and his higher headquarters, the three RCTs, all in motion from the November 2 to 4, became realistic players in a German war game. When the 28th attacked, German Army Group B, commanded by Model, and his senior commanders were at army headquarters in Cologne, Germany. The senior officers were playing a war game based on a scenario where American troops attacked toward Schmidt in the Hürtgen Forest. When an actual attack occurred, Model detached a couple of his key commanders to take charge of operations on the ground, and the remainder stayed in Cologne, playing the exercise based on realistic events in progress. Given American interest in continuing operations into this forested area, Model ordered the 116th Panzer Division, the "Greyhounds," to advance toward the 28th from the north and the German 89th Infantry Division to move up from the south. As German reinforcements advanced, the situation rapidly deteriorated for the 1st Army, and especially for the 28th Infantry Division. German strength was building and, to complicate the situation, the 28th's attack had the attention of Model, well known as an officer skilled in defensive strategy. From the start of the operation, the 28th Division was in serious trouble as the result of a flawed corps plan and an increasingly powerful enemy force.

Nonetheless, at 9:00 am on November 2, the 28th Infantry Division began its attack. The main avenue of advance for the 109th RCT was in a heavily forested area parallel to the road that led to Hürtgen. Initially, this RCT's 1st Battalion made good progress, but its 3rd Battalion stalled and made very little progress. As was standard practice, the Germans responded with two well-organized counterattacks that the Americans repulsed. By November 6, the 109th was essentially in a static position, and the Germans, who had excellent pre-sighted artillery fire, continued hitting them with tree bursts that rained shards and tree fragments on the Soldiers. The 109th attempted to renew its attack, but the Germans, laid down a heavy carpet of fire on the 109th flank making any further attacks far too costly.

The 28th's second RCT, the 110th, fared little better when it began its attack in coordination with the 109th. The 110th struck through a heavily wooded area that German engineers had seeded with mines, booby-traps, barbed wire entanglements, and well-emplaced bunkers. Despite early Army estimates about the limited capabilities of the German defenders, the 110th faced determined and well-prepared German troops. The American effort became a repeat of the 1918 battle in the Argonne Forest, complete with the accompanying casualties. For 3 long days, the 110th fought hard to accomplish its assigned mission. By November 5, German defenses were still firmly holding their positions. By this time, the 110th RCT had taken heavy casualties and was no longer an effective fighting unit.

The 28th's main effort, however, was the attack by the 112th RCT. The task assigned to the 112th, commanded by Lieutenant Colonel Carl Peterson, was not easy. He assigned his three battalions a separate task that dissipated the 112th's strength, a problem that was inherent in the overall division attack. Despite these factors, by November 3, it seemed likely that the 112th would accomplish its mission. Unlike the other two RCTs, this unit appeared to have made a clear breakthrough in the German defenses. By the end of the day, Peterson reported that his battalions had taken Kommerscheidt and Schmidt. Corps and Army headquarters had every reason to be pleased with the 28th's success and congratulated the division's headquarters for its achievement. Finally, it seemed that the 1st Army's plan to clean out the Hürtgen Forest was on track. The euphoria of a seemed victory, shared by the Division, Corps, and Army headquarters, obscured two very significant problems. First, the 112th's successful advance had essentially been an infantry operation with armor to follow. Thus, the infantry did not have the necessary heavy weapons to support its position. Second, the line of communication through this area of advance moved through an area known as the Kall Trail. Choosing this as a suitable line of communication demonstrated Vth Corps' ignorance of the terrain. The Kall Trail was at best a path, suitable only for the advance of a couple of infantrymen abreast and not for the movement of armor or heavy trucks.

Division officers attempted to get heavy weapons into Schmidt by sending a platoon of five tanks to reinforce the weary 112th's infantry. Only three tanks reached the 112th due to the poor road conditions. At about 9:00 am on November 4, as the limited armor assets approached the town, the Germans had already seized the initiative and had counterattacked from three directions. The German pressure mounted and was relentless. On the following day, German artillery and mortar fire rained down on the G.I.s. In order to pressure the defenders, the Germans attacked the 112th's positions about every 4 hours, fatiguing the infantry beyond their endurance. To complicate the situation, German troops were regularly operating in the Kall Gorge, threatening to cut the American line of communications. At this point, the 112th's defenses

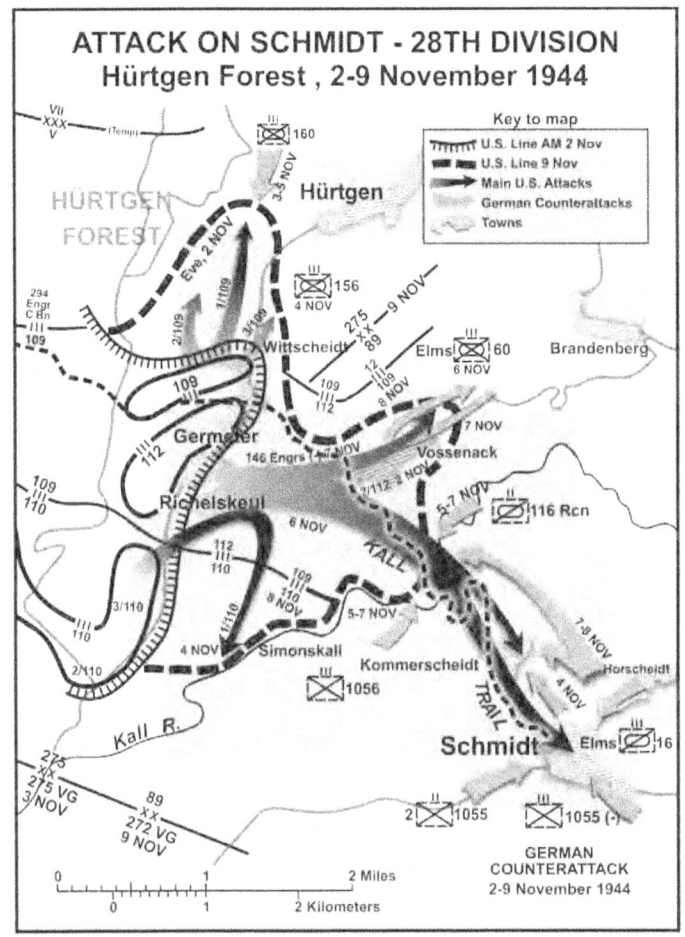

Source: U.S. Army War College.

Map 7-4. Showing the Area where 28th Division attacked.

simply began to fall apart. The limited armor permitted American forces to hold on to the nearby town of Kommerscheidt, but the 28th could not hold Schmidt.

The Corps staff had designated Schmidt as a decisive point, and "Dutch" Cota had received accolades from both Corps and Army headquarters for taking it. As a result, Cota was unwilling to allow it to remain in German hands without a fight. In succession, Cota created two task forces. The first, Task Force Ripple commanded by Lieutenant Colonel Richard W. Ripple, attempted to retake Schmidt. The weather was poor on November 6 and prevented observed artillery fire or close air support. This support could have helped the task force immeasurably, unfortunately, Task Force Ripple's attempt failed. At the same time, German panzers and artillery exerted pressure on Kommerscheidt that forced some American Soldiers to leave their positions and run to the rear. The defense managed to hold until November 7. On that day, the Germans unleashed a firestorm on the American defenders. German commanders followed this attack with a combined arms strike by panzer and infantry assets from the 89th Infantry Division. Under heavy pressure, more 112th infantry broke and left their positions. The Germans pushed the remaining G.I.s out of Kommerscheidt, and the remaining infantry took refuge outside the town in the surrounding woods.

Sometime in the November 5-7 time period, American officers became aware of another problem. Division, Corps, and Army headquarters did not have a clear understanding of the seriousness of the situation or the circumstances facing the American Soldiers in the dank woods. This was evident when Hodges first visited Cota's headquarters on November 5 and expressed considerable displeasure to the 28th's commander about his division's lack of progress.[26] No one thought it appropriate to note that the higher headquarters plan was at least in part responsible for the lack of progress. The shortcomings of the plan included the Corp's failure to concentrate forces, its ignorance of the terrain, and the failure to recognize the tough German resistance. Cota's determination to regain Schmidt and hold the terrain that the 28th Division had taken resulted in the creation on November 7 of Task Force Davis. Commanded by Cota's assistant division commander, Brigadier General George Davis was charged with retaking Schmidt. Task Force Davis never really had a chance. The units available for Davis' assigned task were badly battered and were insufficient to tackle the growing German strength in the Hürtgen. Cota's inability to hold Schmidt and achieve 1st Army's goals resulted in additional criticism. On November 8, Hodges severely dressed down Cota for his inability to keep track of his units in the Hürtgen and for the 28th's inability to achieve its goals.[27]

Davis' inability to get the task force attack off the ground and a frank situation report personally delivered by the 112th Commander, Lieutenant Colonel Peterson, about the status of American units in the field caused Cota to reevaluate the 28th's position. After considering the condition of his troops, he sent a request to Vth Corps Headquarters to allow his division to withdraw across the Kall River. As remnants of the 112th, 707th, and 893rd Tank Destroyer Battalions were withdrawing, the Germans continued to exact casualties from the survivors. The units completed the withdrawal between November 8 and 9.

The cost for the 28th Division had been staggering. From November 2-14, a division of 13,447 Soldiers had suffered 5,028 in cumulative losses.[28] The vast majority of these were in the division's rifle battalions where it lost the preponderance of its forces. For example, the 112th Infantry had 2,093 Soldiers killed, wounded, and missing. The attached 707th Tank Battalion lost 31 of its 52 M4 tanks. In all, the division and its attached units were exhausted and had to be relieved for reconstitution.[29]

Regrettably, the 28th Infantry Division would not be the last American division to be gutted in the still puzzling attack into the "green hell" of the Hürtgen; perhaps only the most famous, due to the numerous accounts concerning the Kall Trail and the battle for Schmidt.[30] Despite what had happened to the 9th Infantry Division and the 28th, Hodges persisted with attempts to take the Hürtgen. On November 19, Hodges ordered another division, this time the fresh 8th Infantry Division to relieve the exhausted 28th and attack on November 21. Corps staff provided the divisional goals based on specified geographical objectives, none of which related to the Roer Dams. Hodges pressured the division commander Major General Donald Stroh, much as he had Cota, until finally on November 27 the exhausted Stroh was relieved at his own request. In that brief period, the last week of November, the 8th Infantry Division suffered 1,092 battle casualties, including 154 officers and men killed in action and another 1,317 nonbattle casualties. They were able to take the town of Hürtgen, but neither the forest nor the dams were in U.S. hands.[31]

The fate of the 9th, 28th, and the 8th was also be shared by the 1st and 4th Infantry Divisions, units that were also thrown into single division attacks against a well-entrenched enemy force in highly defensible terrain. Corps and Army commanders fed them into the fray, one at a time, and each element suffered considerable casualties, with no advantage for the Allied cause. The fighting in the Hürtgen Forest did produce German casualties, but it did not destroy the German forces or their will to fight, as can be seen through the events of December 16 and the days following. The Hürtgen Forest remained in German hands until February 1945.

As November closed, given the determined German resistance facing two divisions in succession, the 1st Army intended to initiate another Operation COBRA style operation. This attack included a massive air assault by heavy bombers, and the planners designed the bombings to blast a path for U.S. troops so they could advance to the Rhine River. Thus, on November 7, Hodges attended a meeting with representatives from SHAEF, 12th Army Group, 9th Air Force, 1st Army, and the IX and XXIX Tactical Air Commands to finalize the air attacks. The plan called for 1,200 heavy bombers from the AAF's 8th Air Force to drop their loads on the German line facing the VIIth Corps. An equal number of aircraft from the RAF would hit selected Roer Valley cities, while medium bombers belonging to the IX Tactical Air Command would concentrate on German Army rear areas. As Collins' units moved forward, the IX aircraft would provide direct support for the advancing corps elements. Planners recalled the fratricide problems in Operation COBRA and planned the bombing runs to avoid American positions. On November 16, with the lavish air assets, VIIth Corps launched its offensive. Poor visibility once again robbed AAF planes of the desired accuracy, although, unlike Operation COBRA, the air strikes did not inflict serious casualties. Much like Operation OVERLORD, the damage to German defenses was minimal. In short, the leadership had failed to comprehend that strategic aircraft were designed for strategic bombing campaigns and should be used for the purpose intended, not to support tactical events.[32]

The Hürtgen in Retrospect.

As one considers the Hürtgen campaign and the horrendous casualties suffered there, one must ask the question: How did the Hürtgen attacks contribute to achieving the Army's objectives in the European Theater? The answer is simply—very little; a type of inertia on the part of the Corps, Army, and Army Group commanders seemed to drag unit after unit into this vortex with no one seriously asking why were they doing this. As months dragged on, Hodges, with Bradley's agreement, threw division after division into the wooded area, forgetting the casualties the Argonne Forest had cost Army divisions in 1918. A blind combativeness seemed to seize Bradley and Hodges causing them to ignore other options that would have helped to reach the Rhine River. Far better terrain existed in the 12th Army Group's area of responsibility, the Losheim Gap and the Monschau corridor, but no one seemed to recognize the potential for maneuver warfare using this favorable terrain. Had Bradley or Hodges initially recognized the potential threat of the Roer Dams, they could have conducted an offensive southeast of the Hürtgen Forest where the terrain was much more favorable for the attacking Allied divisions and certainly would have produced less casualties.

Some have noted incidental benefits from the Hürtgen campaign. In a recent study on the Hürtgen, Army historian Robert Rush postulates that this battle in the foreboding woods may have damaged the chance of success for the Ardennes offensive that began on December 16.[33] The Germans did suffer because of the drain of ammunition and fuel caused by operations in the Hürtgen, however, some German units, like the 116th Panzer Division, also suffered losses in the battle that depleted some of the *Wehrmacht's* offensive capabilities. One can hardly attribute the failure of the Ardennes offensive to the Hürtgen. Had the American Army conducted mobile operations in the Monschau Corridor or the Losheim Gap, the damage to a German counteroffensive would have been much more detrimental to the German war effort and with far less U.S. losses than those suffered in the vicious fighting in the Hürtgen.

Eisenhower's official report on European operations, released in 1946, provides a hint that senior leadership might have recognized the campaign was a mistake. The report discusses the campaign efforts to take Aachen and the Stolberg corridor, but mention of the Hürtgen is scant. The reader is left with the impression that the battle may not have occurred.[34] Despite the efforts of dedicated Soldiers in the Hürtgen, the U.S. Army entered a quagmire that its senior leaders refused to extricate themselves from. Eisenhower could have stopped it. Instead, he chose to let it continue, perhaps because it kept pressure on the German Army. This episode is strangely reminiscent of World War I where both French and British commanders conducted their battles from rear area headquarters, oblivious to the actual conditions at the front. A study of the literature available on the Hürtgen indicates that senior officers from Bradley to various division commanders in the 1st Army did not fully understand the conditions in the forest or the terrain where they ordered their troops to fight. Perhaps James M. Gavin best summarized the situation when he did a reconnaissance of the battlefield in early February 1945 and later stated:

The thought crossed my mind that the disaster that had befallen the 28th Division in the Kall River Valley might have had some relationship to the lack of understanding in the higher headquarters of what the actual situation on the ground was.[35]

Equally serious, the Hürtgen effort was not directly linked to the campaign's overall objectives. The changing rationale for attacking in this foreboding forest, with all of the senseless loss of life, means that even today, after over 60 years, the Hürtgen campaign remains puzzling. The Battle of the Hürtgen Forrest weakened a U.S. Army already short on infantrymen and made it less capable of immediately achieving the objectives of the campaign. It would also be the first of two episodes where Allied intelligence and Allied commanders tragically underestimated German capabilities.

ENDNOTES – CHAPTER 7

1. James M. Gavin, *On to Berlin: Battles of an Airborne Commander, 1943-1946*, New York: Viking Press, 1978, p. 268.

2. Is is acknowledged that there were a few exceptions to this statement. American patrols crossed into Germany at the end of the first week in September. Thus, American Soldiers were on German soil, but there were no major troop movements into Germany until the drive in October to capture Aachen.

3. The Canadians cleared the last Germans blocking Scheldt access on November 8. Finally, the Allies were able to secure a usable high volume port in northern France. The first Allied convoy would not dock there until November 28, a full 85 days after the British had taken the city of Antwerp.

4. Evidence points to the fact that Montgomery was not altogether keen on finishing the Antwerp operation; rather he seemed more interested in his sharp rapier-like thrust into the North German Plain. Montgomery's unwillingness to dedicate the supply resources to take this important port was revealed to Eisenhower by Admiral Bertram Ramsey, and at that stage Montgomery was specifically told to finish the job of opening the port. See Williamson Murray and Allen Millet, *A War to be Won: Fighting the Second World War*, Cambridge MA: Harvard University Press, 2000, p. 458.

5. Joseph P. Hobbs, ed., *Dear General: Eisenhower's Wartime Letters to Marshall*, Baltimore, MD: Johns Hopkins Press, 1999, p. 60.

6. The order establishing the *Volksturm* and additional correspondence on the subject from Heinrich Himmler and Martin Bormann can be found in Karl Pawlas,"Die Waffen des Deutshen Volksturms" ("The Weapons of the German Volksturms"), *Waffen Review*, 4th Quarter, No. 71, 1988, pp. 20-35.

7. Omar N. Bradley, *A Soldier's Story*, New York: Henry Holt and Company, 1951, p. 434. The reader should, of course, remember that this explanation is included in his postwar memoirs.

8. In many respects, the battle of Aachen started as a comedy of errors. The officer charged with the defense of the area, *Generalleutnant* Gerhard Graf von Schwerin, was averse to defending the beautiful old city, due to the destruction that would result, and penned a letter to the American commander who was to take Aachen (General J. Lawton Collins), asking him to take care of the civilian occupants. In the meantime, Collins had decided to bypass the city, a plan that later changed. When Hitler found out what Schwerin had done, he ordered the general's arrest. In the end, American troops attacked the city. See Charles B. MacDonald, *The Siegfried Line Campaign*, Washington, DC: U.S. Army Center of Military History, 1990, pp. 70-72.

9. David W. Hogan, *A Command Post at War: The First Army Headquarters in Europe, 1943-1945*, Washington, DC: U.S. Army Center of Military History, 2000, p. 162.

10. MacDonald, *The Siegfried Line Campaign*, p. 323. According to MacDonald, the Hürtgen sat on the right flank of Collin's

VII Corps, exposing this corps to a potential German flank attack. An American Army had faced the threat of a flank attack from the Argonne Forest 26 years before. The memory of the Argonne appears to have been the initial reason for the Hürtgen, since to Collins and Hodges that area seemed to be a logical assembly area for a German counterattack.

11. The 9th Infantry had warned, as early as October 2, 1944, that the dams posed a significant threat to the U.S. advance. At that time, the 1st Army G-2 Colonel Benjamin "Monk" Dickson disagreed, and thus the month went by without consideration of the dam's significance. As late as October 29, Bradley found the dams to be no threat, but on November 7, Hodges, reacting to a new G-2 report from Dickson, ordered the Vth Corps to develop plans for the seizure of these dams.

12. Dwight D. Eisenhower, *Crusade in Europe*, New York: Doubleday and Company Inc, 1948, p. 329.

13. J. Lawton Collins' narrative is quite revealing on the issue of the Roer Dams. Collins states that, in terms of objectives, "No mention was made of the two major dams on the Roer and its Urft tributary south of Schmidt, nor were they assigned as objectives of the VII Corps." J. Lawton Collins, *Lightning Joe: An Autobiography*, Novato, CA: The Presidio Press, 1994, p. 273

14. Edward J. Drea, *Unit Reconstitution – A Historical Perspective*, Ft. Leavenworth, KS: Combat Studies Institute, 1983, p. 33.

15. Ralph Johnson, "A Soldier's Story, 1941-1946," in Dorothy Chernitsky, ed., *Voices From the Foxhole*, Connellsville, PA: Connellsville Printing Company, 1991, p. 13.

16. Edward G. Miller, *A Dark and Bloody Ground: The Huertgen Forest and the Roer River Dams, 1944-1945*, College Station, TX: Texas A&M University Press, 1995, p. 33.

17. *Ibid.*, p. 32.

18. Robert S. Rush, *Hell in the Hürtgen: The Ordeal and Triumph of an American Infantry Regiment*, Lawrence, KS: University of Kansas Press, 2001, p. 125.

19. Chester Wilmot, *The Struggle For Europe*, Old Saybrook CT: Konecky and Konecky, 1952, p. 566.

20. Hogan, pp. 162-163. The author of this authoritative study also notes that production shortfalls in the United States contributed to this problem as well.

21. Field Order 30, Headquarters, V Corps, October 21, 1944, in *Historical and Pictorial Review of the 28th Infantry Division in World War II*, Nashville, TN: The Battery Press Inc, 1946.

22. The official Army history notes that "not until 7 November, six days after the start of the second attack on Schmidt, was the First Army to call for any plan to seize the [Roer] dams." MacDonald, *The Siegfried Line Campaign*, p. 342.

23. A new objective for the Hürtgen campaign had emerged. In the official history of the Siegfried Line Campaign, the author notes, "There was a growing realization of the defensive importance to the Germans of the Roer River Dams." At the same time MacDonald noted, "Present plans of this Army do not contemplate the immediate capture of these dams." MacDonald, *The Siegfried Line Campaign*, p. 406.

24. The original Corps order established the target date of November 1, but after October 29, the weather turned ugly resulting in the first postponement. *Historical and Pictorial Review of the 28th Infantry Division in World War II*, Nashville, TN: Battery Press, 1980.

25. Drea, p. 33.

26. Hogan, p. 185.

27. Although Cota had indeed lost touch with his units, he could hardly be blamed entirely for the predicament into which the Vth Corps and 1st Army headquarters had thrust his command. *Ibid.*, p. 185.

28. Authorities give various figures for Hürtgen casualties. Drea's Combat Studies Institute paper states that 3,637 battle losses were incurred in the Hürtgen by the 28th Division, and 1,391

nonbattle losses. Cole's book on the Ardennes lists casualties for the 28th as 6,184 casualties, p. 179.

29. The Army's official history has described the 28th Division's action in the Hürtgen as "one of the most costly division actions in the whole of World War II." MacDonald, *The Siegfried Line*, p. 373.

30. The 28th Infantry Division was one of several U.S. divisions to suffer in the Hürtgen fighting in 1944. The 9th Division, which the 28th had replaced, suffered 4,500 casualties from October 5-11, 1944. See John S. D. Eisenhower, *The Bitter Woods*, Nashville, TN: Battery Classics, 1969, p. 86; and Drea, p. 33.

31. Miller, p. 152.

32. Hogan, pp. 185-186.

33. Rush, p. 345. Rush bases his opinion on the comment made after the War by General G. V. von Gerdorf, Chief of Staff of the German VIIth Army, which was the southern flank shoulder for the German offensive.

34. Dwight D. Eisenhower, *Report by the Supreme Commander to the Combined Chiefs of Staff on the Operations in Europe of the Allied Expeditionary Force, June 6, 1944, to May 8, 1945*, Washington, DC: U.S. Army Center of Military History, 1994, pp. 68-70. Eisenhower's report mentions the "slugging matches" of October and November, and his desire to use the "space between our front and the Rhine as a 'killing ground'." This was clearly successful for both armies (p. 69).

35. James M. Gavin, *On to Berlin: Battles of an Airborne Commander, 1943-1946*, New York: The Viking Press, 1976, p. 266.

CHAPTER 8

THE ARDENNES OFFENSIVE

> Taken by surprise, Eisenhower and his commanders acted swiftly, but they will agree that the major credit lies elsewhere. In Montgomery's words, The Battle of the Ardennes was won primarily by the staunch fighting qualities of the American soldier.[1]
>
> Winston S. Churchill

THE MANPOWER CRISIS

After the bitter fighting in Aachen, Germany, the Hürtgen Forest, and the battle to take Metz, France, the American Army was suffering from significant problems. There were still limitations on some categories of supplies in the field, although taking Marseilles and opening Antwerp had significantly improved the logistical situation. More than the materials of war, the American Army was short on Soldiers. The casualty figures enumerating the losses suffered in the campaign across France, Operation MARKET GARDEN, Aachen, and Metz, as well as numerous other engagements in Europe and in other theaters, do not accurately reflect what was happening to the U.S. Army. Casualties were not equally suffered by all branches or all types of units. The preponderance of the casualties in the summer and fall fighting of 1944 were in the infantry rifle companies. As noted by Bradley:

> To replenish those losses and halt any further decline in Infantry strength, we combed the ETO [European Theater of Operations] for emergency replacements.

But though truckloads of hastily trained riflemen were bundled off to the front, they could not offset the litter cases that passed them headed rearward. The drain continued until December 15 when G-1 reported the 12th Army Group was short 17,000 riflemen among its 31 divisions on the line.[2]

Bradley lamented the added problems of 12,000 casualties from trench foot and the "bankrupt replacement system." In reality, the problem facing the U.S. Army was twofold. The fall casualties, particularly the attacks in the Hürtgen by one division after another, wrecked the combat power of a number of divisions. The casualties experienced by the 9th Division, for example, are particularly revealing regarding the impact that the fighting had on the division since their entry into combat operations. See Table 8-1.

Month	Killed	Wounded	Exhaustion	Nonbattle	Total
July	712	2,989	520	1,315	5,536
August	376	1,809	280	1,540	4,005
September	218	1,551	161	1,457	3,387
October	384	2,224	280	2,158	5,046
Total	1,690	8,573	1,241	6,470	17,974

Source: HQ, 9th Infantry Division, Report of Operations, July-October 1944, 309-0.3, Box 7326, Record Group 407, National Archives II.[3]

Table 8-1. 9th Infantry Division Casualties, July 1-October 31, 1944.

A comparable chart included in an Army Combat Studies Institute study on unit reconstitution shows a day-by-day breakdown of casualties from November 2 through November 18, 1944, suffered by the 28th Infantry Division. The study's authors indicate that of the 4,878 replacements received by the division following the Hürtgen offensive, 4,458 were infantry specialties. The study emphasizes that, "The division was able to replace its heavy personnel losses, but the influx of replacements was so great that the individual regiments of the division were no longer combat effective."[4]

The indications of the heavy attrition of infantrymen can also be seen in Patton's attempts to destroy the defensive positions at Metz. As soon as SHAEF had given the 3rd Army the authorization to begin its Lorraine, France, offensive on September 3, Patton's two corps, U.S. Army Lieutenant General Manton Eddy's XIIth and U.S. Army General Walton Walker's XXth, pressed hard to clear Lorraine. Walker's XXth Corps, however, came up against Metz, which Adolf Hitler had declared a fortified city. This was a "tough nut to crack," because the XIIIth SS Corps was responsible for its defense. Walker, much like Joseph Collins and Courtney Hodges in the Hürtgen Forest, had no real understanding of the terrain his Soldiers faced.[5] Nonetheless, on September 6 he first sent the 7th Armored Division, followed by the 5th Infantry Division and the 90th Infantry Division into the Metz vicinity. Although Patton prided himself on his knowledge of historic battles and relished being on these battlefields, he too ignored the fact that Metz was heavily fortified. Romans had fortified the town, and it had been significantly and repeatedly strengthened for centuries, even up through the period after World War I. The

5th Infantry Division fought hard through October 16 to take this fortified city. After its failure to take Metz, division personnel began training on how to take fortified areas. By that time, almost half of the division's assault forces had become casualties. It was not until November 3 that division staff officers developed a scheme of maneuver instead of using a direct assault. Even then, the last fortification of Metz did not surrender until December 8.[6]

Problems suffered throughout the fall, however, were only part of a larger situation that had begun to emerge even before the Normandy landings. In his preliminary war plans, Albert Wedemeyer had called for a much larger Army than was actually created. The War Department did not seriously consider his recommended force structure of 215 combat divisions, and staff officers subsequently reduced it. Wedemeyer did recommend that the Army ground and air components should consist of 8,795,658 Soldiers. Ultimately, the size of the Army did come close to this proposed force size when its total strength reached 8,291,336 uniformed personnel. The problem was not insufficient Soldiers, but an insufficient number of Soldiers in the appropriate units necessary to fight and win the war. The Army needed combat arms Soldiers, particularly infantrymen. Simply put, too many men were going into the wrong specialties. For example, the AAF trained more pilots and aircrew members than were needed for the demands of the war. The War Department staff began to recognize that they had underestimated the number of combat arms Soldiers necessary to win the war. In 1944, the AAF transferred about 24,000 air cadets to Army ground forces to be retrained as infantrymen.[7]

Another example of the recognition of the impending manpower crisis was the cutbacks in the Army

Specialized Training Program. With insight and an eye on the future, Marshall had originally agreed to create a program, proposed by Secretary of War Henry Stimson, called the Army Specialized Training Program. This program took Soldiers with high academic potential, based on their high Army General Classification Test scores, and enrolled them in college to complete degrees. Program designers envisioned that the Army would place these candidates in both wartime and post war positions of responsibility. By February 1944, however, War Department planners determined that this program was consuming too much manpower, and Marshall reduced it to 30,000 Soldiers. This action released 120,000 Soldiers for service in units.[8] Even with the reductions in the number of high aptitude Soldiers and Airmen admitted into this special program, the Army faced a looming crisis.

As early as July, Army offices throughout Washington and Europe became aware of the impending manpower crisis, but bureaucratic wrangling between headquarters and commands caused the problem to drag on without any real resolution.[9] The growth of headquarters staffs and support troops caused part of the problem. A military headquarters is inherently a bureaucracy, and the standard practice for virtually every bureaucracy is that it perpetuates itself and continues to grow. Not only did this bureaucracy continue to grow throughout 1944, the greater coordination between joint and combined forces added to the expansion. Eisenhower recognized this problem and tried to resolve it, where possible, he combed supply and service units to find Soldiers that were available for retraining as infantrymen. In some cases, the Army used female Soldiers from the Women's Army Corps to fill administrative positions in headquarters or in service units so that male Soldiers could be relieved to perform front line duty.[10] Patton levied 5,000 men from his Corps and Army headquarters, and from various noncombatant positions and sent them to be a retrained as riflemen replacements at a center in Metz.[11] Even this was not enough; the Army still suffered from a manpower shortage in its infantry units. It was a shortage unlike that suffered by the British Army, since London simply did not have more men to use as soldiers. The American Army had men in uniform, but these men were simply in the wrong specialties. Another reason for the shortage of personnel was the growth of complex technologies of the day. Advanced communications, maintenance, medical support, and other capabilities required a cadre of extensively trained personnel. If the War Department wanted to maintain a large AAF or armored vehicle fleet, then many well-trained personnel were needed.

AN ABSENCE OF OPERATIONAL THINKING

This leads to yet a third and very important issue, the strategy used by Allied commanders who were waging the European war. The Normandy landings had been unbelievably successful and had opened up the heartland of France to Allied armies. After Allied forces blunted the Mortain offensive and the combined American-British forces closed the Falaise Gap, the Allies implemented the broad front strategy. In the period following Operation COBRA, the most innovative operation attempted by the Western Allies was Operation MARKET GARDEN. Other than Operation MARKET GARDEN, operations on the ground took a largely tactical approach. Critics frequently raised the question, were the broad front strategy operations focused on the destruction of German forces in the field or on seizing terrain? Martin Blumensen, among others, has criticized the Army leadership of the period for their tactical approach in its European operations. In his words,

> The basic Allied motive was . . . geographical and territorial. The intention was to overrun land and liberate towns. In which direction were the Allies going? Toward the enemy homelands, specifically the capitals. Seizing the cities, the Allies believed, was sure to win the war.[12]

Certainly, war waged on the ground is about taking terrain and tactical operations, but as one considers strategy and achieving strategic goals for the campaign, tactical approaches alone are not efficient methods of achieving those goals. One can see an example of a terrain and tactical approach to the battlefield by reviewing the operations of Eisenhower's premier maneuver element, the 12th Army Group. Its commander, Bradley, was an infantry officer who seemed to have a largely tactical view of war. He often recognized larger opportunities on the field of battle. Martin Blumenson stated that Bradley ". . . initiated potentially brilliant maneuvers, then aborted them because he lacked confidence in his ability to see them through to completion."[13] By nature, Bradley was a conservative commander, but one who had caught the eye of the press and public. The press made him famous as the "Soldier's general." Still, in spite of this popular acclaim, he was never successful in making his mark as a great operational commander in World War II.[14] From the time that the breakout began, with Operation COBRA, through the end of the Ardennes campaign in January 1945, Bradley was unable or unwilling to bag and destroy a German force. Planners offered Bradley several opportunities to do this and thereby more rapidly achieve the stated purpose of the campaign.[15]

Depending on your perspective, it is possible to be critical of Bradley or his 1st Army commander, Hodges. In fairness, what military strategists now call operational thought had not entered into the American Army's lexicon of war.[16] The promotion of operational art did not enter the American Army's literature until the late 1970s and early 1980s. Some American officers, however, were ahead of their time. For example, Patton intuitively understood the concept and Collins seemed to accept and practice it, though not consistently. The adversary, the *Wehrmacht*, practiced what we now call the operational art. It was not doctrine, it reflected their way of war, as emphasized from the mid-19th century through World War II. Though not referred to as operational art it was, nonetheless, classic operational thinking.[17]

THE GHOST FRONT

The casualties from the summer and fall fighting, the bitter and at times attritional battles that seemed to focus more on terrain rather that enemy forces, and the growth of headquarters and service troops meant that the U.S. Army was physically unable to adequately cover Eisenhower's broad front strategy.[18] One historian declared: "It was not that the broad front strategy was wrong; the more basic trouble was that the alliance had not given Eisenhower enough troops to carry it out safely."[19] The front was indeed broad as described by Eisenhower: "We were disposed along a line which, beginning in the north on the banks of the Rhine, stretched 500 miles southward to the border of Switzerland."[20] Despite the growing shortage of front line Soldiers, Eisenhower felt obliged to maintain pressure on the Germans, particularly with the operations in progress by the 12th Army Group. This meant that Patton's operations in Lorraine would continue, as well as Hodge's abortive attempts to take the Hürtgen region. To continue the pressure in these areas, the Allied command had to stretch the 12th Army Group's center. Thus, there developed on the right flank of the 1st Army what some have called a "ghost front," a minimally manned quiet area situated along the German and Luxembourg border.

The "ghost front" was indicative of a shortage of American ground units on the continent and, to further complicate the American position, the U.S. Army was without any reserves in the European Theater other than the XVIIIth Airborne Corps, composed of the 82nd and 101st Airborne Divisions. One might question whether this corps was actually a SHAEF reserve, as has been claimed, or more accurately Eisenhower's elite airborne troops that were refitting after Operation MARKET GARDEN and preparing for another drop. To compensate for the personnel shortages in the 12th Army Group, Bradley had to stretch his VIIIth Corps to continue the initiative on the northern and southern flanks of the 12th Army Group. As he described it:

> We would stretch Middleton [Troy Middleton's VIII Corps, Hodges First Army] as taut as we dared thus the Ardennes was deliberately thinned to thicken the winter offensive.[21]

Though he was a cautious and conservative commander, Bradley saw no problem with stretching his center so thin. Troy Middleton, commander of the VIIIth Corps, expressed concern about his badly extended divisions. Bradley told him, "Don't worry Troy, they won't come through here."[22] He explained his assessment by telling Middleton:

> when anyone attacks he does it for one of two reasons. Either he's out to destroy the hostile forces or he's going after a terrain objective. Neither objective could be attained in the Ardennes, for nowhere were we more thinly dispersed than across the wooded front and nowhere in the length of the allied line was a sector more devoid of industrial resources, transportational facilities and worthwhile terrain objectives.[23]

Bradley's stated rationale betrays a tactical mindset, an inability to see beyond the immediate battlefield and think on operational terms. According to his own comments, he only mentally surveyed the battlefield about 20 miles to the rear of the Ardennes lines.[24] Bradley did not seem to be unnecessarily concerned with his lack of strength in his center, opposite of the Ardennes. From October to December, he was focused on the 1st Army's actions in the Hürtgen Forest and 3rd Army's advance into Lorraine. Though after the Ardennes, Bradley would claim that he had taken a calculated risk by stretching Middleton's center so thin, in reality his actions and his own words indicate that his analysis of the battlefield dismissed any real risk to the 12th Army Group's center.[25]

Thinning the VIIIth Corps' center required Soldiers to cover about 88 miles of front line. In early December, the major elements in Middleton's Corps were two veteran divisions, the 4th and 28th Infantry Divisions—both of which were refitting after the Hürtgen—the green 106th Infantry Division, and elements of the new 9th Armored Division. At that time a division front was generally about 8 miles. In the

VIIIth Corps center, the 28th Infantry Division's front was about 25 miles.[26] Eisenhower, despite his desire to maintain the broad front, expressed his concern on several occasions about the thin front opposite the Ardennes. On one occasion, he stated, "the badly stretched condition of our troops caused constant concern, particularly on Bradley's front."[27] Bradley did attempt to address Eisenhower's concerns about this area on several occasions. Once he even purportedly conducted a wargame for Eisenhower of a possible incursion into the Ardennes.[28] After indicating on the map the limits of any possible German incursion, he assured Eisenhower of the remoteness of such an advance and stated:

> Why, even if the Germans were to bust through all the way to the Meuse (which Bradley felt that he could hold), he wouldn't find a thing in the Ardennes to make it worth his while.[29]

While Eisenhower felt he had to trust the judgment of a valued subordinate, he was clearly concerned about the badly extended VIIIth Corps Ardennes front.[30] Perhaps Carlo D'Este best summarized the error in Allied thinking when he stated:

> The German Counteroffensive in the Ardennes would turn out to be the latest example of the principle learned and relearned the hard way by the Allies in World War II: Expect the unexpected. . . . Thus, it should not have not come as the surprise it did that, with Allied operations at a standstill and the Third Reich on the verge of invasion from both east and west, Adolf Hitler elected to gamble the fate of Germany on a last ditch attempt to salvage the war by a sudden lightning thrust through the Ardennes.[31]

D'Este's comments also highlight another problem. Allied commanders failed to recognize that the dominate force in military operations in December of 1944 was none other than Hitler.[32] Since the Allied landings on June 6, 1944, Hitler had sought to take the war to the Allies through offensive operations. Against all sound military advice, he had attempted to do this with his ill-fated Mortain offensive that only weakened German forces. Still, the concept of a new offensive never left Hitler's mind. Unless he could inflict a punishing blow on the Allies, Hitler could not conclude any type of peace that would be favorable to Germany. As a consequence, on August 19, even as German armies were falling back in disarray through France, Hitler told the Chief of *Oberkommando der Wehrmacht* (OKW) *Generalfeldmarschall* Wilhelm Keitel, Chief of the Army Staff General Walter Buhle, and Minister of Armament Albert Speer that in November, when Allied Air Forces cannot operate, German military forces must be prepared to move 25 divisions to the west and take the offensive. So began the planning for the Ardennes Offensive or, as the U.S. Army referred to it, the "Battle of the Bulge."

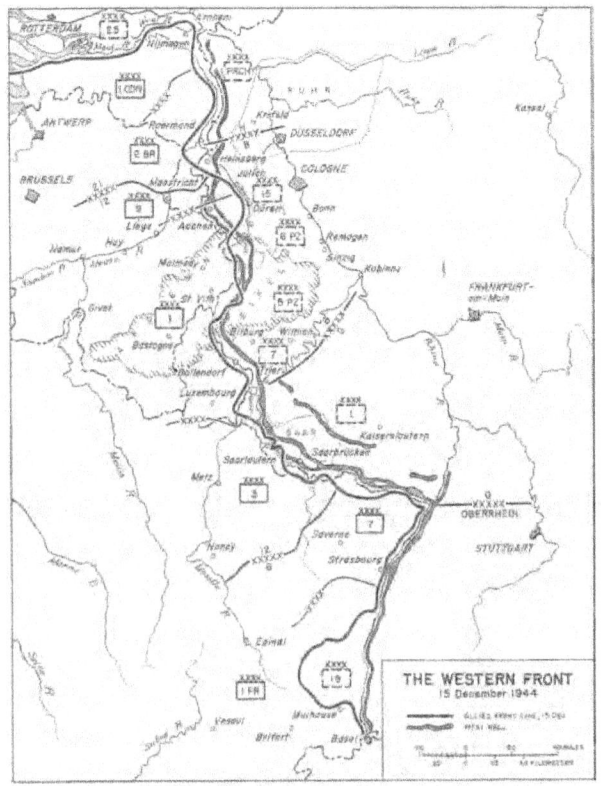

Source: Hugh M. Cole, The Ardennes: Battle of the Bulge, Washington, DC: Chief of Military History, 1965, p.53.

Map 8-1. The Western Front: December 15, 1944.

Hitler's Surprise Offensive.

Before conveying unnecessary criticism on the Army's leadership for being surprised on December 16, 1944, it is important to consider that Hitler's plan did, in fact, violate conventional military wisdom. The Allies were on the offensive, they had dominance on the battlefield, and American and British forces were obviously in the process of preparing for a final push into

Germany. Conventional wisdom would have called for the Germans to hold their limited reserves for staging counterattacks against major U.S. offensives toward the Rhine, Ruhr, or the Saar Rivers. This was a logical assumption, considering the losses suffered by the *Wehrmacht*, and would have been the likely course of action by a professional officer corps, either German or American. Allied leaders knew that Hitler had appointed *Generalfeldmarschall* Gerd von Rundstedt, an experienced professional German General Staff officer, to become German Commander in the West. Allied military leadership assumed that the Germans would follow traditional military wisdom. The major error in this assumption was that Rundstedt was not actually the dominant force in German military operations, Hitler was.[33]

The failure to understand Hitler's role in military affairs was one element of another problem facing the Western Allies, a number of major shortfalls in intelligence gathering and analysis. Since the beginning of the European Campaign, the Allies had two very significant advantages in intelligence gathering. First, on a daily basis they could use information obtained from ULTRA to discern at least some of the German military capabilities. ULTRA gave Allied intelligence analysts access to OKW messages, German *Kriegsmarine* message traffic, and the ability to decipher the state railway system's (*Reichsbahn*) messages. The railway information provided detailed intelligence concerning the of transportation of military assets and the state of the economy. ULTRA did not tell the Allies everything about German intentions, but it did consistently disclose solid order of battle information.

Secondly, from June to early September, the Allies had innumerable human intelligence (HUMINT) resources from the citizenry in occupied France,

Belgium, and Holland. As the European Campaign successfully liberated these areas, HUMINT sources quickly dried up. By the fall of 1944, Allied units were on the German border, which meant that very limited HUMINT was available. Adding to the drought of HUMINT sources, there was an underestimation of the German Army's capabilities, across the front. For example, Brigadier General Edwin Sibert, Assistant Chief of Staff, G-2, Headquarters, 12th Army Group, made such an underestimation when on December 12, 1944, less than a week before the German offensive, he reported that "it is now certain that attrition is steadily sapping the strength of the German forces on the Western Front, and that the crust of defense is thinner and more vulnerable than it appears on our G-2 maps or to the troops in the line."[34] Obviously, Sibert had not been in the Hürtgen in November or December to personally observe this "thin crust" or the weakening of German forces. At the same time, the 21st Army Group G-2 developed a similar conclusion about German capabilities. The 1st Army's G-2 reports were sometimes better, but these reports and the G-2 himself were at best erratic concerning their analysis of German capabilities.[35] The overall intelligence problem in Europe was that the G-2 reports reflected the opinions and analysis that the leadership wanted to see, rather than what they needed.

For a strategic offensive, the plan that Hitler had instructed his staff to develop was an excellent concept, that is, if resources had been available to accomplish it. Hitler selected an offensive plan to attack through the Ardennes region with 28 divisions and drive through Belgium to the port of Antwerp. This would drive a wedge between the British 21st and the American 12th Army Groups. Once this wedge separated the two armies, the German Army could inflict casualties on the British reminiscent of levels of World War I. Hitler hoped that this would set the stage for separate peace negotiations with the Western Allies. Once the Allies and Germany concluded this peace, the German Army could turn its full strength on the Russians who were the main and most dreaded adversary. Senior German commanders, however, lacked the necessary resources for such an offensive. Rundstedt later stated, "If we had reached the Meuse, we should have got down on our knees and thanked God — let alone tried to reach Antwerp."[36]

Given the problems with the offensive, two experienced generals, both of whom had impeccable National Socialist credentials and were directly involved in the operation, argued against the offensive. *Waffen*-SS General and long time Hitler associate "Sepp" Dietrich opposed the offensive into the Ardennes, and Walter Model, one of Hitler's favorites, reportedly stated, "This plan hasn't got a damned leg to stand on."[37] Worried about squandering their dwindling resources, Rundstedt, in cooperation with Model, proposed the small solution where a double-wing envelopment would occur east of the Meuse River and pinch off as many as five American divisions. Hitler was adamant. The Ardennes offensive would be executed as planned, but the date of execution was moved from December 1 to December 16.[38] The forces mustered for the Ardennes were impressive. The 5th and 6th Panzer Armies were the main maneuver elements on the battlefield. The German 7th Army, positioned on the southern shoulder of the advance was a force designed to protect the left flank of the German advance, since planners expected a thrust into this flank by Patton's 3rd Army once the offensive was in motion. The

6th Panzer Army, under the command of Dietrich, was the heaviest force and it was the main effort of the offensive since it was on the shortest axis of the advance routes to Antwerp. Composed of six divisions and a panzer brigade, over half of this force should be regarded as elite units. Dietrich's Army had several elite units. Dietrich could rely on the 1st SS Panzer Division, the 12th SS Panzer Division, the 3rd Parachute Division, and the 150th Panzer Brigade. Both of the SS divisions had 22,000 men each and possessed the latest German equipment.

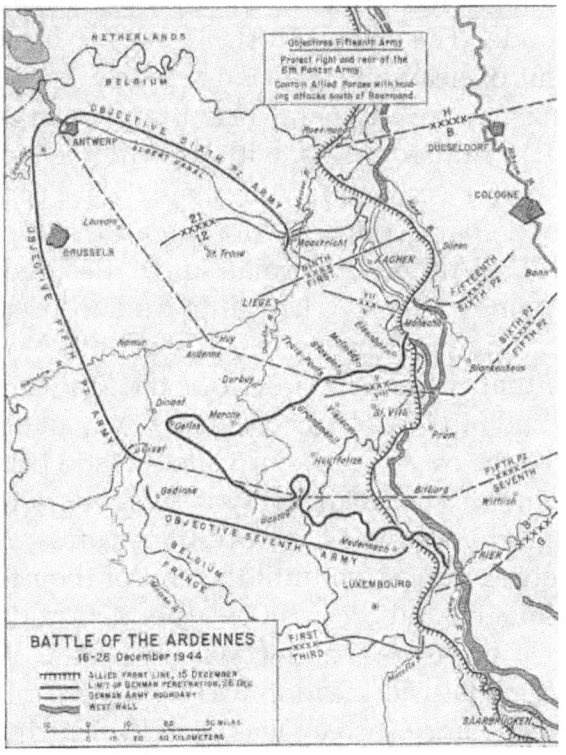

Source: U.S. Army Center of Military History.

Map 8-2. This map clearly shows the overall objectives for the Ardennes Offensive and for each of the three German armies.

The 5th Panzer Army was on a longer avenue of advance and was not the main effort. It did have excellent resources. It was composed of seven divisions, including three panzer divisions, the 2nd, the Panzer *Lehr*, and the 116th. All of the divisions had excellent reputations. Its commander was *General der Panzertruppen* Hasso von Manteuffel, one of Germany's best known armor officers. The 5th Panzer had important objectives for the campaign, such as securing the road net which led to the city of Bastogne, a key transportation node. The main effort, as shown by the employment of heavy SS divisions, clearly involved the 6th Panzer Army. General Eric Brandenberger's 7th Army, had limited assets, with no armored divisions, limited firepower, and few mechanized assets.

Like a page out of Montgomery's Operation MARKET GARDEN, German units designated for the Ardennes offensive had little time to prepare for the attack due to secrecy. It was not until November 6, 1944, that the chiefs of staff of the 7th Army, and the 5th and 6th Panzer Armies, the key maneuver elements for the operation, were called in and briefed for the offensive.[39] German Army commanders received briefings on December 2 and division commanders did not receive notification until the end of the first week in December.[40] Subordinate commanders did not receive their briefs until a few days before the offensive began. Such late notification was hardly a formula for success, but since secrecy was crucial, security necessitated last minute notification. When commanders were briefed for the offensive and the role of their units, they were told that the most important factors for the operation would be "first-SURPRISE, and next-

SPEED!"[41] For this offensive to succeed, both were necessities. In planning the operation, planners assumed that German forces would have about a week in which weather would make it extremely difficult for Allied tactical air to interdict German movements.

Neither the commander nor the headquarters staff of the 12th Army Group had any idea of what was about to hit Middleton's VIIIth Corps in the Army Group's center. On the eve of the German offensive, the 12th Army Group commander had again renewed his fixation on the Roer Dams that, by December, had been determined to be a bona fide objective. Thus, on December 13, on orders from Bradley, Hodges began an attack to seize Schwammenual and Urftalsperre. These targets were decisive points for the Roer Valley dam system. The attack seemed to be going well. However, on the next day, the attack bogged down. In conducting the attack, the Vth Corps commander, Gerow, employed two divisions. Bradley and Hodge's eyes were on the Vth Corps and its actions, not the VIIIth Corps. On the evening of December 15, *Wehrmacht* leaders had positioned 20 German divisions to strike the 99th, 28th, and 106th Infantry Divisions in a classic surprise attack.[42] When Hitler launched his offensive in the early morning hours of December 16, he began the largest ground campaign fought by the U.S. Army in World War II, the "Battle of the Bulge."

The Bulge: Initial Phases.

With weather restricting air power, it looked as though the German Army had a chance for at least limited success with their offensive. To be successful, the German offensive *Wacht am Rhein* (Watch on the Rhine) had to accomplish two important objectives.

First, German forces had to achieve surprise across the American front. Second, once the Germans caught their foe unaware, assault companies had to dislodge the American defenders from their positions along Skyline Drive and reach the far side of the Clerf River. This task seemed feasible because as it turned out the German estimates that American defenses contained only a thin crust of resistance were correct. Once the attacking German units broke through the defenses, speed was critical in order to accomplish all remaining objectives. If German units moved rapidly, then they could reach their objectives before Allied air commanders could react, and ground defenses could be reinforced. The ability of German forces to reach Antwerp depended on these factors and a good deal of luck. Supplies to support the German attack were definitely short, and waging combined arms operations, particularly using tactical airpower which had been so important in early German victories, was conspicuously absent.

When the German attack struck, the Allied senior leadership at Army level and above was short of readily available reserves for a rapid response. On December 16, Bradley was not even at his headquarters. As discussed earlier in this chapter, the pressing problem confronting all Allied commanders by the late fall was a shortage of infantrymen. This issue caused Bradley to leave his headquarters at Luxembourg City and travel by road to Paris to plead for more infantry replacements. Additionally, Eisenhower was getting his fifth star, and Bradley wanted to attend the promotion ceremony for his old West Point classmate. In short, for the first day of the German offensive, Bradley and Eisenhower were not aware of the crisis that was emerging in the 12th Army Group's center. For

Bradley and Eisenhower, December 16 was generally a pleasant day, culminating with Eisenhower's promotion. At dusk, SHAEF G-2, Major General Kenneth Strong, interrupted the generals to inform them that the Germans had attacked and had penetrated American lines. Neither initially seemed concerned with the report, and it was not until late in the evening that Eisenhower and Bradley left their relaxed and celebratory atmosphere and went to the situation room. Bradley looked at the map and quickly assessed that the Germans were staging a spoiling attack. He speculated that the Germans had hoped to discourage his attack toward the Roer dam system. Eisenhower, looking at the map was much more perceptive. He snapped, "that's no spoiling attack," and immediately recommended to Bradley that Middleton needed to have two armored divisions for reinforcements. Eisenhower suggested to Bradley that he use the 7th Armored Division from the U.S. 9th Army and the 10th Armored Division from Patton's 3rd Army. When Bradley expressed considerable concern about Eisenhower's recommendation, Eisenhower overruled Bradley with obvious impatience.[43]

At the front lines, the senior commander most affected by the German attack was Hodges. His G-2 had given increasingly ominous warnings about German capabilities, but the intelligence official did not initially indicate that the Ardennes was an area for concern. These estimates, caused Hodges some concern, and on December 13, Hodges asked Bradley to give him two additional divisions for Middleton. Bradley turned down Hodges' request.[44] Despite his uneasiness prompted by his G-2's reports, on December 16 Hodges was preoccupied with the Vth Corps' attack into the Roer Dam area. When news of the Ardennes

German attack reached his headquarters, he refused to cancel the Vth Corps attack. It was not until December 17, that Hodges and his headquarters staff began to realize how serious the situation facing the 1st Army was.[45] On the first day of the offensive, it was business as usual for the 1st Army, another attempt to secure the Roer Dam complex.

As the situation worsened for the American Army, two senior officers quickly emerged that exhibited a solid understanding of the battlefield, Eisenhower and his old colleague, Patton. Patton was the earliest senior commander to understand what could happen in the Ardennes. The 3rd Army G-2, Colonel Oscar Koch, was perhaps one of the best intelligence officers in the European theater.[46] Patton required Koch to track the buildup of any significant enemy armored formations, even outside his area of responsibility. In early December, he reported that there were eight to nine German armored divisions out of the line; in addition, he identified some parachute and *Panzergrenadier* units which could not be located. Koch became very concerned about the potential for a counterattack.[47] Patton came to share this concern and even earlier in late November noted in his diary that Bradley and Hodges were making a serious mistake by leaving Middleton's units static in the Ardennes for so long.[48] Koch, through hard work, had made Patton aware of the problem in Middleton's area.[49]

Eisenhower had repeatedly expressed concern to Bradley about the thin coverage in the Ardennes area. He had expressed this on several occasions, but in many respects, Eisenhower was a victim of his own strategy. The broad front strategy and his desire to keep the Germans under pressure, at least in selected areas, resulted in the thin center of Bradley's command. There were additional troops for Europe in the "pipeline," but they had not yet arrived in the theater. His concern increased shortly before the attack when Major General Kenneth Strong, chief of intelligence for SHAEF, became concerned about the German buildup and warned Eisenhower about a possible attack in the Ardennes sector. After addressing this assessment, Strong, at the insistence of Bedell Smith, briefed Bradley for 45 minutes. Bradley told Strong that he had considered the possibility of such a German move and that he had units designated to cover such an eventuality. Thus, having warned Bradley, Eisenhower saw no reason to intervene.[50] To his credit, late on December 16 when Bradley again dismissed the gravity of the situation, Eisenhower immediately took command. For the remainder of the Ardennes offensive, Bradley was, at best, on the margins of the American response. As the "Bulge" developed, due to Bradley's center caving in, German units drove a wedge between American units in Bradley's left and right flanks. Since Bradley's headquarters was positioned in Luxembourg, the German effort separated him from his 1st and 9th Armies, making communication tenuous. German units wrecked or compromised much of the wire network. German communications and intelligence analysts could eavesdrop on American radio transmissions. Consequently, Bradley had difficulty in controlling his northern armies.

The deteriorating situation called for a high-level session, and Eisenhower, clearly in command, ultimately called for one, but not until December 19. In the meantime, the leadership to counter the most serious German attack during the European Campaign was in the hands of junior grade officers and senior enlisted personnel. Without them, in the days from December

16 to 20, the German threat could have been far more serious, the German successes more striking. Several notable cases illustrate this point. In the area of the main effort, the green 99th Infantry Division held terrain that was on the right flank of the heaviest force assembled by the Germans for the offensive, the 6th Panzer Army. The 99th, a part of Gerow's Vth Corps, had only been in the line since November. Given the stagnation of positions at that time in the war, it had not been involved in any major operations.

As a battalion of the German 3rd Parachute Division moved up the road near the little Belgian town of Lanzerath, they encountered the Intelligence and Reconnaissance (I&R) platoon of the 394th Regiment from the 99th Infantry Division. Commanded by a 20-year old lieutenant, Lyle Bouck, the I&R platoon's 17 men, after surviving the preparatory shelling in their foxholes overlooking the Belgian village, engaged the German paratroopers with small arms fire. With nothing heavier than a .50 caliber Browning machine gun in their inventory, Bouck and his small band of Soldiers held their position until the latter part of the afternoon, exacting a horrible toll on the advancing Germans. One author states that the Americans caused over 50 percent casualties on their foes.[51] The most serious casualty inflicted on the Germans was on the time schedule for the German 3rd Parachute Division. For a day, 18 men had deprived the Germans of the use of the important Lanzerath Road and had deprived the 3rd Parachute Division of what it needed most, speed. This was a significant accomplishment for a small group of Soldiers, who held at all costs.

In the center of the U.S. positions was another green division commanded by Major General Alan Jones. This division had two of its RCTs forward of the main U.S. line, with some of the companies occupying bunkers that were once a part of the German Siegfried Line. When Manteuffels' 5th Panzer Army launched its attack, elements of his 18th *Volksgrenadier* Division conducted a classic double-wing envelopment, thereby bagging Jones' 422nd and 423rd RCTs and setting them up for destruction. Over the following 3 days, the Germans pounded these two units until they finally surrendered on December 19. The surrender of these two RCTs was the largest single surrender of U.S. troops since the fall of the Philippines, indeed an embarrassment to the U.S. Army. One of the division's RCTs, however, remained ready to resist, the 424th. This unit was joined by Combat Command B of the 7th Armored Division, led by a newly promoted Brigadier General Bruce C. Clarke. Recognizing his inability to command, Alan Jones relinquished command of the remnants of his division to Clarke, an officer junior in rank and seniority. Clarke, though junior, was an energetic officer, and he created an ad hoc defense force centered on the Belgian town of St. Vith. Like Bastogne further south, this town was a road junction that was extremely important to the Germans since they needed paved roads for their mechanized forces. With Clarke's hard-nosed determination, the ad hoc force succeeded in denying the Germans the necessary westward road network.

Further south of the Luxembourg town of Hosingen, two companies of the 28th Infantry Division sat astride the important north and south roadway known as Skyline Drive. Situated essentially in the center of Manteuffel's advance route toward the key road junction of Bastogne, Germans surrounded both companies, K Company of the 110th Infantry Regiment and B Company of the 103rd Engineer Regiment, shortly after dawn on December 16. Manteuffel had his lead units strike after midnight. At dawn, German units were bypassing Hosingen. Much like at Lanzerath and St. Vith, because the companies defended the road net, Manteuffel's lead division, the 26th *Volksgrenadier* Division, had to take this town. From December 16 through the morning of December 18, the Germans gradually reduced the defensive perimeter held by the two companies. With heavy casualties and virtually no ammunition, the two companies held out until 9:00 am on December 18, when they had to surrender.[52] Although German units had bypassed Hosingen, they had to capture it because it dominated the road network. The American companies exacted heavy casualties from the attacking German regiments, but like Bouck's 394th Infantry Regiment I&R platoon, the greatest casualty they inflicted on the Germans was on their time schedule. At Hosingen, the German divisional commander recognized and even personally congratulated the two company grade officers for their bravery.

At Lanzerath, Hosingen, St. Vith, Baraque De Fraiture, and many other locations, from December 16 to 19, small unit actions deprived the Germans of the speed that they needed to accomplish their offensive objectives. For example, as Manteuffel sought to have his panzer units in Bastogne by late December 16 or, at the latest, early on the 17th. They did not reach the outskirts of Bastogne until early December 19. The 26th *Volksgrenadier* Division commander *Generalmajor* Heinz Kokott emphasized the need for speed and the necessity of taking Bastogne when he said:

> Success or failure of the entire operation depends on an incessant and stubborn drive westward and north-

west. The forward waves of the attack must not be delayed or tied down by any form of resistance. . . . If at all possible Bastogne should fall on the second day of the offensive or at least be encircled by then. [53]

The German Offensive Stalls.

As the Battle of the Bulge was developing, the Germans were unable to achieve the necessary speed to advance first to the Meuse and then to Antwerp. Again, speed was necessary so the German spearheads could reach their objectives before the overcast cleared and the Allies could organize air and ground reinforcements to counter the German offensive. The response to the German attack by U.S. Army platoons, companies, and regiments deprived the Germans of the rapid advance they desperately needed to make the offensive a success. Initially, the American response to the German attack came from small units scattered over the front since communications between higher headquarters were chaotic at best. Furthermore, for the first few days of the offensive, higher headquarters had difficulty in determining what was occurring on the front lines.

What was not immediately obvious to the American Army, due to the surprise and the shock of the initial attack, was that the German Army had lost many of the capabilities that made it so successful in earlier campaigns. Hitler never really seemed to appreciate the role that combined arms operations had in the German victories of 1939-42. In France, the Low Countries, and the Russian Steppes, German tactical aircraft dominated the airspace, strongly and effectively supporting German units in contact with Soviet forces. Similarly, German artillery was very important from 1939 through the campaign into the Hürtgen. However, during the Battle of the Bulge, when weather allowed, the Allied air forces totally dominated the airspace; and even though there were still many experienced German artillery units, there was a critical shortage of ammunition.[54] German leadership had made Tiger and Panther tanks available to tank units in increasing numbers, but experienced crews and fuel were in short supply. Even in locations like Lanzerath, Belgium, where Lyle Bouck and his platoon had achieved so much, it was obvious that the young German paratroopers from the 3rd Parachute Division were poorly trained in basic tactics. In short, German military forces had been at war too long, and experienced soldiers and aviators were in limited supply, as were many basic materials of war. As the days, even weeks, of the offensive continued, it would become obvious that the German Army was expending its last fresh units, but as Christmas 1944 approached, this eventuality was far from obvious.

Eisenhower, as ground component commander, had begun his response to the sudden German offensive shortly before midnight on December 16 when he overruled Bradley and ordered the 7th and 10th Armored Divisions to assist in the defense effort. On the following day, with Bradley's encouragement, he set the 82nd and 101st Airborne Divisions in motion to shore up the American position. Bradley also asked Patton what he was able to do to assist. With a response beginning to emerge, Eisenhower announced his intention to launch a counterattack as soon as possible. With this goal in mind, he ordered Devers to stop all of his offensive operations and lengthen the 6th Army Group's line, so that Bradley's 12th Group's lines could be shortened. To firm up his plans for a counterattack, Eisenhower called for a meeting of his senior commanders at Verdun, France, on December 19. Senior officers in attendance were Bradley, Devers, Patton, Bedell Smith, Arthur Tedder, and Eisenhower. Absent was Montgomery who sent a representative, his Chief of Staff, Major General Frederick ("Freddy") Guingand.

As the meeting began, Eisenhower was grim faced, but he told all present that they should regard the German counterattack as an opportunity. After all, the Germans had emerged from their defensive mode and they were out in the open, vulnerable to attack. Patton totally agreed and added, "Hell, let's have the guts to let the sons of bitches go all the way to Paris. Then we'll really cut 'em up and chew 'em up." After the laughter had subsided, Eisenhower stated, "George, that's fine. But the enemy must never be allowed to cross the Meuse." Continuing, Eisenhower directed that once the German drive had culminated, Patton, under Bradley's overall command, was to launch the counterattack. Eisenhower told Patton to attack with at least six divisions and then asked when he could start. Patton quickly responded, "as soon as you're through with me." Then, the SHAEF commander asked, "When can you attack?" Patton responded, "The Morning of December 21st with three divisions." Eisenhower was clearly irritated and responded, "Don't be fatuous, George."[55] In fact, Patton was deadly serious. His staff had been working on plans to counter a German attack shortly after enemy forces penetrated the American lines. Koch had likely started Patton thinking about possible responses with his briefing on December 9, where he showed the general that German units appeared to be concentrating opposite Middleton's Corps.[56] Once Eisenhower's meeting was over, Patton phoned his headquarters and gave the code word that would result in what was one of his most spectacular accomplishments; stopping his army and turning a part of it 90 degrees to attack the German flank.

From December 19-20, Eisenhower announced two significant decisions that would affect the course of the Battle of the Bulge. The first, at Verdun he placed Patton in charge of an attack into the German left flank. Patton was still under Bradley's command, but nonetheless it was his counterattack. The second and more surprising decision was for his 12th Army Group commander. Eisenhower called Bradley on December 20. He informed his old friend that the 1st and 9th Armies, now geographically separated from their 12th Army Group commander by the German Bulge, were going to be placed under the command of Montgomery until the Allies could reduce the threat of the German bulge. By December 20, command relationships on the Western Front had changed substantially. Montgomery's 21st Army Group had expanded in terms of terrain and the number of armies. Devers' 6th Army Group had also expanded, and the 12th Army Group, for all practical purposes, was defunct, other than Bradley's "supervision" of Patton's counterattack. No one recognized this better than Bradley.[57] Bradley never cared much for Montgomery, and after December 20 that dislike increased substantially. Much more, the stage had also been set for a renewal of Montgomery's disagreement with Eisenhower over strategy. Montgomery's main concern regarded Eisenhower's overextension of his span of control, i.e., serving as both Supreme Commander and ground component commander.

Again, as had happened at the Falaise Gap and in the discussion of driving deep toward the Seine River to cut off the mass of the western German Army, the question quickly emerged about what would be the appropriate orientation of Patton's attack. The "Bulge" had resulted in the formation of a classic salient into the American line, and a logical military option would have been to conduct an attack at the base of the salient from the north and south and pinch off the German units, setting them up for destruction. This was clearly Patton's preference, but as the general noted, "that isn't the way those gentlemen up north fight."[58] With the execution of classic double-wing envelopment, there were innumerable problems despite the desirability of such a maneuver. When the 101st Airborne Division moved into Bastogne, Belgium, on the early morning hours of December 19 and became surrounded, there was the obvious need to relieve this beleaguered light division. Map 8-3 clearly shows that Bastogne was in the center of the Bulge, not the base. It was also illogical to consider having the 101st Airborne Division withdraw from Bastogne, even if they could, because it was a vital road junction. Any withdrawal, without outside assistance, would have been difficult. Besides, by December 24, the stand by the 101st, the "Battered Bastards of Bastogne," was providing a psychological boost for the American Army that could find few, if any, victories in that first week of the German offensive.[59]

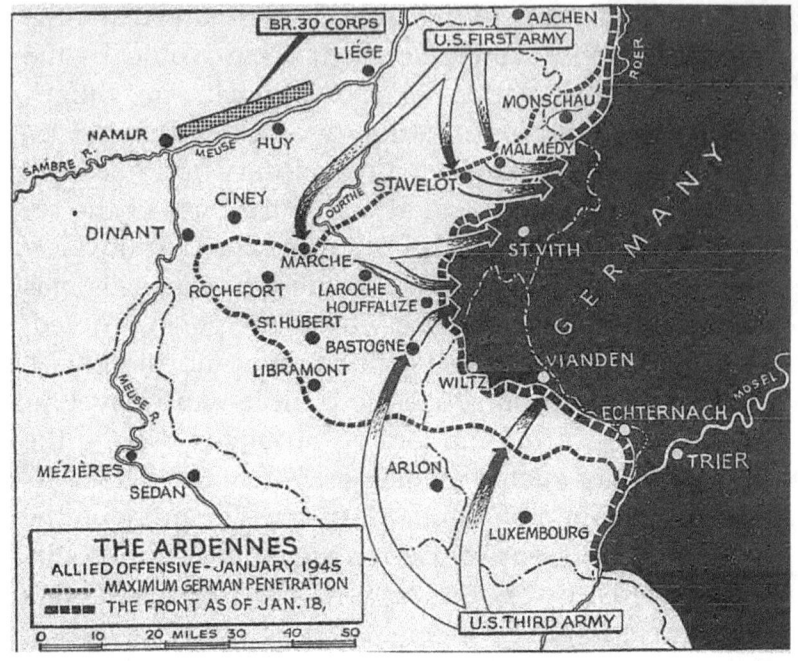

Source: Dwight Eisenhower, *Crusade in Europe*, Garden City, NY: Doubleday and Company, 1948, p. 364.

Map 8-3. Allied Counteroffensive Against the Bulge.

A Crisis in Command.

A second constraint that worked against envelopment was the nagging manpower issue. Since insufficient numbers of American troops meant that the broad front could not be adequately manned, there was a real concern that American units did not have sufficient power to hold the shoulders of the contested area and conduct a double-wing envelopment. There were Soldiers available in the continental United States

(CONUS) and even in England, but that hardly mattered since they were not immediately available on the battlefield.[60] Additionally, the initial German offensive strength was not known, and the force shown by the Germans in the first week came as a shock to the American Army. Thus, the question was, did the U.S. Army have the strength to surround more than 20 German divisions and then destroy them?

Finally, there was the question that if a decision was made to encircle the German force and elements of Patton's 3rd Army struck the base from the south, who would command the northern pincer? Obviously, it would have to be composed of elements from Montgomery's enlarged command. Giving Montgomery such a task and his role in countering the Ardennes offensive was yet another problem for Eisenhower. Up until the time that Eisenhower transferred the command of American units north of the Bulge to Montgomery, the Bulge had been an American operation, an American concern.[61] Now it was an Allied one.

When Montgomery was given authority over the 1st and 9th Armies, he attacked the problem with energy and his cocky self confidence. Finding the disorganization and gloom that seemed to permeate the 1st Army Headquarters and its commander, Montgomery initially wanted to relieve the exhausted Hodges. After hinting this possibility to Eisenhower, the latter politely expressed his confidence in Hodges' capabilities.[62] Since alliance politics made it unwise for a British field marshal to relieve a senior American general, Montgomery quickly found Hodges to be competent to handle the situation. Nonetheless, as described by one of his own British officers, Montgomery descended on 1st Army Headquarters like "Christ come to cleanse the temple."[63] He began the process of reorganizing the American front and almost immediately began to talk about a counterattack. Looking at his potential assets, he logically sought Collins to spearhead this move.

Conversely, as time elapsed, Montgomery's actions become difficult to explain. He wanted to counterattack, but seemed to want some type of validation that the Germans had, in fact, culminated their attack before he struck. Montgomery recognized Collins' aggressiveness on the battlefield but, with his meticulous nature, he wanted to pull him and his Corps out of the line for reorganization and refitting prior to any offensive action. Eisenhower stewed about what he regarded as Montgomery's inaction. When he received word on December 27 that Montgomery was finally considering offensive operations, he could only say, "Praise God from whom all blessings flow."[64] On December 28, Eisenhower was able to meet Montgomery and to discuss plans, hoping to gain a commitment from him on when he would launch his counterattack. A commitment from the Field Marshal proved to be elusive, even though Patton had his attack well under way and Bastogne had been relieved on December 26. Montgomery appeared to be proceeding at a relatively slow pace. He was still waiting for one more big German push, for the shattered 1st Army to be reorganized, and for some reserves to be built up in the 1st Army area. Eisenhower, however, wanted a rapid response. He was impatient and indicated that if the Germans did soon resume their offensive, Montgomery must launch his attack on January 3. In the midst of a rather tense meeting and as Eisenhower was feeling the weight of command, Montgomery elected to bring up the issue of ground component command. He wanted permanent control of the 12th Army Group, resuscitating the argument that had started in September about the need to have a single ground component commander. Eisenhower and Montgomery met in private, without staffers, but when it was over, it was clear that the meeting had been a burden for the SHAEF commander. On December 30, 2 days later, relations between the two reached a crisis.

Montgomery precipitated the crisis by sending a message to Eisenhower that simply enraged the SHAEF commander. Montgomery again pressed his point that he needed permanent control of both Army groups and indicated that if Eisenhower did not agree, additional failures could result.[65] For the case of Allied unity, it was indeed fortunate that there was a peacemaker in the wings. Montgomery's Chief of Staff Major General Francis "Freddy" de Guingand, an officer well liked by his American peers, sensed that a crisis was about to erupt. Taking great personal risk, given the weather, he flew to Eisenhower's headquarters to patch things up. Guingand's worst fears were realized when he found that Eisenhower had already drafted a message to Marshall stating that conditions between he and Montgomery had reached a crisis and that he could no longer work with the Field Marshal. Simply, either Montgomery or Eisenhower would have to go. Horrified by the news, Guingand asked Eisenhower for time to resolve the dispute. Eisenhower allowed 24 hours for resolution.[66]

In actuality, Montgomery would likely have to go. The same rationale that determined the final decision about who would be SHAEF Commander meant that if Marshall and the Combined Chiefs of Staff took Eisenhower's ultimatum seriously, Montgomery's position was tenuous. The American Army had the preponderance of troops on the ground; American industry was supplying a substantial amount of the war effort; and in all, America had the resources to conclude the war in all theaters. This made any decision extremely unlikely that Eisenhower could be required to step aside since he had, by this time, achieved tremendous popularity among the troops and across the nation. However, at the same time, the British press had also canonized Montgomery for his victories in North Africa and in Europe. How could he be relieved?

Guingand had 24 hours and, to his credit, he used it well. He convinced Montgomery that Eisenhower was asking for his relief and that he would likely ask for Field Marshal Alexander as a replacement. A deflated Montgomery let Guingand write the message to Eisenhower, apologizing and asking Eisenhower to tear up his message of December 30. Guingand averted the crisis, although relations between the two for the remainder of the war were rocky at best.[67] Eisenhower was, nonetheless, frequently perturbed with Montgomery during the last week of December and the first week of the New Year, due to Montgomery's slow and measured buildup in preparation for a counter attack. Montgomery's perceived caution, wanting to ensure that the German advance had culminated, was not what Eisenhower wanted. He sought a rapid and decisive action comparable to that provided by Patton. Instead, he got one delay after another. Montgomery would not launch his counterattack until January 3, 1945. When the attack from the north was initiated, it proceeded more slowly than Patton's brilliant 90-degree turn of his 3rd Army elements. In fairness, one should acknowledge that Collins' advance from the north did suffer some significant disadvantages. For example, in executing their counterattack, 1st Army elements were up against the heaviest and best equipped German force.[68]

Ardennes: The Closing Phases.

By January 3, the Allied response around the perimeter of the Bulge was finally in motion. The German Army, despite its initial tactical successes, had stalled. Though it was not immediately obvious to Allied soldiers on the ground, the German attack had been in trouble from the onset. Their key vulnerabilities were a lack of fuel and a lack of adequate air support. Even if they had captured the major U.S. fuel dumps, fuel supply was one of the German Army's "Achilles heels." Mechanized units were critical for the speed they needed, but they simply did not have the necessary fuel to keep their advance in motion.

Even as the Allied response was proceeding, beginning with Patton's attack, the Allies would have to contend with two additional complementary German offensives. In the initial planning for the Ardennes offensive, the likelihood of a flank attack by the 3rd Army was recognized by the German planners. As a result, the Germans devised a ground offensive in the region focused on Alsace, France. German officers designated this operation, NORDWIND, which was designed to relieve the pressure on the German spearheads that were trying to reach Antwerp. Devers' 6th Army Group was responsible for countering Operation NORDWIND. In many respects, this was not an easy task because, when the Ardennes offensive was launched, Devers had been required to extend his group's boundary northward in order to allow Patton's 3rd Army to withdraw divisions and make its 90-degree turn. This extension of Devers' line caused his 6th Army to cover a front close to 200 miles. To complicate the 6th Army Group's task, part of its force was composed of Free French units, which were not up to American training or capabilities. Devers, like 12th Army Group, was also suffering from a shortage of replacements.

Devers was fortunate that German officers did not impose the same secrecy level for Operation NORDWIND as it did for the Ardennes offensive. Since late November, intelligence indicators pointed to the possibility of a German attack. Devers and Eisenhower had the opportunity to plan for a likely second offensive. By Christmas Eve 1944, a German attack seemed a certainty, the only question being when. The Germans answered that question on New Year's Eve when, without any artillery preparation, the Germans attacked.

With some seven infantry and three panzer divisions for the assault and a follow-on force of some three to five additional divisions, the German Army launched Operation NORDWIND. For the first 5 days, they pressed the American and French troops hard as anticipated, and achieved some limited, if temporary, tactical successes. Eisenhower, having determined the Ardennes to be the greatest threat and with no additional divisions to give the 6th Army Group, had instructed Devers to surrender terrain to include falling back to the Vosges Mountains for a better defensive position. Surrendering the geography that Eisenhower suggested meant that an area of Alsace, possibly to include Strasbourg, could revert to German control. Militarily shortening the line made sense, although Devers was unsure that this would be necessary; but surrendering Alsace was yet another matter. Eisenhower made a logical decision, telling Devers to surrender ground, if necessary, but it ignored the French mystique about Alsace and Lorraine. The issue of who should control Alsace and Lorraine had originally emerged following the Franco-Prussian War. In 1945, the issue was still alive. When the French discovered that Eisenhower might shorten the line, inviting the fall of Strasbourg, General Charles De Gaulle, leader of the Free French, vehemently objected. He told Eisenhower that if he allowed the fall of Strasbourg, then he, De Gaulle, would pull Free French forces out from under Eisenhower's command to save Strasbourg from reoccupation by the Germans. Furthermore, De Gaulle, as the new leader of France, sent messages to both Churchill and Roosevelt, questioning Eisenhower's judgment.

A second German offensive had caused another disagreement in the Western Alliance. To resolve the disagreement, Eisenhower and De Gaulle held a meeting on January 3. Churchill and Alanbrooke also attended the discussion. Eisenhower was under considerable pressure. The Bulge was still a bitter battle for American troops, Montgomery was to launch his attack on the same date, and 2 days previously on New Year's Day, the German *Luftwaffe* had launched an attack on American airfields. The *Luftwaffe* officers designed Operation BODENPLATTE to neutralize Allied tactical airpower. Largely ineffective, although Montgomery's personal Dakota aircraft was one of the casualties, this action again proved the resilience of the German armed forces, even at this late time in the war. Two surprise attacks in a 2-week period were an embarrassment for Allied forces. In the midst of all of these crises, another Alliance problem emerged, this time with the French.

The meeting between De Gaulle and Eisenhower was a classic showdown between two strong willed and influential leaders. In the course of the meeting, both at times, lost their tempers and engaged in intense arguments. As the meeting concluded, however, both Eisenhower and De Gaulle found the necessary compromises. De Gaulle, recognized the military wisdom of Eisenhower's initial decision, but he emphasized that the Allies could not surrender Alsace and Lorraine. As an emotional event for France, the liberation of Strasbourg had been second only to that of Paris. Strasbourg and the Alsace-Lorraine area held a special meaning for the French. The Germans had wrested this territory from France in 1870 and again in 1940. On this issue, the French would not negotiate or compromise. At the same time that Eisenhower faced the possibility of disorder in France if he had to order an evacuation from the Alsace-Lorraine area, he found military justification for holding Strasbourg to ensure the safety of his lines of communications.[69] The strength of the Alliance and its leaders were clearly on display in this time of crisis.

German military forces had shown surprising resilience in the Ardennes with both Operations BODENPLATTE and NORDWIND. German military strength was declining, but the *Wehrmacht* still flashed signs of life. By January, the Germans had clearly lost the initiative in the Ardennes and, without the key force multiplier of surprise, coupled with a shortage of reserves, their success with Operation NORDWIND would be fleeting at best. Granted, the "Battle of the Bulge" would not end officially until January 28, many German officers in higher command positions knew as early as December 19 that the offensive had failed. Astute German military general officers like Rundstedt and Model knew it never had a chance. German units failed to achieve any of Hitler's objectives, other than to achieve surprise. Overall, the operation was unsuccessful. Hitler ordered the withdrawal of a number of elite SS formations from the Bulge on January 8.

The same issues that disturbed critics of American leadership in the early stages of the European Campaign, i.e., tactical approach to warfare, became the cause of additional criticism concerning the Allied response to the Bulge. An overview of Allied operations shows that the Bulge reached its culmination on December 23, but when that culmination was reached, there were insufficient forces available to counterattack and begin the destruction of the German forces in the salient, or as the Americans called it, the Bulge. SHAEF reserve, if it was truly a reserve, consisted of two light divisions (the 82nd and the 101st Airborne Divisions), hardly suitable to contest the array of armored forces the Germans had in the expanding penetration. Patton created a suitable response force for a southern arm of a pincer movement, but there was not the same type of innovative leadership available on the northern side of the salient to create a swift, powerful pincer to complete the encirclement. Even if Allied forces could execute a double-wing envelopment, it is unlikely that they would have had sufficient strength to hold the Germans and ensure their destruction, given the unreliability of tactical air in the December skies. Thus, in the end, once Bastogne had been relieved on December 26 and Montgomery had finally launched his attack on January 3, two arms of a pincer movement began to proceed toward encirclement. The 3rd and 1st Armies, however, would not join hands until January 16, and their juncture was at Houffalize, Belgium, a location that was closer to the center of the salient, rather than at its base. The Allied response to erase the Bulge was more systematically pressing it back to its pre-December 16 boundary, rather than cutting it off.

The Ardennes offensive was the defining part of the European Campaign for the American Army. Although Montgomery entered the battle on December 20 as a commander and brought with him some elements of the British Army, the Ardennes was largely an American battle. It proved that the American Soldier and the squad, platoon, company, and regimental leaders had learned and applied the art of war in a winning way. Hit by an attacking force that achieved total surprise, units on the ground showed maturity and resilience in Battle of the Bulge. The battle was a significant test for American forces because without consistent air support, which had so dominated the European Campaign, the American Army had to fight head-to-head with the once mighty *Wehrmacht*. The American Soldier clearly showed his competence.

The Battle of the Bulge, however, raised some serious questions about some of the American Army's leadership. In the Ardennes offensive, two trusted commanders failed, Hodges and Bradley. For the first few days of the offensive, Hodges seemed in shock and was not at all in control of himself, let alone the 1st Army.[70] Despite all of the arrogance and pomposity exhibited by Montgomery, it is not difficult to see why he thought Hodges should be relieved from command. Bradley, though never in shock, in the weeks prior to the German attack, denied the threat to his center. Even when the attack occurred, he initially attempted to deny the crisis that faced American forces. Eisenhower, however, who had expressed concern about the 12th Army Group's center on several occasions, quickly and decisively became the ground component commander by overruling Bradley on troop dispositions before the day of December 16 was over. He then mastered the crisis facing the American Army by turning to a trusted old friend and an early practitioner of operational warfare, Patton, and entrusted him with constructing the initial American response. To address the crisis, Eisenhower effected a change in command relationships.[71] Eisenhower allowed Bradley to remain the nominal commander, but in practice, Patton and his staff organized and implemented the southern wing of the 12th Army Group's response. Patton's counterattack to the flank of the German offensive was his finest hour.[72] The 12th Army Group commander would not even lead his troops on the northern part of the Bulge. Instead, Montgomery was given the role of organizing the Allied response and fighting the battle in that sector.

Eisenhower, despite his lack of any direct combat experience, emerges as one of the most competent senior leaders in the crises of late 1944. However, he still allowed some problems to fester. Granted, perhaps he should have watched more closely and personally intervened in the senseless Hürtgen Forest action. He did not pay enough attention to the manpower drain since it exacerbated the infantry replacement shortage facing the U.S. Army. Instead, he depended on trusted associates, Bradley and Hodges. When the crisis erupted on December 16, he quickly and decisively took charge of crafting the response. Whether the readers agree with his choice of strategy or not, Eisenhower was at least consistent. From the onset to the end of the campaign, he persevered with his broad front strategy.

From the standpoint of this analysis, one of the most regrettable elements of the Ardennes Offensive, or for that matter the European Campaign, was the inability of the Western Allies to quickly and efficiently fulfill one of Eisenhower's key objectives, the destruction of Germany's armed forces. Within the Ardennes area were elements of the German Army that Berlin could not simply replace in terms of elite formations and experienced soldiers. The fighting in 1944 had already been costly for the German Army. A Soviet summer offensive had forced a collapse of Army Group Center and had blown a hole in the German defenses on the Eastern Front. In this disaster, the *Wehrmacht* had already experienced the loss of about 25 divisions. Bagging a substantial amount of the forces in the Bulge would have left a hole in the German line that would have been impossible to plug.

In all likelihood, the Western Allies did not have, on the continent, the available resources to capture or destroy the German force in the Bulge. The Allies did not have many commanders who were willing and able to take the necessary risks to undertake an encirclement of German forces. Patton would have loved the opportunity to attempt such a maneuver, but it is highly unlikely that Montgomery would have done so, at least in a timely fashion.[73] Eisenhower wanted to conduct such an operation, but Montgomery moved far too slow to for such an aggressive maneuver. Much like at Falaise and the Seine, the main body of the German force was able to extricate itself, though with heavy casualties.

In the end, the cost to the German Army was still substantial. The *Wehrmacht* suffered from 81,000 to 98,000 casualties, depending on whose figures one uses.[74] Through either actual battle damage or abandonment due to lack of fuel, the Germans also lost between 600-800 tanks and assault guns. These armored forces amounted to virtually half of the inventory of the German units in the Ardennes. For the *Luftwaffe*, the cost was even higher. In the Bulge, Operations NORDWIND and BODENPLATTE cost the *Luftwaffe* close to 800 aircraft, some 280 on New Year's Day alone. The destruction of these aircraft, together with the accompanying loss of too many experienced pilots, meant the death of the *Luftwaffe* on the Western Front. By the end of the Battle of the Bulge, the European Campaign was entering its final phases.

ENDNOTES - CHAPTER 8

1. Winston S. Churchill, *Triumph and Tragedy*, Boston, MA: Houghton Mifflin Company, 1953, p. 281.

2. Omar N. Bradley, *A Soldier's Story*, New York: Henry Holt and Company, 1951, p. 444.

3. Peter R. Mansoor, *The GI Offensive in Europe: The Triumph of American Infantry Divisions, 1941*, Lawrence, KS: The University of Kansas, 1999, p. 191.

4. Edward J. Drea, *Unit Reconstitution: A Historical Perspective*, CSI Report No. 3, Fort Leavenworth, KS: Combat Studies Institute, December 1983, p. 33.

5. Walker's biographer noted that the drafters of Field Order # 10, which directed the operation against Metz, "appeared to consider the Moselle only a minor obstacle and that the XXth Corps would quickly reduce Metz . . . the commander and his staff were overly sanguine in light of the virtual lack of intelligence concerning the terrain stretching east before them. . . ." Wilson A. Heefnor, *Patton's Bulldog: The Life and Service of Walton H. Walker*, Shippensburg, PA: White Mane Books, 2001, p. 80.

6. Michael Doubler, *Closing with the Enemy: How GIs Fought The War In Europe, 1944-1945*, Lawrence, KS: The University of Kansas Press, 1994, pp. 127-136. Doubler noted Fort Julien, one of the Metz forts, had such strong doors that 10 rounds from a 155mm howitzer could not breach the door. At this stage in the European Campaign, given the experience of Aachen, the Hürtgen, and Metz, the lessons should have been obvious; if at all possible, bypass strong points.

7. In addition, the AAF also transferred another 6,000 potential pilots or aircrew members to the service forces of the Army. See Bernard C. Nalty, ed., *Winged Shield, Winged Sword: A History of the United States Air Force*, Vol. I, Washington, DC: U.S. Air Force, 1997, p. 325. Eisenhower noted that General Spaatz gave the Army 10,000 AAF personnel for retraining as infantrymen, see Dwight D. Eisenhower, *Crusade in Europe*, New York: Doubleday & Co., Inc., 1948, p. 333.

8. That the program enrolled the right kind of people should be obvious by noting some of its alumni: Henry Kissinger, Gore Vidal, Kurt Vonnegut, Robert Dole, and Edward Koch, among others.

9. Russell Weigley notes in *Eisenhower's Lieutenants: The Campaign of France and Germany, 1944-1945*, Bloomington, IN: Indiana University Press, 1990, pp. 372-373, by September the Army Inspector General identified that the replacement pool in the European Theater was 49,000 above the 70,000 authorized.

10. Eisenhower, *Crusade in Europe*, p. 333.

11. Martin Blumenson, *The Patton Papers, 1944-1945*, New York: Da Capo Press, 1996, p. 588.

12. Martin Blumenson, "A Deaf Ear to Clausewitz: Allied Operational Objectives in World War II," *Parameters,,* Summer 1993, pp. 16-17. See also Williamson Murray and Alan Millet, *A War to be Won: Fighting the Second World War*, Cambridge, MA: Belknap Press, 2000. The authors state, "The problem (i.e., the failure to encircle and destroy German armies) was that Bradley and Montgomery were focusing on the gaining of territory rather than the destruction of German forces in France."

13. Martin Blumensen, *The Battle of the Generals, The Untold Story of the Falaise Pocket*, New York: William Morrow and Company, 1993, p. 268.

14. Patton noted: "Omar is O.K. but not dashing." Blumenson, *The Patton Paper*, p. 517; Williamson Murray and Allen Millet, *A War to be Won: Fighting the Second World War*, Cambridge, MA: Belknap Press, 2000. In this recently published book, the authors find Bradley jealous of Patton, suspicious of the British, unimaginative, and dour.

15. Allied military leaders considered a plan to bag the majority of the German forces west of the Seine River, but despite Patton's enthusiasm to strike deep into the base of the German penetration and essentially capture a substantial number of the German forces, this was not attempted. Instead, there was the attempt to do the short envelopment at Falaise. Bradley halted Wade Haislip's advance that could have closed the trap. In the

end, Bradley blamed Montgomery, his superior, for his failure to advance quickly enough to cut off the German retreat. Much later, he acknowledged that his failure to "force the issue" at the Falaise was a decision he questioned. See the Diaries of Major Chet Hansen, Carlisle, PA: U.S. Army Military History Institute, March 28, 1945.

16. Army Doctrine of the period did not promote operational concepts. Reviewing *Field Manual (FM) 100-15, Field Service Regulations*, refers to Army groups as tactical in nature. Granted, Americans of the period were notorious for ignoring doctrine, but the absence of an intermediate level of war between theater and tactical in doctrine is curious.

17. See Robert Citino, *The German Way of War; From the Thirty Years War to the Third Reich*, Lawrence, KS: University of Kansas Press, 2005; and Sam Newland, *Victories are not Enough: Limitations of the German Way of War*, Carlisle, PA: Strategic Studies Institute, U.S. Army War College, 2005.

18. Weigley, *Eisenhower's Lieutenants*; Stephen Ambrose, *Citizen Soldiers: The U.S. Army from the Normandy Beaches to the Surrender of Germany*, New York: Simon and Schuster, 1997, p. 142. As both Ambrose and Weigley have noted, it was the strategy of U. S. Grant, the strategy of attrition.

19. Weigley, *Eisenhower's Lieutenants*, p. 464.

20. Eisenhower, *Crusade In Europe*, p. 322.

21. Bradley, *A Soldier's Story*, pp. 437-438.

22. John S. D. Eisenhower, *The Bitter Woods*, Nashville, TN: Battery Classics, 1969, p. 100.

23. Bradley, *A Soldier's Story*, p. 453.

24. Bradley acknowledged that the Germans had used the Ardennes in previous campaigns. He never seemed to consider the obvious fact that the Germans had used the Ardennes as a corridor for higher value targets in 1914 and 1940. Bradley claimed in his post war memoirs that he had seriously considered the precedent, but neither his papers at the Military History Institute in

Carlisle, PA, or those of his aide, Major Chet Hansen, confirm this. See Bradley, *A Soldier's Story*, pp. 453-454.

25. A presentation by Colonel Robert Doughty, Chairman of the History Department at the United States Military Academy, titled: *A Calculated Risk, The Ardennes, 1944,* January 14, 1995, delivered at a Strategic Studies Strategy Conference, essentially concludes that the calculated risk may have been warranted, given the end results of the destruction of the reserve that the Germans had built up. Like the authors of this book, he finds it difficult to determine if this was a calculated risk and if Eisenhower and Bradley understood the risk.

26. See George E. Dials, "Send Up the Yardstick," *Army*, May 1973, p. 27. A distance of 8 miles is generally accepted practice, not doctrine.

27. Eisenhower, *Crusade In Europe*, p. 337.

28. In his post war memoirs, Eisenhower produced a map that purported to show Bradley's evaluation of the potential Ardennes threat. It is curious that this depiction, drawn after the fact, closely follows the actual limits of the German penetration. No such map ever existed. Eisenhower was merely providing a graphic description of Bradley's sweep of the hand on a map, See Eisenhower, *The Bitter Woods*, p. 101.

29. Bradley, *A Soldier's Story*, p. 454.

30. Of the two senior commanders, Eisenhower seemed more aware of the risk than did Bradley. Eisenhower exhibited concern on several occasions about the extended line and the thin center of the 12th Army Group. He even had Sir Kenneth Strong, his G-2, brief Bradley on the eve of the Ardennes Offensive. Bradley brushed off this warning. See, for example, Eisenhower, *Crusade in Europe*, p. 344.

31. Carlo D'Este, *Eisenhower: A Soldier's Life*, New York: Henry Holt and Company, 2002, p. 654.

32. Belatedly, in his second memoir written with Clay Blair, Bradley recognized the significance of this error stating, "We

were all wrong, of course — tragically and stupidly wrong." Omar N. Bradley and Clay Blair, *A General's Life*, New York: Simon and Schuster, 1983, pp. 350-351.

33. Rundstedt was opposed to an offensive of this magnitude because the *Wehrmacht* did not have the necessary resources to stage it. The professional German officers consequently developed what was termed the small solution. Hitler vetoed the solution.

34. Brigadier General Edwin Sibert, Assistant Chief of Staff, G-2, Headquarters, XIIth Army Group, Intelligence Summary No. 18, Carlisle, PA: U.S. Army Military History Institute, December 12, 1944.

35. The 1st Army G-2 was Colonel Benjamin "Monk" Dickson who Russell Weigley reports that "Dickson's colleagues regarded him as not only bursting with the pretentiousness of a man deeply self doubtful . . . stereotypical G-2 pessimist." Weigley, *Eisenhower's Lieutenants*, p. 460.

36. Danny S. Parker, *Battle of the Bulge: Hitler's Ardennes Offensive, 1944-1945*, Conshohocken, PA: Combined Books, 1991, p. 34.

37. D'Este, *Eisenhower*, p. 639.

38. *Generalfeldmarschall* Gerd von Rundstedt, "Interview with *Generalfeldmarschall* Gerd von Rundstedt," *The Battle of the Bulge, The German View: Perspectives from Hitler's High Command*, Danny Parker, ed., Mechanicsburg, PA: Stackpole Books, 1999, pp. 182-183.

39. *General der Panzertruppen* Erich Brandenberger and *Generalmajor* Freiherr Rudolf von Gersdorff, *Ardennes Offensive of The Seventh Army* (16 Dec 1944 - 25 Jan 1945), Foreign Military Studies MS# A-876, Historical Division, U.S. Army Europe, 1945, pp. 14-15.

40. *General der Panzertruppen* Hasso von Manteuffel, Fifth Panzer Army, Ardennes Offensive Preparations (16 Dec - 25 Feb 1945), Foreign Military Studies MS # B-151, Historical Division, U.S. Army Europe, 1945, p. 21; and *Generalmajor* a.D. Heinz Kokott, Ardennes Offensive, Foreign Military Studies MS # 22, Historical Division, U.S. Army Europe, 1949, p. 7.

41. *General der Panzertruppen* Erich Brandenberger and *Generalmajor* Freiherr Rudolf von Gersdorff, *Ardennes Offensive of The Seventh Army (*16 Dec 1944 - 25 Jan 1945), Foreign Military Studies MS# A-876, Historical Division, U.S. Army Europe, 1945, p. 16.

42. On the southern shoulder was a slice of the U.S. 9th Armored Division and elements of the 4th Infantry Division. On the seam between the 99th Division and the 106th Division, the 14th Cavalry Group was positioned, and a portion of the 2nd Armored Division was engaged in another attack toward the Roer dam system.

43. Eisenhower, *The Bitter Woods*, p. 215.

44. Forest Pogue, *The Supreme Command*, Washington, DC: U.S. Army Center of Military History, 1989, p. 370. See also Stanley P. Hirshson, *General Patton: A Soldier's Life*, New York: Harper Collins Publishers, 2002, pp. 568-569.

45. Hodges had been warned as early as December 10, 1944, by his G-2, Colonel Benjamin "Monk" Dickson that the Germans had reconstituted a force capable of counterattack. Then on December 14, Dickson projected that there would be a German offensive, perhaps to give Aachen back to the *Führer* as a Christmas present. On the eve of the attack, he concluded the attack would be in the Ardennes. Having given this dire projection, Dickson then took a 4-day leave to Paris.

46. In an interview in 1992 with Colonel (Ret.) Leroy Strong, who after the war worked in the intelligence community, Dr. Sam Newland asked him who, in his opinion, was the best G-2 in the European Theater. Without hesitation, Strong said, "Oscar Koch." When asked why, Strong replied, "He had no choice."

47. Brigadier General Oscar Koch, *G-2: Intelligence for Patton*, Philadelphia, PA: Whitmore Publishing Co., 1971. See pp. 82-82, in particular, for Koch's assessments.

48. Blumenson, *The Patton Papers*, p. 582. While expressing concern about the static front, in a press conference on November 24, Patton, when asked if the Germans could stage a counteroffen-

sive, answered, "Not in my opinion." Koch's reports, however, would soon cause him to change his opinion.

49. The question immediately comes to mind, did Patton share Koch's concerns with his higher headquarters? Bradley later stated, "I, of course, did not see these Koch reports. Even if I had, they would not have unduly alarmed me." Bradley and Blair, p. 354.

50. Pogue, p. 365. Despite his claim, Bradley had failed to make any such plans. After this briefing, he issued no alerts and developed no contingency plans. Behind the ghost front there were no additional units, no reserves, and certainly none designated to blunt a German attack, as claimed by Bradley.

51. In *The Bitter Woods*, p. 192, John Eisenhower is highly complementary of the performance of Bouck and his I&R Platoon, as is Stephen E. Ambrose in *Citizen Soldiers: The U.S. Army From the Normandy Beaches to the Surrender of Germany, June 7, 1944-May 7, 1945,* New York: Simon and Schuster, 1997, p. 195. The full epic of this platoon, whose contribution to American victory was long overlooked, can be found in Alex Kershaw's recent book, *The Longest Winter: The Battle of the Bulge and the Epic Story of World War II's Most Decorated Platoon,* New York: Di Capo Press, 2004.

52. The private unpublished journal of Captain William H. Jarrett, Commander, B Company, 103rd Engineer Regiment, 28th Infantry Division, details the struggle of the two companies for the 2+ days of their resistance. Captain Frederick Feiker, K Company, 110th Infantry Regiment, actually negotiated the surrender and was personally congratulated by 26th *Volksgrenadier* Division commander *Generalmajor* Heinz Kokott for his stubborn stand. See *Generalmajor* Heinz Kokott, *The 26th Volksgrenadier Division in the Ardennes Offensive,* Foreign Military Studies, MS#B-040, Historical Division, U.S. Army Europe, 1946, p. 32.

53. Kokott, p.12.

54. Rundstedt, when interviewed after the war about the reasons for the failure of the Ardennes offensive cited American air dominance and also adds the shortage of fuel as key factors. "Interview With *Generalfeldmarschall* Gerd von Rundstedt" in Parker, ed., *The Battle of the Bulge,* pp. 182-183.

55. D'Este, *Eisenhower*, pp. 644-645.

56. Oscar W. Koch, *G-2: Intelligence For Patton*, Atglen, PA: Schiffer Military History Publications, 1999, pp. 92-93.

57. Bradley bitterly and loudly reacted to Eisenhower's call and threatened to resign. Following the end of the conversation, Bradley paced the floor in an unusual display of temper, laced with expletives. Bradley's reaction is recorded in the diaries of his aide, Major Chester Hansen, USMHI.

58. Carlo D'Este, *Patton: A Genius For War*, New York: Harper Collins Publishers, 1995, p. 678.

59. That the German advance was highly vulnerable became obvious on December 23 when, for the first time since the attack started, skies were clear and the Allied air forces had a literal field day with all of the German equipment that stretched from the German border to 6 kilometers from the Meuse.

60. Late on December 18 and before the Verdun meeting, Eisenhower was building up American strength on the continent. He first ordered the 11th Armored Division and the 17th Airborne Division, then training in England, to prepare for deployment in Belgium along the Meuse, should the Germans reach the river. At the same time, the British 6th Airborne Division was ordered to move by sea as quickly as possible to strengthen the 21st Army Group. See Weigley, *Eisenhower's Lieutenants*, p. 504.

61. This statement is generally true. Although as Montgomery became aware of the German penetration, he became more concerned that a German rush to Antwerp would cut the British off from their source of supply and would, in fact, isolate the British and Canadian force.

62. Stephen E. Ambrose, *The Papers of Dwight D Eisenhower: The War Years*, Vol. IV, Baltimore, MD: The Johns Hopkins University Press, 1970, p. 2369.

63. David W. Hogan, *A Command Post at War: First Army Headquarters in Europe, 1943-1945*, Washington, DC: U.S. Army Center of Military History, 2000, p. 219.

64. This consideration was because of Collins presenting to Montgomery on December 27 three plans for offensive action. Two options proposed meeting Patton's thrust around Bastogne, and the other included an attack much closer to the actual base of the "Bulge" at St. Vith. See Weigley, *Eisenhower's' Lieutenants*, pp. 540-541. See also J. Lawton Collins, *Lightning Joe: An Autobiography*, Baton Rouge, LA: Louisiana State University Press, 1979, pp. 289-293.

65. Never a fan of American officers, even Field Marshal Lord Alanbrooke sensed trouble. In his diary entries for December 23-30, he noted that Montgomery had another meeting with Eisenhower. Alanbrooke then stated, "I do not like the account of it. It looks to me as if Monty, with his usual lack of tact, has been rubbing into Ike the results of not having listened to Monty's advice." "Monty" was known among his peers as an officer lacking tact, and in this case Alanbrooke's assessment was exactly right. Alanbrooke, *War Diaries, 1939-1945*, Berkeley, CA: University of California Press, June 2003, p. 638.

66. D'Este, *Eisenhower*, pp. 656-657.

67. Even after the December 30 crisis, Montgomery continued to antagonize Americans in general, and Eisenhower in particular. In a news conference held on January 7, 1945, at 21st Army Group Headquarters, Montgomery discussed the Ardennes offensive and how he had recognized the problems, how he had taken steps to counter the German attack, and how the battle had some similarity to the situation he had to resolve at El Alamein. Eisenhower was furious over Montgomery seeming to take an inordinate amount of credit for stopping the Ardennes offensive, prompting him to consider sacking Montgomery again. The British press was also unkind to American performance in the battle.

68. The 1st Army had been hit extremely hard by the Ardennes offensive, whereas the 3rd Army had not initially been affected by the attack. The 1st Army was short on tanks, radios, rations and, most importantly, riflemen. In the 1st Army official history, the author notes that between December 16-31, 1st Army reported 41,166 losses but received only 15,295 replacements. Hogan, *A Command Post at War*, p. 225.

69. Eisenhower, *Crusade In Europe*, pp. 362-363.

70. Dempsey Allphin, who was the secretary and aide for the 1st Army's Chief of Staff Major General William Kean, reported that on December 17, Kean and Hodges arrived in the headquarters at 8:30 am. Hodges went directly into his office where he remained for the entire day. For the next 2 days, he stayed there alone, not taking calls, visitors, or seeing members of his staff. Hogan, *A Command Post at War*, p. 212.

71. Eisenhower was irritated with Patton's quick response to a request at the December 19 meeting to supply reinforcements during the Battle of the Bulge. He was worried that Patton would respond far too quickly and thus suffer a defeat.

72. No one knew this better than Patton. He stated, "Destiny [Eisenhower] sent for me in a hurry when things got tight. Perhaps God saved me for this effort." Martin Blumenson, *Patton: The Man Behind the Legend*, New York: William Marrow and Company, 1985, p. 252.

73. Resources aside, Alanbrooke's diary entry of January 5, 1945, is interesting because Montgomery mentions the under strength U.S. forces that he was now commanding, but states that between he and Bradley, they could handle the western end of the salient. The base would prove more difficult. Alanbrooke suggested reinforcements from Italy, but apparently he took no action about this issue. Alanbrooke, p. 643.

74. In contrast, the U.S. Army lost 80,987 men in the Ardennes, and the British Army suffered an additional 1,408 casualties. The basic difference was the Germans had scraped the bottom of the barrel — American losses could be replaced.

CHAPTER 9

THE RUHR OR BERLIN

May I point out that Berlin is no longer a particularly important objective.[1]

Dwight D. Eisenhower
March 30, 1945

Berlin was the prime and true objective of the Anglo-American Armies.[2]

Winston S. Churchill

As January 1945 came to an end, and with it the conclusion of the Ardennes campaign, the Western Allies faced the challenge of reaching, then crossing, the Rhine. By crossing the Rhine, the Allies would enter Germany therefore necessitating the destruction of the German military. The weakened *Wehrmacht* was still powerful enough to offer resistance, but that power was rapidly being destroyed. In February, after refitting from the bitter winter and the losses suffered in the Ardennes, the Western Allies again began their push to reach, and then cross the Rhine River. Once the Allied forces crossed into the heartland of Germany, the Allied leadership had to come to grips with what the focus of operations would be to destroy Nazi Germany?

Reaching and then crossing the Rhine were not new tasks for the Western Allies. When Operation MARKET GARDEN was launched in mid-September 1944, its intended result was reaching, then crossing, the Rhine. After American and British forces accomplished the crossing, the North German Plain would be open for a rapid advance eastward that could result in the capture of Berlin. Operation MARKET GARDEN died an embarrassing death, but in March after the Allied forces crossed the Rhine the opportunity existed to resuscitate the drive for, and the capture of, Berlin. Such a rapid advance was possible due to Allied efforts to solve the logistical problems that had plagued them from August through early December 1944. Allied leaders used trucking, rail, and other modes of transportation to ship supplies from Antwerp, Belgium; Marseilles, France; and a logistical center at Amsterdam, the Netherlands. The resource limitations that crippled American and British forces in their drive through the western occupied countries were no longer as debilitating.

The Allied armies in the west had also grown noticeably adding capability to achieve the original goals of Operation MARKET GARDEN. By March, the Western Allies had 2,553,000 American, British, and Canadian troops poised to complete the destruction of Nazi Germany and its military forces. These 91 well-equipped, and supplied Allied divisions faced a German Army whose resources, men, equipment, and terrain diminished daily.[3] American and Allied efforts pressuring the Germans in the west was much smaller than the Soviet efforts on the Eastern Front. By January 1945, Moscow had opened a winter offensive, and Soviet troops advanced on the Oder River in Germany. With the Soviet Army consisting of 555 divisions, it seemed unlikely that the depleted *Wehrmacht* had any chance of stopping them. Josef Stalin pushed the Germans with four massive fronts consisting of almost four million soldiers. The Soviets relentlessly sought a clearly defined goal, the capital of the Third Reich—Berlin. As spring arrived, the question quickly emerged: Was taking the German capital still a priority for the Western Allies?

Eisenhower had several options as he sought to conclude the European Campaign. The Western Allies could engage in a race with the Soviets to try to seize Berlin, or the Allied effort could focus on dissecting Germany into several pieces with a major effort that would cut through the Third Reich. American and British forces could make their move near Kassel and separate Berlin from Munich, the headquarters of the National Socialist movement. Through most of 1944, Eisenhower had been consistent in stating that the goal of the Anglo-American force should be to take Berlin, but by February 1945, he no longer believed that Berlin had any type of strategic importance for the Western Allies.[4] As he noted on March 31, "That place has become, as far as I am concerned, a geographical location, and I have never been interested in these."[5] On the other hand, directly in front of the American 1st Army was the Ruhr industrial district, a well-known center for the production of German war materials. The AAF and RAF CBO had taken a toll on the Ruhr's industrial capacity, reducing production by 25 to 30 percent. The destruction of the area's transportation network had also reduced the resource inflow and product outflow to and from the area, but the reputation of the Ruhr as the German industrial center still made it an objective of military value.[6]

There was an additional factor that added to the value of the Ruhr River Valley: Over 300,000 German troops were located in the area that stretched from the vicinity of Bonn north to Essen along the Rhine River, and to the east from Marburg to the German training facilities at Paderborn. If American and British forces could surround the Ruhr River Valley, then the Germans would lose the industrial basin of Western Germany and over a quarter of a million men. Whether he was aware of this or not, Eisenhower was recognizing that the old Clauswitzian concept of the enemy's capital being a center of gravity was not as relevant in 20th century warfare as it had been in 18th and 19th century wars. Thus, Eisenhower could see little purpose in subjecting the Western Allied armies to potentially heavy casualties for terrain that had already been designated as being in the Soviet zone. [7] As a result, Eisenhower dropped the capture of Berlin as a priority. On March 28, Eisenhower ordered the encirclement of the Ruhr. His plan was to first capture the Ruhr and then cut Germany in half on an east-west axis.

Eisenhower's decision to allow the Soviets to capture Berlin, rather than British and American troops was unpopular in London. Eisenhower did not consult Churchill or the senior British commanders about this decision concerning the change of a major strategic objective. As was often the case, the Prime Minister had his own ideas about the priorities for finishing the war. In addition, Eisenhower's staff sent the advance route information for the 12th and 21st Army Groups, once the Allies took the Ruhr, directly through the American Military Mission in Moscow to Stalin, without coordination through the Combined Chiefs of Staff or without informing Eisenhower's British Deputy, Arthur Tedder. Churchill strenuously objected to Eisenhower's direct submission of his plans to Stalin. Conversely, Eisenhower saw no reason not to directly communicate his plans to Stalin, since the Soviet leader was the commander of his nation's military forces. From Churchill's perspective, however, Stalin was the head of state and an increasingly worrisome dictator.

Churchill enumerated the reasons why Berlin could not be left to the Soviets. In a message to General Eisenhower on March 31, he stated:

> I do not consider myself that Berlin has yet lost its military and certainly not its political significance. The fall of Berlin would have a profound psychological effect on German resistance in every part of the Reich. While Berlin holds out great masses of Germans will feel it their duty to go down fighting ... while Berlin remains under the German flag it cannot, in my opinion, fail to be the most decisive point in Germany.[8]

Of equal significance, Churchill, in a message to U.S. President Franklin Roosevelt warned:

> The Russian armies will no doubt overrun Austria and enter Vienna. If they also take Berlin will not their impression that they have been the overwhelming contributor to our common victory be unduly imprinted in their minds and may this not lead them into a mood which will raise grave and formidable difficulties in the future?[9]

Another issue that rankled British sensitivities was Eisenhower's planned reversion of the U.S. 9th Army to 12th Army Group's control, once the Ruhr was taken. Loss of the 9th Army from British Field Marshal Montgomery's command meant that the combat power of the 21st Army Group was diminished. Thus, the 21st Army Group would lack the combat power to make a dash for Berlin, even if allowed to do so by SHAEF. In the eyes of the British leadership, Eisenhower's proposed shift from Berlin to an axis of advance that would lead from the vicinity of Kassel to Leipzig would mean that the smaller 21st Army Group would be in a backwater sweeping along the coastal areas and likely never even reaching the Elbe River in Germany. The British felt that Eisenhower relegated their forces to a secondary position in military operations.

Eisenhower, however, had the backing of both the American military and political leadership. There was considerable logic to his position. As early as January, lead Russian units were some 40 to 50 miles from Berlin, and by the second week of March, less than 30 miles from the capital. By early March, the Western Allies had yet to cross the Rhine River. Additionally, if the Germans were determined to defend their capital, then the American and British forces were sure to suffer high casualties in the urban fighting that would ensue. The American and British populace would find taking heavy casualties at this time in the war distasteful. Since Allied leadership agreed to the postwar boundaries, taking Berlin would require American and British units to capture terrain and then return it to Soviet control. The cost of capturing this territory seemed far too high for a bit of glory. Thus in Eisenhower's plan, American and British forces would stop at the Elbe River, well before Berlin, and meet the Soviets at a clearly identifiable demarcation line. This action would also avoid any problems with fratricide.

At the same time, Eisenhower understood the importance of alliance harmony, and worked to assuage British sensitivities. In his message to Churchill on March 30, he emphasized that he was not relegating the British-Canadian force to a secondary role; rather he was changing the axis of advance. Eisenhower also emphasized the critical role British troops would have in clearing the northern German ports, which were important for the Allies.[10] Churchill seemed to feel more at ease with Eisenhower's intentions, but at the same time, he replied the following day once again trying to convince the Supreme Commander that the 9th Army should remain with Montgomery's 21st Army Group. If Eisenhower did not make this move, then it would weaken operations. Churchill again made a strong case to Eisenhower and Roosevelt that Berlin should remain the focus of Allied operations. The Prime Minister's insistence irritated the SHAEF Commander. Eisenhower did not respond negatively to Churchill, even though he often found the Prime Minister difficult. The alliance was too important.[11]

With new objectives and a new axis of advance, the emphasis for the Western Allies was now on the 12th Army Group and the operations planned by General Bradley. According to his messages sent to Stalin and Montgomery, Eisenhower's plan was to:

> (1) ... encircle and destroy the enemy forces defending the Ruhr ... by developing offensives around the North of the Ruhr and from Frankfurt to Kassel until the ring is closed. The enemy enclosed in this ring will then be mopped up.[12]

> (2) As soon as you (Montgomery) have joined hands with Bradley in this Kassel-Paderborn area. . . . Bradley will be responsible for mopping up and occupying the Ruhr and with the minimum delay will deliver his main thrust on the axis Erfurt-Leipzig-Dresden to join hands with the Russians.[13]

In many respects a fortuitous event happened on March 7, the seizure of the Remagen Bridge. Elements of the 12th Army Group crystallized Eisenhower's thinking and put Bradley in a position to have a stronger role in the push across Germany. The bridge's capture by 1st U.S. Army, still under the command of General Hodges, was far ahead of their northern peers. The 1st Army elements had crossed the Rhine over the captured Remagen Bridge before Eisenhower's plan was revealed on March 7. Given the Remagen Bridge's location, this meant that the 1st Army was already posed to be the southern pincer of the proposed encirclement.[14]

Nonetheless, the 21st Army Group was to have an important role in the encirclement, the first potential major bag of German troops since the partially successful episode at Falaise, France. Montgomery's preparations for the 21st Army Group crossing of the Rhine were detailed or, according to his detractors, laborious. While elements of Hodges' 1st Army were crossing the Rhine, Montgomery was in a preparation mode which, given the immense buildup would have been difficult, if not impossible, to hide from the *Wehrmacht*. Lieutenant General William H. Simpson, the 9th Army's commander, had urged an earlier attempt at crossing the Rhine. Montgomery was unwilling to do so without an extensive buildup. The intent of Montgomery's Rhine crossing operations, entitled Operation PLUNDER, was to use over a quarter of a million men to execute and exploit his crossing. Before the British started the crossing, Montgomery requested that Eisenhower provide him with 10 American divisions to ensure the success of his operation. SHAEF denied the request. Preparatory fires began in the middle of February with the RAF's Bomber Command and the 8th Air Force pounding German targets. In the second week of March, tactical air forces joined the heavy bombers. Thus, Operation PLUNDER exhibited neither the spontaneity of the 9th Armored Division's Remagen crossing or that of the 5th Infantry Division from Patton's 3rd Army on March 22.

Elements of the 21st Army Group began their crossing on March 23 with considerable fanfare to include the Prime Minister, Alanbrooke, and Eisenhower as spectators. Eisenhower was there since the 9th Army was a participant. By this time, the 12th

Army Group already had two crossings secured. Once Montgomery's massive assault had succeeded, his American units—Simpson's 9th Army—were included in Eisenhower's envelopment plan. The pincer from 21st Army Group designed to move around the Ruhr from the northwest was comprised of Simpson's forces. Bradley was slated to regain control of this American unit after the Ruhr encirclement, but for all practical purposes, the 9th was under his command from the beginning of the operation. When the U.S. 1st and 9th Armies joined hands at Paderborn, the 12th Army Group consisted of 1,300,000 Soldiers, making it by size alone the primary focus of operations on the Western Front.[15]

In accordance with Eisenhower's directive, the group of armies from the north, essentially the 9th Army, and the Allied forces in the south were to proceed toward the Paderborn-Kassel area, where they were to link up. Allied forces were to envelope and then isolate the Ruhr Valley.[16] The Allied forces would create a pocket bounded in the west by the Rhine River with the city of Cologne and Dusseldorf and the smaller cities of Rüthen and Nuttlar in the east. Altogether, the potential pocket comprised almost 4,000 square miles and was 55 miles from north to south, and 70 miles from east to west. Initially, Allied planners estimated that 150,000 German soldiers under Model's Army Group B were in the Ruhr Pocket.[17] This intelligence calculation undercounted the actual enemy strength; Army Group B contained more than double the forces provided by the original intelligence estimate.

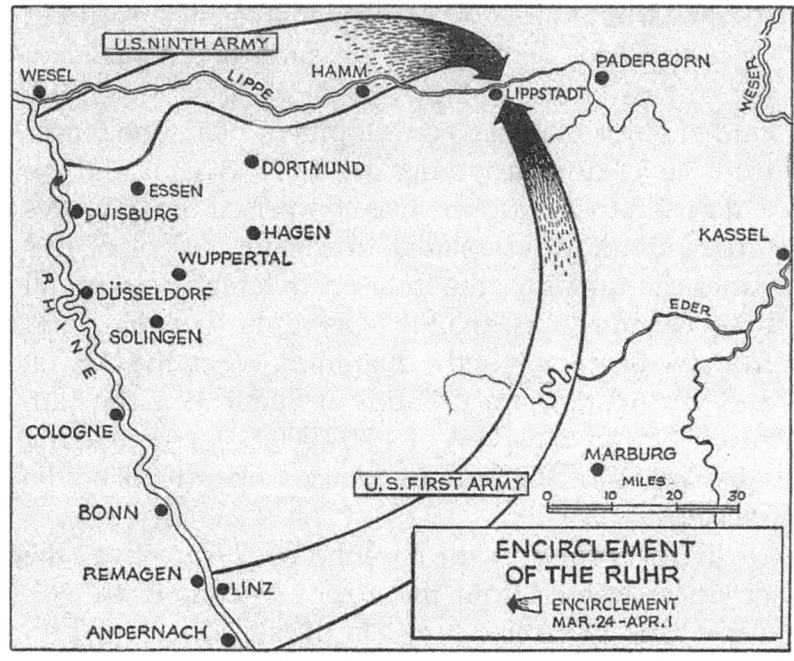

Source: The Author's Collection.

Map 9-1. The double envelopment concept for the Ruhr as planned and executed.

Model's Army Group B included remnants of many German units. The 5th Panzer Army, which had been troubling to the American Army in the Ardennes, was there, as was General Gustav von Zangen's 15th Army. Forces from two corps of the German 1st Parachute Army were in the potential bag as was the Headquarters of Army Group B. The effects of the previous years fighting had weakened these units and replacements and supplies were at best limited. The German commander could have withdrawn 300,000 men before the Allied pincers closed. He could then have broken out of the pocket and linked up with Army Group H in the north or Army Group G to the south. However, Model did have a major constraint. Hitler had ordered no retreats or surrender of German territory to the Allies. In particular, Hitler wanted to retain the Ruhr Valley, despite its reduced capacity. Flexibility for commanders in the field was not in Hitler's policies, particularly at this time in the war.

On March 29, Simpson ordered his 9th Army to advance toward Paderborn to meet elements of Hodges' units. Hodges' lead armored division, the 3rd, raced ahead, rapidly eating up German terrain. The 1st Army, like the 9th, would encounter some pockets of determined resistance, but both pincers continued to make steady progress. By this time, the U.S. Army had veteran commanders and divisions highly capable of executing this complex maneuver and enveloping the enemy. For example, Major General William M. Miley's 17th Airborne Division, with combat experience in the Ardennes campaign and Operation VARSITY, was a part of 9th Army's force.[18] Light forces, like the 17th Airborne Division, were not capable of delivering the necessary punch that would enable the two armies to link up. On April 1, Easter Sunday, elements of the 2nd Armored Division, a part of the 9th Army, and the 3rd Armored Division from the 1st Army joined hands at Lippstadt, only a short distance from Paderborn, thereby completing the encirclement of German forces in the Ruhr Valley.

Model had expected that Hodges would, after immediately crossing the Rhine, maneuver north to Cologne or Dusseldorf. Protecting the Ruhr from this threat was Model's top priority. Though Hodges' forces did take Cologne, he did not focus on cities along the Rhine; rather, his attention was on Paderborn.[19] After Model recognized Hodges' intentions, he attempted to slow or stop the American advance, but his efforts came to naught. Simply, Model lacked the necessary resources and, in addition, he lacked the flexibility to maneuver, given the specificity of Hitler's orders. Model had forces from seven corps that included elements of 19 divisions, but they were surrounded and lacked adequate transport, fuel, and air support to properly conduct operations.[20] Simpson and Hodges began to methodically destroy Model's divided resources.

The German military units in the Ruhr Valley found themselves cutoff from all possible help. Allied armored forces and airpower maneuvered unhindered as the 1st and 9th Armies completed their link up a short distance from Paderborn. A few weakened *Wehrmacht* units did attempt to break out, but were unable to do so. On April 1, the German 3rd *Panzergrenadier* Division could only muster four tanks to try to breech the U.S. 415th Infantry Regiment's defenses at Medebach.[21] Other German units tried to emulate the 3rd *Panzergrenadier* Division's attempt to escape, but all failed. These weakened units could only wait for the inevitable surrender. Simpson's 9th Army was assigned to clear the industrial northern areas of the Ruhr while Hodges was assigned occupation of the south.

Initially, some of Model's formations resisted surrender. Still, American Army units met a sea of white surrender flags in German cities. The tightening encirclement of Model's Army Group B reduced the capabilities of his forces to stem the American tide. Shortages of food, ammunition, and equipment made surrender an attractive option for the Germans. American units began gathering prisoners at the rate of 2,000 per day by the middle of April, up from 500 soldiers daily in late March.[22] Commanders within Army Group B pressed Model to surrender and to end hostilities. He continued to refuse; a German field marshal did not surrender. The 1st and 9th Armies had almost divided the Ruhr Pocket by the first week in April. Some German forces, especially *Waffen*-SS units, continued to offer stiff opposition in cities. Earlier strategic bombardment efforts to curtail economic efforts by the Allies inadvertently gave Army Group B forces the opportunity to improve their defensive efforts in the rubble. Despite these efforts, the defeat of Army Group B became inevitable.

By April 14, all resistance ended north of the Ruhr River, and the area was under control by the 9th Army.[23] The 1st Army had pushed into the southern Ruhr and had separated the territory into two major regions. Model could do nothing but wait. Model's staff and headquarters dissolved Army Group B to avoid surrender on April 17.[24] The next day, all German resistance ended, and the remaining German forces became prisoners. Model, true to his word, did not surrender; he went into the woods and committed suicide. The American military effort "bagged" 317,000 prisoners, to include 25 generals and an admiral.[25] The effort also allowed the Allies to liberate forced laborers struggling to support the dying German economy and industry.

The Ruhr Pocket operation was, in many respects, a milestone. Eisenhower had ordered a classic double-wing envelopment, and the U.S. 9th and 1st Armies had executed it perfectly, destroying or capturing the major German units which could have slowed the Allied advance to the Elbe River. Obviously, the *Führer's* orders to hold the Ruhr against impossible odds and the weakened state of German troops in the pocket helped Eisenhower to achieve his goal. Even so, American commanders and their Soldiers had learned the lessons of war very well. Though in no way to denigrate the capabilities of the British soldier, one could only wonder how long it would have taken Montgomery, given his consistent tendency to engage in lengthy preparations, to accomplish such a task.

Eisenhower's decision to bypass the opportunity to capture Berlin in lieu of the Ruhr was an extremely astute move, despite all of the disagreements he had to endure from his British colleagues, particularly the Prime Minister. In light of the progress of the advancing Soviet forces in the east, it is highly questionable whether the Western Allies could have reached the Third Reich's capital before the Soviets. Furthermore, the experience of World War II clearly shows that electing to fight in an urban area is ill advised, as the experiences of Stalingrad, or for that matter, Aachen, clearly demonstrate. It could have been even worse for the British-American forces had they attacked Berlin, given the Western Allies tendency to use strategic air assets to obliterate targets and thus convert them into excellent defensive positions. Even after Monte Cassino, Italy, the Western Allies seemed to ignore this lesson.

What had occurred in the Ruhr pocket was clearly important for Eisenhower's plans, but at the same time, the Third Reich was rapidly unraveling. Without the fanfare and publicity of Montgomery's Rhine crossing, Patton's 3rd Army had crossed the Rhine and rapidly advanced across Germany, reaching the Czechoslovakian border and again bisecting Germany. Patch's 7th Army from the 6th Army Group did much the same, driving across Bavaria and preventing the Germans from executing any attempt to further the war. The U.S. 9th Army raced across the North German Plain. By the middle of April, American forces had reached the Elbe. The 1st Army's success was likewise spectacular. Hitler's Thousand-Year Reich was only days away from its passage into the dustbin of history.

Eisenhower's order to ignore Berlin and encircle the Ruhr, coupled with his handling of the Battle of the Bulge, indicate that he was a far better field commander than as implied by his critics. He was also able to function exceptionally well as a commander of a joint Allied force and was able to capably deal with the multiple and often difficult personalities within the Allied governments. Under his guidance, the priorities set by Marshall and the objectives set by Roosevelt, ultimately the end of the European Campaign, were all in sight.

ENDNOTES – CHAPTER 9

1. Message from General Dwight D. Eisenhower to General George C. Marshall, dated March 30, 1945, in Dwight D. Eisenhower, *Crusade in Europe*, Garden City, NY: Doubleday and Company, Inc., 1948, p. 400.

2. Winston S. Churchill, *Triumph and Tragedy*, Boston: Houghton Mifflin Co., 1953, p. 456.

3. Russell Weigley, *Eisenhower's Lieutenants: The Campaign of France and Germany, 1944-1945*, Bloomington, IN: Indiana University Press, 1990, p. 668.

4. In Eisenhower's message to Marshall, he stated, "May I point out that Berlin itself is no longer a particularly important objective. Its usefulness to the German has been largely destroyed and even his government is preparing to move to another area." Eisenhower to Marshall in a memorandum dated March 30, 1945; Dwight D. Eisenhower, *Crusade in Europe*, New York: Doubleday and Company, 1948, pp. 400-401.

5. Alun Chalfont, *Montgomery of Alamein*, New York: Atheneum, 1976, p. 270.

6. Weigley, p. 674.

7. This was not the first time the Western Allies had faced such a quandary. On January 22, 1944, the U.S. Army had made a surprise landing at Anzio. The stated purpose of this operation was to cut the lines of communication that supported the German Xth Army on the Gustav line and restart the stalled British-American advance up the Italian peninsula. From the time American troops landed, the Allies seemed to lose focus. Their commander on the ground set up a defensive perimeter instead of moving eastward to cut the German lines of communication. General Mark Clark and the British, notably Churchill, seemed to forget the original purpose of the operation and began to focus their intentions on liberating Rome, rather than unraveling the German defense.

8. Winston S. Churchill, *Triumph and Tragedy*, Boston, MA: Houghton Mifflin Co., 1953, p. 463.

9. *Ibid.*

10. Dwight D. Eisenhower, *The Papers of Dwight D. Eisenhower: The War Years*, Vol. IV, Alfred Chandler *et al.*, eds., Baltimore, MD: The Johns Hopkins Press, 1970, p. 2563.

11. *Ibid.*

12. Eisenhower, *The Papers of Dwight D. Eisenhower*, Vol IV, p. 2363.

13. *Ibid.*, p. 2364.

14. The crossing of the Rhine by the 21st Army Group was, in many respects, anticlimactic except in Montgomery's mind. A task force from the American 9th Armored Division reached the Remagen Bridge on March 22. George Patton's 3rd Army began crossing the Rhine on March 6. Simpson's 9th Army under 21st Army Group command could have also crossed the Rhine in early March, but Montgomery refused to give Simpson permission to

do so. In what was Montgomery's hallmark, he developed his own plan for a massive assault later in the month which, while successful, seemed clearly overkill.

15. Weigley, p. 684.

16. Eisenhower, *The Papers of Dwight D. Eisenhower*, Vol. IV, p. 2542.

17. Weigley, p. 677.

18. Operation VARSITY was a part of Montgomery's PLUNDER activities. On March 24, 1945, 21,680 paratroopers, transported by 1,696 transports and 1,348 gliders, deployed to support Montgomery's advance. For the 17th Airborne Division, it would be its first combat jump of the war, although its first combat was in the Ardennes.

19. Forrest C. Pogue, *The Supreme Command*, Washington, DC: U.S. Army Center of Military History, 1996, p. 438.

20. *Ibid.*

21. Weigley, p. 677.

22. Charles Whiting, *Ike's Last Battle: The Battle of the Ruhr Pocket April 1945*, Barnsley, South Yorkshire, UK: Leo Cooper, 2002, p. 162.

23. Pogue, p. 440.

24. *Ibid.*

25. Weigley, p. 680.

CHAPTER 10

CONCLUSIONS AND OBSERVATIONS

This book is about a campaign, the European Campaign of World War II. It concerns how strategy and operations affected this campaign. Before considering either of these two subjects, one should first consider the basis of the military strategy, the goals and objectives established by a nation's leadership. The United States in World War II gives the student of military affairs an outstanding example of the national command authority determining the nation's goals and objectives. Beginning in late 1938, even before the war began, the nation's goals and objectives began to emerge. At that time, U.S. President Franklin D. Roosevelt had expressed great concern about the aggressive acts perpetrated by Germany, Italy, and Japan. His concern focused on German aggressive actions in Europe. In a meeting at the White House, he instructed the national and military leadership to begin producing weapon systems, initially aircraft, which would be available to assist friendly powers in resisting aggression. With this goal in mind, his basic strategy was to provide military equipment to democratic countries that faced aggression. Considering the mood of the country, the President's strategy was logical. As the decade concluded, he had to consider additional options to oppose Germany and Japan's actions. But, his goal and fundamental strategy, assisting nations threatened by the Axis powers, did not waver.

Although his initial strategy provided the means for potential victims of fascist aggression to resist their powerful adversaries, such a strategy would prove insufficient because the world situation continued to degenerate. As it worsened, he first expanded the practice of aiding endangered countries with such programs as the Lend-Lease Act of March 1941. Again, this strategy of providing military assistance to countries facing aggressors supported his goal. The world situation, however, was so volatile that he and his advisors soon realized that the supply of the weapons of war to U.S. allies would not be enough to halt the Axis powers. Their aggression continually pushed the United States closer to war. Thus, even while retaining the hope of avoiding direct American involvement in the war, the administration began expanding military forces. The passage of a peacetime draft and the National Guard and Reserve mobilization in 1940 ultimately gave America a more robust military force. Still, the nation's leadership was not fully committed to war. Although both of these measures expanded the nation's military, they were limited since they were effective for only a year. The United States was still struggling to develop a national consensus. At this point, the President's goal was still preventing the expansion of fascist moves through assistance to the threatened countries. Roosevelt's leadership, seen through his establishment of a clear objective and his ability to stick with it, provides an excellent example of solid executive leadership.

By 1941, the nation was rapidly being drawn into active participation in the war. War plans, actual military strategies, were in desperate need of revision. On several occasions Roosevelt had expressed his concern that the prewar plans were contingencies, not detailed war plans. The prewar Rainbow Plans and the AAF's AWPD/1 were available, but they did not provide the necessary detailed basis for conducting a war. The military leadership also foresaw the need for early planning and began the process of improving its prewar plans. Brigadier General Leonard T. Gerow created the first detailed plan when he ordered Wedemeyer to develop the "Ultimate Requirements Study," called by one author the "Victory Plan of 1941." The principles of how Wedemeyer outlined and created the strategy provide a good model of how to think about planning for war, no matter whether the war is a short war, counterinsurgency, or a full-scale worldwide conflict.

Wedemeyer's methodology for developing a war plan began with attempting to clearly ascertain the nation's objective. He simply asked, "What is the national objective of the U.S.?" Reading all that he could on the subject, Wedemeyer grasped the President's priorities, his intent, but he needed to develop a clear objective statement for the basis of the plan. After considerable research he determined the objective was "to eliminate totalitarianism from Europe and, in the process, to be an ally of Great Britain; further to deny the Japanese undisputed control of the Western Pacific."[1]

In this accepted objective, three statements stand out. First, Europe was preeminent in any consideration of American involvement in war. Second, Great Britain was an important element in Roosevelt's plans. Third, Japan was a concern, but it was not the primary focus; rather it was a secondary effort in America's war plans. As Wedemeyer developed the Victory Plan, some of the specific force structure assumptions he made were incorrect, but the objective and priorities he developed were correct. He had captured Roosevelt's intent, and the nation never wavered from these stated objectives. As noted by the late Charles E. Kirkpatrick, "the Victory Plan established the model for modern strategic planning."[2] Although changes and modifications were made to Wedemeyer's plan, the central thrust of the strategy remained remarkably constant. His example provides a great case study to view the development of strategy in the context of modern conflict.

This Victory Plan based on the Roosevelt's priorities, in turn, directly led the nation to the planning for and the execution of the European Campaign. National leadership must tie military strategy to the political objectives of the state. As noted by Colin Gray, strategy becomes a bridge that links military capability and forces to political purposes. In this case, it was done well. Once the war began, Roosevelt strengthened his objectives and perhaps clarified his intent. Eliminating totalitarianism meant the unconditional surrender of America's totalitarian enemies, not merely compelling the surrender of their military forces.

National leadership should develop and create military strategies based on clearly stated and achievable objectives. Without achievable objectives and strategies, which are within the means of a nation, tactical, and even operational successes will come to naught. The German experience in World War II demonstrates what can happen if objectives and strategy are ill-conceived or unrealistic, or are beyond a nation's means. Here again, the United States was fortunate. Despite a slow recovery from a worldwide economic depression, it was perhaps at the height of its industrial era. Such industrial power gave the United States the means to wage war in two widely separate theaters, as well as to assist Great Britain, the Soviet Union, Nationalist China, and a host of other minor players. Both factories and agricultural output far exceeded what the nation needed to accomplish Roosevelt's objectives. Thus, the nation had what was required in terms of the means, the resources for war.

Although the pre-conflict plans seemed reasonable in Washington circles, they often had to be amended or changed due to political reasons, the unexpected action of the enemies, and actions by Allies in accordance with their national interests. Personalities, both within American military circles as well as political leaders, had a decided effect on Allied plans and strategies. For example, demands from Joseph Stalin to open a second front to relieve pressure on the Soviet Union dogged Roosevelt and British Prime Minister Winston Churchill throughout the war and helped make the European Campaign a virtual necessity. The concept of invading the continent of Europe was decidedly a part of American plans, but Stalin's insistence on a second front made it even more important. Churchill's concern about the Mediterranean, the British interest in peripheral strategies, and their postwar interests were responsible for repeated attempts at changing the plans and strategies of the Western Allies. National political and military leaders had the political backing, priorities, and service capabilities to accommodate these various factors.

As a final and important element leading to a nation's potential success, what military strategy did the Allies adopt to achieve the objectives? The American strategy centered on the engagement of the German *Wehrmacht* and its destruction. This would be the nation's first priority; the Pacific Theater was to be a secondary effort. Virtually from the onset, in Marshall's mind, American forces would have to enter the continent of Europe and engage and destroy the German military on its "home turf." In addition to the efforts of American ground forces, the American intrusion into Europe would also come from the air. Naval forces would support combat sustainment, and

Allied air forces would conduct a Combined Bomber Offensive, an effort in the tradition of Italian General Giulio Douhet, to bring German industry and the will of its people, to their knees. The United States and its military leadership never changed from these basic principles, despite distractions from within and from our major Western ally, the British. Roosevelt had to accept some compromises to ensure that the coalition of disparate Allies would hold together to fight Germany. Fears of a Japanese-conquered China, its incursion into India, and expansion throughout the Pacific caused some American military leaders, notably naval leadership, to question the primacy of a Europe first strategy, but Europe first and the invasion of the European continent endured.

The question has been repeatedly raised by both historians and students of military strategy and operations as to whether American and Western allied operations in the European Campaign were directly focused on the destruction of the enemy force. This intent of American strategy is evident, the destruction of once mighty *Wehrmacht*, but were operations clearly focused on the destruction of Germany's military machine? One can provide repeated examples to show that Allied operations sometimes seemed to center more on the seizure of terrain and the taking of cities, a charge that has been made by both Martin Blumenson and Williamson Murray. One can wonder, even after over 60 years, how anyone can explain, logically, the Hürtgen Forest, an unbelievable slugging match that hardly profited the American Army. Furthermore, it will likely be debated into infinity as to why American and British forces tarried so long in closing the Falaise Gap in France; or why the Allies were unable to pinch off the Bulge, rather than just hammer German forces back to their starting position. There were, in fact, few examples in the European Campaign of the Western Allies engaging in strategic or operational maneuver, a type of warfare exhibited first by the Germans and later by the Russians, who learned well from their adversaries.

Instead, on the ground, Western Allied armies pursued Eisenhower's favored broad front strategy, the strategy of general advance. One can still ask the question, did the Western Allies have the experienced commanders on the ground in the early phases of the campaign enabling them to conduct Cannae-type operations (Second Punic War in Italy), where a military force enveloped and annihilated a foe?[3] Certainly American military doctrine did not include anything comparable to what would later be called the operational art. In fairness, the concept existed, but the doctrine did not. One is left to wonder if critics of the war's conduct, i.e., the lack of operational thinking, realize that although Eisenhower's broad front strategy was neither imaginative nor dashing, but it was a strategy that the Germans were least able to handle. Faced by the 500-plus Russian divisions on the Eastern Front, and the Western Allies resources, the Germans were simply unable to adequately handle all of the crises that confronted their forces in the field.

Still, as the war reached its conclusion, Allied forces finally concluded with a classic example of enveloping a major enemy force in what was called the Ruhr Pocket. Prior to this episode, the Western Allies seemed unwilling or unable to conduct such a maneuver. In the end, the German Army was destroyed, and American and British units so completely defeated their opponents that there could never be the possibility of another "stab in the back" legend comparable to 1918 that could grow among German politicians and officers.

American military strategy allowed Washington, and ultimately London, and Moscow, to accomplish their primary objective in World War II, the unconditional surrender of National Socialist Germany and the destruction of its armed forces. The European Campaign, coupled with the overall history of World War II in Europe, illustrates to students of military operations a very clear lesson. The adoption of achievable objectives and strategies, both national and military, are keys to a nation's success.

Military strategy does not exist by itself, rather it supports the political object of the war; and World War II in general, and the European Campaign in particular, serves as a classic example. A student of World War II can see the interplay of political objectives and the impact that they had on strategy. The war was conducted consistent with Carl von Clausewitz's dictum that, "[s]trategy is the use of engagement for the purpose of the war."[4]

The relationship between military strategy and political purpose has not changed despite the passage of over 60 years. Whether one believes in the theories of Clausewitz, Henri Jomini, Sun Tzu, or countless other strategists past and present, strategy and its development is a timeless art. Beliefs in particular military theories, service agendas, claims for particular roles and missions, doctrine, education, resources, leadership styles, and political realities molded many of the military strategies before and shortly after America's entry into World War II. These same issues face political and military leaders today.

One could say that in today's world, strategy, both national and military, must be more flexible. In World War II, the chief vehicle to defeat Germany was military force. Conventional militaries squared off in the air, on land, and at sea, to vanquish their respective opponents. Although the nation must still have this capability, the rise and importance of other elements of power and the wider range of potential conflicts raise questions as to the primacy of exclusive military options. Events have forced strategists to adopt approaches that affect not only more coordinated joint actions, but joint, interagency, intergovernmental, and multinational aspects too. Strategy has become a complex mix of interactions between players. Technology has advanced so much that military actions happen with greater speed and can have unparalleled precision. Similarly, global media can take an innocuous action and turn it into a pivotal event that changes the character and direction of a conflict. Coupled with a dynamic environment that forces national and military leaders to continually review their objectives, policies, and resources, the potential for vast differences between strategy and political ends seem great.

Despite the introduction of higher technology and a host of systems and organizations to ensure military strategy supports national objectives and interests, the problem of establishing achievable objectives and the strategies to achieve them remains. Today's environment may be more complex than the one American Army leadership faced in the 1940s, but many of the lessons from World War II remain significant. Leadership differences, differing national interests within an alliance even as close as Britain and the United States, and the upsets caused by unanticipated enemy reactions can all be seen through a study of the European Campaign.

This highlights the point that strategy, national and military, has always been dynamic and likely always will be. Possessing the flexibility and imagination to respond to political changes are an absolute must for military strategists. Few situations, if any, would dictate a fixed, set-piece strategy. What has changed is the speed of communications and the reaction time to the events that have an impact on a nation's interests. Still, practitioners and students of military strategy have at least one consolation. Many of the problems faced today and in the future most likely have never been encountered before. However, not all is lost. A study of military history sheds light on many present issues and ones that a nation will face in the years to come. Strategy and operations, like those covered in this book on Allied operations in Europe, will always be a dynamic activity. The impact of personalities, improved technology, differing agendas within an alliance, and differing interservice agendas will all force changes in strategy, much as they did in World War II. That the world, like war, has seen many changes should be obvious, but the problem of creating a coherent strategy in order that a nation may protect its interests and achieve its objectives still exists and likely always will. A study of history cannot solve this quandary, but it can provide important insights.

ENDNOTES - CHAPTER 10

1. Charles E. Kirkpatrick, *An Unknown Future and a Doubtful Present: Writing the Victory Plan of 1941,* Washington, DC: U.S. Army Center of Military History, 1990, p. 63.

2. *Ibid.,* p. 123.

3. In 216 B.C., the Carthaginian General Hannibal lured his Roman opponent into a pocket, then closed the flanks and rear of the pocket leading to the annihilation of the Roman force.   The name "Cannae" has since become synonymous in the study and practice of the military art with envelopment and annihilation on the battlefield.

4. Carl Von Clausewitz, *On War*, Michael Howard and Peter Paret, eds., Princeton, NJ: Princeton University Press, 1976, p. 177.

BIBLIOGRAPHY

Government Documents.

Chief of Staff to Supreme Allied Commander, History of COSSAC, Historical Sub-Section, Supreme Headquarters, Allied Expeditionary Force, N.P., May, 1944.

Documents on German Foreign Policy, 1918-1945, Washington, DC: U.S. Department of State, 1949.

Eisenhower, Dwight D., *Report by the Supreme Commander to the Combined Chiefs of Staff on Operations in Europe of the Allied Expeditionary Force 6 June 1944 to 8 May 1945,* Washington, DC: U. S. Army Center of Military History, 1994.

Marshall, George C., *Biennial Reports of the Chief of Staff of the U.S. Army to the Secretary of War, 1 July 1939 - 30 June 1945,* Washington, DC: U.S. Army Center of Military History, 1996.

Middleton, General Troy, VIII Corps After Action Report on the Ardennes, April 6, 1945, U.S. National Archives.

Sibert, Edwin, Assistant Chief of Staff, G-2, Headquarters, XIIth Army Group, Intelligence Summary No. 18, December 12, 1944, U.S. Army Military History Institute, Carlisle, PA.

U.S. Army Air Forces, IXth Troop Carrier Command, "Air Invasion of Holland: IX Troop Carrier Command Report on Operation Market," January 1945.

U.S. War Department, *Field Service Regulations,* FM 100-5, *Operations,* Washington, DC: Government Printing Office, 1941.

Primary Sources.

Alanbrooke, Field Marshall Lord, *War Diaries, 1939-1945,* Alex Danchev and Daniel Todman, eds., Berkeley, CA: University of California Press, 2001.

Bennett, Ralph, *Ultra in the West: The Normandy Campaign, 1944-45*, New York: Charles Scribner's Sons, 1979.

Bradley, General Omar N., *A Soldier's Story*, New York: Henry Holt and Company, 1951.

Brandenberger, General der Panzertruppen Erich, and Gersdorff, General Rudolf von, Ardennes Offensive of Seventh Army (16 December 1944 - 25 January 1945) Foreign Military Studies, No. MS A-876, Historical Division, U.S. Army Europe, n.d.

Chandler, Alfred, Stephen E. Ambrose *et al.*, eds., *The Papers of Dwight D. Eisenhower: The War Years*, 5 vols. Baltimore, MD: The Johns Hopkins Press, 1970.

Churchill, Winston S., *Their Finest Hour*, Boston, MA: Houghton Mifflin Co., 1949.

Churchill, Winston S., *The Grand Alliance*, Boston, MA: Houghton Mifflin Co., 1950.

Churchill, Winston S., *The Hinge of Fate*, Boston, MA: Houghton Mifflin Co., 1950.

Churchill, Winston S., *Closing the Ring*, Boston, MA: Houghton Mifflin Co., 1951.

Churchill, Winston S., *Triumph and Tragedy*, Boston, MA: Houghton Mifflin Co., 1953.

Collins, J. Lawton, *Lightning Joe: An Autobiography*, Novato, CA: The Persidio Press, 1994.

Corlett, Charles H., *Cowboy Pete: The Autobiography of Major General Charles H. Corlett*, Santa Fe, NM: Sleeping Fox Publisher, 1974.

Eiler, Keith, ed., *Wiedemeyer on War and Peace*, Stanford, CA: Stanford University Press, 1987.

Eisenhower, Dwight D., *Crusade in Europe*. Garden City, NY: Doubleday and Company, 1948.

Eisenhower, John S. D., *General Ike: A Personal Reminiscence*, New York: The Free Press, 2003.

Gavin, James M., *On to Berlin: Battles of an Airborne Commander, 1943-1946*, New York: The Viking Press, 1976, p. 266.

Goschler, Constantin, ed., *Hitler: Reden, Schriften, Anordnung, Februar 1925 bis Januar 1933* (*Hitler, Speeches, Writings, and Orders, February 1925 to January 1993*), Munich, Germany: Saur Verlag, 1994, Vol. 4, p. 95.

Groener, Wilhelm, *Der Weltkrieg und Seine Probleme: Ruckshau und Ausblick* (*The World War and Its Problems: Retrospect and Projections*), Berlin, Germany: Martin Warneck Verlag, 1930.

Jodl, Generaloberst Alfred, *Invasion and Normandy Campaign*, Foreign Military Studies, MS# A-913, U.S. Army Europe, Historical Division, 1945.

Koch, Oscar W., *G-2: Intelligence for Patton*, Atglen, PA: Schiffer Military History Publications, 1999.

Kokott, Generalmajor a.D. Heinz, *Ardennen Offensive* (*The Ardennes Offensive*), Foreign Military Study MS# 22, Historical Division, U.S. Army Europe, 1949.

Kokott, Generalmajor a.D. Heinz, The *26th Volksgrenadier Division* in *the Ardennes Offensive*, Foreign Military Studies MS# B-040, Historical Division, U.S. Army Europe, 1946.

Kokott, Generalmajor a.D. Heinz, *The 26th Volksgrenadier Division in the Arc: Lennes Offensive* (16 December 1944 - 25 January 1945), Foreign Military Studies No. MS# A-876, Historical Division, U.S. Army Europe, n.d.

Kruger, General der Panzertruppen Walter, LVIII *Panzer Corps in the Ardennes Offensive* (16 *December* 1944 - 11 *January* 1945), Foreign Military Studies MS# B-321, Historical division, U.S. Army Europe, n.d.

Johnson, Ralph, "A Soldier's Story, 1941-1946," in Dorothy Chernitsky, ed., *Voices From the Foxhole,* Connellsville, PA: Connellsville Printing Company, 1991.

Liddell Hart, B. H., ed., *The Rommel Papers,* London, UK: Collins Press, 1953.

Luck, Hans von, *Panzer Commander: The Memoirs of Colonel Hans von Luck,* New York: Dell Publishing, 1989.

Manteuffel, General der Panzertruppen a.D. Hasso von, *Fifth Panzer (Ardennes Offensive Preparation)* (16 *December 1944 - 25 February* 1945), Foreign Military Study MS# B-151, Historical Division, U.S. Army Europe, n.d.

Manteuffel, General der Panzertruppen Hasso von, *Fifth Panzer Army (Ardennes Offensive Preparations)* (16 *December 1944 - 25 February* 1945), Foreign Military Studies, MS# 151A, Historical Division, U.S. Army Europe, 1946.

Montgomery, Field Marshall the Viscount of Alamein, *Normandy to the Baltic,* Boston, MA: Houghton Mifflin Publishing, 1948.

Montgomery, Bernard, *The Memoirs of the Viscount Montgomery of Alamein, K.G.,* New York: The World Publishers, 1958.

Roosevelt, James, *My Parents: A Differing View,* Chicago, IL: The Playboy Press, 1976.

Rundstedt, Generalfeldmarschall Gerd von, "Interview with Generalfeldmarschall Gerd von Rundstedt," Danny Parker, ed., *The Battle of the Bulge, The German View: Perspectives from Hitler's High Command,* Mechanicsburg, PA: Stackpole Books, 1999.

Schlieffen, General Field Marshal Count Alfred von, *Cannae,* Ft. Leavenworth KS: 1992.

Schram, Percy E., *Hitler: The Man and The Military Leader,* Chicago, IL: Quadrangle Books, 1971.

Schramm, Percy E., *The Preparation for the German Offensive in the Ardennes, September* to 16 *December* 1944, Foreign Military Study MS# A-862, Historical Division, U.S. Army Europe, 1945.

Stimson, Henry L. and McGeorge Bundy, *On Active Service in Peace and War,* New York: Harper and Brothers, 1949.

Speer, Albert, *Inside the Third Reich,* New York: The MacMillan Company, 1969.

Waldenburg, Generalmajor Siegfried von, *Commitment of the 116th Panzer Division in the Ardennes* 1944/45, (First part from 16-19 December 1944), Foreign Military Study MS# A-873, Historical Division, U.S. Army Europe, 1945.

Warlimont, Walter, *Inside Hitler's Headquarters, 1939-1945*, Novato, CA: The Presidio Press, 1964.

Wedemeyer, Albert C., *Wedemeyer Reports,* New York: Henry Holt and Company, 1958.

Weinberg, Gerhard, ed., *Hitler's Second Book: The Unpublished Sequel to Mein Kampf,* New York: Enigma Books, 2003.

Interviews, Letters, Memoranda, Diaries, and Manuscripts.

Dinardo, Richard L., *Twentieth Century Soldier in a Busby: August von Mackensen.* A paper delivered at the annual meeting of the Society of Military History, 2005.

Doughty, Robert, United States Military Academy, *A Calculated Risk, The Ardennes, 1944,* January 14, 1995, delivered at a Strategic Studies Strategy Conference.

Hansen, Chester, "The Diary of Major Chester Hansen, Omar N. Bradley's Aide during the European Campaign," Carlisle, PA: U.S. Army Military History Institute, n.d.

Jablonsky, David, "The Paradox of Duality: Adolf Hitler and the Concept of Military Surprise," Carlisle, PA: Second Annual Conference on Intelligence and Military Operations, May 1987.

Jarret, Captain William H., Commander B Company, 103d Engineers, 28th Infantry Division, an unpublished diary on his service in the European Theater of Operations and captivity, entries from December 16-18, 1944.

Johnson, Warrant Officer Ralph, Assistant Adjutant, 110th Infantry Regiment, 28th Infantry Division, Battle of the Bulge-World War II ETO, 16 December 1944, a typed manuscript by Ralph Johnson, Philadelphia, PA, February 15, 1984.

Kasdorf, Bruno, Oberst der Bundeswehr, "The Battle of Kursk: An Analysis of Strategic and Operational Principles," Carlisle, PA: U.S. Army War College, 2000.

Strong, Leroy, Colonel (Ret), aide to General Alan Jones, Commander of the 106th Division, later assistant G-3, 28th Infantry Division, in an interview in April 1992 with Sam J. Newland regarding intelligence in the European Theater.

Periodicals.

Blumenson, Martin, "A Deaf Ear to Clausewitz: Allied Operational Objectives in World War II," *Parameters,* Summer 1993.

Dials, George E., "Send Up the Yardstick," *Army,* May 1973.

Klein, Friedhelm und Karl Heinz Freiser, "Manstein's Gegenschlag am Donec: Operative Analyse des Gegenangriffs der Heeresgruppe Süud in Februar/Määrz 1943" (Manstein's Counterstroke on the Donets: Operational Analysis of the Counterattack of Army Group South in February/March 1943); Militärgeschichte: Zeitschrift für Historische Bildung, Heft 1, 1 Quartal, 1999, 9. Jahrgang (Military History Magazine for Historical Education, Number 1, 1st Quarter, Vol. 9, 1999), pp. 12-18.

Miller, Edward G. and David T. Zabecki, "Tank Battle in Kommerscheidt," *World War II,* November 2000, pp. 42-48, 88-89.

Morton, Louis, "War Plan Orange: Evolution of a Strategy," *World Politics,* January 1959, pp. 221-250.

Pawlas, Karl, "Die Waffen des Deutshen Volksturms," (The Weapons of the German Volksturm"), *Waffen Review*, 4th Quarter, No. 71, 1988.

Reardon, Mark J., "A Warning From the Woods," *World War II*, December 2006, pp. 36-41.

Weigley, Russell, "From the Normandy Beaches to the Falaise-Argentan Pocket," *Military Review*, September, 1990, p. 46.

Secondary Sources.

Ambrose, Stephen, *Band of Brothers: E Company, 506th Regiment, 101st Airborne From Normandy to Hitler's Eagle's Nest*, New York: Simon and Schuster, 1992.

Ambrose, Stephen, D-Day: *June 6, 1944: The Climactic Battle of World War II*, New York: Simon and Schuster, 1994.

Ambrose, Stephen, *Citizen Soldiers: The U.S. Army from the Normandy Beaches to the Surrender of Germany*, New York: Simon and Schuster, 1997.

Anderson, Duncan, "Remember, This is an Invasion," in Jane Penrose, ed., *The D-Day Companion: Leading historians explore history's greatest amphibious assault*, London, UK: Osprey Publishing Co, 2004.

Badsey, Stephen, *Arnhem 1944: Operation Market Garden*, London, UK: Osprey Publishing, 1993.

Michael Barrett, *Operation Albion: The German Conquest of the Baltic Islands*, Bloomington, IN: Indiana University Press, 2007.

Bennett, Ralph, *Ultra in the West: The Normandy Campaign, 1944-45*, New York: Charles Scribner's Sons, 1979.

Blumensen, Martin, *The Battle of the Generals, The Untold Story of the Falaise Pocket*, New York: William Morrow and Company, 1993.

Blumenson, Martin, *The Patton Papers, 1940-1945*, New York: Da Capo Press, 1996.

Blumenson, Martin, *Patton: The Man Behind the Legend,* New York: William Marrow and Company, 1985.

Brokaw, Tom, *The Greatest Generation,* New York: Random House, 2004.

Buckley, John, *Air Power In the Age of Total War,* Bloomington, IN: Indiana University Press, 1999.

Buell, Thomas et al., *The Second World War: Europe and the Mediterranean,* Wayne, NJ: Avery Publishing Group, 1989.

Carafano, James J., *After D-Day: Operation Cobra and the Normandy Breakout,* Boulder, CO: Lynne Reiner Publishers, 2000.

Carver, Field Marshall Lord Michael, *The Imperial War Museum Book of the War in Italy 1943-1945: A Vital Contribution to Victory in Europe,* London, UK: Pan Macmillan, 2001.

Chalfont, Alun, *Montgomery of Alamein,* New York: Atheneum, 1976, p. 270.

Chun, Clayton K. S., *Aerospace Power in the Twenty First Century: A Basic Primer,* Colorado Springs, CO: United States Air Force Academy, 2001.

Chun, Clayton K. S., *Thunder Over the Horizon: From V-2 Rockets to Ballistic Missiles,* Westport, CT: Praeger Press, 2006.

Citino, Robert M., *The German Way of War: From the Thirty Years War to the Third Reich,* Lawrence, KS: The University of Kansas Press, 2005.

Clausewitz, Carl Von, *On War,* Princeton, NJ: Princeton University, 1989.

Clark, Jeffery J. and Robert Ross Smith, *Rhine to the Riviera,* Washington, DC: U.S. Army Center of Military History, 1993.

Coffman, Edward M., *The Regulars: The American Army 1898-1941,* Cambridge, MA: The Belknap Press of Harvard University Press, 2004.

Cole, Hugh M., *The Ardennes: Battle of the Bulge,* Washington, DC: Chief of Military History, 1965.

Cooper, Matthew, "Die Luftwaffe--Strategically a Failure," in Simon Goodenough, ed., *Hitler's War Machine,* London, UK: Salamander Books, 1975.

Corum, James S., *The Roots of Blitzkrieg: Hans Von Seeckt and German Military Reform,* Lawrence, KS: The University of Kansas Press, 1992.

Corum, James S., *The Luftwaffe: Creating the Operational Air War, 1918-1940,* Lawrence, KS: University Press of Kansas, 1997.

Craig, Gordon A., *Germany 1966-1945,* New York: Oxford University Press, 1978.

Crane, Conrad, *Bombs, Cities, and Civilians: American Airpower Theory in World War II,* Lawrence, KS: University of Kansas Press, 1993.

DiNardo, Richard L., *Germany and the Axis Power: From Coalition to Collapse,* Lawrence, KS: The University of Kansas Press, 2005.

Doubler, Michael, *Closing with the Enemy: How GIs Fought The War In Europe, 1944-1945,* Lawrence, KS: The University of Kansas Press, 1994.

Doubler, Michael, *I am the Guard: A History of the Army National Guard, 1636-2000,* Washington, DC: U.S. Government Printing Office, 2001.

Drea, Edward J., Unit *Reconstitution-A Historical Perspective (CSI Report No.3),* Fort Leavenworth, KS: Combat Studies Institute, December 1983.

D'Este, Carlo, *Decision in Normandy,* New York: Konecky & Konecky, 1983.

D'Este, Carlo, *Eisenhower: A Soldier's Life*, New York: Henry Holt and Company, 2002.

Deist, Wilhelm, "The Road to Ideological War: Germany 1918-1945," in Williamson Murray *et al.*, eds., *The Making of Strategy*, Cambridge, MA: Cambridge University Press, 1994.

Dupuy, R. Ernest, and Trevor N. Dupuy, *The Harper Encylopedia of Military History: From 3500 B.C. to the Present*, 4th Ed., New York: Harper Collins, 1993.

Eisenhower, John S. D., *The Bitter Woods*, Nashville, TN: Battery Classics, 1969.

Erhart, Robert C., Thomas A. Fabyanic, and Robert Futrell, "Building an Intelligence Organization and the European Theater," in John F. Kreis, ed., *Piercing the Fog*, Washington, DC: Air Force History and Museums Program, 1996.

Futrell, Robert Frank, *Ideas, Concepts, Doctrine Volume I Basic Thinking in the U.S. Air Force 1907-1960*, Maxwell AFB, AL: Air University Press, 1989.

Geyer, Michael, "German Strategy in the Age of Machine Warfare, 1914-1945," in Gordon Craig, Felix Gilbert, and Peter Paret, eds., *The Makers of Modern Strategy from Machiavelli to the Nuclear Age*, Princeton, NJ: Princeton University Press, 1986.

Gordon, Andrew, "The greatest military armada ever launched" in Jane Penrose, ed., *The D-Day Companion: Leading historians explore history's greatest amphibious assault*, London, UK: Osprey Publishing Co, 2004.

Gray, Colin, *Modern Strategy*, Oxford, UK: Oxford University Press, 1999.

Greenfield, Kent Roberts, *American Strategy in World War II*, Malabar, FL: Robert E. Krieger Publishing Company, 1982.

Gole, Henry G., *The Road to Rainbow: Army Planning for the Global War, 1919-1940*, Annapolis, MD: Naval Institute Press, 2003.

Gropman, Alan L., *Mobilizing U.S. Industry in World War II*, McNair Paper # 50, Washington, DC: National Defense University Press, 1996.

Hallion, Richard, *D-Day 1944: Air Power Over the Beaches and Beyond*, Washington, DC: U.S. Government Printing Office, Program, 1994.

Hansell, Haywood S., Jr., *The Strategic Air War Against Germany and Japan*, Washington, DC: Office of Air Force History, 1986.

Harclerode, Peter, *Arnhem: A Tragedy of Errors*, London, UK: Caxton, 1994.

Harrison, Gordon A., *The European Theater of Operations: Cross Channel Attack*, in the series, U.S. Army in World War II, Kent Roberts Greenfield, ed., Washington, DC: Office of the Chief of Military History, 1951.

Hastings, Max, *Bomber Command*, New York: Dial Press/J Wade, 1979.

Heefnor, Wilson A., *Patton's Bulldog: The Life, and Service of Walton H. Walker*, Shippensburg PA: White Mane Books, 2001.

Herwig, Holger, "Strategic Uncertainties of a Nation State: Prussia-Germany, 1871-1918," in Williamson Murray, Macgregor Knox, and Alvin Bernstein, eds., *The Making of Strategy: Rulers, States and War*, Cambridge, UK: Cambridge University Press, 1994, pp. 257-263.

Hirshorn, Stanley, *General Patton: A Soldier's Life*, New York: Harper-Collins Publishers, 2002.

Hobbs, Joseph P., ed, *Dear General: Eisenhower's Wartime Letters to Marshall*, Baltimore, MD: Johns Hopkins Press, 1999.

Farrar-Hockley, Anthony, *Airborne Carpet: Operation Market Garden*, New York: Ballantine Books, 1969.

Harvey, A. D., *Arnhem*, London, UK: Cassel, 2001.

Hogan, David W., *A Command Post at War: The First Army Headquarters in Europe, 1943-1945,* Washington, DC: U.S. Army Center of Military History, 2000.

Holley, Irving Brinton, Jr., *Buying Aircraft: Materiel Procurement for the Army Air Forces,* Washington, DC: U.S. Army Center of Military History, 1989.

Hughes, Thomas Alexander, *Overlord: General Pete Quesada and the Triumph of Tactical Air Power in World War II,* New York: The Free Press, 1995.

Jacobs, W.A., "The British Strategic Air Offensive Against Germany in World War II," in R. Cargill Hall, ed., *Case Studies in Strategic Bombardment,* Washington, DC: Air Force History and Museums Program, 1998.

Kagan, Donald, *On the Origins of War and the Preservation of Peace,* New York: Anchor Books, 1995.

Kershaw, Alex, *The Longest Winter: The Battle of the Bulge and the Epic Story of World War II's Most Decorated Platoon,* New York: Di Capo Press, 2004.

Kershaw, Ian, *Hitler 1934-45: Nemesis,* New York: W. W. Norton and Company, 2000.

Kirkpatrick, Charles E., *An Unknown Future and a Doubtful Present: Writing the Victory Plan of 1941,* Washington, DC: U.S. Army Center of Military History, 1990.

Langer, William L. and S. Everett Gleason, *The Undeclared War,* New York: Harper and Brothers, 1953.

Larabee, Eric, *Commander in Chief: Franklin Delano Roosevelt, His Lieutenants and Their War,* New York: Simon and Schuster, 1987.

Lykke, Arthur F. Jr., "Toward an Understanding of Military Strategy," in Joseph R. Cerami and James F. Holcomb, Jr., eds., *U.S. Army War College Guide to Strategy*, Carlisle, PA: Strategic Studies Institute, 2001.

MacDonald, Charles M., *A Time for Trumpets,* New York: William Morrow and Co., Inc.

MacDonald, Charles B., "The Decision to Launch Operation Market Garden," in Kent Roberts Greenfield, ed., *Command Decisions*, Washington, DC: Office of the Chief of Military History, 1960.

MacDonald, Charles B., *The Siegfried Line,* Washington, DC: Chief of Military History, 1990.

Magenheimer, Heinz, *Hitler's War: Germany's Key Strategic Decisions 1940-1945,* London, UK: Cassel Publishing, 1998.

Mansoor, Peter R., *The G.I. Offensive in Europe: The Triumph of American Infantry Divisions, 1941-1945,* Lawrence, KS: University of Kansas Press, 1999.

Mark, Edward, *Aerial Interdiction: Air Power and the Land Battle in Three American Wars,* Washington, DC: Center for Air Force History, 1994.

Marshall, S. L. A., *Bastogne: The First Eight Days,* Washington, DC: The Infantry Journal Press, 1946.

Mason, David, *U-boat: The Secret Menace,* New York: Ballantine Books, 1968.

Matloff, Maurice, "The Anvil Decision," in Kenneth Roberts Greenfield, ed., *Command Decisions*, Washington, DC: U.S. Army Center of Military History, 1959.

Mattloff, Maurice, *Strategic Planning For Coalition Warfare* , in the series, U.S. Army in World War II, Kent Roberts Greenfield, ed., Washington, DC: U.S. Army Center of Military History, 1959.

Matloff, Maurice, *American Military History,* Washington, DC: Office of the Chief of Military History, 1969.

Mauer, Mauer, *Aviation in the U.S. Army, 1939-1939,* Washington, DC: Office of Air Force History, 1987.

McFarland, Stephen L. and Wesley Phillips Newton, "The American Strategic Air Offensive Against Germany in World War II," in R. Cargill Hall, ed., *Case Studies in Strategic Bombardment*, Washington, DC: Air Force History and Museums Program, 1998.

Miller, Edward G., *A Dark and Bloody Ground: The Hürtgen Forest and the Roer River Dams, 1944-1945*, College Station, TX: Texas A&M University Press, 1995.

Miller, Edward S., *War Plan Orange*, Annapolis, MD: Naval Institute Press, 1991.

Millet, Allan R. and Peter Maslowski, *For the Common Defense*, New York: The Free Press, 1984.

Milward, Alan S., *War, Economy and Society 1939-1945*, Berkeley, CA: University of California Press, 1979.

Ministry of Defense (Navy), *The U-Boat War in the Atlantic*, Vol. II, January 1942-May 1943, London, UK: HMSO, 1992.

Mitchell, Ralph M., *The 101st Airborne Division's Defense of Bastogne*, Fort Leavenworth, KS: Combat Studies Institute, 1986.

Mitcham, Samuel W., Jr., *Eagles of the Third Reich: The Men Who Made the Luftwaffe*, Novato, CA: Presidio Press, 1997.

Mortensnen, Daniel R., *A Pattern For Joint Operations: World War II Close Air Support North Africa*, Washington, DC: Office of Air Force History and U.S. Army Center of Military History, 1987.

Morton, Louis, "Germany First: The Basic Concept of Allied Strategy in World War II," in Kent Roberts Greenfield, ed., *Command Decisions*, Washington, DC: U.S. Army Center of Military History, 1984.

Murray, Williamson, "A Visitor to Hell: On the Beaches," in Jane Penrose, ed., *The D-Day Companion: Leading historians explore history's greatest amphibious assault*, London, UK: Osprey Publishing Co, 2004.

Murray, Williamson and Allen Millet, *A War to be Won: Fighting the Second World War,* Cambridge, MA: The Belknap Press of Harvard University Press, 2000.

Murray, Williamson, *Strategy for Defeat, the Luftwaffe 1933-1945,* Maxwell AFB, AL: Air University Press, 1983.

Nalty, Bernard C., ed., *Winged Shield, Winged Sword: A History of the United States Air Force,* Vol. I., Washington, DC: United States Air Force, 1997.

Nalty, Bernard C., John F. Shiner, and George M. Watson, *With Courage: the U.S. Army Air Forces in World War II,* Washington, DC: Air Force History and Museums Program, 1994.

Newland, Samuel J., *Victories are not Enough: Limitations of the German Way of War,* Carlisle, PA: Strategic Studies Institute, 2005.

Oakley, Robert W. and Richard M. Leighton, *Global Logistics and Strategy, 1943-1945,* Washington, DC: U.S. Army Center of Military History, 1968.

Orange, Vincent, "Getting Together: Tedder, Cunningham and Americans in the Desert and Tunisia," in Daniel R. Mortensnen, *A Pattern For Joint Operations: World War II Close Air Support North Africa 1940-1943,* Washington, DC: Office of Air Force History and U.S. Army Center of Military History, 1987.

Overy, Richard J., *The Air War 1939-1945,* Chelsea, MI: Scarborough House, 1980.

Overy, Richard J., *War and Economy in the Third Reich,* Oxford, UK: Clarendon Press, 1994.

Overy, Richard J., *Why the Allies Won,* New York: W. W. Norton and Co., 1995.

Pape, Robert A. A., *Bombing to Win: Air Power and Coercion in War,* Ithaca, NY: Cornell University Press, 1996.

Perret, Geoffrey, *Winged Victory: The Army Air Forces in World War II,* New York: Random House, 1993.

Phillips, Robert H., *To Save Bastogne*, New York: Stein and Day, 1996.

Price, Frank James, *Troy H. Middleton: A Biography*, Baton Rouge, LA: Louisiana State University, 1974.

Pogue, Forest, *The Supreme Command*, Washington, DC: U. S. Army Center of Military History, 1989.

Roth, Günter, Brigadier General (Doctor), "Operational Thinking of Schlieffen and Manstein," in Militärgeschichliches Forschungsamt Freiburg im Breisgau, eds., *Development, Planning and Realization of Operational Conceptions in World Wars I and II*, Bonn, Germany: E.S. Mittler and Sohn, 1989.

Ruppenthal, Roland G., "Logistics and the Broad-Front Strategy," in Kent Roberts Greenfield, ed., *Command Decisions*, Washington, DC: Office of the Chief of Military History, 1960.

Rush, Robert S., *Hell in the Hürtgen: The Ordeal and Triumph of an American Infantry Regiment*, Lawrence, KS: University of Kansas Press, 2001.

Ryan, Cornelius, *A Bridge Too Far*, New York, Simon and Schuster, 1974.

Sherry, Michael S., *The Rise of American Air Power: The Creation of Armageddon*, New Haven, CT: Yale University Press, 1987.

Showalter, Dennis, *Patton and Rommel: Men of War in the Twentieth Century*, New York: The Berkley Publishing Group, 2005.

Sligh, Robert Bruce, *The National Guard and National Defense: The Mobilization of the Guard in World War II*, New York: Praeger, 1992.

Spector, Ronald H., *At War At Sea: Sailors and Naval Combat in the Twentieth Century*, New York: Viking Press, 2001.

Stewart, Richard W., ed., *American Military History: The United States Army in a Global Era, 1917-2003*, Washington, DC: U.S. Army Center of Military History, 2005.

Stoler, Mark A., *Allies and Adversaries: The Joint Chiefs of Staff, the Grand Alliance and U.S. Strategy in World War II*, Chapel Hill, NC: University of North Carolina Press, 2000.

Terraine, John, *The Right of the Line*, Hertfordshire, UK: Wordsworth Eds., 1997.

Thompson, W. F. K., "Operation Market Garden," in Philip de Ste. Croix, ed., *Airborne Operations*, New York: Crescent Books, 1978.

Tuchman, Barbara W., *The Zimmerman Telegram*, New York: The Viking Press, 1958.

Urquart, R. E., Major General, *Arnhem: Britain's Infamous Airborne Assault of World War II*, Los Angeles, CA: Royal Publishing Company, 1995.

The United States Air Force, *USAF Airborne Operations: World War II and the Korean War*, Washington, DC: USAF Historical Division, 1962.

Warnock, A. Timothy, *Air Power versus U-boats: Confronting Hitler's Submarine Menace in the European Theater*, Washington, DC: Air Force History and Museums Program, 1999.

Watson, Mark Skinner, *The War Department, Chief Of Staff: Pre War Plans and Preparations*, Washington, DC: U.S. Army Center of Military History, 1991.

Watts, Barry D., *The Foundation of US Air Doctrine: The Problem of Friction in War*, Maxwell AFB, AL: Air University Press, 1984.

Weigley, Russell F., *History of the U.S. Army*, New York: The MacMillan Co., 1967.

Weigley, Russell F., *The American Way of War: A History of the U.S. Military Policy and Strategy*, Bloomington, IN: University of Indiana Press, 1973.

Weigley, Russell F., *Eisenhower's Lieutenants: The Campaign of France and Germany, 1944-1945,* Bloomington, IN: The University of Indiana Press, 1981.

Weinberg, Gerhard L., *Visions of Victory: The Hopes of Eight World War II Leaders*, Cambridge, MA: Cambridge University Press, 2005.

Whitlock, Flint, *The Fighting First: The Untold Story Of the Big Red One on D-DAY,* Boulder, CO: The Westview Press, 2004.

Whiting, Charles, *Ike's Last Battle: The Battle of the Ruhr Pocket April 1945,* Barnsley, South Yorkshire, UK: Leo Cooper, 2002.

Wilmot, Chester, *The Struggle For Europe*, New York: Konecky and Konecky, 1952.

Wray, Timothy A., *Standing Fast: German Defensive Doctrine on the Russian Front During World War II, Prewar to 1943*, Combat Studies Institute Research Survey No .5, Ft. Leavenworth, KS: U.S. Army Command and General Staff College, 1986.

APPENDIX I

DEVELOPING STRATEGY: A LOOK AT THE OTHER SIDE

> ... they [The National Socialists] aimed at a reconstruction of German society and the German state on the basis of conquest, annihilation, and subjugation.[1]
>
> Michael Geyer

Over the years, some have criticized the inability of American World War II military leadership to deal effectively with the influence of President Franklin D. Roosevelt or various Service chiefs, particularly Admiral Ernest King, for promoting their Service interests vice the development of a true joint or coalition approach. Also criticized was British Prime Minister Winston Churchill's perceived ability to persuade Roosevelt to ignore his military advisors and acquiesce to British preferences. For those who find flaws with the development of American wartime strategies, a review of the problems faced by our major adversary in developing and implementing strategy provides an interesting perspective.

While Washington entered the post-World War I era as a major though reluctant power in world politics, Germany entered the period as a defeated nation. One writer succinctly noted, "Germany's situation did not permit a foreign policy with a military accent or the development of any strategy that included the use of armed forces."[2] After World War I, when America was playing an important role in the arms limitation talks and its military leadership was considering the possibilities of a future war, Germany, the pariah among the major powers, was simply trying to survive. The first challenge for Berlin was the need for stability; in 1918, this was not an easy task. The German Kaiser had abdicated and with that, the political and social structure of Germany was in the process of rapid and often chaotic change. In the 1920s, the German political leadership had to establish a new democratic government that, from the onset, had a myriad of problems to resolve.

This task would not be easy because in 1920 Germany as a nation was only 50 years old. Granted, the German states had existed for centuries, but a unified German nation-state had only existed since 1871. Thus, it was in fact, much younger than the United States, a country that many in Europe considered a novice in international politics. Consequently, there was a decided immaturity in the German nation and many of its political systems. For example, the German system was a curious blend of democracy and autocracy. From 1871 to 1918, the German chancellor, the equivalent of a prime minister, served at the pleasure of the Emperor, not Parliament. From 1871 to 1889, Chancellor Otto von Bismarck dominated German foreign policy and, to a large extent, military policy. After Bismarck left office, Kaiser William II and his key advisors developed foreign and military policies through procedures used by most parliamentary systems.[3] When World War I began, the military came to dominate the affairs of state, and Germany essentially became a military dictatorship.

When Germany unconditionally surrendered at the end of World War I, a new democracy, the Weimar Republic, came into being, and the German government resembled a parliamentary democracy. Conversely, the new democratic government faced a number of critical issues. Two issues in particular were galling to most Germans: the limited sovereignty permitted by the Allies for the new German government and the inability of Germany to defend itself.[4] Of considerable importance to most citizens was the pressing need to restore the economic wellbeing of the country. Above all, there was general agreement within the new government, its political parties, and the populace, that the Versailles settlement was an abomination that had to be overturned.

Two important priorities faced the Weimar government and were in need of rapid resolution. The preeminent issue confronting Weimar politicians was the need to promote economic recovery, an elusive goal for the new Republic. For the average citizen, the economy was certainly the most important issue. The cessations of territory demanded by the Allies severely affected the German economy. The Allied powers gave the province of Posen, together with a corridor to the sea, to Poland, and the German city of Danzig was made an international city. Additionally, the French government wanted German territories west of the Rhine River totally and permanently demilitarized. The Saar River area was rich in mineral deposits and coveted by France. The German government lost control of the area because the Allied powers insisted that the area should be under international control for a period of 15 years. Following this period of foreign control, the people in the territory would hold a plebiscite to determine whether permanent control would become German or French. Under the terms of the Versailles Treaty, three-fourths of Germany's iron resources and one-fourth of its coal was in foreign hands.[5] Allied powers also stripped Germany of all of its colonies, which also amounted to a significant financial loss. These factors, together with the inadequate methods used by the Kaiser's government to finance the war, meant that Germany was in serious financial straits. To further complicate the Weimar's problems, poor financial policies caused rapid inflation in the years from 1921 to 1923. Financial collapse was inevitable.[6] In 1923, these problems were further exacerbated by the occupation of the German industrial heartland, the Ruhr Valley, by French and Belgian troops when the Germans failed to make their required reparations payments.

With a sympathetic ear from the United States and Great Britain, the Germans received some relief from reparations payments. Throughout 1924 to 1929, Germany appeared to be on the road to recovery for the first time since the end of the war. What choices the Weimar government might have made, what course it might have set for the people and their new democratic government is difficult to say, because in October 1929 the Great Depression struck. The economic progress made by the Weimar government evaporated almost overnight. Thus, from October 1929 until 1933, economic issues related to mere survival were once again the most crucial concern for many Germans.

A second major priority for the new German republic was the revision of the so-called Versailles *Diktat*. The German government and people suffered territorial losses in Europe, but the Germans were also forced to: accept full responsibility for initiating the brutal war that turned into a bloodbath for Europe; relinquish all of their colonies; destroy their air force; and surrender most of their navy. The army was limited to a mere shadow of its former self, truncated to 100,000 personnel, including an officer corps of only 4,000. This meant that Germany was simply unable to defend itself from any external threats such as incursions from France or Poland, both of which were realistic threats, as the early 1920s would show. In reality, the army only had the resources to handle missions related to Germany's internal security. The restoration of full sovereignty over German territory, like the Rhineland and the Saar, remained an important issue throughout the 1920s. The power to regain these territories and defend the nation from future incursions, like those by France in 1923, rested in the hands of the military. Further complicating the problem was the fact that German military forces were not always in good stead with the new German government, since Socialist and Communist leaders regarded "militarists" with great suspicion.[7] While some pragmatic Social Democrats recognized the importance of a strong military for defense and for the maintenance of internal order, many Social Democrats were wary of the military and its leadership. Julius Leber, a leading Social Democrat, warned his party at a 1929 conference "that a republic in which there was an unbridgeable gulf between the armed forces and the working class could not possibly survive."[8] Regrettably, the citizens and their elected representatives ignored this prophetic warning.

As the Weimar government faced repeated crises, many of which were due to the economy's poor state, German military officers systematically studied issues relating to the country's defense. In short, the Army's leadership sought to understand what had gone wrong in the operations of 1914 to 1918 resulting in stalemate on the Western Front and the German defeat. The objective of these analyses was to determine how to defend Germany in the future. The German army held a great deal of bitterness toward the Allies and toward the new republic that agreed to the draconian terms of the peace treaty.[9] In the wake of its defeat that many soldiers refused to acknowledge or accept, the army conducted its postwar reorganization and studies under Hans von Seeckt, Chief of the German *Truppenamt* and head of the German *Reichswehr*.[10]

Seeckt was an intellectual and a man of refinement, but at the same time, he was a military commander with considerable field experience. During the Great War, Seeckt had served on the Western and Eastern Fronts. While on the Eastern Front, he was Chief of Staff for the Armies under General August von Mackensen. The latter was likely one of the most competent field commanders in the German Army during World War I.[11] As head of the *Reichswehr*, Seeckt had two important goals: to develop a highly professional force despite the strictures of the Treaty of Versailles and to place a restored German army in the virtually semi-autonomous role it held in the period from 1889-1918. To facilitate this process, he commissioned studies, previously mentioned, which were a very important element in the process of restoring both the Germany army and Germany's traditional way of war.

The *Reichswehr's* postwar studies concluded that trench or positional warfare, as conducted on the Western Front in 1914-18, was an aberration and should be rejected as a basis for future wars. The German Army had initiated its World War I campaigns on the Western Front with a war of movement or maneuver. Nonetheless, this now famous or infamous large-scale single wing envelopment, the Schlieffen Plan, had failed despite meticulous planning.[12] Thus, the war of movement, the *Bewegungskrieg* promoted by the German officer corps, had bogged down in 1914 and became a *Stellungskrieg*, positional warfare. The studies commissioned by Seeckt concluded that the concept of using maneuver warfare on the tactical and operational level was still valid and desirable for future warfare. Simply, in 1914 maneuver warfare had been executed poorly, but the basic concept was still sound. Seeckt himself was a strong advocate of waging war within the tradition of Helmuth von Moltke (the elder) and Alfred von Schlieffen, wars of movement and encirclement. As one notable historian stated, with good justification, Seeckt was a "restorer rather than an innovator."[13] Thus, in the interwar years, the German army's leadership promoted a return to wars of movement. Studies conducted by key German officers were well within the German tradition of warfare in that they centered on the tactical level through the operational levels of war, but they did not include matters such as national military strategy or national security policy. These military officers failed to recognize that one of the major failings prior to the outbreak of World War I was the erratic nature of the Kaiser's national security policy and the tendency of German policymakers — particularly in the Kaiser's inner circle — to exercise all too quickly, the military instrument of power.[14] Seeckt sought to recreate an elite professional force, which could avoid or counterbalance the excesses or the influence of both the extreme right and left of the German political spectrum. Thus, his plan was for an army and a professional leadership cadre similar to the pre-1914 Imperial Army. In retrospect, Seeckt's studies missed several important issues that put the Germans at a disadvantage as compared to their future adversaries, the United States and Great Britain. German military leadership ignored three important areas: the need for the nation to develop sound political and military strategies; the importance of establishing workable joint and combined alliance headquarters; and the importance of using alliance and coalition warfare as a force multiplier for its military efforts.

Source: The Author's Collection.

Hans von Seeckt, Chief of the German *Truppenamt* and head of the German *Reichswehr*.

These issues and failings were nothing new for Germany. They had their origins in the Imperial era, and officers continued to struggle with them in the Weimar period. For example, once Otto von Bismarck resigned from the role of Chancellor in 1889, consequently Germany lost a firm hand on the German tiller of state, at least in terms of developing achievable objectives and a sound national strategy. Immediately after the wars of unification in 1870, Bismarck had designed and exercised a system where Germany was a hegemonic power on the European scene, but at the same time avoided the appearance of being one. Thus, the German nation from 1871 to 1889 consistently exercised its power, pursued objectives that were within its national interests, and attempted not to antagonize its European neighbors, other than the French. Once Bismarck left the Chancellorship, the country, under new leadership, failed to wisely exercise its power in Europe or, for that matter, throughout the world. National security policy and national military strategy were jumbled and, at times, all but nonexistent.

In terms of developing coalitions and alliances that would link Germany with countries that had common goals and interests, Germany was politically, economically, and militarily far behind its potential adversaries. German leadership could attribute some of the issues to political immaturity or perhaps the failure to recognize the additional power that strong alliances provide. In the German Wars of Unification of 1864 to 1871, Prussia's coalition partners had been some of the German states that shared a similar cultural heritage and at least some common interests. When Germany went to war in 1914, it was a member of the Triple Alliance. That alliance proved to be a dysfunctional one. While the Germans had some common interests with the Austro-Hungarian Empire, they shared little in terms of common interests or goals with the Italians. A basic problem with their alliances was that they tended to be military compacts rather than alliances based on mutually identified interests.[15] This became obvious when Italy failed to support their German Allies and, within a year, the Italians bolted and joined the British and French to wage war against the Germans. Even working with their closest ally, the Austrians, the Germans dealt with them in a haughty and often condescending fashion. In short, in the first 2 decades of the 20th century, the Germans had an extremely poor record of working within alliances. Even after the war, studies that analyzed the conduct of the war seemed to ignore this problem. This is surprising, since Hans von Seeckt, the Chief of the *Reichswehr*, had served as Chief of Staff to *Generalfeldmarschall* August von Mackensen, perhaps Germany's most accomplished alliance warfare practitioner.[16]

The *Reichswehr* officer corps, however, did not all march in step with Seeckt. There were elements within the *Reichswehr*, led by Werner von Blomberg and Joachim von Stulpnagel—both of whom became general officers— that wanted a mass popular army rather than a professional elite, that could harness the energies of German society. These advocates of the *Volkskrieg*, the people's war, attempted to promote their concepts, particularly during the French occupation of the Ruhr Valley, when the German Army was too weak to defend its territory. Another faction led by Kurt von Schleicher and Wilhelm Groener took a broader look at Germany's problems, and their conclusions were perhaps the most realistic. Groener postulated that Germany could not rebuild its military power unless it had a significant economic recovery.[17] Thus, Germany's priority had to be rebuilding economic power, restoring the fragmented domestic situation and, after these issues had been resolved, the restoration of political power and influence. Nonetheless, in the end, Seeckt's vision of a skilled professional force dominated military thought and planning, at least within military circles.

Obviously, Seeckt's preference for a professional German army had its limitations, since it was so small it could only serve as a cadre for a future force. With the Versailles Treaty limiting the size as well as the weapons systems of the *Reichswehr*, German officers could only postulate about wars of maneuver. Only through the use of covert facilities, which were available to the *Reichswehr* as a result of the Treaty of Rapallo in Kazan, had limited development and exercise of motorized units been possible.[18] Seeckt's vision was in many respects limited, since it focused on operational and tactical approaches to war, rather than a strategic vision. Despite the implications of the various studies that had been conducted, Seeckt commissioned his army to be a nucleus for the *Wehrmacht*, to function with an operationally focused leadership, rather than one that functioned at the strategic level.

Striking differences and similarities are evident between Germany and the United States during this period, as it relates to strategy and national defense. After 1918, the American citizenry and the politicians that represented them wanted to avoid another major war, within the National Socialist leadership and certain elements of the German army there was actually an enthusiasm for war. In 1933, the militaries in both countries were small and underfunded. In the event of another war, both countries would have to undergo a major economic mobilization of the manpower base. In the United States, force structure limitations were due to domestic politics and priorities, whereas in Germany, external constraints imposed by the Treaty of Versailles limited Berlin's actions. In 1933, the United States was not prepared to expand its military, whereas in the same period, the new German government under Adolf Hitler was anxious to do so. Although the small but efficient *Reichswehr* had diligently studied operational and tactical warfare in the postwar era, the Germans were inadequately prepared for another war, since any type of national military policy strategy was problematic.

Source: The Author's Collection.

Throughout the interwar period the German Army was extremely short on mechanized equipment. This photo from the late 1930s shows German troops still using horse drawn equipment.

It is difficult to assess what type of national strategy or national military options might have been developed by the new German government had the Weimar Republic survived. Why, because the enduring theme of the Weimar government, in its 14 years of existence, was crisis, it never really had the opportunity to adequately chart its political, economic, or military future. Due to the Versailles Treaty, the Weimar government lacked the ability to forge a national security policy and a foreign policy that allowed for the exercise of military power. On the other hand, from 1925 through 1929, the Weimar government was somewhat successful in restoring the economy and in regaining some national sovereignty. Unfortunately, the 1929 worldwide economic collapse drove the final nail in Weimar Republic's coffin. As a result of this worldwide depression, Germans turned to the right or the left rather than stay in the Weimar center, to solve the problems of the nation. Thus, after a period of political instability from 1929 to 1933, the National Socialists assumed power. Although the National Socialist policies were ultimately negative for the world in general, and the German people in particular, at the time they seemed to offer solutions that could resolve the numerous and challenging problems confronting the German people.

Source: Jim Haley Collection.

Once the war started with the invasion of Poland on September 1, 1939, Hitler increasingly wore his military uniform, rather than party or civilian clothing.

As the National Socialist era dawned, its national strategy and military policy consistently migrated into the hands of Adolf Hitler. Hitler was by no means a traditional or a rational strategist, but from the end of January 1933 until 1945 he set clear objectives for his movement, a factor that would ultimately provide a quandary for German military leaders. Hitler served as the undisputed leader of the National Socialist Party, the arbiter of its ideology, the head of state and, by the end of the decade, its military leader. Hitler established early on in his political career the interests and goals of his National Socialist movement and, once in power, served as the undeniable author of German national strategy and foreign policy. His basic concepts were reiterated numerous times in speeches throughout Germany, but they were fairly well outlined by Hitler as early as 1924. In his rambling and poorly organized book, *Mein Kampf*, and his 1928 lesser known "Second Book," which was not made public until long after World War II, Hitler clearly enunciated his goals.[19]

After becoming Chancellor, Hitler immediately called for the economic recovery of Germany, the elimination of the restrictions from the Treaty of Versailles, full rearmament of Germany to include the restoration of the German navy and air force, and the restoration of territories taken from Germany at the end of World War I. These goals strongly resonated with the German public because they had widespread acceptance in Germany throughout the postwar era. What the leadership of the German army, and for that matter the leadership of the Western democracies failed to recognize, was that Hitler's goals went beyond what some might regard as reasonable goals and objectives. He espoused expansionistic goals for the new Germany that seemed limitless. While many observers in Germany and in the Western democratic countries regarded Hitler's bombastic speeches to be little more than propaganda and not realistic goals, they would soon learn that his plans for territorial expansion and the elimination of Jews and Slavs were, in fact, real. Thus, Hitler believed that it was in the national interest of Germany to have large tracts of land in the east, as well some territory in the west for *Lebensraum* — living space — for the German people. In a 1930 speech delivered to the students and faculty at Erlangen University, Hitler clearly stated his expansionistic goals, by saying: "No people had more of a right to fight for and attain control of the globe than the Germans."[20] Perhaps he understood that Germany, which is situated in the center of Europe and with a growing need for raw materials and foodstuffs beyond its borders, was in a vulnerable situation. Therefore, what critics considered to be propaganda, Hitler's consistent call for the achievement of his goals and what he believed to be in the national interest of Germany, in reality formed the framework of the National Socialist world vision. These goals, despite the ebb and flow of Germany's military fortunes, were essentially the same in 1944 as those enunciated in 1924 when Hitler initially penned *Mein Kampf* in Landsberg Prison.[21]

Hitler fully intended to achieve his national goals through the use of the military element of power. Hitler did not appreciate the advantages of using economic power, and he was impatient with negotiations and political power. To Hitler, power was synonymous with military power, and not just the threat of military power, but the actual employment of military power. To achieve what he sought for a new Germany required war, not just one war, but a series of wars with no end. Initially, he duped the world's major political leadership by putting aside his brown uniform and wearing suits, top hats, and tails, and engaging some of his adversaries in negotiations. Hitler moved with a degree of caution trying not to alarm the world community, since Germany in the early 1930s was not ready for any type of confrontation. For example, in 1934, Hitler signed a nonaggression pact with a nervous Polish government. In 1935, however, he threw off all pretensions and announced that, despite the restrictions imposed by the Treaty of Versailles, Germany would rearm. Hitler capped this action with an introduction of compulsory military training for all males and an expansion of the German navy, made possible through a negotiated agreement with Great Britain.[22]

The German armed forces welcomed its expansion with euphoria because the *Reichswehr* had two important goals — expansion and rearmament. In this regard, Hitler and the military leadership agreed. The German military however, mistakenly assumed that it could manage, or influence the policy of this new regime similar to the strong role it played in manipulating the Kaiser in the period immediately prior to the beginning of World War I. Unfortunately, the German military realized all too late that their post-1918 studies had focused largely on the expansion of the German army coupled with the operational and tactical methodology necessary for succeeding in the next war. What the German military could not have realized was that their new Chancellor had what seemed to be almost limitless and expansive goals for the rapidly expanding German armed forces. As the 1930s ended, it was Hitler, not the diplomats or the military that would develop strategies for the new Germany. How then were German military planners to prepare for the struggles that were to come?

In the areas of tactics and operational thinking, the German military forces were far superior than their competition. Seeckt's army had determined to wage the next war in the traditional German/Prussian method, wars of movement. Wars were to be short wars in which the army would focus on the decisive defeat, if not annihilation, of the enemy force.[23] The talented *Generalleutnant* Ludwig Beck who served as the Chief of the revived German General Staff from 1933-38 undertook the army's preparation for war. In 1935, serious preparations began to move Germany from its post-1918 state of defenselessness to an ability to first defend itself and then to wage offensive war. A plan dating from December 1933 sought to address these objectives by expanding the size of the *Reichswehr* from a 100,000-man army consisting of seven infantry and three cavalry divisions to a total of 21 divisions by March 1938.[24] In August 1936, a second phase of the German rearmament plan emerged with goals set for the building of an army consisting of 36 infantry divisions, three armored divisions, three light divisions, a single mountain division, and a cavalry brigade. These goals were not achieved by the target date of 1939, because all branches of the German armed forces faced a significant problem that was foreign to American military planners; limited raw materials necessary for war.

Germany had gotten its start as a modern industrial state in the 1880s, at least in part due to the abundance of coal deposits which, together with iron ore, were the building blocks of the early industrial age. Iron ore was available to Hitler through Sweden, but aluminum, oil, and rubber were not readily available in the greater German Reich. As the age of the National Socialist sponsored military expansion dawned, Germany's significant natural resource was still coal. Within the borders of the Reich, there were insufficient deposits of iron ore and inadequate supplies of oil, both prerequisites for an army waging modern wars of movement. From almost any perspective, Germany lacked the necessary raw materials for war, especially if foreign powers cut Germany off from international markets. A bellicose Germany, with insufficient natural resources, could in the event of war, face a situation comparable to 1914-18 where both its military and mercantile fleets were bottled up in the North and Baltic Seas. This is in stark contrast to the United States that had more than adequate resources. Nonetheless, the Germans designed a 5-year rearmament plan that Berlin adopted in August 1936. The German army was prepared to engage in defensive operations through this period, but it was not prepared to wage offensive war until 1940. The planning assumed that Germany would likely face a two-front war. Given the restrictions that the Allies had imposed by the Treaty of Versailles and the lack of raw materials necessary for a modern war, a 5-year period to prepare for offensive war was hardly adequate, something the military leadership understood. Hitler, however, refused to be bound by logical thinking or reasonable restrictions.

This problem affected more than the German army's buildup, it affected the other services, especially the navy. When Hitler became Chancellor in 1933, the German navy was hardly competitive with the other major powers. It had flourished under the Kaiser who had stated that "[o]ur future lies on the water, the trident must be in our hands."[25] The Imperial era naval power had allowed Berlin to exploit its colonies in Africa, the Pacific, in China, and to show the flag throughout the world. With the defeat of 1918 and the restrictions imposed by Versailles, German naval strength after World War I was hardly a shadow of its former self. Germany was allowed to keep eight obsolete pre-dreadnought class battleships, eight light cruisers, and 32 destroyers and torpedo boats. The German submarine fleet was totally disbanded. In 1933, rebuilding the German navy to its 1914 level would be a monumental challenge.

The truncated interwar German navy, populated by many former Imperial naval officers who had remained as active members of the service pressed Hitler in 1933 to start a naval construction program. From 1892 to 1918, the Imperial Navy's nemesis was the British navy. In the mid-1930s however, the immediate threats to National Socialist Germany were France and Poland. Since Hitler's initial expansion focused on the continent, Britain was not presumed to be an immediate adversary until a decade later. *Großadmiral* Erich Raeder, the Navy's commander in chief, initially pushed for parity with France and 50 percent parity with the Royal Navy.[26] Obviously, such efforts would have required a massive naval buildup even though Germany was still in the grips of the depression and, at the same time, faced with competition for resources by the other services. Thus, the leadership of the *Kriegsmarine* had the task of fighting both the army and the *Luftwaffe* for resources and at the same time constructing a formidable naval force with a severely restricted shipbuilding industry. Given the limited industrial and economic capability of the Germans in the mid 1930s, the *Kriegsmarine* faced the prospect of going to war as an underequipped and undermanned service if war came too soon.

Before any naval expansion could begin, Germany had to find a way to eliminate the restrictions imposed by the Versailles Treaty. Negotiations with the British resulted in the Anglo-German Naval Agreement of 1935 that helped to resolve this problem. This agreement allowed Germany to buildup to 35 percent of the Royal Navy's battleship tonnage. The rationale given for a larger British fleet was Britain's need to protect its colonial empire. Germany, on the other hand, had lost its colonies and only needed sufficient surface ships for duty in the Atlantic. With this new authority, Raeder began expanding the German navy, but he believed that in the next war fleets would again engage each other on the high seas with capital ships. With his concepts of naval warfare rooted firmly in the tradition of the old Imperial Navy, he promoted a high seas fleet mentality. Some German Naval leaders believed they could ensure parity with the British by expanding U-boat construction, but they were in the minority as were those officers who appreciated aircraft carrier based warfare.[27]

Source: Author's collection.

Großadmiral Erich Raeder, Commander-in-Chief of the German Navy and a strong supporter of the large fleet Navy. Note that Raeder wears his Nazi party membership badge on his military uniform.

Complementing the Anglo-German Naval Agreement, Hitler believed that political agreements or even an alliance with Britain might avoid or delay a direct confrontation with the British before the German navy was adequately prepared to do so. Raeder and the rest of the *Kriegsmarine* leadership fully trusted Hitler's assurances that there was no intent to become confrontational with Britain in the immediate future, or at least until the entire German military obtained the appropriate trained and equipped forces.[28] Despite his assurances, as early as the Czechoslovakian crisis, Hitler enthusiastically prepared to conduct his first campaign that seemed likely to include the use of military force. A military campaign seemed necessary because he wanted not only to bring the Sudeten Germans home to the Reich, but to also destroy Czechoslovakia. The possibility of war, prompted by Hitler's high-risk strategy, long before Germany was prepared to engage in conflict forced some of the German military leaders to protest, including the resignation of Beck in the summer of 1938.

While some regard the Czech crisis as Hitler's masterpiece of diplomacy and coercion, the *Führer* later defined it as one of his great mistakes. He believed the resolution of this crisis deprived him of his first military campaign where he could achieve a desired goal, the destruction of Czechoslovakia,[29] despite the fact that none of his forces, particularly the navy, seemed ready for war. Interestingly, many key German military leaders, including Raeder, Blomberg, Seeckt, and many others, whose cultural roots were firmly planted in the Imperial era, thought the resurgent German military would have the autonomy for planning and the development of strategy much like the old army had during the Imperial era. From the onset of his Chancellorship, however, Hitler clearly intended to dictate the military's priorities and dominate Germany's strategy. The logical sequential planning and budgeting necessary to accomplish his goals seemed beyond the dictator's grasp.[30]

Raeder's initial assumption that Hitler would, in fact, give the *Kriegsmarine* the necessary time to rebuild was a dream. Nonetheless, only months before Germany initiated its attack on Poland in January

1939, Hitler approved a long-range plan for the fleet's expansion. This Z-Plan called for the completion of 10 battleships, two aircraft carriers, three pocket battleships, three battleship cruisers, five heavy cruisers, 13 light cruisers, 47 destroyers, and 194 U-boats by 1947.[31] Upon the completion of this plan, the *Kreigsmarine* would be able to contest even the Royal Navy's dominance of the seas. See Table Appendix I-1.

Ship Category	1939	40	41	42	43	44	45	46	47	Final Target
Battleship Type H	-	-	-	-	2	6	6	6	6	6
Battleship Types *Gneisenau* and *Bismarck*	2	2	3	4	4	4	4	4	4	4
Pocket Battleships (a) Type Deutschland	3	3	2(b)	1(c)	3	3	3	3	3	3
Battleship Cruisers Type P	-	-	-	-	3	3	8	8	10	12
Aircraft Carriers	-	1	2	2	2	2	2	3(d)	4	8
Heavy Cruisers	2	5	5	5	5	5	5	5	5	5
Light Cruisers Type M(e)	-	-	-	3	3	4	5	8	12	24
Scout Cruisers	-	-	-	2	6	9	12	15	20	36
Destroyers	22	25	36	41	44	47	50	53	58	70
Torpedo Boats	8	18	27	35	44	54	64	74	78	78(f)
U-Boats-Atlantic	34	52	73	88	112	133	157	161	162	162
Coastal	32	32	32	32	33	39	45	52	60	60
Special Purpose	-	-	6	10	16	22	27	27	27	27

(a) Armament of *Scharnhorst* and *Gneisenau* to be upgraded 1941-42.
(b) *Scheer* to be converted-1941.
(c) *Graf Spee* and *Deutschland* to be converted-1942.
(d) First two carriers to be followed by smaller type.
(e) Five light cruisers of *Köln* and *Leipzig* class, plus
(f) Twelve torpedo boats of *Möwe* and *Wolf* class, from 1942 to be relegated for training purposes.

Note. In the interests of clarity, all training, experimental, and auxiliary craft (such as motor minesweepers and motor torpedo boats) have been omitted from the table. Their planned production figures adhered to the general pattern and are of little historical importance.[32]

Table Appendix 1-1. The "Z-Plan" Long-Term Production Plan for the German Navy, 1939-47.

In the Z-Plan, Raeder and his planners assumed that war with Britain would occur no earlier than 1945. Unfortunately, war began when German military units crossed the Polish border on September 1, 1939. Hitler hoped for limited opposition to this aggression, but his assessment proved erroneous when Britain and France declared war against Germany 2 days later. In 1939, the *Kreigsmarine* was forced to confront two major powers on the high seas with only a fraction of the Z-Plan requirements. In September 1939, the surface fleet had no modern battleships or aircraft carriers, and it only had two battle cruisers, three pocket-battleships, two heavy cruisers, six light cruisers, and 34 destroyers and torpedo boats, and a few pre-dreadnought battleships.[33] The German navy operated only 57 submarines, a figure that included several training boats. On the other hand, the Royal Navy could outgun the German forces with 15 battleships and battle cruisers and six aircraft carriers. In addition, the French also possessed a large fleet, which further added to the *Kriegsmarine*'s woes.

The German navy was unprepared for major naval operations against either the French or the Royal Navy. The *Kreigsmarine* could not conduct extensive surface operations to support a major conflict at least in part due to an ill-prepared industrial base and an economy not yet mobilized for war. The existing German high seas fleet was a mere shadow of its 1914 level, and the limited size fleet would never be able to produce a significant threat to the Allied military or merchant marine fleets. The German navy's first aircraft carrier could not be completed due to shortages of both workers and raw materials, as well as inter-service rivalry.[34] When the German navy did venture out of its Baltic lair, the Allied navies relentlessly hunted its ships like the *Bismarck* and the *Tirpitz*. Surface vessels had to restrict themselves to conducting mostly raiding actions, not the direct fleet confrontation that Raeder assumed would happen. Instead, as the war continued, German naval operations would have to concentrate on submarine activities to threaten the Allied sea lines of communications. Yet, even in this infamous activity, the *Kriegsmarine* was unprepared due to possessing an insufficient number of U-boats that would be necessary to strangle its adversaries. German records indicate that on September 1, 1939, the *Kriegsmarine* had 57 U-Boats commissioned, only 45 of which were fully serviceable. When the war broke out, only 19 were in a standby position in the North Atlantic.[35]

The *Kriegsmarine* never achieved its ultimate vision of building a robust force and subsequently challenging the Royal Navy. The Allies were able to out-resource and out-build the German navy and ultimately to dominate the sea lanes. Its basic problem was not a lack of planning or vision on the part of its leaders, but rather the problem was attributable to Germany's master strategist, Hitler, whose plans and policies defied logic and ignored resource limitations. Without major surface, and later U-boat opposition, the Allies were able to blockade Germany and prevent it from receiving vital raw materials and foodstuffs. Allied control of the seas facilitated the supply of the Soviet Union with critical resources, the curtailment of Axis capabilities in North Africa, and enabled major amphibious operations in the Mediterranean and, of course, the invasion of Europe on June 6, 1944.

While the Versailles Treaty restricted German naval development, it prohibited the existence of an air force. The treaty did allow civilian and commercial air activity as well as sport flying clubs, but not military air activities. The 15-year prohibition on military airpower initially proved to be a considerable problem for the fledgling *Luftwaffe*. German engineers and manufacturers would need time and resources to produce technologically advanced aircraft. The depression of the 1930s and competition with the army and the *Kriegsmarine* for limited resources for defense production also initially hindered aircraft development.

Once the creation of a new air force was authorized, German air power advocates much like their ground war colleagues, were faced with an immediate objective; protecting the borders of the Reich, rather than projecting power. This was a difficult, if not impossible task, for when Hitler assumed power, no branch of the German military had the capability to defend Germany's borders. Nonetheless, when the creation of the *Luftwaffe* was authorized, this was its first mission. The *Luftwaffe*'s main objective was to assist in deterring the French and Polish military from waging a preventative war against Germany.[36] France had become more secure and thus less threatening to Germany as a result of the completion of the Maginot Line, which was constructed between 1929 and 1932, but it remained suspicious of its eastern neighbor's intentions. However, Polish intentions remained a concern for Germany throughout the mid 1930's.

As the German air arm began expanding, the leadership of the *Luftwaffe* at the strategic level was a serious problem. While the German navy had a professional career naval officer to lead its reconstruction, the commander in chief of the *Luftwaffe*, wearing a second hat as the Air Minister, was Hermann Göring. One of Germany's air heroes from World War I, Göring seemed to offer multiple advantages as leader of the air arm.

With his military record, his experience as a member of the *Reichstag*, and his position as Minister President of Prussia, he had both military and political credentials. Göring, however, was a victim of his excesses, including an addiction to drugs, and by 1939, it was doubtful that he could even fit in a cockpit like that in which he had achieved so much fame in 1918.

Source: Jim Haley Collection.

Reichsmarschall Hermann Göring, Commander-in-Chief of the German Air force, and a former pilot who had long ago lost touch with the needs of military aviation.

Despite his reputation as a World War I ace, Göring's experience in the air was dated. In these later years, Göring the politician had a tendency to promise results, which neither he nor his air service could deliver. Faced with the virtual absence of a German Air Force from 1918 to 1933, he first supported a policy of numeric rather than qualitative superiority over Germany's opponents.[37] He was also an advocate for the tactical focus of the air force. Some German air leaders however, observed and promoted the need for other than tactical capabilities for the fledgling air force. Walter Wever, the first Chief of Staff of the *Luftwaffe* from 1933 to 1936, was a strong advocate of a comprehensive air power doctrine that included the development of a strategic bomber force. Even though he was a former infantry officer who appreciated the ground support role of the *Luftwaffe* and their needs to neutralize, if not destroy, the enemy's air power, he believed that the *Luftwaffe* also required a strategic bombardment capability.[38] Wever's premature death while still in office stalled the development of a German strategic bomber fleet.[39]

Beyond the issues of leadership and mission, the *Luftwaffe* suffered from two additional problems. The *Reichswehr's Truppenamt*, under the firm direction of Seeckt, conducted the immediate postwar studies, synthesizing the lessons learned from World War I. These studies found that wars of maneuver, using a combined arms approach, could prevent a positional war like that of 1914 from occurring in the future. Combined arms for this type of warfare required the *Luftwaffe* to support ground troops. That the *Wehrmacht* was so proficient in combined arms operations, so dominating the air space over Europe in the early part of the war, is clear evidence that they learned these lessons well. At the same time, a review of the types of aircraft produced between 1939 to 1940 shows that the *Luftwaffe*'s primary objective at its inception was first air superiority, closely followed by close air support and interdiction missions to support ground operations. Thus, the early *Luftwaffe* depended on a force of dive-bombers, medium bombers, and fighters. These initial designs were excellent airframes for the short term, but as early as the Battle of Britain, the short range of fighter aircraft and the limited bomb loads carried by medium bombers posed a serious problem for the *Luftwaffe*. These problems demonstrate both a continental and tactical approach to airpower, from which the *Luftwaffe*, despite its early successes, would never recover.

This short-term tactical approach was strongly supported by Hans Jeschonnek the fourth Chief of the Staff of the *Luftwaffe* who served in that capacity from early 1939 until mid 1943.[40] A World War I army officer schooled in the traditional German way of war, Jeschonnek assumed that wars fought by Germany's military forces would be short and intense actions, and that virtually all air resources would be committed during times of conflict.[41] German pilots from operational, training, and test units would all be called upon to fight the war; *Luftwaffe* officials did not hold back any assets in these short intense wars. Jeschonnek failed to invest in training and long-term planning, which ultimately had a negative impact on the *Luftwaffe's* performance and future.[42] Under Jeschonnek's administration, emphasis was given only to combat aircraft in all training and procurement decisions.[43] *Luftwaffe* planners relegated reconnaissance and transport aircraft to a secondary priority. Since they were planning for short wars in Western Europe, the *Luftwaffe*'s leadership failed to make a leap forward in technology, permitting their service to develop longer-range aircraft and in sufficient numbers to meet the demands of an expanding and long war. It was not until well after 1940 that designers attempted to analyze the latest trends and technologies affecting airpower; too late to change the course of the *Luftwaffe's* first aerial failure, the Battle of Britain.[44] German ground operations could call on dive-bombers and fighter aircraft to support operations, but they were merely an extension of long-range artillery.[45]

In essence, the *Luftwaffe* entered World War II as a force designed primarily to support ground operations. Germany's initial victories over Poland, France, Norway, Belgium, and the Netherlands gave the military leadership confidence in its combined arms strategy, often erroneously called *Blitzkrieg* strategy.[46] Jeschonnek seemed to have delivered the right force to the fight. They did, in fact, have the correct force for a short, tactical, continental campaign, but not a long global conflict. The AAF, in contrast, had developed its strategy under AWPD/1 based primarily on the strategic bombardment concept. With this strategy, hardly a short war approach, America could win a conflict by the destruction of economic targets. The AAF recognized that the United States would ultimately conduct an amphibious invasion of Europe and would need sufficient tactical air forces to support Allied ground operations. As a result, the AAF did develop a series of pursuit aircraft to protect many of the U.S. bases, overseas and domestic, as well as to provide support for ground operations. Geography also played a role because the large geographic distances over which the United States would have to project power; and America's industrial capacity allowed American air leaders to plan for different types of aircraft.

The *Luftwaffe* did have advocates, even after Walter Wever's early demise, for strategic bombardment campaigns, but neither the *Luftwaffe's* bomber or pursuit force could fight over long distances. The *Luftwaffe's* force of short-range fighters, dive-bombers, and a limited medium bomber force could not support simultaneous operations. The force was not capable of conducting sustained bombardment against industry or economic targets that supported British and Soviet military forces. Germany's limited mobilization of military industries, its continental approach to the air war, and the competing demands from the other services forced it to abandon its ambitious plans for longer-range aircraft in the late 1930s.[47]

The Battle of Britain demonstrated the first major crack in the *Luftwaffe's* armor. The German air force failed to obliterate the RAF and achieve air superiority to allow for the planned invasion of England, Operation SEALION. The failed German attempts to achieve air superiority ensured that its bombardment campaign against British industrial and civilian targets would also fail. Consequently, German military operations continued to evolve from that of a lightning campaign designed to knock England out of the war, to a more complex, broader effort against the Soviet Union. The easy German military victories from 1939 through 1940 gave Berlin a false sense of superiority that allowed its leaders to ignore the need for, or at least slow the acquisition of, a second generation of aircraft.

The German military establishment, but especially the *Kriegsmarine* and the *Luftwaffe*, both of which were capital intensive forces, faced seemingly endless problems as they attempted to wage Hitler's wars. The *Luftwaffe* was constantly confronted with the lack of basic resources, particularly petroleum. Long-range planning was nonexistent, since Hitler refused to be constrained by the advice from his military leaders. Complicating this factor, from the onset, the German economy reflected the short war philosophy. Building complex weapon systems required a well-trained, organized armament industry, which initially Germany did not possess. At the start of World War II in 1939, Germany devoted 21.9 percent of its industrial workforce to its war effort. By 1940, it accelerated its commitment to 50.2 percent and crept up to 61.0 percent in 1943.[48] Worker productivity in the armament industry, from 1940 to 1942, actually declined starting in 1939.[49] Adolf Hitler commented that the economy had been "mismanaged" despite the change by 1939 to a global war footing, and he was correct.[50] What he failed to acknowledge was that he was a large part of the problem specifically due to his inability to logically and sequentially plan for Germany's future.

A remarkable turnaround in worker output productivity occurred from 1943 to the end of the war, despite aerial bombardment and a maritime blockade. By 1944, work productivity in the arms industry increased by 60 percent per worker compared to the productivity averages in 1939. Other industry showed similar improvements. Steel, petroleum products, synthetic rubber, iron ore, and coal output all increased significantly from 1939 to 1943. At least some of the progress in war production was due to the addition of resources and factories from numerous occupied countries. While production increases forestalled the *Wehrmacht's* demise, it was too little and too late. Pressure from Allied attacks from the west, south, and east started to take its toll by the fall of 1944 as economic capacity slowly degraded through the loss of large blocks of occupied territory, and ground and aerial attacks.

By this stage in the war, the many poor decisions made by German leaders helped to seal the nation's fate. German leaders needed to adapt and change to another generation of weapons and tactics. However, changes in weapon systems were expensive and time consuming to produce, test, train, acquire, and field. Fighting a broad, two-front, campaign spelled disaster for the *Luftwaffe*, because it could not adequately replenish itself and compete against the other services for resources. The dedication of the workforce and the bravery of the *Luftwaffe*'s pilots could not overcome inadequate *Luftwaffe* planning and an overall flawed strategy.

Limited resources were a serious problem for the German armed forces, but competition among the various branches of service for resources proved to be a cutthroat parochial situation that accelerated throughout the war and consequently diminished the impact that the available resources could have produced. For example, Hermann Göring was a consummate empire builder and, although he often overextended himself and the *Luftwaffe*, he consistently raided the other services for force structure and missions. Thus, in 1938 he was able to wrest control of German army paratroopers to make them a *Luftwaffe* asset for the remainder of the war. In 1942, he created the Hermann Göring Panzer Division, clearly a ground unit that nonetheless belonged to the *Luftwaffe*'s force structure. In the same year, the *Luftwaffe* began creating field divisions, infantry units created by and for the *Luftwaffe* command that competed with the army for missions and equipment. Göring was also able to retain control of proposed naval aviation, even though it deployed on naval vessels. His control of aviation for carriers was, to say the least, detrimental for Raeder's plans to deploy a functional aircraft carrier as early as 1941, when Raeder informed Hitler that the *Graf Zeppelin* was 85 percent complete. Göring reported that aircraft could not be made available for the carrier until 1944. To meet the *Kriegsmarine*'s needs, he offered ME 109Es, an aircraft that had been used in the 1940 Battle of Britain and which was being phased out of the *Luftwaffe*'s first line inventory.[51]

Source: The Author's Collection.

Photo of *Waffen*-SS

The battle for resources and force structure grew to include nonmilitary elements as well, and made the competition for resources between the U.S. armed services look like child's play. As expansion of the armed forces proceeded in the late 1930s, the SS, led by Heinrich Himmler, a pseudo military commander, formed *Waffen*-SS divisions. First, Himmler created infantry units, but subsequently the SS fielded panzer divisions. Through their performance in the Russian Campaign in 1941-42, SS units earned Hitler's respect. Their expansion continued in 1942-44, at least some of which was possible by recruitment through various ethnic German communities in southern and Eastern Europe. Their reputation and Hitler's distrust of the traditional German military, particularly after the July 20, 1944, attempt on his life, meant that for the 1944 Ardennes Offensive, "Sepp" Dietrich, an SS general officer, would lead the main effort. Two heavy SS Panzer divisions dominated the main assault force.

All of these failures in planning were symptomatic of a larger problem faced by Nazi Germany; the Third Reich functioned in an administrative morass which was of Hitler's making. Critical thinking, national strategy, long-range planning — if there was any — and military priorities, were all supervised or determined by Hitler. The epitome of German military efficiency, the General Staff, had begun preparations for war in 1935, and for the next 2 years, it worked to develop plans and strategies as Germany's ability to defend itself increased. At the end of 1937, Hitler called into question the military's strategies and the plans for the systematic buildup and deployment of German troops. Thus, rather than strategies, Germany would have to contend with essentially spontaneous military opportunities, which would produce what today's military might call crisis action planning: the 1939 invasion of Poland led to the invasion of France, the Low Countries, Denmark, and Norway; and the spring 1940 campaigns led to the air campaign against Great Britain; the lack of success with Britain ushered in Barbarossa, the attack against the Soviet Union. Where was the strategy and planning with all of this? There was none. One war led to another, one campaign led to further opportunities. Granted, Hitler had a vision for a Europe dominated by Germany, but to say that he had a plan, a strategy, for the conquest of Europe, is inaccurate. Systematic strategy formulation and war plans died a quick death sometime in 1938. German leadership could not resuscitate the effort in the prewar or wartime era.[52]

For the Third Reich, there would never be a General Marshall, Major Wedemeyer, or any type of victory plan. With this chaotic method of administration, National Socialist Germany tended to function more like a group of interrelated fiefdoms, rather than a hierarchical dictatorship. A lack of resources, chaotic leadership, bitter competition within and between the services, and poor, if not nonexistent, planning meant that even though Germany seemed well prepared for war, it was in fact, merely better prepared than its adversaries at that time.

The skeptic might ask if their economy and their strategy were so tenuous, how was it that they did so well in dominating military campaigns from 1939-42. The logical answer is, beginning with Hitler's assumption to power in 1933, Germany relentlessly prepared for war. In Hitler's mind, this was not preparation to defend National Socialist Germany, but rather preparation to wage war. At the same time, the German army had studied and digested the lessons of World War I perhaps better than any other major power, thereby putting Germany ahead of the other nations particularly in terms of combined operations and maneuver warfare. While Hitler's military forces were diligently preparing for war, the U.S. Government focused on domestic politics and domestic woes. Washington was expending neither funds nor intellectual energy on defense. Britain too, was bemoaning the loss of a generation on the fields of Europe as was evident by Chamberlain's attempts at avert war over Czechoslovakia The Soviet Union, despite the enormity of its army, was in turmoil with repeated purges that struck the Soviet Army's leadership with a vengeance. In short, in 1939 the Germans had the initiative, and they were far better prepared than their adversaries. The absence of an achievable set of objectives, a strategy to achieve them, and a strong economic base to support the war effort, meant that in the end, these advantages would be squandered.

ENDNOTES - APPENDIX I

1. Michael Geyer, "German Strategy in the Age of Machine Warfare, 1914-1945," in Gordon Craig, Felix Gilbert, and Peter Paret, eds., *The Makers of Modern Strategy from Machiavelli to the Nuclear Age*, Princeton, NJ: Princeton University Press, 1986, p. 596.

2. Wilhelm Deist, "The Road to Ideological War: Germany, 1918-1945," in Williamson Murray *et al.*, eds., *The Making of Strategy: Rulers States and War*, London, UK: Cambridge University Press, 1996, p. 357.

3. The writers are quick to acknowledge the influence of Helmuth von Moltke on military policy during Bismarck's tenure as Chancellor (1871-89) and the heavy influence of Army advisors and Admiral Alfred Tirpitz on defense policy during 1890-1914. As noted by Günter Roth, Chief of the Militärgeschichliches Forschungsamt, post-Bismarck politicians squandered the Chancellor's legacy, and when the political leaders found Germany encircled by unfriendly powers and had few, if any, solutions to offer, "the vaacum was filled by the generals." See Brigadier General (Doctor) Günter Roth, "Operational Thinking of Schlieffen and Manstein" in Militärgeschichliches Forschungsamt, Freiburg

im Breisgau, eds., *Development, Planning and Realization of Operational Conceptions in World Wars I and II*, Bonn, Germany: E. S. Mittler and Sohn, 1989, p. 7.

4. A German Army was permitted but restricted to 100,000 men. The small size of the army, and the prohibition of an air force and certain categories of weapons, meant that Germany did not have the means to defend itself. Consider that the French had a peacetime army of 750,000 men and Poland, 300,000. Thus, when the French and Belgians invaded the Ruhr Valley in 1923, the Germans were without recourse. They simply did not have resources to defend their nation.

5. That the Versailles settlement was punitive seems obvious, but had the Germans won, their peace settlements with their former adversaries would have been at least as draconian, if not more so. A classic example of their intentions is the 1917 Treaty of Brest-Litovsk, which gave Germany essentially a quarter of Russia's population and much of its available resources. Additionally, seizures of land by the victor and concessions by the loser were well within the European tradition, as exhibited through the Napoleonic wars.

6. To illustrate the impact of inflation on the average German, consider that from 1922 to 1923, inflation reduced the German mark to 4.2 trillion to the U.S. dollar. Inflation accelerated at such a rapid rate that owners paid workers daily since, on the following day, the mark would be worth even less.

7. There was considerable mistrust between the government and the German military. The Social Democratic Party (SPD) dominated the postwar government. The SPD was a party that rightfully claimed credit for the creation of the new German Republic. The SPD had a reputation of being anti-military, in part due to its socialist heritage, and in the years after the war the SPD failed to improve relations with the military leadership. With suspicion, it watched the involvement of military personnel in the various splinter parties, particularly on the right, and the support by some of the military establishment in the Kapp Putsch and Hitler's 1923 Beer Hall putsch.

8. Gordon A. Craig, *Germany 1866-1945*, New York: Oxford University Press, 1978, p. 501.

9. The reader should, however, understand that while the Allies imposed harsh peace terms on the Germans, had the Germans won, their peace terms would have been equally severe. A case in point is the Treaty of Brest-Litovsk in 1917, concluding a separate peace with Russia. Through this treaty, Russia lost control of the Baltic provinces, Ukraine, Finland, and Poland, regions which had about one-quarter of Russia's population and much of its prewar industrial and agricultural wealth.

10. The *Truppenamt* was the successor to the German General Staff, an organization forbidden by the Treaty of Versailles. The *Reichswehr* was the name of the post-1918 German Army.

11. For an excellent paper on this topic, see Richard L. Di Nardo, "Twentieth Century Soldier in a Busby: August von Mackensen, 1914-1918," paper delivered at the annual meeting of the Society of Military History, 2005. As this author noted, Von Mackensen was also adept at coalition warfare, an ability many of his peers lacked.

12. Schlieffen's pre-1914 Cannae studies had focused on the campaigns of Carthaginian commander Hannibal in the Second Punic War. These were published immediately prior to the outbreak of World War I and were made available to the German military community. They were brought to the attention of the U.S. Army in 1916. See General Field Marshal Count Alfred von Schlieffen, *Cannae*, Ft. Leavenworth KS: U.S. Army Command and General Staff College Press, 1992.

13. Martin von Creveld, *Fighting Power*, Westport, CT: Greenwood Press, 1982, p. 134. See also James S. Corum, *The Roots of Blitzkrieg: Hans Von Seeckt and German Military Reform*, Lawrence, KS: University of Kansas Press, 1992, pp. 25-50.

14. The paranoia in military circles about Germany's encirclement and the urging of the Kaiser's military advisors to use the military instrument of power is well described in Holger Herwig, "Strategic Uncertainties of a Nation State: Prussia-Germany, 1871-1918," in Williamson Murray, Macgregor Knox, and Alvin Bernstein, eds., *The Making of Strategy: Rulers, States and War*, Cambridge, UK: Cambridge University Press, 1994, pp. 257-263.

15. As highlighted in a current study, relations between the Germans and their allies in the early 20th century "were marred by a disingenuousness that evolved into an escalating pattern of deceit and dishonesty on the part of both Germany and Austria." Richard L. Di Nardo, *Germany and the Axis Power: From Coalition to Collapse*, Lawrence, KS: The University of Kansas Press, 2005, p. 22.

16. *Ibid.*, pp. 10-11, 14.

17. Wilhelm Groener was an intriguing individual. In World War I, he served as the chief administrator of the War Office. He succeeded Eric Ludendorff when the latter resigned in 1918. He clearly demonstrated his political talent when on November 9, 1918, he called Friedrich Ebert and placed the Army at the disposal of the new German Republic. From 1928-32, Ebert served as the Minister of Defense for Germany. Much of his thinking about Germany's problems can be found in his book, *Der Weltkrieg und Seine Probleme: Rueckshau und Ausblick* (*The World War and Its Problems: Looking Back and Current Views*), Berlin, Germany: Martin Warneck Verlag, 1930.

18. Note, experimentation with aircraft and aircrews was conducted at Liptesk, about 220 miles from Moscow by the *Reichswehr*. See James S. Corum, *The Roots of Blitzkrieg: Hans Von Seeckt and German Military Reform*, Lawrence, KS: the University of Kansas Press, 1992, particularly Chapter 7, pp. 144-168.

19. See Adolf Hitler, in Gehard L. Weinberg, ed., *Hitler's Second Book: The Unpublished Sequel to Mein Kampf*, New York: Enigma Books, 2003.

20. Constantin Goschler, ed., *Hitler: Reden, Schriften, Anordnung, Februar 1925 bis Januar 1933* (*Hitler: Speeches, Writings, and Orders, February 1925 till January 1933*), Vol. 4, Munich, Germany: Saur Verlag, 1994, p. 95.

21. One document introduced at the Nuremberg Trials, the Hossbach Memorandum, outlined the goals enunciated by Hitler in a fall 1937 meeting between the *Führer*, his military, and political leadership. While it was used at the trials to provide damming evidence of Hitler's desire to wage aggressive war, the statements

made by Hitler were really restatements of policy goals made on many other occasions. See *Documents on German Foreign Policy, 1918-1945*, Washington, DC: U.S. Department of State, 1949.

22. It is significant to note that at the same time, Chief of Staff of the U.S. Army Douglas MacArthur was pleading in vain for the President not to cut the U.S. Army's already small budget. During MacArthur's tenure, the Army's budget and manpower reached all time lows and, despite his efforts, he could not persuade the then domestic focused President Roosevelt to place more emphasis on defense.

23. A highly recommended work discussing the German way of war is Robert M. Citino's *The German Way of War: From the Thirty Years War to the Third Reich*, Lawrence, KS: The University of Kansas Press, 2005.

24. Wilhelm Deist, "The Rearmament of the Wehrmacht," in Wilhelm Diest *et al.*, eds., *Germany and the Second World War*, Vol. I, London, UK: 1990, pp. 405-408.

25. Richard Humble, *Hitler's High Seas Fleet*, New York: Ballantine Books, 1971, p. 10.

26. *Ibid*, p. 377.

27. Chris Bishop and Adam Warner, *German Weapons of World War II*, Edison, NJ: Chartwell Books, 2001, p. 36.

28. The worsening world situation in 1938 and the confrontations over Czechoslovakia and Austria caused Raeder to fear that Hitler's policies were pushing Germany toward war with Britain, even though his earlier planning had focused on the threat posed by France and Poland. He was exactly right.

29. Hitler's attitudes toward waging war in this period are, at times, contradictory and confusing. In the case of Czechoslovakia, Hitler sought the destruction of that state, an irrational but important goal to the *Führer* due to his hatred of Czechs that developed while he was an Austrian citizen. Neither France nor Britain would have likely acquiesced to the total destruction of the state, but their agreement to dismember Czechoslovakia if nothing else

irritated Hitler because the Munich agreement robbed him of the chance to destroy it in one swift and singular move. See Ian Kershaw, *Hitler 1934-45: Nemesis,* New York: W. W. Norton and Company, 2000, pp. 87-88, 163-64.

30. The disconnect between having necessary resources and the achievement of Hitler's goals was the subject, at least key military leaders thought it was, of the fall 1937 meeting at the Reichs Chancellery which produced the Hossbach Memorandum. Instead of analyzing the needs of the services for rebuilding Germany's military forces, the military chiefs were the recipients of a two-hour Hitler monologue about his future goals. Competing demands for scarce resources were ignored.

31. Humble, p. 34.

32. Cajus Bekker, *Hitler's Naval War,* Garden City, NY: Doubleday and Company, 1974, p. 372.

33. Paul Kennedy, "Die Kreigsmarine" ("The German Navy"), in Simon Goodenough, ed., *Hitler's War Machine,* London, UK: Salamander Books, 1975, p. 162.

34. Two carriers were ordered, but only one, the *Graf Zeppelin,* was launched on December 8, 1938. Beset by conflicting construction priorities, the still incomplete *Graf Zeppelin* was scuttled by the Germans on April 25, 1945. The other keel, which was to be the *Peter Strasser,* was scrapped in 1940, due to the same problems.

35. Bekker, p. 374.

36. Williamson Murray, *Strategy for Defeat, the Luftwaffe 1933-1945,* Maxwell AFB, AL: Air University Press, 1983, p. 14.

37. Matthew Cooper, "Die Luftwaffe – Strategically a Failure," in Goodenough, ed., *Hitler's War Machine,* p. 112.

38. Wever's philosophy was embodied in *Luftwaffe* Regulation 16, *The Conduct of Aerial War.* A good discussion on the impact of Wever's leadership and this doctrine is included in James S. Corum, *The Luftwaffe: Creating the Operational Air War, 1918-1940,* Lawrence, KS: University Press of Kansas, 1997, pp. 137-144.

39. In all fairness, it should be noted that a strategic bomber fleet, at the level produced by Great Britain and the United States, would have been too resource intensive for Germany. Four-engine strategic bombers and the fuel it would take to mass a strategic bombardment campaign would have been difficult for Germany. After all, its resource problems were a large part of its difficulties in even attempting to launch two aircraft carriers.

40. Samuel W. Mitcham Jr., *Eagles of the Third Reich: The Men Who Made the Luftwaffe*, Novato, CA: Presidio Press, 1997, p. 27.

41. The concept of the brief and intense war, as the German way of war, has been recently covered in detail by Robert M. Citino, *The German Way of War from the Thirty Year War to the Third Reich*, Lawrence, KS: The University of Kansas Press, 2005; and Samuel J. Newland, *Victories are Not Enough: Limitations of the German Way of War*, Carlisle PA: Strategic Studies Institute, 2005.

42. Corum, *The Luftwaffe*, p. 231.

43. *Ibid.* p. 231.

44. Wilhelm Deist, "The Road to Ideological War: Germany 1918-1945," in *The Making of Strategy*, p. 376.

45. Mitcham, p. 130.

46. The term *Blitzkrieg* is too often used, and misused, to describe the German method of war during the first few years of the war. What is termed *Blitzkrieg* is actually joint and combined warfare, wars of movement, or in modern terminology operational warfare. See Karl Heinz Frieser, *The Blitzkrieg Legend: The 1940 Campaign in the West*, Annapolis, MD: The Naval Institute Press, 2005.

47. Williamson Murray and Allan B. Millet, *A War To Be Won: Fighting the Second World War*, Cambridge, MA: The Belknap Press of Harvard University Press, 2000, p. 33.

48. R. J. Overy, *War and Economy in the Third Reich*, Oxford, UK: Clarendon Press, 1994, Table 9.15. German and British war effort: selected statistics, 1939-1944, p. 312.

49. *Ibid*, pp. 366-367.

50. *Ibid*, pp. 312-313.

51. The *Graf Zeppelin* was to be equipped by the *Luftwaffe* with upgraded versions of the ME-109 a version called the ME 109 T. The E version was already being supplanted, but more up to date versions (like all ME 109s, the E and T) had a narrow track undercarriage which was prone to collapse even under the best of conditions. The FW 190 would have been a much better craft for carrier landings. At the same time, it was to have had a naval version of the JU 87 (E), an aircraft which was only suitable for combat missions, if absolute local superiority of the airspace could be guaranteed.

52. Michael Geyer, "German Strategy in the Age of Machine Warfare, 1914-1918," in Peter Paret, ed., *Makers of Modern Strategy: From Machiavelli to the Nuclear Age*, Princeton, NJ: Princeton University Press, 1986. See in particular pp. 570-572.

APPENDIX II[1]

TO SUPREME COMMANDER ALLIED EXPEDITIONARY FORCE

12 February 1944

1. You are hereby designated as Supreme Allied Commander of the forces placed under your orders for operations for liberation of Europe from Germans. Your title will be Supreme Commander Allied Expeditionary Force.

2. *Task.* You will enter the continent of Europe and, in conjunction with the other United Nations, undertake operations aimed at the heart of Germany and the destruction of her armed forces. The date for entering the Continent is the month of May, 1944. After adequate Channel ports have been secured, exploitation will be directed towards securing an area that will facilitate both ground and air operations against the enemy.

3. Notwithstanding the target date above, you will be prepared at any time to take immediate advantage of favorable circumstances, such as withdrawal by the enemy on your front, to effect a reentry into the Continent with such forces as you have available at the time; a general plan for this operation when approved will be furnished for your assistance.

4. *Command.* You are responsible to the Combined Chiefs of Staff and will exercise command generally in accordance with the diagram at Appendix. [See the

original for the Appendix and the associated diagram]. Direct communication with the U.S. and British Chiefs of Staff is authorized in the interest of facilitating your operations and for arranging necessary logistic support.

5. *Logistics.* In the United Kingdom the responsibility for logistics organization, concentration, movement, and supply of forces to meet the requirements of your plan will rest with British Service Ministries so far as British Forces are concerned. So far as U.S. Forces are concerned, this responsibility will rest with the U.S. War and Navy Departments. You will be responsible for the coordination of logistical arrangements on the continent. You will also be responsible for coordinating the requirements of British and U.S. forces under your command.

6. *Coordination of Operations of other Forces and Agencies.* In preparation for your assault on enemy occupied Europe, Sea and Air Forces, agencies of sabotage, subversion, and propaganda, acting under a variety of authorities, are now in action. You may recommend any variation in these activities which may seem to you desirable.

7. *Relationship to United Nations Forces in other areas.* Responsibility will rest with the Combined Chiefs of Staff for supplying information relating to operations of the Forces of the U. S. S. R. for your guidance in timing your operations. It is understood that the Soviet Forces will launch an offensive at about the same time as OVERLORD with the object of preventing the German forces from transferring from the Eastern to the Western front. The Allied Commander in Chief, Medi-

terranean Theater, will conduct operations designed to assist your operations, including the launching of an attack against the south of France at about the same time as OVERLORD. The scope and timing of his operations will be decided by the Combined Chiefs of Staff. You will establish contact with him and submit to the Combined Chiefs of Staff your views and recommendations regarding operations from the Mediterranean in support of your attack from the United Kingdom. The Combined Chiefs of Staff will place under your command the forces operating in southern France as soon as you are in a position to assume such command. You will submit timely recommendations compatible with this regard.

8. *Relationship with Allied Governments – the re-establishment of Civil Governments and Liberated Allied Territories and the administration of enemy territories.* Further instructions will be issued to you on these subjects at a later date.

ENDNOTES - APPENDIX II

1. Dwight D. Eisenhower, *Report by The Supreme Commander to the Combined Chiefs of Staff on Operations in Europe of the Allied Expeditionary Force, 6 June 1944 to 8 May 1945*, Washington, DC: U. S. Army Center of Military History, 1994, p. v.

www.ingramcontent.com/pod-product-compliance
Lightning Source LLC
Chambersburg PA
CBHW071618170426
43195CB00038B/1347